DEADLY SWINDLE

PATRONS OF THE SOCIETY

Professor Constance Backhouse
Chernos, Flaherty, Svonkin, LLP
Gowling WLG
Hull & Hull LLP
Mr. Wayne Kerr
The Law Foundation of Ontario
McCarthy Tetrault
Osler, Hoskin & Harcourt LLP
Pape Chaudhury
Paliare Roland Rosenberg Rothstein LLP
The Hon. Robert Sharpe
Torys LLP
WeirFoulds LLP

The Osgoode Society is supported by a grant from
The Law Foundation of Ontario

The Society also thanks The Law Society of Upper
Canada for its continuing support

DEADLY SWINDLE

An 1890 Murder in Backwoods Ontario
That Gripped the World

IAN RADFORTH

Published for The Osgoode Society for Canadian Legal History by
University of Toronto Press
Toronto Buffalo London

© Osgoode Society for Canadian Legal History 2024
University of Toronto Press
Toronto Buffalo London
utorontopress.com
Printed in the USA

ISBN 978-1-4875-6023-2 (cloth)
ISBN 978-1-4875-6025-6 (EPUB)
ISBN 978-1-4875-6024-9 (PDF)

Library and Archives Canada Cataloguing in Publication

Title: Deadly swindle : an 1890 murder in backwoods Ontario that gripped the world / Ian Radforth.
Names: Radforth, Ian Walter, 1952– author. | Osgoode Society for Canadian Legal History, issuing body.
Series: Osgoode Society for Canadian Legal History series.
Description: Series statement: Osgoode Society for Canadian Legal History series | Includes bibliographical references and index.
Identifiers: Canadiana (print) 20240371380 | Canadiana (ebook) 20240371402 | ISBN 9781487560232 (cloth) | ISBN 9781487560249 (PDF) | ISBN 9781487560256 (EPUB)
Subjects: LCSH: Birchall, Reginald, 1866–1890. | LCSH: Benwell, Frederick Cornwallis, 1865–1890. | LCSH: Swindlers and swindling–Ontario–Case studies. | LCSH: Murder–Ontario–Case studies. | LCSH: Trials (Murder)–Ontario–Woodstock–Case studies. | LCGFT: Case studies
Classification: LCC HV6535.C32 O65 2024 | DDC 364.152/309713–dc23

Cover design: Ingrid Paulson
Cover image: Newspaper clippings from proquest.com and newspapers.com

We wish to acknowledge the land on which the University of Toronto Press operates. This land is the traditional territory of the Wendat, the Anishnaabeg, the Haudenosaunee, the Métis, and the Mississaugas of the Credit First Nation.

University of Toronto Press acknowledges the financial support of the Government of Canada, the Canada Council for the Arts, and the Ontario Arts Council, an agency of the Government of Ontario, for its publishing activities.

Contents

List of Illustrations   VII
Foreword   IX
Acknowledgments   XI
List of Principal Characters in the Benwell–Birchall Case   XIII

1 Introduction   3

2 The Murder Mystery   13

3 Arrests at Niagara   30

4 The Net Tightens   42

5 In Woodstock Jail   62

6 Pelly's Story   80

7 The Great Detective?   96

8 The Trial Begins   110

9 The Defence and Conclusion   143

10 Aftermath of the Trial   165

11 Birchall's Own Story   190

12 Pleading for Mercy   214

13 The Hanging   224

14 A Compelling Story   235

15 Epilogue   239

Notes   245
List of Newspapers Cited   273
Index   275

Illustrations

0.1 Map of Reginald Birchall's travels 2
2.1 In the Blenheim swamp where the body was found 14
2.2 The corpse, photographed in Swartz's undertaking establishment, Princeton, Ontario 18
2.3 Archibald McLay, MD, Woodstock coroner 24
3.1 Frederick Cornwallis Benwell 32
3.2 Reginald Birchall with wife Florence Birchall 35
4.1 Thomas H. Young, chief of the Ontario police in Niagara Falls, Ont 43
5.1 Woodstock Jail, where Birchall remained incarcerated from 13 March to 14 November 1890 64
5.2 Rex Birchall and "Cholly" Dudley kibitzing for the photographer in Woodstock 71
6.1 Douglas Raymond Pelly, the Crown's star witness 84
7.1 John Wilson Murray, Ontario government detective 98
8.1 Old Town Hall, Woodstock, Ont., where Birchall's trial took place 111
8.2 Justice Hugh MacMahon, George Tate Blackstock, and Britton Bath Osler 114
8.3 The Birchall trial under way in the upstairs theatre of the Town Hall 121
10.1 The jury in the Birchall trial 173
10.2 Florence Birchall and her elder sister, Marion West-Jones 176

viii Illustrations

11.1 Pen-and-ink drawing by Birchall made to illustrate his autobiography   196
14.1 Footstool crafted out of wood from where the body was found in the swamp and from the gallows on which Birchall was hanged   243

Foreword

Ian Radforth's *Deadly Swindle* is a fascinating journey into life and law in late nineteenth-century Canada. Its jumping-off point is the murder of Frederick Cornwallis Benwell, whose body was discovered in the woods a dozen miles west of Woodstock, Ontario, in February 1890. From there the author takes us back to the history of how Benwell, John Reginald Birchall, and Douglas Raymond Pelly, well-connected young Englishmen from wealthy families, emigrated to Canada in search of fortune. Benwell and Pelly were lured overseas by Birchall, who dangled the prospect of investing in a horse farm. The horse farm did not exist; Birchall was a swindler, and the resulting disputes ended with him killing Benwell. Birchall was convicted and executed, with Pelly the chief witness for the prosecution. The book then provides a detailed, vivid, and learned analysis of the operation of the criminal justice system in this period. There is also a parallel theme, that of how one localised story was taken up by the press and made into a provincial, then national, then international story. In part, the widespread interest in the case was the result of Birchall's fascinating personality – attractive, charming, charismatic, and self-confident. He had many admirers despite the fact that he was also a cold-blooded murderer. *Deadly Swindle* is a wonderful illustration of legal archeology, using a close study of a particular case to show not just the operation of the criminal justice system, but also the intricacies of how many other aspects of society and politics affected how the law worked in practice.

The purpose of the Osgoode Society for Canadian Legal History is to encourage research and writing in the history of Canadian law. The Society, which was incorporated in 1979 and is registered as a charity, was founded at the initiative of the Honourable R. Roy McMurtry, and officials of the Law Society of Upper Canada. The Society seeks to stimulate the study of legal history in Canada by supporting researchers, collecting oral histories, and publishing volumes that contribute to legal-historical scholarship in Canada. This year's books bring the total published since 1981 to 125, in all fields of legal history - the courts, the judiciary, and the legal profession, as well as the history of crime and punishment, women and law, law and economy, the legal treatment of Indigenous peoples and ethnic minorities, and famous cases and significant trials in all areas of the law.

Current directors of the Osgoode Society for Canadian Legal History are Constance Backhouse, Heidi Bohaker, Brendan Brammall, Bevin Brookbank, Shantona Chaudhury, Paul Davis, Linda Silver Dranoff, Timothy Hill, Ian Hull, Mahmud Jamal, Waleed Malik, Rachel McMillan, Dana Peebles, Linda Plumpton, David Rankin, Paul Schabas, Robert Sharpe, Jon Silver, Alex Smith, Lorne Sossin, Michael Tulloch, and John Wilkinson.

Robert J. Sharpe
President

Jim Phillips
Editor-in-Chief

Acknowledgments

I appreciate the advice I received when I presented a synopsis of this book to the Osgoode Legal History Workshop. As a result of that presentation, Jim Phillips encouraged me to submit a scholarly book manuscript for consideration by the Osgoode Society for Canadian Legal History. He gave me further encouragement and expert feedback on a draft of the book, and he has skilfully shepherded the manuscript through the peer review process. I was fortunate in getting thoughtful advice from the anonymous reviewers. Legal scholar Ian Kyer volunteered to comment on the book manuscript and offered expert advice, which I followed. I appreciate the time Timothy Brook took to read an early draft of the book and make thoughtful suggestions. Lori Loeb kindly provided British history references.

At the University of Toronto Press, my editor, Len Husband, was once again a cheerful, encouraging presence. Christine Robertson guided the book through publication effortlessly, or so she made it appear! As with my last book from UTP, I have been fortunate in having as my copyeditor Matthew Kudelka, whose extraordinary talent contributed to making this book a much better read. Freelancer Nate Wessell produced the map with his usual skill and efficiency.

My good friend Paul Eprile once again read chapter drafts, commented helpfully, and gave endless doses of encouragement. The title resulted from our brainstorming and his clever breakthrough. I very much appreciate all his help. Final thanks must go to my partner, Franca Iacovetta, who always believed this book would see the light of day and gave me the push I needed to bring that about.

Principal Characters in the Benwell–Birchall Case

Baker, George. Woodstock resident; murder suspect.
Ball, Francis Ramsay. Oxford County Crown attorney.
Benwell, Charles. Brother of Frederick Benwell; Crown witness.
Benwell, Frederick Cornwallis. Murder victim.
Benwell, Col. Frederick W. Father of the murder victim.
Birchall (or Burchell or Somerset), John Reginald, "Rex." Tried for murder.
Blackstock, George Tate. Toronto lawyer; lead defence attorney in Birchall trial.
Bluett, Charles. Toronto detective working for Birchall's defence.
Caldwell, Robert. Murder suspect; defence witness.
Cameron, John. Governor of Woodstock Jail.
Crosby, William. Justice of the peace, Princeton, Ont.
Duffy, James. News agent on train; Crown witness.
Elvidge, George and Joseph. Woodsmen who discovered the body in the swamp.
Hay, George. Brakeman on Grand Trunk train; Crown witness.
Hayward, Alfred. Eastwood miller and farmer; Crown witness.
Hellmuth, Isidore F. Passenger aboard *Britannic*; London, Ont., lawyer; a defence attorney in Birchall trial.
Hill, Andrew Gregory. Police magistrate, Niagara Falls, Ont.
Ivey, Charles H. London, Ont., law partner of Hellmuth; counsel for the Birchalls in Niagara Falls.

Leatham, Arthur. Montreal resident; friend of Reginald Birchall.
MacMahon, Hugh. Judge at Birchall trial.
MacMurchy, Dugald. Toronto lawyer; assisting defence attorney in Birchall trial.
McDonald, William. Acquaintance of Reginald Birchall; agent in farm-pupil business.
McKay, Samuel G. Woodstock lawyer; a defence attorney in Birchall trial.
McLay, Dr. Archibald. Woodstock, Ont., physician and coroner.
Mowat, Oliver. Attorney general and premier of Ontario.
Murray, John Wilson. Ontario government detective.
Osler, Britton Bath. Toronto lawyer; Crown attorney in Birchall trial.
Pelly, Douglas Raymond. Fraud victim; Crown witness.
Pelly, Raymond Percy. Rector in Saffron Walden, Essex; father of Douglas Pelly.
Pickthall, Neville Hunter. Farmer near Woodstock; friend of Reginald Birchall.
Radclive, John Robert. Birchall's executioner.
Staples, Dr. Charles R. Woodstock physician; co-conductor of Benwell's autopsy.
Swartz, James H. Undertaker, Princeton, Ont.
Taylor, Dr. Oliver. Woodstock physician; co-conductor of Benwell's autopsy.
Thompson, Sir John. Minister of Justice.
Wade, William H., Rural Dean; Reginald Birchall's confessor in jail.
Watson, W.J. Princeton, Ont., constable.
West-Jones, Marion. Sister of Florence Birchall.
Willis, H.R. chief of police, Woodstock.
Young, Thomas H. Chief of Ontario Police, Niagara Falls, Ont.

DEADLY SWINDLE

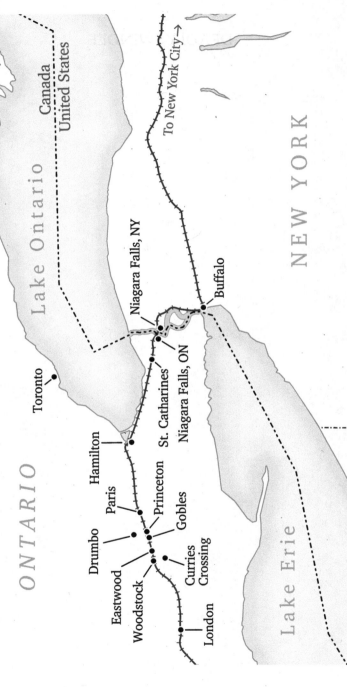

0.1. Map of Reginald Birchall's travels.

1

Introduction

"The whole of England, and especially London, is aroused as it never was before over this murder in the lonely Canadian swamp," declared a report from London, England, in March 1890. The story referenced a murder that had taken place in southwestern Ontario near Woodstock. At the conclusion of the legal proceedings, *The Times* observed that "the Atlantic cable has certainly never borne eastward so heavy a daily reporting of proceedings in a court of justice." The *Daily Post* of Birmingham, England, explained that the nature of the crime "was such as to cause a peculiar thrill of horror, and almost of dread, in a great many English homes."[1]

The story that grabbed so much press attention began on Friday, 21 February 1890. Brothers George and Joseph Elvidge were cutting wood in the Blenheim Swamp twelve miles west of Woodstock, Ont., when they discovered the dead body of a young man. Frozen and partly covered in snow and ice, he lay face-up on a brush pile in the lonely spot. The back of the head had a bloody hole. Suspecting foul play, the Elvidges immediately called in two local authorities, one a justice of the peace and the other a part-time constable in the nearby village of Princeton. After surveying the scene, the authorities decided to move the body to an undertaker's establishment in the village, where it was left to thaw so that an autopsy could be performed. Remarkable was the high quality of the man's clothing and especially the "fine new and clean underclothing."[2] Also notable was the fact that the clothing had been loosened and all labels snipped off. There was no identification on the body, and no local individual recognized the dead man.

Newspapers reported what they dubbed "a murder mystery," the identity of both victim and perpetrator being initially unknown. Soon, Canadian, American, and British newspapers picked up the story. As more and more information circulated about the case, interest ballooned. An autopsy showed that the dead man had been shot by a revolver twice in the back of the head. It became known that the murder victim, the alleged perpetrator, and the Crown's star witness, all upper-class men in their early twenties, had recently arrived in Canada from England. The chief suspect, John Reginald Birchall, appeared to have been swindling the other two men – Frederick Cornwallis Benwell and Douglas Raymond Pelly – by luring them to Ontario and getting them to invest in a horse farm that didn't exist. The story's appeal was enhanced by its main character, Reginald Birchall, represented in the press as a gentleman with a colourful past, charisma, a jovial demeanour, good looks, and unflinching self-confidence, features that gained him many admirers even though it appeared he had committed a cowardly, cold-blooded crime.

The Benwell–Birchall case had legs. Newspaper readers in Britain were fascinated by a murder involving a swindle of England's wealthy sons in an emigration scam. At the time in Britain, there was enormous interest in emigration matters. The murder suggested an explanation for the disappearance of many young Englishmen who had gone overseas and never been heard from again. Newspapers in the United States were drawn to a lurid murder story, a staple of their columns. Moreover, American commentators revelled in a case that exposed the gullibility of privileged Englishmen and brought them down a peg. Newspaper readers in Canada enjoyed the sensational coverage of a Canadian story, as well as the attention Canada was suddenly receiving in the international press. The timing of the crime mattered, too. It coincided with the height of British imperialism and thus with the fascination English-speaking Canadians, and especially Ontarians, had for England's power and global reach that enhanced the young Dominion's own place in the world.

Especially the trial of the alleged perpetrator of the crime drew national and international press attention. In the courtroom, class was put on trial. Spectators watched as the prisoner's behaviour in Ontario revealed intriguingly both how a gentleman given the best English education had resorted to swindling men of his class and how, if the

Crown's case was believed, he had shot a gentleman in cold blood. It was certainly not what most people expected of England's gentry.

The Newspaper Industry

Today we talk of "the media" in reference to the wide range of forms in which news reaches us: via a dizzying array of internet platforms, television, radio, and newspapers. In the late nineteenth century, however, newspapers alone disseminated the news on a commercial basis, making the press more important than it is today and a growing rather than shrinking industry.

In late nineteenth-century Canada, the United States, and Britain, population growth and advances in literacy thanks to mass schooling presented a ready consumer market for newspapers and their advertisers. Low capital costs encouraged the entry of precariously funded publishers, with the result that newspapers proliferated. Big cities created population densities that enabled dailies to prosper and to afford technological innovations in printing, such as the rotary press.[3]

Newspapers were changing in the second half of the nineteenth century. Earlier, most were political journals that devoted the bulk of their coverage to party politics in an intensely partisan way. Increasingly, the availability of fast presses and the appearance of the much cheaper "penny dailies" fed a mass readership. In the meantime, the emergence of the "new journalism" changed both the content and the style of many newspapers, whose editors now aimed to maximize profits by attracting a wide, popular readership. Gripping tales, including stories of crimes and disasters, distinguished the content of the new popular press. The *New York Herald* developed the sensational style that other mass dailies emulated. In mid-Victorian Britain, with the arrival of the "new journalism" and London's Sunday newspapers, editors who faced competition from broadsheets and pulp semi-fictions "began to assign more space and bigger headlines to any murder that contained even modest amounts of mystery and gore."[4] That change sparked an elitist complaint about sensationalism and the vulgarity of newspapers, but the new approach attracted an enormous mass readership. Somewhat behind, Canadian newspapers adopted the "new journalism" in the 1880s. In Toronto, the "people's journals" of the 1880s were afternoon and evening papers (with the exception of the *World*) and sold for one cent. Quality newspapers were morning publications and sold for two or three cents.[5]

The sheer number of newspapers that carried reports on the Benwell–Birchall case is astounding. While by no means providing a complete count of newspapers covering the story because of its limited coverage outside the United States, www.newspapers.com gives an indication. A search for "Benwell murder" produces 704 hits for the United States, 528 for the United Kingdom, and 60 for Canada. A search for "Reginald Birchall" results in 212 hits for Kansas alone.[6] Much of this coverage derived from reports telegraphed from Niagara Falls and Woodstock. By 1890, telegraph wires criss-crossed the globe, and reliable undersea cables linked the continents.

News agencies greatly assisted the spread of the news. They had been formed to facilitate the distribution of the news and to cut individual publisher's costs by sharing telegraph costs. Two American services, United Press and its rival Associated Press, fed stories across North America and beyond. The great, London-based news agency Reuters cabled sober reports from correspondents in Canada to London, and the New York-based Dalziel Agency sent the English press more colourful reports. Canada lacked its own associated press until 1903, although in 1890 journalists representing the US-based Associated Press sent out stories from Canadian places.[7] It was claimed that no previous event of any kind had occasioned such extensive use of telegrams as the Birchall trial. On its last day, telegraphers sent out 115,710 words from Woodstock. Overseas transmissions made it "an unprecedented feat in the history of the Atlantic cable."[8]

The telegraph and news agencies enabled even small newspapers to carry wire-service accounts of the Benwell murder and Birchall trial. Editors could fill columns with wire copy that they didn't need their own reporters to write. That helps explain why so many words were telegraphed from Woodstock and why so many newspapers covered the story. Wire-service reports tended to have a sobering effect on the style of reporting. Because each word cost money to transmit, journalists composing the stories adopted a terse and unadorned style.[9] Wire-service reporting countered some of the industry's trend towards florid sensationalism.

Toronto newspapers provide important sources for this book. Toronto, Ontario's largest city, with a population of about 180,000 in 1890, had six daily newspapers: the *Empire, Globe, News, Mail, Telegram*, and *World*.[10] This book draws from all them, as well as from other Canadian journals, especially Hamilton's *Spectator*, London's *Free Press*, and Montreal's *Gazette*. Of the Toronto dailies, the *World* picked up the

Benwell murder and ran with it like no other.[11] The venerable *Globe*, with its exceptionally deep reach into the markets of southwestern Ontario, covered the story closely if less flamboyantly. Reporters, many of them from the Toronto newspapers, fed stories to newspapers in places as far away as Allahabad, India, Panama City, Mexico City, Georgetown, Guyana, and Toamasina, Madagascar.[12]

Woodstock, where the Birchall trial took place, had two daily newspapers in 1890 to serve the town's population of 8,500: the *Sentinel-Review* and its rival the *Evening Standard*.[13] The *Sentinel-Review* of 1890 demonstrates how aggressively a small-town paper could cover the news. Its reports are a crucial source for this study. Owned by the Pattullo family, the *Sentinel-Review* was edited in 1890 by Andrew Pattullo, described as one of Ontario's most able journalists.[14] In 1890, he was chosen president of the Canadian Press Association, and in 1896 he was elected as a Liberal to the Ontario legislature. Thomas Dufferin "Duff" Pattullo, Andrew's nephew, was in 1890 working as a junior employee on the journal, long before he became premier of British Columbia in 1933. In the 1890s, the *Sentinel-Review* had a small staff of journalists who immediately spotted "the swamp murder" as a promising story. Their colourful reporting drew the interest of editors of mass dailies in Toronto and elsewhere, who took up the story. Small-town journalism near the site of the crime in southwestern Ontario provided the catalyst for the wave of reporting.[15]

The Historical Literature

Ever since the time of the 1890 murder, the Benwell–Birchall case has had its chroniclers. Authors have been drawn to it because of the dramatic story, and every author's purpose has been to entertain readers with a compelling account. Some writers have taken what they understood to be the basic facts of the case and run with them, using their imaginations to fill in gaps in the story. In 1890, the *Police Gazette* of New York published a short book that sold for twenty-five cents titled *The Benwell Murder: A Tragedy That Startled Two Continents*. In a sensational style, it brings the story to life with imagined dialogue and vivid illustrations.[16] Another 1890 publication, *The Swamp of Death or, The Benwell Murder*, appeared from a Toronto publisher.[17] The first half of the book, set in England, imagines the lives and romantic entanglements of the case's main characters well before the murder in Canada. Also imaginative, though purporting to be otherwise, is the account published in

1904 by the Ontario government's lead detective in the case, John Wilson Murray, and discussed in chapter 7 below.[18] Other authors relied on Murray's account, notably W. Stewart Wallace in his 1931 collection *Murder and Mysteries: A Canadian Series*.[19]

The Benwell–Birchall case has continued to attract imaginative storytellers in the twenty-first century. A black-and-white video dramatizing the case, *The Cultured Criminal*, directed by Canadian Florin Marksteiner, was released in 2012. It embellishes the known facts in a series of short scenes acted in the style of silent movies.[20] Also focused on storytelling is a book that is much more thorough and better researched (although not footnoted), *The Swamp of Death: A Tale of Victorian Lies and Murder* (2004) by Rebecca Gowers. The author is an English journalist and the great-granddaughter of Douglas Pelly, the Crown's star witness at Birchall's murder trial. In 2015, Alan J. Bytheway, another British author, told the story in his *Murder as a Fine Art: A Story of Fraud, Betrayal, and Murder across Two Continents*, which speculatively "links Birchall's psychological mindset to the writings of the essayist, Thomas de Quincey."[21]

This book differs from previous accounts of the case because, while it also relies on narrative, it is scholarly and analytical and contextualizes the case. Contributing to the well-established field of Canadian legal history, this book is a case study that illuminates how the legal process played out in a particular situation. Furthermore, it examines how contemporary newspapers developed the sensational story they related, one that travelled around the English-speaking world and beyond. Along the way, press representations of gender – of Reginald Birchall's performance of masculinity and his wife's upper-class femininity, for example – provide a topic for analysis.

Studies of legal cases from the past now form a significant genre in the field of legal history. By focusing on a single case, such studies demonstrate how the law worked at particular times and in particular settings. They highlight the fact that the application of legal processes is not determined strictly by the formal law, but rather varies depending on the players, places, and period.

Many legal history case studies share the purpose of revealing the lives and circumstances of ordinary people who otherwise have left little historical record of themselves. Natalie Zemon Davis's path-breaking *The Return of Martin Guerre* inspired many scholars to discover in legal archives new knowledge and insights about people that history has overlooked.[22] Her book is an outstanding example of micro-history, a genre that takes a single, focused historical "moment" and uses it to shed light on broad themes and a wider world.[23] Micro-histories rely on legal records to uncover everyday people's experiences in the past and to allow readers to feel a connection to that past. By contrast, the main players in *Deadly Swindle* were scarcely dispossessed. The victim, the alleged murderer, the chief Crown witness, and the leading lawyers were all privileged men of means and social standing. Only around the edges of the case do ordinary people speak to us from the past. Witnesses at Birchall's trial included farmers, woodsmen, railway employees, and female shop assistants. In the pages that follow, then, we glimpse aspects of the lives and cultures of both the well-to-do and folks of modest means.

Particularly helpful in writing about the legal processes of the Benwell–Birchall case has been Robert Sharpe's authoritative case study, *The Lazier Murder: Prince Edward County, 1884*.[24] Peter Lazier was murdered at a farmhouse near Bloomfield, Ont., on 21 December 1883, and three neighbours were arrested and charged with murder. Based on archival and newspaper accounts, the book reconstructs the Lazier murder case and attempts "to place the legal issues in their proper historical context." Because the case also took place in rural Ontario and only six years before the Benwell murder, Sharpe's insights into how the law worked are highly pertinent. Comparisons between the two cases, moreover, reveal similar themes: how the community-based and amateur tradition of justice administration was shifting towards professionalism and expertise; the powerful role of public opinion as expressed by the press in shaping outcomes; and the presence of some onlookers troubled by the possibility of wrongful conviction.

Historical case studies that examine legal processes pursue other themes raised by the case. Martin Friedland's *The Case of Valentine Shortis*, for example, which deals with a 1895 murder in Valleyfield, Quebec, provides an entrée into the history of psychiatry because of the trial's insanity defence and because the convict served a part of his sentence in a facility for the criminally insane. In *Walk towards the Gallows* Rheinhold Kramer and Tom Mitchell explore melodrama because the murderer, a female domestic servant living in Brandon, Manitoba, in 1899, was deeply affected by her reading of literature. In *Murdering Holiness* authors Jim Phillips and Rosemary Gartner connect the 1906 murder of a self-proclaimed prophet and sect leader in Seattle, Washington, to the then popular holiness movement in American religion.[25] Legal case histories thus shed light on themes well beyond the law, as does *Deadly Swindle* when exploring the role of the press in the Benwell–Birchall case.

Authors of histories of legal cases depend heavily on contemporary newspaper coverage of them because it enables historians to expand on surviving legal records. Newspaper articles help us contextualize a case by providing information and gossip circulating in the community and more widely. The press is an essential source in gauging the impact of public opinion on the legal process and its outcomes. Of course, newspapers are not a straightforward gauge of public opinion, but it would be many decades before public opinion polls began to be taken in Canada. For the Benwell–Birchall case, newspaper sources hugely augment the disappointingly sparse archival sources on the case.[26]

Of course, the content of newspapers cannot be counted on to provide a reliable record of events or an accurate indication of public attitudes in the past. News reports and commentary must be read, like all historical sources, with a measure of scepticism, and where possible, they should be tested against other sources, including the content of other journals. Good history always treats critically what was said in the past, benefiting from the historian's temporal distance from the events to analyse them afresh. Certainly, in the Benwell–Birchall case it is necessary to appreciate that journalists treated it as a sensational story and did their best to appeal to readers by playing up the drama and intrigue.

A key reason why reports on the Benwell–Birchall case found a place in so many newspapers was that it fit neatly with the press's long-standing interest in sensational news about crime and especially murders. Lurid publications about crimes in England date back as far as the 1650s,[27] and sensational reports of them only increased with time. In 1830s New York, James Gordon Bennett of the *New York Herald* paved the way for other publishers when he discovered that featuring racy accounts of crimes gave a boost to circulation and profits.[28] In nineteenth-century Britain, where crime journalism was a major industry, "Victorians treated murder news like a form of 'popular entertainment, a spectator sport.'"[29] Critical media scholars go further and emphasize that crime stories provide publishers and journalists with an opportunity to shore up "dominant values governing normative behaviour." As one scholar puts it, the media's preoccupation with deviant behaviour "is not because it is intrinsically interesting, but because it is intrinsically instructive." By restating social rules and warning that violators will be prosecuted, "the wayward are cautioned and the righteous are comforted."[30] Relatedly, L. Perry Curtis argues that in Victorian England newspaper editors saw crime stories as having a dual appeal: they fed the appetites of the prurient, which sold newspapers, and they offered an opportunity "to reinscribe the code of respectability."

The Locale

The part of southwestern Ontario where Benwell's murder took place had been first settled by the Neutral/Attawandaron people of the longhouse, but they had abandoned their villages by 1650. Colonization of the area was made possible under British law by treaties that the Crown signed in the late eighteenth century with the Mississauga First Nation and the Chippewa First Nation.[31] The first wave of colonizers came from south of the Great Lakes because of the American Revolution, while later waves arrived from Great Britain. With the Baldwin Act (1849), which democratized local government structures, Oxford County became a self-governing county with an elected council.[32] After mid-century, population growth slowed because the good land had been colonized, but villages and towns servicing the rural population and economy continued to grow.

According to the 1891 *Census of Canada*, Oxford's population of nearly 50,000 was overwhelmingly Canadian-born and of British descent. Some Americans and German-speakers were added to the mix, but other groups were tiny.[33] Earlier, white Quaker abolitionists in Oxford had welcomed African Americans, many of them people escaping enslavement. The 1881 *Census of Canada* counted 158 "Africans" in Oxford, but their numbers soon dwindled. In 1891, Blacks numbered only fifteen in Woodstock.[34] In all of Oxford County, the 1891 census counted only eight Jews and just four individuals born in China. That census showed that the county's population was overwhelmingly Protestant, with Roman Catholics making up only 6 per cent of those who reported a religion.[35] In 1890 Canada, Protestant–Catholic conflicts were intense, but in Oxford, local sectarian tensions were slight, perhaps because of the small Catholic presence and, relative to many other parts of Ontario, the small Irish Protestant population.[36]

Most of the settlers came to the area seeking an independence on the land, and many met with success. Family farms sustained the great majority of inhabitants, who were soon producing a range of agricultural products for home consumption and local exchange. Wheat was their most important cash crop. During the second half of the nineteenth century, dairying became increasingly important, and Oxford's cheese put the county on the map as a major producer for British markets as well as Canadian ones. The prosperity of local agriculture fostered the growth of an urban population that serviced the farming sector. Villages dotted the countryside, and two substantial towns emerged: Woodstock, Oxford County's administrative centre with its courthouse and county jail, and Ingersoll, Woodstock's more industrialized rival.

Woodstock's population stood out from the rest of the county because it was first settled by an unusually large number of pensioned officers of the Royal Navy and British army. For a time, it continued to attract well-off English newcomers, who were drawn by the town's elite and their equestrian-centred leisure pastimes of riding to the hunt and steeple chasing.[37] Woodstock and vicinity also drew a large number of "farm pupils." Firms in England charged well-off young men for placements on Canadian farms, where they worked without pay but supposedly learned local farming methods in preparation for establishing their own farms. Reginald Birchall first came to Woodstock as a farm pupil and stayed for a while to enjoy its horse culture.[38]

The following chapters tell the story of the Benwell murder and Birchall's trial mainly as reported by 1890 newspapers. Readers of this book learn more and more about the case just as newspaper readers in 1890 did from daily reports. The book is, on the one hand, a history of a crime, the related legal processes, and the punishment meted out by authorities, and on the other, a history of the press – how it handled a sensational case. Other sources, especially memoirs,[39] supplement newspaper sources and enable insights into the vivid characters at the heart of the drama.

2

The Murder Mystery

The murder story broke the day after the Elvidge brothers found the body in the Blenheim Swamp near Princeton, Ont., a small village on the Governor's Road in Oxford County.[1] On Saturday, 22 February 1890, local and regional newspapers provided the first details of the body's discovery after being fed a wire-service report from Princeton. Like all such reports, the story had no byline; authorship is unknown. Toronto's *World* and the *Free Press* of London, Ontario, carried nearly identical reports from Princeton dated Friday, 21 February. The *World* headed its report "Probably a Murder," and the *Free Press* headline was "Found Dead in the Woods."

The accounts explained that when the Elvidges entered the Blenheim Swamp at 11 a.m. to cut wood, they discovered the body of a young man with "an ugly head wound just back of the left ear." Some blood had dropped onto the snow beneath the body and had frozen solid. No weapon had been found, and there were no traces of a struggle. Investigators found footprints that looked to have been made by large moccasins between the corpse and the nearby Blenheim second concession road. The dead man wore a brown felt hat and was dressed in an overcoat with a cape made of brown checked tweed, black pants with a grey stripe, high-quality new and clean underclothing, and a freshly laundered, linen shirt having pearl cuff buttons marked "W. West." No money or papers were found on the

2.1. In the Blenheim Swamp where the body was found. Posed second from the left is Detective John Murray, and on the right is farmer John R. Rabb, who lived just west of the swamp entrance.

Source: Woodstock Museum, image 1988.22.10.

body, and the inscribed marks on the clothing identifying the owner had been cut out as if to foil identification of the corpse. The Elvidge brothers helped take the body by sleigh to Swartz, the undertaker in Princeton.

That same day, 22 February, Woodstock's *Sentinel-Review* immediately shaped the narrative by featuring the story as "A Murder Mystery." It focused on speculations about the murdered man's identity, in which local residents were showing "considerable interest." So far, no local person had been able to identify him. A Woodstock man had been asked to visit Princeton to see whether the remains were those of a young man from the town who had disappeared mysteriously. The body appeared to be of a man about twenty-three or twenty-four years of age. That same day, the other Woodstock daily, the *Evening Standard*, also featured the local story, reporting, for instance, on a search party scouring the Princeton area.

Authorities on the Scene

Upon discovering the body, the Elvidges followed legal procedure in the case of a suspected crime by immediately fetching the local magistrate and nearest police constable, the faces of the local state. In rural Ontario during the nineteenth century, the justice of the peace and the constable were pillars of the community justice system inherited from England. It was intended that justices of the peace be men of social standing who could command authority in their communities. Property qualifications helped ensure the standing of appointees.[2] Justices of the peace held a wide range of responsibilities in the field of local administration, from highway planning and maintenance to liquor licensing. Although legal training was by no means a requirement of the post, they were crucial figures in justice administration, having the power to investigate crimes, decide bail and trial committals for serious offences, and adjudicate minor offences. They also had the power to recommend the appointment of constables.

The justice of the peace who appeared promptly at the crime scene in Blenheim Swamp was William Crosby, a farmer who resided in or near Princeton. In 1890, Crosby, age sixty-two, was married with four children. The *Sentinel-Review* referred to him respectfully as "Squire Crosby."[3]

Constables were appointed by the Quarter Sessions on the recommendation of justices of the peace. Throughout rural Ontario, constables were part-time and paid on a fee-for-service basis. The compensation was modest at best, sometimes even failing to cover expenses. Essentially volunteers, they lacked training in criminal investigation. By the 1880s, some people in Ontario were voicing considerable criticism of the amateurism of local constables and calling for the appointment of full-time, salaried constables.[4] The constable on the scene in the Blenheim Swamp was W.J. Watson, a house painter in Princeton.[5] His occupation of painter is typical of the modest occupational status of local constables at the time.

Crosby and Watson were hardly a formidable state presence at the murder scene. Nevertheless, the community would have seen the pair with their local connections as entirely appropriate authorities. The *Sentinel-Review* had precious little to say about them, taking for granted their identities and roles. Much less mundane was the eventual arrival in Princeton of John Wilson Murray, one of just three detectives employed by the government of Ontario to provide professional expertise mainly in small towns and rural areas like Princeton and vicinity. Woodstock would have been familiar with Murray's name and reputation from the many newspaper articles that reported his detecting activities throughout Ontario. His arrival locally would thus have been newsworthy.[6]

Although newspapers did not report it at the time, also on the scene before the body was removed to Princeton was Dr. Oliver Taylor, one of the two doctors who would soon conduct the autopsy. When he arrived at the swamp, he found that the clothing of the deceased was frozen to the ground.[7]

Pondering the Identity of the Deceased and the Murderers

Of great interest to reporters was local speculation and gossip about who the deceased could be. The *Sentinel-Review* reported on 24 February that James Swartz, the Princeton undertaker, said that in December, he had seen the man, an "Indian" (Indigenous man) or someone like him, performing Indian war dances in Drumbo, a village near Princeton, on Nomination Day. ("Nomination Day" was a social occasion, the day kicking off an election campaign, when men gathered to select candidates.) Swartz's recollection fit with the moccasin footprints. The *Sentinel-Review* gave further credence to Swartz's story by saying that the man's "features were strikingly Indian." His face was dark, his hair black, his nose Roman, his lips full, and his eyes light grey. The *Sentinel-Review* made the most of the mystery by reporting that the body, although found in the woods, had on a white shirt that "still looked as if it were fresh from the laundry." The *Evening Standard*, however, discounted the story of the deceased's racial difference. Coroner McLay declared the body to be "perfectly white" except for the face, which had been exposed to the frost.[8]

On 24 February, Toronto's *Globe*, the province's most prestigious newspaper, published its first article on the "Murder Mysterious." Because the deceased had not readily been identified by local residents, people believed he had been lured to the area and killed, or killed elsewhere and the body dumped near Princeton. The *Globe* challenged the speculation that the deceased was an Indigenous person, quoting Coroner McLay about the whiteness of the body. Moreover, the gold plate and fillings and the man's clothes denoted "refinement and opulence." It appeared more likely that the well-dressed victim was a young Englishman newly arrived in Canada. The racialized depiction of the victim, then, was almost immediately dismissed.

That Monday, the *Sentinel-Review* provided more information and speculation. Many people had visited Swartz's undertaking establishment on the Sunday to view the murdered man's remains, which were lying on a stretcher upstairs under a cloth. The body measured five feet seven-and-a-half inches and weighed 140 pounds. The many visitors had failed to identify him, however. In Woodstock it was rumoured that a local man, together with a fellow from Sarnia recently tried for robbery, had perpetrated the murder, but the Woodstock man visited police and denied the story. "Rumors are flying thick and fast," commented the *Sentinel-Review*, "and if one believed everything ... he would find that the man had been identified several times and in several ways and that several people had already been arrested for the murder."

To assist with identification, Woodstock photographers C.E. Perry and A.G. Westlake had dressed the man's upper body in his clothes and had taken three photographs of him lying on his back with his upper body and head slightly raised. Prints of them were widely distributed to Ontario newspaper offices.[9]

On 26 February, Toronto's *World* provided details about the condition of the body, presumably as reported by the doctors performing the autopsy. Two bullets had been fired from a revolver into the deceased's head. Either one would have killed him instantly. One bullet wound was found behind the left ear, and another just where the nape of the neck joins the head. Both thirty-two-calibre bullets found in the skull had been flattened out. The path of the bullets showed the gun had been fired in an upward direction. The hair around the wound at the neck was burned, indicating that the shot had been fired from a revolver at point-blank range. A quantity of powder surrounded the other wound. Two yellowish-green bruises were found, a large one on the right groin and a smaller one on the stomach. It was thought that they might have been caused in the removal of the body or by contact with the limb of a tree. A kick could not have caused them.

On a return visit to the swamp on the day after the discovery, the Elvidge brothers found things probably belonging to the murdered

18 Deadly Swindle

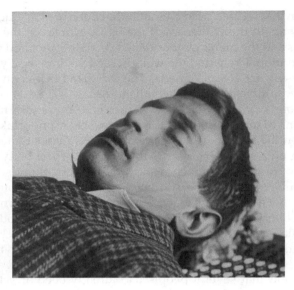

2.2. The corpse, photographed February 1890 in Swartz's undertaking establishment, Princeton, Ont., by C.E. Perry and A.G. Westlake. Copies of this image appeared in the windows of newspaper offices throughout Ontario, and it was the basis for drawings published in many newspapers.
Source: Woodstock Museum, image 1988.22.7.

man, including a cigar-holder and a pair of gold-rimmed spectacles with "Peebles" lenses, that is, thick lenses with strong magnification for reading. Another discovery was of a cigar-box with a name written on it: "F. C. Benwell."[10] The *Sentinel-Review* made no comment. It turned out to be a crucial clue, but its significance went unrecognized at first because no one knew whether the name referred to the victim, a perpetrator of the crime, or someone else. The *Evening Standard* maintained that it might have belonged to one of the parties who carried the deceased into the swamp or perhaps "it had been placed there for the sake of throwing the authorities off the trail."[11] The *Globe* and the *Mail*, the Toronto dailies with the largest readerships, took several days to report the discovery of the cigar-box.

It was eventually explained that the Elvidge brothers lived on a Princeton-area farm owned by William Hersee and worked for him. A couple of miles away, Hersee owned 250 mostly forested acres where the swamp was located and where the brothers had gone to work on 21 February.[12]

A reporter for the *Sentinel-Review* showed initiative by following up on the Benwell name by investigating a tip that a James W. Benwell kept a hotel in Brantford, Ontario. Telephone inquiries ascertained that the hotel-keeper knew nothing of any F.C. Benwell. The newspaper observed: "the mystery is still as mysterious as ever."[13]

The *Sentinel-Review*, which featured the story the following day, reported that the photographs of the dead man had been posted in windows in Woodstock and examined by a great many people. Still, his identity remained unknown.[14]

Various residents of Woodstock thought they had seen a man resembling the deceased selling cheap jewellery in town on Dominion Day (1 July), 1889. Some said the peddler was Jewish, thus racializing the stranger. However, this line of speculation was quickly dismissed. An enterprising reporter had consulted town records, which showed that no licence to sell jewellery had been issued for Dominion Day. The only Jewish jewellery peddler on record was Levi Isaac, whose face did not resemble the dead man's.[15] In rural Ontario during the late nineteenth century, the occasional visit from a Jewish peddler introduced a foreign "other," who in this instance provided a convenient focus for speculations about the stranger's identity.

The *Sentinel-Review* gave details concerning Princeton-area residents' suspicions about two men, one from Woodstock and the other from Sarnia, thought to be the murderers. Late at night, both men "full of liquor" had left Woodstock for the nearby village of Drumbo. One of them was said to have carried considerable money, which he claimed he had gotten from his uncle. The drunken pair stopped at several houses along the way, waking the residents, and feigning the need for directions to Princeton. In fact, they were doing so out of "pure cussedness." The *Sentinel-Review* said that as the story was discussed, it "assumed wonderful shapes," but in fact the spree could well have had nothing to do with the murder. It reasoned that the murder was committed by "no drunken brawler" because it was "too well done." The newspaper surmised that, given the clothing was free from blood, either the man had been undressed when shot or his clothes had been changed after he died. Probably, too, given that the clothing was so clean, the murder had been done in some building or under cover and then taken to the site where it had been discovered. It was significant that the identification labels from the clothing had been neatly and methodically removed by "cunning hands." Clearly, it was "no ordinary case of highway robbery."[16]

On Wednesday, 26 February, the *Free Press* and the *World* took the story further. The London paper reported on two identifications of the body. A man resembling the deceased, but with a light moustache, was said to be a coachman employed by a Mr. Yates of Brantford, to whom some of the clothing and the cigar-box had been sent for identification. Another theory was that the deceased was a man who had been around Woodstock selling polishing compound for use by barmen. The *Free Press* reported that many people around Princetown were saying the man was murdered while naked in "a house of prostitution." That explained the lack of blood on his clothes. Murdered while naked in the brothel, he had then been dressed and taken to the woods. Because the clothing showed that scissors had been used to cut the identifying labels, it was all the more likely the murder had taken place indoors, where scissors would be close at hand. Furthermore, it was believed the deceased's face had been shaved after his death. Noting these same "facts," the *Evening Standard* concluded: "a woman must be involved." It urged the police to arrest everybody connected with the brothel, "as there is no more likely scene for committal of such a diabolical crime than such a den." Locating the much-discussed brothel near Princeton proved impossible, however.[17]

On 26 February, the *World* committed to making the story its main preoccupation, which it would remain for several weeks. "Who Is This Man?" asked the headline, which was followed by "Princeton's Murder Mystery Unsolved." The coverage, which took up half the front page of the Toronto newspaper, boasted an artist's rendering of the widely distributed photograph of the dead man. (Reproducing photographs in newspapers was beyond the means of the Ontario press at the time.) "It is hardly possible," surmised the newspaper, "that among The World's thousands of readers there will not be some who will recognize ... the features and thus solve a most important element in the problem." The article repeated what the press had previously reported and then some. Clearly the editor was banking on the story selling newspapers.

The *World* speculated that the murderer or murderers had intended to carry the body into the swamp, taking a trail that leads to a small lake where it would not be found. However, the going had been too tough and so the body had been deposited only ten yards or so from the road, where a pile of brush made farther access difficult. The *World* also provided additional details, such as the fact that the underclothing was made of "the finest French wool" and that the cigar case, inscribed inside with the name F.C. Benwell, was of "strong leather."

The reporters from the *World* became amateur detectives, working to identify the body. One of them, who had gone to Woodstock, inquired of a local haberdasher and found that the inscription "W. West" found on the man's buttons was simply the name of a well-known button-maker. There went that clue. The *World* placed a photograph of the deceased in the front window of its newspaper offices on Toronto's King Street, where thousands of passers-by examined it. Within half an hour, two men had come into the office and said the photograph was of a moulder they knew who had worked in a foundry in St. Catharine's, Ont. (A moulder was a skilled craftsman who shaped wooden moulds to produce metal goods and parts.) The men couldn't remember his name.

World reporters made inquiries among Toronto moulders at the Gurney foundry and the Labour Hall. When shown the photograph of the corpse, various moulders thought they had seen him and believed he might have been employed at the Massey works during the previous spring and might have boarded at 844 King Street West. The fellow resembled the man in the photograph, except that he had a light, red mustache. The keen reporters then visited the boarding house, where Miss Cameron thought the image resembled her former boarder named Slack, although it was hard to be certain because the man in the photo lacked the moustache. She said that Slack had left for Rochester, New York. Detective Wasson, who was in Galt, Ont., during a recent strike of moulders, "distinctly recognized" him as a man he had seen there, an imported moulder who acted as a strike-breaker.

The next day (27 February), however, the *World* reported that a Mr. Matthew Howie of Toronto rejected "the moulder theory." Moulders did not wear fine clothing. If the deceased had anything to do with the Galt strike, he would be an American detective hired by the companies to watch the strikers. "The description tallies with that kind of man," he observed. Clearly, the tense labour relations of the period affected perceptions of whose body it might be. The *Sentinel-Review*, in reprinting the moulder story from the *World*, dismissed the moulder hypothesis, declaring that "the deceased had no appearance of being a moulder or mechanic of any kind."[18]

The *World* asked Det. John Newhall, a senior member of the Toronto Police Force, for his assessment of the case. Surprisingly, given the evidence about the two shots, he maintained that it was likely a suicide. The man was well-dressed, which, he said, was typical of suicides, who generally make themselves as presentable as possible. The absence of a weapon and the empty pockets could be accounted for by a robbery of the body by a passing tramp.[19]

The *World* reported that a local man in Princeton was certain the man was a young tenderfoot recently arrived from England, adding that there were about two hundred such men living with farmers in the area. The *Sentinel-Review* reported that Mr. Fred Cheeswright, an English tailor and long-time resident of Princeton, had examined the deceased's clothes and declared them to be definitely made in England.[20] The Woodstock *Evening Standard* quoted prominent local resident T.C. Patterson, who believed the deceased was one of two brothers who had come from England and visited him on his farm. His son, however, said that the deceased's boots had thin soles, unlike the heavy boots worn by the English brothers.[21]

Both the *World* and the *Sentinel-Review* carried similar stories about further discoveries.[22] Blood on the man's collar showed that he had not been undressed at the time he was shot, thus discrediting the story about the elusive brothel. More than 1,000 curious people had visited Princeton to view the corpse.

Newspapers also carried reports that the body had been identified as being that of Oscar Scarff, who worked in British Columbia's seal fishery. He had visited the Turnbulls, people in the neighbourhood, three or four weeks earlier and then had gone to Sarnia. He had had $600 on him. The Turnbulls went to see the body and identified it as being Scarff by a scar on the leg. Scarff wore a dark moustache, but it was surmised that it had probably been shaved off after his death to throw off identification. Both newspapers reported, however, that a telegram sent from Sarnia said that Scarff had left by train for British Columbia.

Swartz had embalmed the body immediately after the autopsy so that it could continue to be viewed by people seeking to identify it. On 27 February, the *Sentinel-Review* reported that the people of Princeton had turned out and given the deceased a Christian burial in their cemetery, the burial service having been read by the warden of the local Anglican Church. "The remains were encased in no pauper's box," declared the *Sentinel-Review*, "but in a good casket." The newspaper said that "the whole sad affair," had been handled well by Princeton's inhabitants and especially by Swartz, the undertaker.

The Coroner's Inquest

While newspapers reported on developments and speculations, further information reached the public through reports of the official proceedings. The legal process had gotten under way within hours of the body's discovery when the coroner at Woodstock issued a warrant directing the Princeton constable to summon a jury of at least twelve men for an inquiry. The law required coroners to investigate any death caused by violence, unfair means, or negligence, as well as deaths in prisons.[23] Investigations were "to be held with as little delay as possible."[24] Clearly, the body in the swamp required investigation. Wherever possible, coroners' reports identified the cause and perpetrator of the death, and for the community's benefit recommended steps to avoid similar deaths in future.

The coroner in this case, Dr Archibald McLay, was a man of standing in the community. Born in Glasgow, Scotland, in 1843, McLay had immigrated at age eleven with his large family, who settled in Southwold Township, Elgin County, to the south and west of Oxford. McLay married a young Southwold woman in 1869, and they took up residence in Woodstock, where McLay built his practice. Physicians competed for appointments as coroner because it brought status and fees. Applicants for the position generally needed political pull with members of the Ontario legislature. Expertise in investigating crimes was not a requirement of the job; manuals provided helpful advice, as they did for men playing other roles in the community justice system.[25] By 1890, there were critics of this long-standing, community-based system of justice, who called for reforms to bring greater central control and professional expertise.[26]

McLay quickly appointed a jury to investigate the swamp death, drawing from the men who had assembled at Princeton at the first news of the body's discovery. As required by law, the coroner and jury first convened at the site of the death, in this case, in the snowy woods of the frozen swamp. McLay would have instructed the jury to examine the body closely, checking for injuries and observing its position and immediate surroundings. They would also have looked for any weapon and signs of struggle, and paid attention to any footprints in the snow.[27]

Also on the scene were Const. Watson, the Elvidge brothers, and two Woodstock physicians tasked with conducting an autopsy. Once the coroner and jury had completed the on-site portion of their inquiry, the Elvidges loaded the body onto a sleigh and removed it to

24　Deadly Swindle

2.3. Coroner Archibald McLay, MD, the Woodstock coroner who undertook the February 1890 inquest in Princeton, Ont.
Source: Western University, D.B. Weldon Library, Archives and Special Collections.

Princeton, where it was expected that the inquiry would resume with witnesses called to testify under oath. Before much progress could be made, however, the coroner wanted an autopsy completed, which was impossible until the body had thawed. It was left in the upstairs room of Swartz's funeral parlour with a woodstove providing the necessary heat.

The inquest resumed on Monday, 24 February, in Dake's Hotel, Princeton. The report on the autopsy was ready. In the written opinion of Drs. Oliver Taylor and Charles R. Staples, "Death was produced by injury to the brain caused by two pistol shots fired by some hand as yet unknown, but other than the deceased's, either one of which was sufficient to produce death." They remarked that the shots had been fired at close range and that the nature of the wounds meant that there would have been little blood.

Having dealt with the autopsy, Coroner McLay then called on the Elvidge brothers to explain under oath about the discovery of the body.

Two witnesses followed who spoke to the identity of the deceased. George Fowler of Drumbo, who owned a furniture store in Waterford, testified that a year earlier in Waterford, he saw a jewellery and tinware pedlar who resembled the deceased. The man was a party to running jewellery stores in Brantford and Waterford. Alfred Laycock, a miller and farmer near Gobles, thought he had seen the deceased four years earlier selling jewellery and again just a year ago peddling jewellery in Woodstock on Dominion Day.

At this point, McLay kept reporters from hearing the remainder of the day's testimony. The law permitted a coroner to exclude people from an inquest, although the advice was "to err on the side of publicity." The *Sentinel-Review* reported that three residents testified about visits late the previous Wednesday evening and early Thursday morning by two men. The inquest then adjourned.

On the evening of Wednesday, 26 February, the inquest resumed at Dake's Hotel. Now Oxford's Crown attorney, Francis Ramsay Ball of Woodstock, was in attendance, indicating the Crown's increased interest in the proceedings. John McKay, proprietor of the North American Hotel in Woodstock, and James Oliver, bartender at the hotel, each testified that the deceased resembled a man who had visited the hotel selling polish some days before the body's discovery. They equivocated, however, and McKay said that, unlike the deceased, the man had had a small, dark moustache.

John R. Rabb, who lived near the swamp on the Second Concession, Blenheim Township, testified that on the Tuesday before the body was discovered, at about six in the evening, he had heard two pistol shots fired, and had talked about them with his neighbour. On the Friday he noticed tracks leading from the direction of where the body was found. Mrs. Rachel Schultz, a nearby neighbour of Rabb's, testified that she had heard one shot fired.

Several witnesses then testified about the movements of two men, Baker and Caldwell, who had called at their homes or businesses either late on the Wednesday evening or early Thursday morning. James Atkinson, hotelkeeper in Drumbo, said the men had called at his establishment at about 3:30 Thursday morning. Samuel Stroud said that at about 11 p.m. on the Wednesday the two men had come to his father's hotel in a muddy buggy. Jerry Dake of Princeton said that the two men had visited his hotel early Thursday morning. Both had been drinking, but he thought they weren't as drunk as they made out. John Rabb, hosteler at Dake's Hotel and the son of a previous witness, said that he saw the two men at the hotel and thought they had "considerable liquor in them." Col. Cowan heard the two men talking at Dake's, saying where they had visited. He thought they had been on a spree and that Caldwell had money with him. James Kipp, wagon-maker in East Oxford, testified that about 1:00 a.m. Thursday, the men had called at his house, saying they were lost.

At this point, the inquest adjourned. McLay announced it would resume on Friday, 7 March.

Getting Serious

On 1 March, the *World* featured its interview with Det. John Wilson Murray, the Ontario government detective, caught on the fly as he was leaving Toronto by train. Murray was confident that the dead man was a recent arrival from England who had never performed manual labour. He said that the hypotheses that he was a Jewish pedlar, or a moulder, or the sealer Oscar Scarff, had all proven to be chimerical. The *World* reported too that there had been excitement around Toronto's Albion Hotel on the previous evening because of a report that a man resembling the deceased had stayed at the hotel from 13 to 19 February. The guest, A.L. Atkinson, had said he was a passenger shipping agent based in London, England, where he was next headed via New York. It was agreed that his clothes resembled the dead man's but were darker. That awkward fact did not deter speculation.

The *World* gave additional details about the two men earlier reported to have been on a spree near Princeton.[28] George Baker of Woodstock and Robert Caldwell, formerly of Blenheim Township but recently working on building the Grand Trunk Railway tunnel at Sarnia, had come to Woodstock on Wednesday, 19 February, where they had done some drinking. They then had hired a rig at Hood's livery and at 1 a.m. had gone out the Governor's Road, which runs parallel to the Second Concession close to where the body was found. Along the road they called on James Kipp, a wagon-maker, asked him the way to Princeton, and invited him for a drink. He recognized them and told them they knew the way. They did the same at Lancaster's farm and got the same reply. At 3:30 a.m., Baker and Caldwell arrived at the Atkinson House in Drumbo and woke up the landlord. They had several drinks and then, after spending the night, had breakfast there before returning to Woodstock. When the pair left, some people in the hotel remarked that "a robbery or some other depredation must have been afoot." The *World* reported that when the pair had accounted for themselves to the detective, their story was "anything but satisfactory."

On 1 March, the *World* published a complete list of the dead man's clothing and effects:

Suit of the very best English gray striped tweed, probably west of England tweed.
White shirt with high stand-up collar, both evidently of English manufacture. Piece cut out of collar where initials had been.
Undershirt and drawers, very fine English flannel: piece removed from the bosom of the shirt, evidently contained initials.
Dark brown knitted socks name removed from front.
Pair of English laced walking boots, slightly worn on inside of soles as if wearer had been in habit of wearing overshoes.
Waterproof ulster with cape, evidently made in London, Eng. as contained half-moon shaped trade mark of English manufacturer.
Brown Christy hat of latest pattern.
Dark blue necktie with white spots.
Pair milky-pearl cuff buttons of silver setting engraved "W. West."
Plain gold shirt studs.
Gold ring (English) in bloodstone, marked 18 carat.
Found beside body:
Brown leather cigar case, with name "F. C. Benwell" written in ink and easy flowing hand, showing writer to have been clever with the pen. Case contained one mutilated cigar.
Cherry wood cigar holder.
Heavy gold plate in mouth, containing three false teeth, two on left side and one on right side. Evidently English workmanship and very fine.
Pair of eye-glasses, suitable for a person slightly near-sighted.

The *World* gave all the details in the hope that it would aid identification of the man.

Identified at Last

That same day, the *Sentinel-Review* observed that it was unfortunate the body had been buried so soon because people were arriving from out of town who wished to make an identification. A married couple had come from Niagara Falls, New York. The man said he had a friend named F.C. Benwell who had gone to examine a farm property near Woodstock or Paris, and he had not returned. From the description of the body, he was certain the man was his friend.

"Mystery Solved" shouted a headline in the late (3 p.m.) edition of the *Sentinel-Review* on Saturday, 1 March. The body had just been disinterred and examined by Mr. J. Burchell, who had come from Niagara Falls and positively identified the remains of F.C. Benwell, a young Englishman just out from the Old Country. According to Burchell, Fred Benwell had left him at Niagara Falls three or four weeks earlier to look for a suitable stock farm to purchase near Woodstock or London. Burchell said he had received a letter from Benwell about three weeks previously from London, Ont., saying he would soon return, but nothing had been heard from him. Burchell maintained he hadn't the slightest doubt that Benwell had been decoyed by some ruffians and murdered for the money in his possession. The local newspapers had the scoop on out-of-town ones. As it was Saturday afternoon, the other newspapers had to wait until Monday to make their reports.

It was reported that once Const. Watson of Princeton learned of the identification, he had telegraphed the attorney general's office in Toronto requesting assistance from Det. John Murray. Murray left for southwestern Ontario immediately, on 1 March.

Thus, in the course of the week following the discovery of the body, Woodstock's local newspapers and the *World* had developed the mystery by citing local people's speculations about the identity of the unknown body as well as reports of the testimony of witnesses at the inquest. It had been suggested that the victim was an Indigenous person who had been seen singing "Indian war songs" in Drumbo, a Brantford hotelkeeper or guest, one of two well-off brothers visiting from England, a Jewish jewellery peddler, a coachman from Brantford, a sealer from British Columbia, a travelling salesman, and a shipping agent from London, England. The ever-evolving list of possibilities kept readers interested in "The Murder Mystery."

The press had also reported on speculations about the identity of the killer or killers. Had it been the two men on a spree, who it seemed were up to no good? Or was the culprit a woman, a prostitute from a local brothel? The evidence from the post-mortem examination showed it had to have been a murder; even so, the *World* reported a detective's hunch that it was actually a suicide followed by a robbery of the corpse.

Journalists had done more than simply report the news. They had played detective, following the leads in an attempt to provide their readers with a scoop. The inscription on the shirt buttons was looked into, as was the Brantford hotelkeeper named Benwell. Adding further intrigue to the tale, the *World* had built an elaborate story around their investigations into the possibility that the body was that of a moulder or a labour spy. The newspapers that focused on the story gave it shape and meaning both by their reports and by their reporters' investigations.

From this point on, newspapers no longer referred to "the Murder Mystery"; they now labelled the case "the Benwell Murder." One mystery had been solved, but the bigger mystery remained: who was the killer?

3

Arrests at Niagara

"Traced at Last," shouted the *World*'s headline on Monday, 3 March. "There are sensational and romantic developments since the Saturday issue of The World ... At the present writing it looks as if this tragedy would prove one of the most interesting crimes ever perpetrated in Canada." The action now shifted from Oxford County to Niagara Falls, Ont., where the Birchalls were staying. Long a tourist destination for the well-to-do, in 1890 Niagara Falls remained a small town with a population of just over 3,000.[1] Because of its location on the Canada–United States border, the town had a customs house with Canadian officials and a small force of provincial police.

By 3 March, many newspapers were beginning to give greater attention to the Benwell murder by publishing wire-service reports from Woodstock and Niagara Falls. However, it continued to be Woodstock's *Sentinel-Review* and Toronto's *World* that produced original copy by their own reporters, who ferreted out the most complete details and speculated about what had happened. In shaping the narrative, they made the story appealing to other journals. Just three days of coverage exposed a great deal of the story.

Revelations

The first of the revelations came on Monday, 3 March, when newspapers reported on a lengthy statement that Reginald Birchall had made to the representative of the Associated Press in Niagara Falls.[2] On

Saturday, 1 March, Birchall (or Burchell, the spelling being uncertain) said: "The dead man's name is Fred. C. Benwell of London, Eng., 24 years of age, is well connected, his father being an officer in the British army. Benwell, [Douglas] Pelly, and myself and wife sailed in the White Star steamer Britannic from Liverpool on Feb. 14, Benwell with the intention of locating in Canada and buying a farm."

Birchall continued, explaining that upon landing in New York, they had stayed at the Metropolitan Hotel. They then had gone by train to Buffalo and registered at the Stafford House. Birchall said that on 17 February, "Benwell left me at the Grand Trunk depot in Niagara Falls, [Ont.], saying he was going to London, Ont." Benwell told Birchall that he was going to look for a farm property and would report back. Benwell took a large valise with him and left Birchall in charge of two trunks in bond that were at the express office in Niagara Falls, Ont. (British goods going to Canada could travel through the United States in bond, that is, without American duties being paid.) Birchall said that on 19 February, he had received from Benwell in London, Ont., a ticket to allow him to collect the trunks from the express office.

Birchall went on to say that on Friday, 28 February, he saw in the *World* the name "F. C. Benwell" in connection with the murder near Princeton. Birchall went directly by train to Paris, Ont., and then drove to Princeton. The next day the body was exhumed, and he recognized the deceased as Fred Benwell. "I knew that he had from $50 to $100 with him when he left me, also a watch and chain," said Birchall. They had not been found on the body. "Taking everything into consideration," observed Birchall, "I feel that he had been foully murdered."

Birchall explained he had known Benwell, a man of temperate habits, for six or seven months before they left England, and he knew the family before that. "It was through no inducement from me that Benwell came to this country," Birchall emphasized. He said that this was one of several trips he himself had made to Canada to buy horses for shipment to England. Pelly had come with him on the same errand and remained with him until he left for New York in search of Benwell. Pelly was expected back soon.

Birchall reported that he had told all this to Det. John Murray in Paris earlier that day. The young Englishman said he was confident that "the detectives would ferret the whole affair out and expose one of the most cruel murders that has ever taken place in Ontario for some years."

Newspapers devoted considerable column space to Birchall's lengthy statement, which on the surface appeared believable. Judging by his

3.1. Frederick Cornwallis Benwell in life. Photographed in England, c. 1887–9. Note the contrast between this image and the one of the corpse.

Source: Woodstock Museum, image 1988.22.9.

actions, Det. Murray found it worth pursuing. When he left Birchall he went to London, Ont., in search of evidence that Benwell had gone there.

After the name "Benwell" had been published in connection with the murdered man, an employee of the Canadian Express Company in Niagara Falls, Ont., informed police that two trunks had arrived from England on 18 February under the name "Benwell." No one by that name had been to pick them up. Police in Niagara Falls made inquiries at the local hotels on the Canadian side and learned that two Englishmen, one with his wife, were staying at John Baldwin's private hotel and that they knew something of the trunks and the dead man.[3]

The *London Free Press* reported on the Monday that after learning that Benwell had possibly gone to London, Ont., one of its reporters had visited the city's better hotels, the Tecumseh and the Grigg, to see whether Benwell had registered at one of them. The guest registers for the previous three weeks had no such name.

The Arrests

That same Monday, newspapers reported a sensational development: police in Niagara Falls had arrested Birchall on suspicion of the murder of Benwell. The *World*'s headline read "Traced at Last." Even more stunning news came well down the story under the subhead, "He's Locked Up."

Thomas H. Young, the chief of police in Niagara Falls, had been busy doing detective work locally and in connection with police in Buffalo, New York. Chief Young took an interest in the Benwell murder when an astute customs officer in Niagara Falls, Ont., read in a newspaper about the cigar-box bearing the name "F. C. Benwell," and made a connection with two large trunks labelled "Benwell" that had not been claimed from the customs office. Intrigued, Chief Young began investigating. He learned that Benwell had been staying with Reginald and Florence Birchall and another Englishman named Douglas Pelly in a Buffalo hotel. Young went to Buffalo and, with the assistance of local police there, learned that Benwell had not returned from a train trip he had made with Reginald Birchall. Young tracked the Birchalls and Pelly to the Baldwins' private boarding house in Niagara Falls, Ont., where the Birchalls were in residence, although Pelly wasn't there because he had gone to New York City. Young placed an officer at the hotel to ensure that the Birchalls didn't abscond, and another officer at the railway station where Pelly was expected to arrive back from New York.[4]

"Things took quite a lively and interesting turn this beautiful Sabbath morning," began the *World*'s report from Niagara Falls. Pelly arrived on the Erie Flyer at 7:30 Sunday morning, and after encountering the policeman waiting for him, he surmised that he would probably be arrested as an accomplice of Birchall in the Benwell murder. Pelly persuaded the police to take him to the office of Andrew Gregory Hill, the Niagara Falls, Ont., police magistrate, who questioned him privately. Pelly's compelling story about Birchall, combined with his diary entries for the trip, diverted police attention entirely to Reginald Birchall. Chief Young promptly arrested him in his bedroom at the Baldwins' boarding house.

According to the report from Niagara Falls, the news spread "like wildfire" through the streets of the small town. People were stunned to think that "the swamp murderer" could be one of the young Englishmen they had frequently seen walking through town during the previous week. The *World*'s reporter attempted to interview Pelly, but he said he had promised the magistrate and police that he wouldn't say anything without their permission.

The *World* described Birchall as having a dark complexion, a black moustache, sharp features, and badly decayed front teeth. He was about five feet nine inches tall, weighed about 150 pounds, and looked to be about thirty years old. He had a tired look around the eyes but was "of a jovial disposition." His wife was a slender, "rather pleasant-looking blonde" and appeared to be "a highly educated and refined English lady." Pelly, about twenty-two years old, was the same height as Birchall but had a slight build, a fair complexion, and a small, light moustache. A well-educated gentleman, he spoke with "a decidedly English accent." It was said he was the son of a clergyman in England, but he refused to elaborate. He did say that he hadn't known Birchall long, although he knew his family well. Both Pelly and Birchall "dressed decidedly English." They wore tweeds, and Pelly had a fore-and-aft English tweed cap, while Birchall sported a light tweed Ulster that reached to his heels. Obviously, Canadian and American men at the time dressed differently from Englishmen.

Florence Birchall was reported to have been "crying bitterly and at times reaching hysterics" since the arrest. Whether this was true or not, her behaviour as described was exactly what was expected from a married gentlewoman in her predicament. Victorian stereotypes of the upper-class lady underscored her feminine fragility and proneness to emotional upsets. Florence Birchall was made to appear vulnerable, in contrast to her husband with his "jovial disposition."

London's *Free Press* reported that a local lawyer, Isidore F. Hellmuth, had visited its office to see the photograph of the victim. (The towering Hellmuth was well known as a tennis champion, the first winner of the Canadian national tennis championship.) He identified the photograph as being of Benwell, with whom he had recently crossed the Atlantic aboard the *Britannic*. He said that Benwell had come aboard at Liverpool with Mr. and Mrs. Birchall, all of them apparently being well acquainted and "very jovial." Birchall had told Hellmuth he frequently visited Canada and had a farm near Niagara Falls. Hellmuth observed to the *Free Press* that "a murderer does not generally identify the victim of his fiendishness, and I cannot think that Mr. Burchell was a party to the tragedy."[5] Hellmuth made a strong point: it was difficult to believe that a murderer would voluntarily identify the victim and so draw official attention.

A prominent barrister in London, Ont., Isidore Hellmuth belonged to that city's establishment. His father was the bishop of Huron, an

3.2. Reginald Birchall with wife Florence Birchall on the right, a photograph taken in England, c. 1889.
Source: Woodstock Museum, image 1990.42.1.

Anglican diocese that sprawled across southwestern Ontario. Isidore was an alumnus of Cambridge University in England, where he had studied in the 1870s. Called to the Ontario bar in 1877, by 1890 he had a practice with barrister Charles H. Ivey.[6] Hellmuth had married in 1880, and he and wife Harriet had two children. They lived comfortably. Their household staff consisted of a cook, a housemaid, and a butler.[7] Hellmuth's social credentials, and perhaps especially his Cambridge education, explain how he travelled in the same circles as the Birchalls, Pelly, and Benwell, saloon passengers all, aboard the *Britannic*. Their shared elite status also accounts for his manly willingness to leap to the defence of the Birchalls even though he did not specialize in the criminal law.

Filling Out the Story

Journalists grasped the extraordinary public interest in the murder story and dug for further details. It was soon reported that Mr. James

Bampfield and his wife, Margaret, the proprietors of the Imperial Hotel in Niagara Falls, Ont., knew the Birchalls from a year earlier when they had stayed there as "Mr. and Mrs. Somerset." When talking with the Somersets recently, they learned from them that they were now travelling under the alias "Burchell," the name of a family connection, so as to facilitate horse trading.

Newspapers reported that many people in Woodstock had known the Somersets, who had lived there for several months the previous winter. Some in Woodstock claimed they understood them to be Lord and Lady Somerset, members of the English aristocracy. Others maintained that Somerset had said he was the son of Lord Somerset. When pressed by friends, he told them "Birchall" (or "Burchell") was his name and that "Somerset" was the title of his father and his own title. His mail had usually been addressed: "R. Birchall (or Burchell), c. Somerset and Co., Woodstock." They had boarded at the home of Margaret McKay, the widow of lawyer John S. McKay.[8]

Birchall had lived the high life during his winter in Woodstock. "The champagne bills were enormous," reported the *Sentinel-Review*. "He had spent money freely and used his credit with as little reserve." The *Evening Standard* discovered that in Woodstock he had been "fond of ostentatious display and had a good deal of 'swagger' about him." It was obvious that he had been "brought up in luxury because he knew intimately the ways of the gentry." The *Mail* reported that he would shock people in church by dropping a $20 gold piece in the collection plate. Birchall's extravagance stood in sharp contrast, no doubt, to the ways of the modest folk around him in Woodstock, where budgets were tight and parsimoniousness prevailed. Extraordinary in Woodstock, too, was Birchall's wife, who appeared "chic and interesting." The *Sentinel-Review* said she "looked like a lady of culture and lived like a woman of the world."[9] She called her husband "Rex," and he called her "Flo."[10] People in Woodstock suspected that while Somerset lived with the woman as his wife, shockingly they had never been legally married. Their outward display invited speculation about an imagined immorality.

On the following day, 4 March, various Ontario newspapers began to cover the story more closely. Publishers eager to sell newspapers jumped at a story that involved well-to-do young Englishmen freshly arrived in Canada, one a murder victim, the other, styling himself an aristocrat, accused of the murder. The *Globe* and Brantford's *Courier* published accounts that had appeared the day before in the *Sentinel-Review*.

That newspaper and the *World* continued to take the lead in providing up-to-the-minute coverage of the story on their front pages.

"As an Accessory: Mrs. Birchall Taken into Custody," read the headline in the *World*. Late the previous evening, Det. Murray, now in Niagara Falls, arrested Florence Birchall as an accessory to the murder. "The woman was almost paralyzed with fear when the officers took her and burst out crying," ran the stereotypical description. The *World* surmised that Pelly's revelations to the authorities had triggered her arrest.[11]

The *World* carried a late report from Niagara Falls, this one filed at 2 a.m. and titled "The Knot Tightens." The reporter had just interviewed Det. Murray, who was headed for bed a tired man but confident he had "a strong chain of evidence wound around Birchall and his wife." Murray said that in jail Birchall was "very reticent," a lawyer having got to him and told him "to keep his mouth shut." Murray had just cabled Benwell's father, Col. Benwell of Cheltenham, Gloucestershire, telling him to come at once. Murray offered that he thought the swindle a "most diabolical scheme to entice young wealthy men away from England to murder them in this country for the money they may bring with them." The self-promoting detective was now using the press to place himself at the heart of the investigation. Murray never mentioned Chief Young, who had actually collected the evidence and arrested Reginald Birchall.

Pelly, who was now willing to talk to reporters, spoke to a representative of the *Sentinel-Review*. He admitted to having paid Birchall £170 ($800) as part of an investment he had thought he was making in a horse farm near Niagara owned by Birchall. The young Englishman said he had been greatly reassured by the respectability and position of Florence Birchall, the daughter of Mr. David Stevenson, a high official in England's London and North Western Railway.[12] As a Victorian lady, Florence Birchall was defined by the respectability and prominence of her father, upon whom she had been economically dependent.

Pelly related sensational stories about how the previous week he had come close to his death at Birchall's hands while in Niagara Falls. At one point, Birchall enticed him down a stairway to the water's edge above the Falls with the suggestion he would get a better view. He had feared that Birchall would push him into the dangerous river, but fortunately, a stranger suddenly appeared and Birchall backed off. Another time, Birchall tried to induce Pelly to go to the edge of the Suspension Bridge, where he could easily have been shoved into "the angry rapids of the Niagara River below."

The *Sentinel-Review* carried reports of people from the vicinity of Woodstock who said they had seen "Somerset" recently. Fred Millman, a grocer in Woodstock, insisted that he saw Somerset in town on 18 or 19 February. He had on black pants, a skin cap, a dark overcoat, and red stockings. The reporter interviewed him twice, not convinced of his sighting. Alfred Hayward of Eastwood, a village with a railway station a few miles east of Woodstock in the direction of Princeton, said he and his wife saw Somerset and another man at Eastwood on 17 February. His niece had seen just one of the men return to Eastwood in the afternoon, via a back way. Hayward was convinced it was Somerset who came back alone. It appears that staff reporters were again doing the work of detectives in tracking down and getting testimony from local people who said they had seen Birchall in February.

The *World* carried a story its reporter in Woodstock had gleaned from a Mrs. J.B. Nelles. "Do I remember Burchell, or rather Somerset?," she asked rhetorically. "Of course I do, and so does every person else who was in Woodstock at the time for he cut a wide swath and for a time distributed gold like chaff." She explained that he had been seen daily in the streets attired in red knee breeches tied with white ribbon making large bows in front and rear. With this flamboyant costume, Birchall was an exotic sight in a town where men dressed sombrely. Mrs. Nelles took note of "a woman had been with him whom he had called his wife." An expert horseman, Somerset frequently had driven four-in-hand (driving a vehicle pulled by hour horses). He said he was "the son of a 'dook' and was doing Canada for pleasure." Mrs. Nelles contended that he had always paid his large bills until his last "carousel," when he had left a debt of $25 or $50. For her, the visitor's extravagance and carousing raised suspicions that his failure to pay his debts confirmed.

A contrasting depiction of the couple came from the daughter of the late Mrs. McKay with whom the Birchalls had boarded. While residing at the house, she said, Birchall "acted in honorable ways," and she did not believe that he had been guilty of the murder. A Mrs. Quinn, who had been a servant in the McKay home, said she had "a very high opinion of Mr. and Mrs. Birchall." She regretted that while in Woodstock he had been "systematically swindled out of his money."[13]

A *World* reporter, playing detective, had tracked down a young man who had travelled across the Atlantic with the people of interest. Mr. H.M. Shannon, of Manchester, Eng., was staying at Toronto's Queen's Hotel. It was frustrating for the reporter because Shannon would say nothing about Birchall because, he averred, he didn't want "to get mixed up in the matter at all." He did say that on the *Britannic* he had played a few games of whist with Pelly, who had seemed to be "a very nice young man." The *World* urged Shannon to come forward and assist the detectives, for "never was a fouler crime committed in Ontario."

The *World* once again dismissed ongoing speculation that Benwell was killed by highwaymen. No highwayman would bother to cut out labels in the clothing. That was done by someone who knew the man and where the labels would be. The *World* wondered whether it was "an Atlantic job," suggesting that the plot had been hatched aboard the *Britannic*. After all, it was common knowledge that those "floating palaces" carried "confidence men, bunco steerers, gamblers, sharps and even worse. Many a job was put upon the credulous while crossing the water."

The *World* left its readers with several questions that undermined Birchall's account of matters. Where was the letter that Birchall said Benwell had written from London, Ont., asking that his trunks be taken out of bond? Birchall was using the possibly non-existent letter to support his contention that Benwell had gone to London. If Benwell really went to London, why was his name not found in a hotel register there? Where was the evidence that Birchall had not gone west with Benwell? Why travel under the names "Somerset," "Burchell," and "Birchall"? When was he a dealer in horses, and with whom did he deal?

The next day, 5 March, the *Sentinel-Review* called the Benwell murder story "one of the most extraordinary in the whole history of crime in this country." City papers that had given the murder little attention were now providing full, overblown, sensational reports. In Woodstock, interest in the crime continued at "a fever pitch." The previous evening edition of the *Sentinel-Review* had sold out its extraordinary print run, and for that reason some of the previous day's coverage was being repeated. The *World* topped the claim of the *Sentinel-Review*, calling the crime "almost without parallel in the history of Canada *or any other country*. It even rivals the most famous murder mysteries of fiction."

The big news that day concerned Birchall's preliminary hearing in Niagara Falls, which will be discussed in the next chapter, but newspapers had a few tidbits to report in addition to that story. Det. Murray talked to reporters and said he now had solid evidence showing that on the afternoon of the crime, Birchall had been aboard a train coming from Eastwood, the railway station nearest the crime scene. At the time his trouser legs had been rolled up and his boots muddy, suggesting he may have been in the woods. The detective said he had examined Benwell's trunks and found letters that incriminated Birchall in a con job. He promised more details to follow.

The *World* reported that a gentleman in Woodstock had said that "Lord Somerset" the previous year had advertised for tenders for the erection of a magnificent stable to be lighted with electricity. The advertisement had caused a great stir and had appeared to confirm that Birchall was a real "dook." He had driven the best horses, smoked the choicest cigars, and given wine suppers that must have cost at least $100. A late riser, Somerset had seldom been seen on the streets before 10 a.m., at which time he had usually appeared with his "lady friend" driving a pair of dashing greys. According to a report in the *Empire*, he had been fond of ostentatious display and had "a good deal of swagger about him." It appears likely that even before Birchall was accused of swindling and murder, people in Woodstock found Birchall's habits morally suspect.

The *World* reported, too, that Birchall was familiar with the area where the body was found. On his many riding outings in 1888–89, he had at least once passed by the Blenheim Swamp on the Hersee property, and he had even put up his horse and had dinner at the Hersee farm.[14] This fact strengthened suspicions about Birchall being the swamp murderer.

A reporter in New York interviewed Thomas Maloney, the ticket agent who had sold the Birchall party train tickets to Buffalo. Maloney said he had gone to the wharf to meet passengers disembarking from the *Britannic*. Reginald Birchall and his party came down the gangplank, and Birchall greeted Maloney warmly. The agent didn't remember him but said that he must have sold him tickets in the past. Maloney described Birchall as "bright and chatty, a very pleasant sort of fellow," and his wife as "a pretty little woman." Maloney was trying to convey a positive image of the suspected murderer and his wife, although his choice of words to describe Florence Birchall was rather demeaning. Maloney saw Pelly again when he visited New York looking for Benwell. Maloney sold him his ticket back to Niagara Falls.[15]

The *Sentinel-Review* picked up a story from Toronto's *Mail* regarding a man in Toronto who had been at school with Benwell. P.C. Goldingham of Goldingham and Pauw, sporting goods agency, Toronto, said he and Benwell had been students together at Cheltenham College. Benwell left school in 1886, and Goldingham hadn't seen or heard from him since. Goldingham said that Benwell had been "a very steady, respectable young fellow, and his family connections were all that could be desired. He was rather fond of football and an all-round jolly good fellow." Later, another old friend of Benwell's explained that the boy's "fastidiousness and attention to dress caused him to keep somewhat aloof from the boisterous horseplay of other youths."[16]

On 5 March, Toronto's *Telegram* published a good example of the sensational reporting complained of by the *Sentinel-Review*:

> The story told by Pelly in the witness box yesterday recalls the numerous instances when the dead body of well-dressed young men, evidently of good birth and family, have been found floating in the Niagara River, buffeted and mangled beyond possible recognition in the terrible maelstrom and rapids seething and swirling down the narrow defilement below the Falls in the Niagara River at Queenston, and consigned to unknown graves at Lewiston and Queenston. "Suicide" everybody said ... Now the fear grows until it is settled belief that some of those unknown persons may, possibly, have been decoyed over to Canada from the old country by unprincipled scoundrels who would not stoop to murder in order to satisfy their greed for gold.

The piece went on to quote from a recent advertisement in England's *Oxford Times* inviting young Englishmen to invest £500 in a Woodstock bakery and fruit business. "It is ... altogether possible," speculated the *Telegram*, "that Birchall is only one of a ring of conspirators who are fleecing young Englishmen ... by inserting bogus advertisements."

At the beginning of March, the Benwell–Birchall murder case was becoming front-page news across North America and beyond. Newspapers farther afield began picking up the story at the beginning of March. An indication of the story's reach comes from a search that shows that on 3 March the Benwell murder was reported by twenty-eight different American newspapers from San Francisco to New York and from Saint Paul to New Orleans.[17] That same day, the story appeared in English newspapers, including London's *Morning Post*. On 5 March, the *New York Evening World*, which specialized in crime reports, commented: "The story related by Pelly adds intense interest to the case and makes it appear as if a plot of fiendish ingenuity had been concocted by Birchall to lure Benwell to his death in an out-of-the-way place."

In just a few days, the story had developed quickly. Although not all the evidence was yet in, it increasingly appeared certain that Birchall had swindled Benwell and Pelly. But was he also Benwell's murderer?

4

The Net Tightens

Preliminary Hearing

On Wednesday, 4 March, both Reginald and Florence Birchall appeared for their preliminary hearings in the Niagara Falls police court presided over by Andrew Gregory Hill, the JP who had heard Douglas Pelly's story that led to Reginald Birchall's arrest.[1] Scottish-born Hill, a resident of Niagara Falls, was about fifty-five years of age in March 1890 and married with four children. He had attended Victoria College in Cobourg, was called to the bar, and in 1861 began practising law in Welland County, the county in which Niagara Falls was then located.[2]

Hill's appointment as police magistrate was an unusual one. In 1874, the Ontario legislature passed an act making "special provision" for a police magistrate and constables in the vicinity of Niagara Falls to protect the "frontier" from criminals crossing the border from the United States and to ensure the safety of tourists.[3] That magistrate had authority throughout the counties of Lincoln and Welland. Rents collected by the province for its properties along the Niagara River and at the base of the Falls were diverted towards the payment of the police magistrate and constables. Soon after the act came into force, Hill was appointed the provincial police magistrate in Niagara Falls.

Magistrate Hill hired Thomas H. Young as his chief of police in Niagara Falls. Scottish-born, Young was about forty-eight years of age

4.1. Thomas H. Young, Chief of the Ontario Police in Niagara Falls, Ont. Chief Young arrested Birchall for murder.
Source: Western University, D.B. Weldon Library, Archives and Special Collections.

in 1890. Standing six feet, three inches, he cut an impressive figure. "His reputation as a police detective had a continental fame," declared Kingston's *British Whig*. "The password of crooks coming into Canada by the frontier was 'Watch the big Canadian "Tom" Young; he will nail you sure.'"[4] Because of the unusual nature of the appointment, he was often referred to as the chief of provincial police in Niagara Falls.

Birchall's hearing took place in what had been constructed in 1847 as the Niagara District Courthouse. Local residents hoped that its construction would ensure the political and administrative dominance of their town. However, in 1866, provincial authorities moved the court to St. Catharines, and the handsome Niagara courthouse became the Niagara Falls Town Hall with a basement police lock-up.[5] The morning of Birchall's hearing, large crowds hovered around the town hall door eager to see the accused and the proceedings. Because of the size of the crowd, many people were turned away. According to John Markey, the *Sentinel-Review*'s own reporter in the courtroom, the prisoner appeared "a little pale but quiet and reserved."[6] In addition to Markey, reporters included one from the *New York World* and several from Buffalo newspapers.[7]

For his American readers, a reporter from the *Buffalo Times* described the courtroom, which for him recalled "the courtroom scenes described by Charles Dickens, for everything savored of the English customs." At one end of the room "on a high judicial chair sat 'His Worship' (not his honor) Police Magistrate Hill." At a nearby table were Det. Murray and Chief Young, who conducted the prosecution "for the 'crown' and not for the people, as on this side of the river." In front of the judge's bench in an enclosed area stood a table where the reporters busily worked, and at one end of that table sat the accused. Birchall, the reporter observed, had "dark glittering eyes" and was "tastily dressed." He borrowed a pencil from Chief Young and spent his time at the desk sketching.[8] Was Birchall feigning disinterest in the case against him?

The charge read out to Reginald Birchall was that he did "feloniously murder Fred C. Benwell on or about 17 February in or around Princeton, Ont." Birchall expected to be represented at the hearing by Isidore Hellmuth, the barrister from London, Ont., whom he had met on the Atlantic crossing aboard the *Britannic*. However, Hellmuth did not appear that morning because he was detained in Ottawa on another case. Birchall was unrepresented. Newspapers make no mention of a Crown attorney's presence that morning.

A preliminary hearing differed from a trial in several respects. The procedure was inquisitorial, with the magistrate asking questions of witnesses to get at the truth, rather than acting like a referee. Unlike in an 1890 trial, the accused were invited to respond to statements made and could speak in their own defence. Sometimes the county Crown attorney acted as prosecutor, but at the Birchalls' preliminary hearings, Det. Murray presented the prosecution's case, testifying himself, introducing evidence such as letters, and determining the order in which witnesses were called.

The hearing got under way when the magistrate asked Birchall how he pled, and he replied "not guilty." Det. Murray, sworn as the first witness, said that Birchall told him Benwell had been in Australia sheep farming and had come to America to find a suitable stock farm to invest in with Birchall. Murray said that Birchall told him that he himself had been to America before but had never gone west of the Falls. Recently, on 5 February, the party had sailed from England, arriving in New York on 14 February, and the next day they had gone to Buffalo. Birchall told him that on 17 February, he, his wife, and Benwell visited the Falls, where Benwell left them, saying he was going to London, Ont. Murray explained that he himself had gone to London to check a hotel register where the name F.C. Benwell appeared, but the signature did not match the one on the cigar-box. Murray testified that Birchall had told him he had received a letter advising him to get Benwell's baggage out of bond in Niagara Falls, Ont.

The next witness sworn was Douglas Raymond Pelly of Saffron Walden, Essex, who testified for several hours. Two or three months previously, he said, he had replied to an advertisement he saw in a London newspaper, the *Standard*, giving details of a stock farm in America and instructions for interested parties to apply to a Mr. T.S. Mellersh with an address at a club in Cheltenham, Gloucestershire.[9] He arranged to meet Mellersh at the club but he didn't show, the steward saying Mellersh was out of town. Then Pelly got a letter from Birchall inviting him to invest in a horse farm he had near Niagara Falls. (Presumably Mellersh had passed on Pelly's name to Birchall.) Pelly said that he and Birchall exchanged several letters. Those from Birchall were still in England; the Niagara Falls police had Birchall's side of the correspondence.

Pelly had understood from Birchall that he had a large stock farm where he raised feed and kept horses that he bought, groomed, and sold at a profit. There was a brick house heated by steam and lit by gas, and a barn lit by electricity. Birchall had said there were several Englishmen at Niagara Falls and that they had a club he had been instrumental in organizing. Its members lived in English style and had English servants. He told him that he and Mrs. Birchall had lived for a time in furnished rooms at Woodstock close to another farm in which he had an interest. Pelly would have found Birchall's description of the farm and the Falls appealing and reassuring because it confirmed this was the sort of opportunity he was seeking and the kind of place where he would be comfortable.

Pelly had decided he was interested in investing, and they signed two copies of a contract. Pelly at that point paid Birchall £170 ($800 at the time, about $33,000 today[10]). In return he was to receive board, expenses, and 22.5 per cent of the sales from their horse farm. Pelly and Birchall travelled together by train from London to Liverpool, their port of embarkation. On the way, Birchall asked Pelly whether he carried a revolver. Pelly told him he had one in his luggage. Birchall then showed him his own revolver, a small one he carried in his pocket.

On the train to Liverpool, Birchall mentioned Benwell for the first time, saying he was coming out to Canada with them. Birchall commented that Benwell was "'not much of a chap' and did not care to have him associate with me." In Liverpool, on the morning of the *Britannic*'s departure, Birchall introduced him to Benwell at his hotel. Pelly, Benwell, and Florence and Reginald Birchall all boarded the *Britannic* at 4 p.m. on 5 February shortly before the sailing.

While crossing the Atlantic, Pelly talked to Benwell several times. Benwell said he had a brother in the artillery and that their father was a colonel in the British army. Birchall told him that Benwell had been out to New Zealand. Pelly testified that he didn't take to Benwell. When Pelly learned that Benwell was also going into partnership with Birchall in the horse business, Pelly said he had showed his annoyance. He threatened Birchall that he would withdraw from their contract. Birchall replied that Benwell was a nuisance and he would get rid of him as soon as he could. He would send him to the farm overseer, William McDonald, who would put him off the agreement. Meantime, Birchall explained that some of the cash that Pelly had given him, he had already invested in horses in England that had been shipped to America.

On 14 February, the *Britannic* arrived in New York, where the party stayed at the Metropolitan Hotel. Benwell arranged to have two trunks shipped in bond to Niagara Falls, Ont. The next evening, after exchanging some money, they left from Jersey City for Buffalo, where they stayed at the Stafford House. Early the next day, 17 February, he had seen Birchall dressed in country clothes – dark blue jacket and waistcoat, a black astrakhan cap, and heavy field boots. Birchall left with Benwell, saying they were on their way to the farm near Niagara Falls. Mrs. Birchall and he stayed behind in Buffalo.

At 8:30 that evening, Pelly received a telegram from Birchall saying he would be arriving late and they were to stay on at the Stafford House. When Birchall arrived soon after the telegram, Pelly asked him where Benwell was. Birchall explained that Benwell had not liked the farm or McDonald, its overseer. Birchall had given Benwell the names of some other farmers whose properties he might investigate, and Benwell had gone off. Birchall expected he would also be going to London to visit Hellmuth, his acquaintance from the *Britannic*. Pelly asked Birchall what he had been doing all day, and he said he had been at the farm, which was in "a beastly state." It would be best for them all to stay in Niagara Falls, Ont., until the farm had been made ready for them.

During the day while Birchall and Benwell were away, Pelly looked at the shops in Buffalo with Mrs. Birchall, who was interested in buying some wallpaper to decorate the farmhouse. Her shopping might have been her way of persuading Pelly that there really was a farmhouse, or alternatively, it might indicate that she had bought her husband's story hook line and sinker.

Next morning, Pelly and Mrs. Birchall had crossed over to Niagara Falls, Ont., and Birchall had followed them there later. In the afternoon, while Mrs. Birchall waited at the Imperial Hotel, Pelly and Birchall found lodgings at the Baldwins' boarding-house. It was a two-storey brick house on ample grounds. Their luggage (but not Benwell's big trunks) cleared customs and was brought there.

In the days following, they spent their time in much the same way each day, strolling about town. With nothing happening, Pelly had grown suspicious. Birchall reassured him that he was expecting money from England and soon everything "would be in full swing." On the Tuesday, Pelly told Birchall things were not as represented in England, to which he replied, "Oh well, then you can please yourself about staying." That day, when Pelly and Birchall came across a stairway going to the Niagara River, Birchall said, "Let us go down here." They had begun their descent when, to Birchall's surprise, they encountered a man coming up, so they left.

On Wednesday, Birchall went to Buffalo about some message he said he had received from Benwell. Pelly went to see a friend, Mrs. Johnson Clench, of St. Catharines, but had found no one home. He returned to the Falls, where the Birchalls said they had had a message from Benwell saying to send his heavy luggage to the Fifth Avenue Hotel in New York.

On the Friday, Birchall burst upon him, saying, "What do you think I have seen in the paper in connection with that man found murdered at Princeton? A cigar-case marked F. C. Benwell!" This news was a shocker. After discussions, it was decided that the Birchalls would take the 1:30 train for Paris, Ont., and proceed to Princeton, and that Pelly would go on the 5 p.m. train to New York to see whether Benwell had gone there.

Pelly had been testifying for four and a half hours, and the magistrate was about to adjourn the case until the next day, but then the court called a man who had just arrived, William McDonald of Woodstock. He testified that he had known the prisoner in town one and a half years earlier as Mr. Somerset, who had driven fast livery horses around town and finally left owing debts. He had been "a regular deadbeat and swindler."

The magistrate then asked Birchall whether he had any questions for the witnesses. Birchall had nothing to say about the long testimony of Pelly, but asked McDonald why he had called him "a swindler." McDonald replied that he had "had his fingers burned." At this point, the court adjourned for the day.

The reporter for the *Sentinel-Review* said that Pelly's story "had every evidence of truth and was exact in every particular. He appeared like a conscientious witness, and his testimony was received with general confidence." Birchall sat through "the whole ordeal with an expression perfectly calm and serenely composed."

The next morning the hearing continued.[11] The Associated Press report from Niagara Falls included an admiring portrait of the prisoner's appearance at the start of the day:

> Birchall is an exquisite personage, with pointed patent-leather shoes and well-kept finger nails ... His finger nails are the index to his carefully-cultivated personal appearance. Birchall stands about 5 feet 9 ½ inches in his stockings. Silk stockings they are too, and he is supple, clean cut and well built. His hair is dark as the raven's wing and cut in the latest mode ... The nose is as delicate as a cameo and from it gleam a pair of steel-blue eyes ... It is a handsome face, but impenetrable.[12]

Testimony began once again with Det. Murray, who reappeared to put on the record some correspondence he had found while examining the luggage of the English visitors. The letters, which were reproduced in the press, concerned the making of business and travel arrangements. The first, dated 3 January 1890, from F.C. Benwell to Birchall, showed Benwell pressing to firm up arrangements for travel to Canada expected to take place later that month. Eventually the *Britannic*'s 5 February sailing was settled upon. Pelly's letter of 16 January enclosed his cheque for £170 and copies of their agreement. The agreement was also reproduced in the press.[13]

Det. Murray testified that in Paris, Ont., when shown the photograph of the body, Birchall had said he didn't recognize the clothes. Later, Pelly had observed to him that Benwell wore clothes made of very distinctive fabrics that were easy to recognize.

Niagara Falls Chief of Police Tom Young testified that he first become involved in the case when he learned about the trunks waiting at the local express office under the name F.C. Benwell, the name on the cigar-box. He had immediately wired Det. Murray telling him to come to the Falls. Young and James Flynn, a Canadian customs officer, went to Buffalo, where Young checked in at police headquarters. Two American detectives accompanied him to the Stafford House, where they found that the Birchalls, Benwell, and Pelly had registered on Sunday, 16 February, and ascertained that two of the party had left the Stafford House for the day on the Monday, but only one had returned. Young figured the absent man was Benwell.

Chief Young said he questioned Pelly and later that Sunday morning arrested Birchall, who took it "quite coolly." Young searched him in the jail and found a receipt for Benwell's bonded luggage, a gold pen and holder engraved "Conny, N.Y., 1869," ninety-five cents in silver, an open-faced watch with chain, a blank bankbook of the Niagara Falls Bank, New York, good for $152, and a bunch of ten small keys. Young went to the Baldwins' boarding house, where he searched the Birchalls' room and luggage and where he had Florence Birchall searched. At this point, Det. Murray arrived. Together they questioned Birchall, who admitted to having gone to Niagara Falls with Benwell. He refused to say whether he had been within ten miles of Woodstock. He also refused to say how he came to have the trunk keys and bond receipt for Benwell's luggage. Young said that in the luggage he found the Birchalls' 1888 marriage certificate from Croydon, Surrey.[14]

At this point in the hearing, Det. Murray asked for an adjournment for eight days. The magistrate agreed the hearing would reconvene on 12 March.

As it turned out, Det. Murray later asked the magistrate to reconvene the hearing on 6 March because he now had witnesses whose testimony he wanted to get on record before they left town for their jobs. The hearing resumed with witness George Hay, a brakeman on the Grand Trunk Railway (GTR).[15] He testified that he saw the prisoner on the platform at Eastwood Station, a few miles from Princeton, on the afternoon of Monday, 17 February – the crucial day. The prisoner boarded the No. 10 eastbound train, the only passenger to have done so at that station. He was wearing a small-checked sack coat and a black curly cap. His pants were turned up at the bottom and his shoes were covered with mud. He had gone into the smoking car, which Hay attended. The man had a single ticket to Hamilton. The passenger asked Hay whether he would have time to stop there for dinner before proceeding to Niagara Falls. Hay told him that if he had dinner in Hamilton, he would have to catch a later train to the Falls. Birchall went into the station at Hamilton and then reboarded the train, now with a ticket through to the Falls, which is where he had gotten off. While on the train the only other person Birchall had spoken to was James Duffy, the news agent. Hay said that he recognized the prisoner from having seen him at Woodstock in 1888. He had taken note of him then because people had been talking about "Somerset."

When the magistrate asked Hay whether he would recognize the cap the prisoner had been wearing, Hay thought that he would. It was placed on Birchall's head, and Hay confirmed it looked like the one he had seen. As the hat was put on his head, Birchall grinned broadly and spectators laughed. On cross-examination by Hellmuth, who by this point had at last arrived to represent Birchall, Hay said that the detectives had taken him to the lock-up and shown him the prisoner, whom he said he recognized. He further testified that while on the train, Birchall had a flask, but that he did not appear drunk.

Pelly reappeared on the stand and testified that detectives had asked him to look through Birchall's trunk, where he found the cap he had seen Birchall wearing. The detectives confirmed the story.

That concluded the testimony. The magistrate remanded Reginald Birchall to the Welland Jail for seven days. Birchall was taken by the 4:30 GTR train to Welland, where the jail, housed in the east wing of the impressive stone courthouse, was more secure than the lock-up in Niagara Falls.

That same day, Florence Birchall was brought into the same police court accompanied by her counsel, Isidore Hellmuth.[16] The *Sentinel-Review* thought readers would be interested in her appearance: "Her petite and pretty figure was hidden by a dark green Newmarket [long, close-fitting cloak] lined with old gold silk and topped with a coachman's beaver collar, a feathered hat with a lace veil concealing her blue eyes from the gaze of the spectators. When not talking to her counsel, she kept her eyes riveted on the magistrate." The reporter for the *Buffalo Evening News* described her eyes as "very large, very blue, and yesterday wore an appealing look."[17]

Magistrate Hill read the charge: "that you did, on or about the 17th of February at Niagara Falls aid and abet one J.R. Burchell to murder and kill F. C. Benwell, that you received and did comfort said Burchell contrary to the statutes." The prisoner pleaded "not guilty." Douglas Pelly testified about what she had told him about the horse farm, but when it came to her involvement in the murder, he said, "I do no know that Mrs. Burchell knew anything of Mr. Burchell's movements on the 17th, nor do I see how she could have known anything more of his movement on that day than I did." He noted that he had been with her in Buffalo all day on the seventeenth.[18]

Magistrate Hill declared that there was not sufficient evidence against Florence Birchall to proceed at the moment and informed her that she was remanded for seven days. Hill instructed Det. Murray on the kind of evidence he would need for the Crown's case to proceed. He had to show that she "knew that the crime was to be committed, and also that she counseled and advised and aided, or commanded it to be committed." Hill did not believe a wife could be convicted of being an accessory after the fact, given that it was a wife's obligation to comfort and support her husband.

Hellmuth implored the judge to allow for bail in any amount for Florence Birchall, saying there was "not one scintilla of evidence against her." Hill would not allow bail, however, because the provincial attorney general and premier, Oliver Mowat, had intervened and directed him to reject bail and remand the prisoner for a week. Hellmuth said that the attorney general must have misunderstood the situation. Moreover, Helmuth declared that it was "an absurdity" for Mowat to act above the magistrate's head. Indeed, interference in the administration of justice in this way was highly inappropriate, although it is possible that it happened frequently.[19] The political intervention drew no newspaper comment; such an intervention today would certainly be cause for criticism. The attorney general did have oversight over Crown attorneys, and he had the power to decide whether a Crown attorney or someone else should prosecute a case.[20] Instructing that bail not be granted was another matter entirely, however. "The lawyer raved and Mrs. Birchall wept," commented the *World* succinctly, applying gender stereotypes to the dismissal of the bail request. In the end the prisoner was allowed to remain under surveillance in Niagara Falls for the night until bail could be discussed with the attorney general. She was taken to the Baldwins' boarding house and placed in the charge of a police officer.

The leniency the magistrate showed Florence Birchall came in for some criticism. "There is a great deal of sympathy for Mrs. Birchall," observed the *Sentinel-Review*. "There always is for a pretty woman in distress." The newspaper feared, however, that an excess of sympathy had resulted in too lenient treatment of her. "Everyone would like to see her escape indignity and establish her innocence, but this is no reason why weak sentiment should interfere with the course of justice."[21] Det. Murray was met with hisses when, during the hearing, he said she was at least guilty of participating in the fraud and should be jailed pending a trial.

While in Niagara Falls for the hearing, Det. Murray spoke to newsmen several times. At 2 a.m. on 4 March, reporters said that "he had not the slightest doubt but Birchall was the murderer of Benwell."[22] The *World* reported on 5 March that Det. Murray had said "there is not the slightest doubt but that Benwell was murdered on the Monday, Feb. 17." Such statements shaped the public's perceptions of the case. Anyone suggesting that the shooting had been done by someone other than Birchall, or that it had occurred on a day later than Monday, was confronted with the detective's apparently authoritative remarks. Of course, it was crucial to Murray's case that the murder be dated to the Monday because that was the only day that Birchall lacked an ironclad alibi – the only day he had not been with Pelly. The *Sentinel-Review* reported on 6 March that some people believed Benwell was murdered on the Wednesday because Benwell's white shirt, which appeared so pristine, would have been damaged by the storm earlier in the week. A Wednesday date would get Birchall off the hook. But public opinion as reported in the press generally followed Det. Murray's lead.

Interest in the Benwell murder was increasing. "Judged by the sale of papers," declared the *Sentinel-Review* on 6 March, interest "reached its highest pitch yesterday." On the streets of Woodstock, readers had snatched papers from the newsboys, reducing their bundles at a frantic pace. The first edition of 1,000 copies had sold out immediately, and more copies were run off. The *Sentinel-Review* boasted that it "had the fullest and most interesting details connected with the case." It was the only Canadian newspaper that had had its own reporter at Niagara Falls for the hearing. Other journals made do with the telegraphed dispatches from the Associated Press reporter on the scene. Still, those papers gave the story front-page treatment, and some of them borrowed copy from the *Sentinel-Review*. New York newspapers were now showing a keen interest in the Benwell murder story. The *World* reported that some New York papers had devoted three columns to it and were asking for more copy.[23]

While the hearing was under way, the *Sentinel-Review* sent staff scouring Oxford County to track down anyone who had seen Birchall on 17 February.[24] The newspaper boasted that it had found several individuals who could testify as to some of Birchall's movements that day. Detectives would follow in the footsteps of the reporters. The *Sentinel-Review* sniffed that the *Mail* was printing news that had appeared the day before in the *Sentinel-Review*.[25]

In an unusual turn of events, Birchall's preliminary hearing was disrupted by the coroner's inquest into the victim's death, and then resumed once the inquest had completed its inquiry. It is unclear why such an unusual arrangement was made. Perhaps it resulted from a power struggle between the police magistrate in Niagara Falls and the coroner in Princeton.

The Inquest Resumes

Coroner McLay and the twelve men of the coroner's jury, including Robert Rutherford, the foreman, had first assembled at Princeton on the day the body was discovered, and ever since, testimony had been heard off and on. The inquest was scheduled to resume in earnest on 7 March with the arrival of witnesses from Niagara Falls. "The peaceful little village of Princeton," reported Toronto's *Empire*, "was never in such a state of intense excitement as today. Hundreds of people from the surrounding country wended their way thither in vehicles, on foot, and by rail till the sleepy little place was literally packed with a throng craving for a sight of the alleged murderer." Pelly, Helmuth, and Murray were subpoenaed to attend. However, Coroner McLay received a telegram from the deputy attorney general, John Robinson Cartwright, asking that the inquest be adjourned until the next day, which was the soonest that key witnesses could get there.[26] McLay decided to go ahead with the witnesses who were on hand.

In Princeton, the railway platform was crowded with men and women eagerly awaiting the arrival of the westbound train. When only reporters got off, disappointed spectators asked, "Where is Pelly? Where is Mrs. Somerset? Is the prisoner here?"[27] It was reported that the journalists included men from most of the Toronto papers and from the *New York World*. Toronto's *News* had an artist there, and a Mr. D.G. Wickson of Paris, Ont., sketched the scene of the crime and various faces for the *Graphic*, the prestigious illustrated newspaper of London, England.[28]

The inquest now was held in Princeton's tiny town hall, which was crammed to the rafters, with spectators "jostl[ing] each other like so many caged cattle."[29] Some of the witnesses called that day were people who had been tracked down by the staff of the *Sentinel-Review*. The trainmen were first to testify.[30] George Hay gave the same evidence that he presented in Niagara Falls. William H. Poole, the conductor on the GTR train, testified that on 17 February, the train had left Niagara Falls at 7:05 a.m. and reached Eastwood Station at 11:14. Only two men had gotten off the train. The baggage man had given "a queer-shaped" box to one of the men. Poole thought the box probably had contained a gun.

Matthew Virtue, a bailiff of Woodstock, testified that he had been aboard the westbound train on 17 February and had seen two men get off at Eastwood, one of them wearing a cape. Alfred Hayward, miller and farmer of Eastwood, said that between 11 a.m. and noon on 17 February, he had seen two men coming along the road from the Eastwood Station, one of them wearing a cape. He said he had told his "woman" when they passed that they looked like two Englishmen going to the home of Mr. Patterson, a neighbour who often had English visitors. One of the pair had thrown a snowball at the Haywards' cat. Another man, the young Blenheim Township farmer John Crosby, son of Squire Crosby, JP, testified that he had seen two young men walking on the Governor's Road just before noon. One had carried a small parcel wrapped in brown paper. They had been between four and five miles from where the corpse was later found.

Alice Smith, sixteen or seventeen, also testified. Male journalists took special note of her appearance. The *Sentinel-Review* called her "a rather handsome young lady ... whose face attracted the pencil of a least one artist present." The *World* reporter, also impressed with her appearance, wrote that "she wore a conspicuous red hat and her somewhat robust figure was encased in a dark costume trimmed with silver braid. She had raven-black hair and sounded intelligent." Identifying herself as the granddaughter of John Hayward of Eastwood, she said she had walked to the Eastwood Station to mail a letter just before the arrival of the three o'clock eastbound train on 17 February. A man there had held out his hand and said, "How do you do?" She had known he was one of the Englishmen she had met a year previously, and had asked him if he was Dudley, Somerset's chum. He had said, "Don't you know me?" Then he had asked after her family and the "old governor," her grandfather. She then had become certain the man was Somerset.[31]

Two more young women of Eastwood had also been at the station that afternoon. Miss Mary Swayzie said she had seen a man she hadn't known talking to Stationmaster Dunn. The man's pants had been turned up and his shoes were muddy. Obviously impressed with the stranger's appearance, she twice described him as having "dark, bright eyes, a dark mustache," and being "very intelligent looking." Miss Ida Cromwell said that she too had seen Dunn talking with a stranger. He had been wearing light pants and a dark coat.

Stationmaster Dunn testified that he had sold a ticket to Hamilton on the afternoon of 17 February to a man with rolled-up pants and boots covered in mud. James Hayward, an Eastwood shopkeeper, said he had seen Mr. Dunn talking to a stranger just before the three o'clock arrival of the eastbound train on 17 February. The man had on a dark coat, light pants, and a cap. His pants were turned up.

At this point the inquest adjourned for the day. It is remarkable how many people said they had taken note of the strangers' presence. Villagers were evidently unaccustomed to seeing many strangers.

That evening, missing witnesses Det. Murray and Douglas Pelly arrived in town. The inquest resumed at 1 p.m. the next day, Saturday, 8 March.[32] The coroner, several jurors, and some 300 spectators accompanied Pelly to the cemetery for his identification of the exhumed body. In brilliant sunshine on a frigid day, Pelly immediately said the deceased was definitely the young man who had accompanied him on the *Britannic*. He told reporters he was surprised that, given the time that had passed since death, Benwell's "features had retained so much of their naturalness." He confided that the experience, which he had been dreading, had not been as bad as he had feared.

Pelly's experience had much to do with the effectiveness of undertaker Swartz's embalming methods. Although only a village undertaker, Swartz claimed to have studied embalming at leading establishments in Boston, New York, and Springfield. Swartz was also a manufacturer of a brand of embalming fluid that grew in popularity after so many people read about the good condition of Benwell's body when disinterred.[33]

The inquest now moved to the courtroom, where all the front seats were filled with women spectators who were said to be eager to see Pelly, a handsome young gentleman of means. Pelly gave the same testimony that he had given at the preliminary hearing, except that, in the view of the *World* reporter, he now emphasized Florence Birchall's involvement in the affair. Pelly noted, for example, that she had emphasized to him that she had lived in the house at the farm and did not like it. She had complained about the servants and had said she planned to replace them with ones brought over from the old country by a clergyman. When she heard of the discovery of the cigar case, she had told Pelly she'd had a presentiment of the trouble in her bad dreams.

Det. Murray, next to testify, related the now well-known story of his involvement in the case, although for the first time he contended that when interviewing Birchall at Paris, he had been suspicious of the story told. During the questioning, Murray said he had asked Birchall about the letter that Benwell had allegedly sent from London, Ont. Birchall had searched through his pockets and had said he didn't know what had happened to it. He had asked his wife whether she knew what had become of it, and she had said she didn't. When shown the photograph of the dead man, both Birchall and his wife had said they had never seen Benwell wearing clothes like the ones on the body. Murray's testimony took up most of the afternoon.

The last to testify was Constable W.J. Watson of Princeton, who confirmed that the body Pelly had just seen was the one found at the swamp.

The room was then cleared so that the jury could deliberate with the assistance of the coroner and the county Crown attorney. According to the *World*, some of the jurymen wanted to delay bringing in their verdict until the prisoners were brought from Niagara Falls. Others were unsure about Florence Birchall's role in the affair. Their deliberations took an hour-and-a-half. In the end, the jury found that Frederick Cornelius Benwell had died from two pistol shots to the head fired "by the hand of Reginald Birchall alias Somerset, with deliberate purpose and wilfully and feloniously to commit murder, on or about the 17th day of February, 1890." The jurors "were of the opinion that Florence Birchall, wife of Reginald Birchall, was accessory to the murder after the fact." Clearly, the Crown attorney's advice to the jury had not excluded the possibility of a wife being accessory after the fact in a murder committed by her husband.

The *Sentinel-Review* observed that, given the considerable circumstantial evidence, the verdict was not at all surprising. People in Princeton who had gathered on street corners expressed their satisfaction with it. The *World* reported that in Princeton, there was "a wide variety of opinion" as to Florence Birchall's knowledge of the murder, but as for Rex Birchall, "there were few who believe it will be possible for him to provide an alibi." The *News* declared colourfully that "the coils tightened almost taut around the neck of Reginald Burchell, while Florence Burchell is caught deep in the meshes."[34]

While newspapers agreed that Pelly had once again been a highly credible witness, they were critical of the young Englishman's naivety. "The Gullibility of Englishmen," was the title of an editorial in the *Sentinel-Review* on 7 March. What particularly caught the attention of Ontario's rural residents was Pelly's acceptance of Birchall's boast that the barn on his Niagara Falls farm was lighted by electricity. That seemed far-fetched at a time when electricity was still a newfangled convenience to which only prosperous townspeople and city dwellers had access. "Think of Pelly handing over his money to this adventurer Birchall on his mere assurance that he owned a farm with barns illuminated by electricity," observed the *Sentinel-Review*.[35]

About the same time, British newspapers were producing editorials critical of parents naive enough to invest with strangers who enticed their sons to faraway places. In mid-March, London's *Standard* printed a long article outlining Birchall's scam and Benwell's murder. "It would be interesting to know," opined the newspaper, "how the flashy adventurer [Birchall] succeeded in imposing so completely on the parents of the two young men who were entrusted in his charge." It bluntly asked: "Did they make no inquiries about him?" After all, the "ranching business" had long had a dodgy reputation.

Fed up with such newspaper commentary, Col. Benwell penned a revealing letter to the *Standard* to correct misunderstandings about Birchall's manner and to defend his own diligence in checking out the man who took his son to Canada. Col. Benwell objected to the press's depiction of Birchall as "flashy," saying in his experience Birchall "was nothing of the sort, either in dress or manner." (No doubt Rex was not wearing his red jodhpurs with white bows when trying to impress the Benwells.) The colonel explained that he had taken the trouble to get the measure of the man both in a two-hour interview at a London club and during a lunch in Cheltenham, where Birchall's "manner, both at table and in conversation, were those of a perfect gentleman, and he appeared to me to be a self-possessed, straightforward, and frank as anybody could be, though all the time he was telling me no end of lies." Son Fred had also checked out Birchall by visiting him at his father-in-law's home, "where he was favourably impressed by what he saw there." Still, the colonel had not agreed to invest until his son had seen the farm and assessed its business prospects. Defending himself, the colonel declared reasonably enough, "I took every precaution against fraud, but it never entered my head to guard my son against murder."[36]

The Preliminary Hearing Resumes

In anticipation of the resumption of the preliminary hearing in Niagara Falls, the hotels were crowded with visitors, including many Americans, eager to attend the proceedings. On the morning of 12 March, a throng gathered on the railway platform at Niagara Falls, expecting to see Birchall arrive from Welland by the eleven o'clock train. Only Pelly and Murray stepped down. Where was the star prisoner? "Immediately all kinds of rumors were spread about," reported the *Empire*. "Many contended that it was a trick on Murray's part and that Birchall had been sent on to Woodstock in utter disregard of Magistrate Hill's order." Chief Young telephoned Sherriff Smith at Welland and learned that Smith had made a mistake. Instead of bringing Birchall to Niagara Falls, he had waited for Murray to pick him up.[37]

People still wondered whether Murray had sabotaged the arrangements, for it was known that at this point he was barely cooperating. He found the shifting back and forth between Niagara Falls and Princeton "unorthodox and faulty," grumbling that the "proceedings are foreign to anything I ever saw in my life." It was also reported that he and Chief Young were "at loggerheads." Murray thought Young had arrested Birchall too early, thus preventing the discovery of much important evidence. Young's supporters maintained that by his swift action he had prevented Birchall from escaping.[38]

Meanwhile, in the Welland Jail, Birchall had gone back to bed with a book. When told he would be going in the late afternoon, he quipped, "Well all right; I presume that the Falls will remain until I get there."[39] Birchall finally arrived at 4:50 that afternoon via the Michigan Central. The accused had "stepped off the train as lightly as if he were a school boy starting a holiday trip," wrote the reporter for the *Mail*. Handcuffed, Birchall was escorted the few steps to the courthouse. "He was as sprightly looking a young man as you can meet anywhere," observed the *World*. The handcuffs were clasped around fine kid gloves. He was impeccably dressed in a black suit with a blue box coat draped over his shoulders. On his head he wore a black bowler hat. He was freshly shaven, except for his mustache, which was waxed and artistically turned up at the corners. "The murderer presented quite a fresh and attractive picture," said the *World*.[40]

Some people in the crowd were unimpressed by the prisoner's appearance. "Confess you fiend and die decent," one fellow was alleged to have shouted.[41]

Shortly afterwards, accompanied by her "lady guard," Florence Birchall arrived at the courthouse wearing a bottle-green dress of fashionable cut. Disappointingly for the crowd, she was so thickly veiled that her features could not be seen at all. Nevertheless, it appeared to the *World* reporter that she had lost her confidence and was but "a shadow of her former self."

Because of the size of the crowd, the hearing was held in the town hall's large upstairs room, which was more often used as a theatre. Its stage was occupied by the officials, the lawyers, and no fewer than thirty reporters – many more than when the hearing began, an indication of the growing interest in the case. Birchall was given a place near the magistrate, between wings of the scenery.[42]

The court dealt with Florence Birchall first. Charles H. Ivey, the London, Ont., law partner of Hellmuth, asked for the immediate discharge of his client because there was no evidence against her. Magistrate Hill asked Det. Murray for his input. "I have nothing to say whatever," he replied grumpily. Sympathizing with Florence Birchall's predicament, Hill preferred to discharge her, but because he knew Det. Murray planned to immediately rearrest her on a warrant issued in Woodstock, he chose to remand her for a further eight days to see whether any evidence surfaced showing her to have been an accessory in Niagara Falls to the murder. The audience applauded loudly. Police removed her to the Baldwins' boarding house.[43] In Niagara Falls, no further action would be taken against her, but at Woodstock on 20 March she was brought before a magistrate and again charged with being an accessory to her husband's murder of Benwell. To a satisfied public, she was immediately released on her own recognizance after posting a $1,000 bail bond.[44]

Having dealt with Florence Birchall, the police court in Niagara Falls turned to her husband, who was also represented by Ivey.[45] Birchall was brought up from a basement cell, nodding to left and right as he passed through the crowd and taking the seat his wife had just vacated. The reporter for the *World* thought it strange that Birchall paid no attention to the witnesses or their testimony: "He seemed to have thorough contempt or unconcern for what they were saying."

First to testify were the four trainmen who had appeared at the inquest in Princeton. Their statements were very similar this time, except that Birchall was now present, which allowed the magistrate to ask whether they recognized him as the man on the No. 10 train. Poole, for instance, replied that the prisoner resembled the man in dark clothes, but he couldn't swear that it was the same man because he hadn't paid much attention to the two passengers dressed like Englishmen.

James Duffy, described by the *World* as "a sharp-looking young news agent," said that on the eastbound afternoon train on 17 February, he had seen the prisoner sitting alone in the front seat of the smoking car. Duffy had put some books beside him and the passenger had paid thirty cents for Mark Twain's *A Tramp Abroad*. He had also bought some cigars and oranges. Duffy said that he had sat down beside him and the two had smoked cigars and talked. Duffy had told him business wasn't very good. The stranger had said that his name was Smith and that he was going to see his brother in Buffalo. He had offered Duffy a drink from a glass flask, which he had refused. Duffy said he had noticed that the man's pants were turned up and his shoes muddy. After the two got off at the Falls, Duffy lost sight of him and never saw him again.

The magistrate asked Duffy whether the prisoner was the man he had seen on the train. Duffy looked him up and down for nearly two minutes and dramatically replied, "That is the man I saw on the train; I am sure of it." Birchall never even glanced at Duffy, but in the eyes of the reporter for the *World*, Duffy's evidence created among the spectators "quite a flutter."

James Flynn, a Canadian customs officer at the Falls, said that on 10 February, Birchall and Bampfield, owner of the Imperial Hotel, had removed a lot of luggage from the customs house, but left two boxes labelled "F. C. Benwell." Later, Flynn had gone to the Imperial to ask about them and Birchall had said he would look after them in a few days as he had charge of them. The boxes had never been taken out. Later, Chief Young had come to look through their contents and Flynn had assisted. They had found that one of the boxes contained clothes and shoes and the other a lot of carpenter's tools.

George Phemister, of the Great Western Telegraph office at the Falls, testified regarding telegrams he had sent out. On the evening of 17 February, he had sent a telegram addressed to "Pelly, Stafford House, Buffalo." It read: "Arrive at Buffalo 9 to-night. Must remain there tonight. Signed Bastell." Phemister was unable to identify the man who had sent the telegram. Another telegram, this one sent on 27 February and addressed to "Burchell, Imperial Hotel," read: "Telegram and letter were sent on to you yesterday to ship heavy baggage to Fifth-Avenue Hotel, New York. Signed Stafford." That concluded the evidence.

Magistrate Hill invited Birchall to make a statement but cautioned him that it would be taken down in writing and could be later used against him. After consulting with Ivey, Birchall declared that he had nothing to say. "Then you are fully committed for trial," declared the magistrate. The next day Birchall would be accompanied to Woodstock to await his trial, scheduled for the fall assizes there.

Birchall's nonchalance throughout the proceedings struck reporters as strange. A reporter from the *Buffalo Times* maintained that the prisoner reacted most when Magistrate Hill committed "some startling crime against the queen's English." Birchall's eyes "would curl up into a contemptuous smile as though a violation of correct rhetoric distressed him more than the gravity of his own situation."[46]

That same reporter thought Pelly was displaying signs of suffering. "The buttons were nearly all off his exquisite English greatcoat yesterday, and a certain tone of pathetic manner in his girlish English drawl excited a feeling of pity for him." The reporter attributed these signs of stress to Pelly experiencing "a mode of life that is as new to him as would be the manners of another planet." The young man "had never had to rub up against the vulgar wicked world before, and it wears on him."[47] In contrast to most descriptions of Pelly, this one by an American reporter showed less deference to the Crown's star witness, impugning his manliness and sheltered existence.

5

In Woodstock Jail

On Thursday, 13 March, the afternoon edition of Woodstock's *Sentinel-Review* excitedly reported the arrival in town of Canada's most infamous prisoner. Reginald Birchall, increasingly referred to by the press as "Rex," had come to town at 10:42 a.m. aboard the express train from "the Bridge," the suspension bridge at Niagara.

Birchall had spent the previous night in the Welland Jail, where, to his surprise, he had encountered someone he knew. It was a former gardener of his father's, now reduced by illness to the life of a tramp. Birchall said that the poor fellow, jailed for vagrancy, had known him instantly and upon learning the charge was murder, he had cried "like a child." Birchall told the story aboard the train to Woodstock, when he sat with Det. Murray, Woodstock Chief of Police H.R. Willis, and a reporter from the *Empire* who for reasons unknown had privileged access.

"I never spent such a night as last night," moaned Birchall according to the *Empire*. The prisoner said he had no bed, no blanket, and no pillow, and quipped that he had "had to lie down on the soft side of a board." Still, he told Det. Murray that he would be all right once he got a meal tucked away. Taking the hint, Murray called a steward, who ten minutes later presented Birchall with a breakfast tray upon which was a large beefsteak, three fried eggs, a pot of coffee, several slices of toast, and a piece of corn bread. "O, I say, you are a jolly fellow, Murray," exclaimed Birchall as he dove into the meal.[1]

In Woodstock

At least 150 people stood on the platform at Woodstock to watch the prisoner descend from the train. Accompanied by Det. Murray and Chief Willis, a handcuffed Birchall walked along the platform, which gave everyone a chance to see him. The reporter from the *Sentinel-Review* observed that Birchall had "a nervous sort of smile" and, apparently looking for old friends, "glanced fervently at the crowd." The curious onlookers watched "in perfect silence" as the three men got into a waiting cab, which drove off quickly in the direction of the jail, a short distance across town.[2]

The Woodstock Jail had been a requirement for the county town once Oxford County was established at mid-century. Hamilton architects Clarke & Murray won a design competition, and construction was completed in 1854. It is an imposing structure of local yellow brick in the Italianate style with Tuscan Gothic details. Tall walls surround the yard around the jail; a grand entryway and a central octagonal tower dominate the building itself. The structure references a castle with strong defences. In Birchall's era, it was known locally as Castle Cameron, after the jail's governor, John Cameron. The historic jail still stands grandly on the edge of Victoria Park, but it now houses public health offices. It is a national historic site, and in the winter of 2019–20 it underwent its most recent restoration, which reconstructed Gothic details earlier removed.[3]

As Birchall proceeded to the jail, he showed a familiarity with people, making his arrival appear like a homecoming. The driver of his cab was John Stuart, a man Birchall knew well. "Old John has driven me before many a time, and a good fellow he is," declared the prisoner. Opposite the Commercial Hotel, Birchall noticed a Black friend and shouted to him at the top of his voice: "Hello, Rants!" The man turned, took off his hat, and bowed. The jail door was opened by turnkey James Forbes, a good friend from 1888–89, who bounded up to Birchall and shook his hand. With a tear in his eye, Forbes said he was sorry to see him there. Birchall responded with a laugh.

In the jail, Birchall shook hands with several reporters waiting there. The journalist from the *Sentinel-Review* thought Birchall appeared "quite cheerful and self-composed, tho' it was apparent that much of his sprightliness was forced and affected."[4] While waiting to be processed, Birchall leafed through the jail register, exclaiming, "Gad, what a lot of Irish there's here!" (The predominance of Irish among the population of

5.1. Woodstock Jail, where Birchall remained incarcerated from 13 March to 14 November 1890.
Source: Author's photograph, 2020.

Ontario's nineteenth-century jails was widely acknowledged.) Birchall's own particulars were then recorded: "J. R. Birchall, gentleman by profession, belonging to the Church of England, married." When asked whether he was temperate, a matter routinely recorded in the register, he appeared puzzled. "Do you take a nip occasionally?" the jailer helpfully asked. "Yes, when I can get it," he replied. Birchall was entered as being "intemperate."[5]

The prisoner was escorted to his cell at the west end of the jail's west wing. It was bright enough but had a limited view. The cell had a table with a couple of books on it, one of them a Bible. An adjoining cell had his bed. Birchall joked about having "a suite of rooms," referencing his days at Oxford University. He shook hands goodbye with Murray, who said, "I'll do anything for you outside of this case." Birchall thanked him warmly. He said goodbye to the reporters and invited them back anytime. "I wish you boys would send me something to read," said Birchall. "Balzac or anything."[6]

This prisoner planned to avoid the jail grub. He said that the food in the Welland Jail had consisted of a piece of fatty meat floating in a bowl of water. He asked his Woodstock jailer to arrange for his meals to be delivered from a nearby hotel. Birchall assured him that he had cashed a cheque so that his attorney would have plenty of funds to cover the cost.

The jail surgeon, Dr. Andrew T. Rice, examined Birchall, declaring him to be "sound in wind and limb." When Rice was asked by a reporter whether he thought Birchall insane, he said it was too soon to tell. He had noticed that the prisoner's eyes were strangely dilated, but said that might be caused by excitement and the great strain he has been labouring under.[7] (It is possible that his dilated pupils were a side effect of laudanum, a tincture with opium then widely available.)

Birchall had various visitors that day. Coroner Archibald McLay came to the cell, and they had a long conversation interrupted by frequent laughter. McLay mentioned that many of the young Englishmen in the area had come by their money easily. Birchall cheekily replied that he had heard many doctors did, too, charging more for medicines than the components cost them and prescribing unnecessary ones.

Visiting reporters had an opportunity to ask him about many things. One matter was at last cleared up: the spelling of his name. He said that different branches of his family spelled it differently, which explained why he went by both "Birchall" and "Burchell."

In the afternoon, the prisoner got his first "airing" in the jail yard. While there, another prisoner, described by the press as "a lunatic," asked him whether he shot Benwell. The only reply was a laugh.

There was a consensus that the ever-cheerful Birchall appeared totally unconcerned about the charge against him. The *Telegram* thought he "must be possessed of enormous self-confidence to maintain so calm an exterior in the face of such an uncomfortable situation." Another observer declared that there was "no apparent difference between the Birchall of Woodstock jail and the old 'Lord Somerset.'" After arriving in Woodstock Jail, he had written several letters to England. The jailer who read them remarked that "strange to say the burden of them [was] all horse-racing or some kindred subject."[8]

Det. Murray brought witnesses to identify Birchall in the jail. Few, if any, precautions were taken to place the accused in a context where his identity would not be obvious. Line-ups were not used. The *Empire* reported that throughout the identifications, only once did Birchall's chipper demeanour break. Charles Buck, a farmer living near the infamous swamp, was brought to the jail one day by Det. Murray to determine whether the prisoner was the man Buck had seen on 17 February just 300 yards from where the body was found. In the dim light of the cell, Buck couldn't see Birchall clearly, so he was brought into the corridor. When the prisoner saw Buck, "the effect was magical," reported the *Empire*. "For the first time since his arrival [Birchall] quaked. His eyes glistened ... and he became deathly pale." Nevertheless, he quickly recovered himself. Buck said he was certain the prisoner was the man he had seen.

That afternoon, the town grew excited when it was learned that Buck was the brother-in-law of Baker, one of the men who had been on a spree and who had first been suspected of the murder. People now doubted Buck's story and his identification. (As it turned out, the Crown never called him as a witness.)[9]

The Farm-Pupil Business

Newspapers explored Birchall's involvement with the farm-pupil business, which looked dodgier than ever after Benwell's murder. In interviews with Birchall and in letters found among his effects in Niagara Falls, journalists pieced together his history in the business.

Early accounts of Birchall's first experiences with the farm-pupil business reveal him to have been a victim of a fraud rather than a con man. In the fall of 1888, in London, he paid £70 to Ford, Rathbone & Co., one of the leading London agencies involved in the business, and became a "farm pupil" bound for Canada. The agreement was that the company's agent in Woodstock would place him on a nearby farm, where, without pay, he would learn how to run a Canadian farm. Like other "pupils" the agency in England placed abroad, he was shown pictures of fine farmhouses and beautiful farms that made the opportunity look enticing. The company also provided him with testimonials, Birchall said, from "bishops, canons, peers and others."[10]

In December 1888, Birchall and his bride came out to Canada to take up their farm placement near Woodstock, where they met William McDonald, the local agent of Ford, Rathbone. McDonald had farmed for thirty years about four miles north of Woodstock. In about 1887 he sold the farm for the princely sum of $9,000 and moved into Woodstock with his wife and children. In 1888, Burgess, the local agent for Ford, Rathbone, died, and McDonald took over the position that summer.

Ford, Rathbone would pay $125 to a farmer for taking on a newcomer, and if he lasted three months on the farm, McDonald would get a commission of $30. McDonald placed several men on farms, although some of them didn't stay long.[11]

In 1888, McDonald sent the Birchalls to a farm placement that Birchall later remembered as having been near Springfield. The couple stayed only one night before returning to Woodstock. They complained to McDonald and to the agency in London, saying that the placement was unsuitable and did not at all resemble what they had been led to expect. From jail, Birchall told a reporter that when they had returned home to England in the spring of 1889, he had threatened to sue the company, although, in the end, he settled for financial compensation.[12] Birchall's disillusionment with the business was shared by many farm pupils. As he told Canadian reporters, English gentlemen were familiar with the ideal of the farm life of the gentry in England and expected to find the same attractive way of life in Canada. They had no wish to rough it or to work at heavy farming tasks, which was generally what was expected of farm pupils in Canada.

As time went on, it became increasingly uncertain whether Birchall had been a victim or a perpetrator of the farm-pupil fraud. A letter found by police in Birchall's possessions in Niagara Falls and reproduced by the press showed that Birchall had actually worked in some capacity for Ford, Rathbone. In the letter written in the winter of 1888–89, Birchall informed the company about the poor record of recent farm placements in the Woodstock area. Farm-pupil Levy had left his farm placement and was now in jail for vagrancy. Childs had skipped town owing $1,300, and the bailiff had just sold off Childs's cattle. Overvey had refused to work anywhere, saying the farmers never pay, and so had just left for the North-West. Pickhorn [sic, Pickthorn] was spending all his time hanging about Woodstock's Commercial Hotel, which was a favourite resort of farm pupils. Radley had been "terribly drunk off and on for over four weeks." Birchall informed the company that the people in Woodstock disliked the farm-pupil business. A clergyman who had come to see him about it said that young men in England should be discouraged from coming out. He planned to make representations to authorities about the fraud.[13]

In fact, the Canadian government, in its emigration materials circulated in Britain, had for several years been including warnings about the farm-pupil business. It explained that paying a premium for a placement on a Canadian farm was unnecessary. Employment was available, and government agents would assist new arrivals in finding a paying job.[14] Canadian agricultural journals similarly warned against the "evil." Any young man willing and able to work hard on a farm could readily find work, learn Canadian farming methods, and be paid. Proper farmers didn't want unpaid loafers about their properties. "No well-to-do farmer who can afford to pay, feed, and house his men will be bothered with men who are not receiving wages," declared the *Canadian Breeder and Agricultural Review*. "They want no drones and 'swells' about their places."[15]

Birchall, like so many other farm pupils, felt burned by the experience, but in his case, it was also an inspiration. Back in England after his Canadian sojourn, when he was casting about for an opportunity, he struck upon the idea of taking advantage of young men from well-to-do families who were interested in making a career in Canadian agriculture. He fell in with T.S. Mellersh of Cheltenham, Gloucestershire, who frequently advertised in the English press for young men wishing to have assistance in finding a farm placement in Canada. Col. Benwell had asked Mellersh to look for a suitable business opportunity for his son Fred. After determining that Birchall was "a gentleman," Mellersh gave him the names of Fred Benwell and Douglas Pelly. Birchall contacted them about investing in his horse farm near Niagara Falls, and so began the steps that brought them to Canada.

The farm-pupil business took on a more sinister aspect following Benwell's murder. It was widely surmised that probably many other young Englishmen who had gone out as farm pupils to Canada and the United States and never been heard from again had similarly been murdered by unscrupulous emigration agents. The *Globe* reported that Benwell's murder had prompted Scotland Yard detectives to trace five well-to-do emigrants bound for Canada who had disappeared. "The theory of their fate," said the report, "is that they have been inveigled into someplace and murdered by a band of desperadoes for the sake of the money which they were carrying with them."[16]

This aspect of the case profoundly disturbed the respectable classes of England, who feared its implications for them. *The Times* observed that in England "men of moderate sagacity" make extensive inquiries into people with whom their sons propose to partner with in business, adding: "The sad fate of Mr. Benwell is a terrible proof that such inquiries cannot be safely dispensed with in the colonies." Putting a positive spin on the murder, London's *Standard* hoped that Benwell's "death will at least emphasise the lesson that too much caution can hardly be displayed in dealing with the originators or the promulgators of those seductive advertisements which tempt so many English lads to face the perils and hardship of the Western wilderness." It was reported that in response to Benwell's murder, people in England were showing a new wariness of the farm-pupil business by removing their names from the books of agencies that placed young men on farms in Canada and the United States.[17]

The Pickthall Mystery

In the period from the time of Birchall's arrest until his incarceration in Woodstock, the newspapers supplemented the main narrative with related stories, one of which concerned the mysterious disappearance of one Neville Hunter Pickthall. He had a farm six miles south of Woodstock, was recently married, and had suddenly and inexplicably left the area on 10 February. No one knew where he had gone, including his young wife. It appeared that Pickthall had deserted his wife, or perhaps he had self-divorced, a long-standing practice that took place beyond the law.[18]

The first news of Pickthall's whereabouts came from Pelly's revelations at the Benwell inquest in Princeton. Pelly testified that the Birchalls had spoken about Pickthall both in England and aboard the *Britannic*. They had said he was an English neighbour at Niagara with a farm adjoining theirs. While staying at the Metropolitan Hotel in New York, Pelly had again heard the Birchalls speaking about Pickthall. Mrs. Birchall had told her husband that she had seen Pickthall in their hotel that very morning. Birchall had said he hadn't noticed him there but had encountered him later that day.[19] Reporters traced Pickthall's movements across the border and to a hotel in New York where he was staying when the Birchall party arrived in town. After that, he had left no trace.

Pickthall's sudden disappearance and the Birchalls' encountering him in New York prompted endless discussion in the press about "the Pickthall mystery." Was it possible that Pickthall had gone to New York to meet Birchall and discuss the plans for fleecing and murdering Benwell and Pelly? It soon came out that the day Pickthall left Oxford County, he had taken out $1,000 in cash by arranging a new mortgage on his farm. Was that money being used to further the plan? Or had he disappeared in New York because Birchall had taken his money and murdered him there? Alternatively, perhaps Pickthall had left Oxford County because of a love affair. That was denied in the *News*, which reported that according to those who knew him best, Pickthall "possessed a singular aversion to women, and avoided their company as far as possible."[20] Yet he had recently married, perhaps best explained by his bride's attractive financial resources.

Journalists reported the rumours that were circulating and also ferreted out the details of Pickthall's biography. Born in Suffolk, England, Pickthall had come to America at the age of seventeen in 1884, arriving in New York with the intention of making a new life as a farmer. He had a small income from his father, a clergyman. Eventually he found his way to Woodstock, where at first he simply enjoyed himself, drinking and doing without work. Nevertheless, around 1888 he managed to get the money together to buy a farm about six miles south of Woodstock at Curries Crossing.[21]

When the Birchalls were living in Woodstock during their first sojourn there, Rex Birchall had made friends with Pickthall. During this period, Pickthall took on a farm pupil fresh from England, S.V. ("Cholly") Dudley, who played the flute. He lasted only one month on the farm but became another one of Rex's drinking pals. A photograph taken in Woodstock of "Somerset" shows him with Dudley, two suave fellows clowning together. Both would become embroiled with the law. Shortly after Birchall's arrest, it was reported that Dudley was in jail in Detroit, accused of having stolen money and clothing from the rooming house where he was staying.

Journalists hinted that Pickthall and Dudley may have been intimate, although such an accusation was of course put in ambiguous language. "Many queer stories are told," said one account, "of the wild life he and Pickthall used to lead while they were keeping 'batch' on the farm."[22] Placed beside statements of neighbours who said Pickthall disliked and avoided women, the gossip takes on added significance.

On 11 March, the *Sentinel-Review* reported that Mrs. Pickthall had at last had news from her husband, who had sent her a letter dated 2 March from Tucson, Arizona. The letter's contents were not divulged, but Mrs. Pickthall said that they shed no light on the reason for his disappearance. At this point a metropolitan newspaper with more resources, the *New York World*, contacted the editor of *Sentinel-Review* and struck a deal. If the Woodstock editor would supply the Tucson address from which Pickthall's letter had come, it would send a reporter to Tucson to interview Pickthall and his report would be shared with

5.2. Rex Birchall and "Cholly" Dudley kibitzing for the photographer in Woodstock, 1888–9.
Source: Woodstock Museum, image 1900.39.15.

the *Sentinel-Review*. Indeed, the Woodstock paper had the scoop on the rest of the Canadian newspapers when, on 14 March, it published what the *World* reporter had found.[23]

The reporter who interviewed Pickthall in Tucson described him as being twenty-four, six feet tall, 164 pounds, and of fair complexion with a light mustache. Pickthall said that in New York he had assumed the name "Jackson" to hide his whereabouts from creditors after taking heavy losses. He hoped to go to California to recover his fortunes. On 14 February he had left New York for the West by train. Upon arriving in Deming, New Mexico, on the US–Mexico border, he had lost his ticket to California, his money, and his baggage. Pickthall eventually had found his way to Tucson. In the newspapers he had seen his name connected with Birchall's and so he had written to his wife back in Woodstock. When prompted by the reporter, Pickthall had reminisced about his contact with Birchall back in 1888–89. Birchall would drive out to the farm two or three times a week for a visit. Pickthall was always mystified by where Birchall got his money and found him "reckless, fast, and unreliable." Still, he could not believe he was a murderer.

Further news of Pickthall's misadventures in the West came from a Mr. Peters, who had travelled with Pickthall. In San Francisco, after reading about the Pickthall mystery in California newspapers, Peters told his story to the *San Francisco Chronicle*. "I fell in with Pickthall at Albuquerque," he recounted, "and came through on the same train with him as far as Deming." Peters described the traveller as "a lively, jovial fellow and easy to become acquainted with. He is very tall in build, and is a blond of the English type."[24] At Albuquerque they drank together and had had "a lively time with the boys." At Deming their train was delayed six hours, so they had gone up town for some fun. Pickthall drank heavily and gambled, losing $100 or $200. Peters had returned to the train on time, but Pickthall, being drunk and possibly hoping to win back his gambling losses, had missed it. At Tucson, Peters had received a telegram from Pickthall asking Peters to look after his baggage (still aboard the train) and take it to the Palace Hotel in San Francisco, where he would meet him. He had not shown up. Peters still had Pickthall's luggage, including an unlocked satchel that contained mortgages and letters in the name of Pickthall, which Peters took to be valuable and to indicate that Pickthall was "a man of means."

On 26 March, the press announced that Pickthall was expected home in Woodstock soon. Early on the morning of 1 April, he registered at the O'Neill House as "N. H. Pickthall, Tucson." Pickthall told a *Sentinel-Review* reporter that he had been "fleeced" in Deming, New Mexico. In a drunken state, he had flashed a large bill and someone had taken advantage of him. "I was stupid," he said. "I was drugged." He had had just enough money left to get to Tucson, which is where he had gone.[25] When asked about why he had left Oxford County in the first place, Pickthall said that he had been drinking and suddenly got it into his head that he should leave his life on the farm, which was not paying the way he had hoped. When arranging for the $1,000 mortgage, he concocted stories about how he was going to invest the money in land and cattle. In fact, he went away without a plan of what he would do. Later, when he sobered up, he grew ashamed of the stories he had told. He hadn't been able to face going home, which was why he stayed away.

The explanation made the whole mystery seem hollow. So much ink, in so many cities, had been expended on what turned out to be quite a mundane tale. The *Evening Standard* took aim at the *Sentinel-Review*, accusing its rival of grossly exaggerating the significance of the

Pickthall story from the start.[26] The possibility remains, however, that Pickthall was lying because he didn't want to divulge his shady business dealings with Birchall, which would have implicated him in the fraud and, possibly, the murder as well.

Further Revelations

Soon after Birchall was charged with Benwell's murder, newspapers began speculating about the backgrounds of the key players and researching who they were. Transatlantic conversations among journalists in England and Canada shed light on the origins and reputations of the men.

The *World* reflected on both Benwell's and Birchall's identities. Efforts to track down Benwell's alleged military family initially failed. Birchall's claim that he had been in the business of purchasing horses in Ontario and shipping them for sale in England could not be confirmed either, but it looked doubtful. Two prominent horse dealers in Toronto said they had never heard of him.[27]

It didn't take long before the *World* was able to confirm Benwell's identity by publishing a report from England.[28] A journalist had interviewed Fred Benwell's father, Col. Frederick W. Benwell, at his home in Cheltenham, the fashionable spa town in Gloucestershire. Col. Benwell had explained that he had wanted to set up his son to farm in Ontario. Birchall had approached him, and it was agreed that young Benwell would go out to Canada to live on Birchall's farm for three months at no cost to him. At the end of the trial, if he liked what he found, the colonel would pay Birchall £500 for a half interest in the farm. The colonel explained that he had last heard from his son in a letter sent when they arrived safely in New York.

The sensational part of the interview with Col. Benwell concerned a letter he had received about the farm investment on 4 March, the day after he had read in the London papers that an F.C. Benwell had been murdered in Canada. The letter was undated but had been posted on 20 February in Niagara Falls. In the letter, Birchall told the Colonel that his son Fred was "so well satisfied with the prospect here that he is ready to go immediately into partnership." Birchall asked him to send to their business in Canada £500 (today more than £58,000 or nearly $100,000[29]). He added that young Benwell was "writing today on the subject." Readers of the article were fully aware that, in fact, Fred Benwell was dead by the time Birchall sent the letter. The news made Birchall look more devious and cold-hearted than ever. Even after murdering Benwell, he was still trying to fleece the young man's father.

The colonel said that upon receiving the letter, he immediately cabled Birchall about the developments but had no reply. Confident in his own high status, the colonel then sent a statement outlining the story to Lord Knutsford, secretary of state for the colonies. In a private letter to Douglas Pelly's father, Col. Benwell declared that he found the letter from Niagara Falls to be "positive proof of Burchell's guilt."[30] Col. Benwell told the reporter he had had growing suspicions of Birchall, whom he was by then catching out in lies. When confronted, Birchall had squirmed out of them, and the colonel, to his regret, had let things ride.

In the interview, Col. Benwell cleared up one matter: the amount of money that his son had with him in Canada. He had left with just £25 and probably had spent £10 aboard the *Britannic*. Still, he had taken a large outfit of clothing. So that there would be no problem at customs, the Colonel had insisted that his son label all his clothing, which Birchall had tried to discourage. (Here was yet more suspicious behaviour.) In closing the interview, the colonel asked the reporter to deny the insinuation that his son and Mrs. Birchall had had "improper relations." They had met only once, at her father's house, with her parents and husband present.

Repeated claims that the Birchalls were never legally married were put to rest when a marriage notice was found in *The Times* from 27 November 1888. It read:

> On the 19th inst. by license at Croydon, Reginald Burchell, youngest son of the late Rev. Joseph Birchall, Rector of Church Kirk, near Accrington, Rural Dean of and Proctor in Convocation for the Archdeaconry of Manchester [married] Florence Stevenson, fourth daughter of David Stevenson of Maberley Road, Upper Norwich.

The notice thus indicated both the respectability of the couple's relationship and their high social standing.[31]

In March, an unidentified English reporter interviewed David Stevenson, Birchall's father-in-law, at his London home. Stevenson, who had a high position in one of England's major railways, said that his daughter had first met Birchall at a party. When introduced to Stevenson, Birchall had represented himself as a rich man, the only question being whether he would settle $100,000 or $200,000 on his bride.

The courtship had been brief – three months – so Stevenson refused to give his approval for marriage. Undeterred, the couple had eloped and immediately afterwards gone off to Canada. While Birchall and his daughter were there, Stevenson had seen notices in the English press placed by creditors looking for Birchall. When he confronted the creditors, Stevenson realized his son-in-law was in serious debt. Nevertheless, when the couple returned from Canada, Stevenson had forgiven them for eloping, and he and his wife had opened their home to them. That is where they stayed, living comfortably, until their second trip to Canada. Stevenson said that during the courtship, he had seen Birchall as "an unprincipled fellow." Yet it now struck him that he was "of manners so amiable that it was difficult to believe that he could commit such a terrible crime as murder."[32]

The same English reporter visited the home of the Rev. Mr. R.P. Pelly, rector of the parish of Saffron Walden, Essex, and father of Douglas. The reporter was shown a letter that Birchall had written describing his farm at Niagara Falls and outlining the investment opportunity. The letter was written in a "bold hand upon fine, tinted paper, with initials and an elaborately stamped black and gold monogram." Both the senior Pelly and Col. Benwell told the reporter they had been impressed by the wealth and standing of Mr. Stevenson, a well-known man of commerce in England.

In Canada, doubts about Birchall's upper-class identity were by then being raised. The *World* observed that there was a strong feeling that Birchall was neither an Oxford man nor from the prominent family of Birchalls in Accrington, Lancashire. The speculation was that "Birchall" must have assumed the identity of *that* Reginald Birchall, which explained how the imposter had succeeded in marrying so well. A young man in Woodstock maintained that he knew Somerset/Birchall was actually the son of a livery-stable keeper outside London, England. That would explain why he did not "act like an Oxford bred man."[33]

This line of speculation might have continued for some time, but news arriving via the Atlantic cable ended it.[34] The unidentified English reporter who interviewed Stevenson and the Rev. Pelly reported that there could be no doubt that Birchall was "an errant scamp" of a well-known Lancashire family and had indeed attended Oxford.

Meanwhile, in England, the public was becoming informed about Birchall's background and reputation, thanks to investigations by reporters in Lancashire. The *Weekly Standard and Express*, published in Blackburn, Lancashire, first expressed disbelief that Birchall was "really a Churchite," that is, that he was the son of the Rev. Joseph Birchall, who for forty years had been rector of Church Kirk in Church, Lancashire. A week later, the same newspaper conceded that, although "painful to think," the swamp murderer was indeed the son of the respectable Lancashire clergyman who had died when Reginald was about thirteen. It observed, "Even a clergyman cannot keep watch and ward over the conduct and morals of his children longer than he lives." A London newspaper learned that Birchall's father was a man of considerable wealth with a financial interest in a large brewery and a good salary from Church Kirk, a prosperous parish.[35]

Canadian newspapers carried a report from London that claimed to describe Birchall's financial affairs. In his will, Rex's father had split his estate among his three children so that Rex was to get the handsome sum of $20,000, but not until May 1891, when he was to turn twenty-five. While at Oxford, Rex ran up debts amounting to $5,000; he escaped his creditors by coming to Canada in 1888. Lawyers for the creditors advertised in English newspapers their plans to sue him, but all they got was a letter announcing his residence in Woodstock, Ontario. Upon his return to England in 1889, Birchall sold his share of his inheritance to his sister for $15,000. He must have used some of that money to ward off his creditors and to keep up appearances with his wife and father-in-law. Probably he was losing money at the races. It appears that by the time he came again to Canada, now with Benwell and Pelly, he had exhausted the $15,000.[36]

Canadian newspapers also began carrying stories about Rex Birchall's misbehaviour while he was enrolled in Oxford University. "His wild ways were notorious through the length and breadth of Oxford," declared one London report that circulated in Canada. "At Lincoln [College] he made the night hideous, and his wild Indian whoop was often heard at night." As the founder of the Black and Tan Club, he had led his colleagues in revelry and troublemaking. After leaving school he had worked as a theatre manager, a profession of doubtful respectability. It was asserted that later still, Birchall had gone into the immigration con business with T.S. Mellersh, "the English swindler who worked the confidence game by sending rich young farmers to Canada."[37] The *New York Herald* printed an article headlined "Wild Career at Oxford," apparently based on interviews in Oxford. It referred to "his love of mischief and his unscrupulousness, and his indulgence in falsehoods," but also evident was "a sort of wild anarchic generosity, a keen sense of humor and an activity of intellect." He liked to draw attention to himself by wearing "gaudy waistcoats" and "some adornment of flaming hue."[38]

In England, too, colourful reports circulated about Birchall's misbehaviour at Oxford University, where he had been a leader of a disreputable set and popular because he threw money around. For the Black and Tan Club, he had designed a blazer that had "broad, perpendicular stripes of most inharmonious shades of olive and pink." He made a spectacle of himself in Oxford's streets. With eyes half closed, he would pass through crowded streets of the town "tapping his stick loudly ... after the manner of the blind man." He loved to attend the theatre and "could be seen in the front stalls during the performances with a bottle of champagne in one hand and a glass in the other, offering refreshment to any who might take his fancy."[39]

Birchall never completed his degree. Although the rector of Lincoln College described him as "a brilliant fellow," his bad behaviour led college authorities on 9 December 1887 to remove his name from the register. The rector observed that, while so promising, Birchall had gone "irretrievably to the dogs."[40]

Previous speculations in Canada about Birchall's doubtful origins were thus quashed. Everyone now knew that he was a genuine blue blood, but wild. At Woodstock, the man who had said he knew that Birchall was the son of a liveryman near London now admitted he had been mistaken. He had been thinking of a liveryman by the name of Somerset.[41]

Meantime, news arrived that prominent people were expressing their support for Douglas Pelly. Cablegrams from England showed concern for him. It was reported that the governor general had received a letter from Sir Robert Herbert, under-secretary of state for the colonies, asking that consideration be shown towards Pelly, a young man of fine character. The message had been communicated to Ontario's attorney general. Pelly, of course, was a key Crown witness whose character was not in question. For journalists, Pelly provided a convenient foil for Birchall, the one an upright aid to the Crown's case, the other a scoundrel and alleged murderer.[42]

Stories also surfaced from people in Canada who knew something of the main players in the drama. A clergyman in Montreal said he had been at Oxford at the same time as Rex Birchall. "He was rather shunned by the Lincoln men," recalled the clergyman, "but all his outside friends looked upon him as a jolly good fellow." When he had known him, Birchall had lived opposite Barnes's livery stables, from which he had taken out horses every day. Mr. Johnson Clench of St. Catharines, the clerk of Lincoln County, said his English wife knew young Pelly and his parents well. Recently Mrs. Pelly had written his wife asking her to keep a watchful eye on her son while he was at Birchall's farm near Niagara Falls. Mr. Clench had gone looking for the farm, had not found any evidence of it, and thus had grown suspicious of Birchall's story.[43]

A man by the name of Joseph Youngheart of the firm Vineberg & Co., wholesale hatters and furriers of Montreal, explained how he had met Fred Benwell aboard the *Britannic*. About five or six days out they formed part of a group of six who played card games. Youngheart remarked: "He was a poor companion. I did not care much for him. He wore an eyeglass and very stylishly cut clothes, so the passengers christened him "the Dude." (In nineteenth-century American slang, a dude was a dandy, or one excessively well-dressed.) "Benwell was unpopular on board," concluded Youngheart, "presumably because of his dudish dress, and was guyed by many."[44] Here Benwell was represented as an unattractive figure lacking in manliness.

The stories of Birchall's connections with respectable English society were made more tangible in Ontario when his wife's older sister, Mrs. Marion West-Jones, and his father-in-law, Mr. David Stevenson, arrived in Woodstock in mid-March to give support to Florence Birchall. Although West-Jones stayed on in town, after six weeks Stevenson left for home. In mid-May, it was reported in England that when Stevenson had arrived in London, he had been presented with a testimonial signed by 750 of the 752 employees in his department.[45] Stevenson was thus depicted as an admired manager.

The Interregnum

Birchall had a long wait in the Woodstock Jail before his trial at the fall assizes, which would open on 18 September. The assize courts were held twice yearly, when a Toronto-based judge travelling on his circuit visited Woodstock to preside over trials of serious offences. The timing of Birchall's committal in Niagara Falls was such that he missed the assizes in spring 1890 and had to wait a full six months for his trial. Once the press had covered his arrival and early days at the jail, understandably interest waned for lack of developments.

A few news items cropped up. It was, for instance, reported that Birchall had made a case to local authorities for having his cell carpeted, the twenty-four-year-old arguing that he suffered from rheumatism.

His request was granted, which underscored that he was no ordinary prisoner. His far superior meals continued to arrive thrice daily from the Commercial Hotel. They were brought to him by his "butler," the young African Canadian, Rants.[46] Birchall's wife Florence, who was staying at a Woodstock hotel along with her sister Marion, six years her senior, visited him often in the jail during the spring and summer. To help pass the time, he sent and received an enormous number of letters. Issues of sporting magazines came his way, many sent by his mother. He decorated his cells with sketches he made of people and horses.[47]

Meanwhile, entrepreneurs were taking advantage of the sensational murder case. Montreal's "Wonderland" introduced a "Chamber of Horrors" featuring Benwell and Birchall. Ten cents bought a ticket to this "Palace of Enchantment."[48]

The press wondered what Douglas Pelly would do during the interregnum. Subpoenaed to give evidence at the trial, he was given a Canadian-government allowance to defray his expenses while he waited. Nevertheless, he wanted a job, preferably outdoor work. Eventually it was arranged for him to work on a survey crew on the Canadian prairies.[49]

During the interregnum, Birchall's lawyers attempted to use the law to prohibit the press from publishing reports that could prejudice the people of Oxford against Birchall and prevent a fair trial. Isidore Hellmuth, representing Birchall's interests, appeared in Toronto courtrooms to argue two cases. In April, he presented a motion to the court calling upon the editor and proprietor of the *Fireside Weekly*, published in Woodstock, to show why he should not be found in contempt. The *Fireside* had advertised that it would be publishing a serial story titled "Who Killed Benwell, or the Mystery of the Blenheim Swamp." Hellmuth argued that such a story would be prejudicial to his client.[50] In June, Hellmuth presented another motion in a Toronto court asking the proprietors of the *Mail* and the *Empire* to show why they should not be committed for contempt for articles stating that Birchall had planned to send a victim in a barrel over Niagara Falls. Both cases became entangled in legal technicalities, and in the end nothing came of them.[51] Clearly, Hellmuth was looking out for Birchall's interests, but in fact many damaging reports about Birchall had been published and widely read in Oxford County. It had long been difficult to imagine how an unbiased jury might be found.

In any event, during the interregnum developments in the story were few while Rex Birchall waited anxiously – or otherwise – for his September trial.

6

Pelly's Story

We are fortunate that in 1933 Douglas Pelly wrote a memoir about his life up to and including his time in Canada, and that the memoir was saved by his family and a copy placed in the Archives and Special Collections of the Weldon Library at Western University in London, Ont.[1] The memoir enables us to get to know Pelly and appreciate his perspective on his involvement with Birchall and his knowledge of the murder. Accompanying the memoir are copies of letters from 1889–90 as well as a "Detailed Account" of Pelly's contacts with the Birchalls up to 23 March 1890. Pelly had prepared this account for the use of the Crown prosecutor. This chapter is based on the memoir and the accompanying sources.

Pelly's reminiscences, written when he was sixty-eight, begin on a modest note. He says that he knows that he cannot write well and that his life is not of much interest or significance, but he explains that his wife and children insisted that he record his life story.[2] In fact, the account is engaging, as well as significant in that it sheds light on the Benwell murder story.

Early Life

Born in 1865 in Micham, Surrey, Douglas Raymond Pelly was reared in a world of privilege. His paternal grandfather, whom Douglas knew well and liked, had made a fortune in banking. Douglas's grandmother was the youngest daughter of Elizabeth Fry, the celebrated Quaker. The grandparents' youngest son, Raymond Percy Pelly, was educated for the Church (the Church of England). In 1864, at age twenty-three, he was ordained a deacon and married a bride of nineteen. Douglas was the first of ten children born to Raymond and Louise Pelly. Helping with the children were various governesses, and the household had other staff as well. The family moved periodically as Raymond, ordained a priest in 1866, took charge of a series of parishes.[3]

As a small boy, Douglas lived with his family in Matlock Bath, Derbyshire, which he writes gave him a lifelong appreciation of the beauties of mountains and rivers. In 1872, the family moved to Woodford Wells, Essex, where his father built a large vicarage, dubbed by his bishop "the little palace." It was a deeply religious home. "Throughout my youth," recalls Douglas, "we lived in a very strictly religious atmosphere, with family prayers twice a day and a long Bible reading after breakfast." The Sabbath was strictly observed. On Saturday night the butler would bring into the parlour a tray with religious tracts for Sunday reading and remove all secular reading material, locking it in a cupboard until Monday morning. During the week there were opportunities, depending on the season, for riding, swimming, skating, and shooting.[4]

At age ten, Douglas attended his first school, Coningham House, in the seaside town of Ramsgate, Kent, where he says the teaching was good but the food and accommodations were dreadful. His health, he says, was "delicate," and he suffered from several illnesses while there. In 1879, he began attending Harrow, the famous public school. Unfortunately, his illnesses continued, which soon led to his departure. He was then tutored privately.[5]

Summers brought pleasant breaks from Douglas's studies. In 1879 the family joined his Aunt Blanche ("Lady Pelly"), who had rented Monorbeir Castle, a medieval castle in Wales that delighted Douglas and his younger siblings. The following summer he enjoyed a holiday in the Scottish Highlands.[6]

In 1882, Douglas's father became vicar of St. John's, Stratford, Essex, a parish that included densely populated working-class neighbourhoods. The work of his father was demanding, even though he had help from four curates and his son Douglas.[7]

While living in Stratford, Douglas became an officer in the Volunteer Force, the citizen soldiery of the United Kingdom. He joined the Third Volunteer Battalion of the Essex Regiment and soon came to love part-time military life, especially the summer camps.[8]

The following year, Douglas became an undergraduate in Emmanuel College, Cambridge University, from which he graduated with a BA three years later. Pelly says little about his studies there, but remarks that he enjoyed rifle-shooting and rowing and was a success at both. Holidays brought opportunities for travel to the Channel Islands, Switzerland, Germany, Italy, and Austria. And his part-time, volunteer military service continued.[9]

Searching for a Career

Douglas hoped for a career in the army, but upon his graduation from university, his father announced that he was to become an insurance underwriter as a member of Lloyd's. Did his father fear that Douglas would stray from religion if he became a professional soldier? Or was his father's concern that Douglas's delicate health would be made worse by army life? In any event, Douglas began an apprenticeship at Lloyd's, where his share of the family resources was now tied up in the firm.[10] He hated the job and blamed his continuing health problems on the sedentary work in a crowded, airless office environment. All was not drudgery, however. He enjoyed his continuing service in the Volunteer Force and his travels to the Middle East, Italy, and Switzerland.[11]

After another bout of illness, a physician removed Douglas's tonsils, a painful operation conducted without anaesthetic. Happily for Douglas, his doctor recommended that he recover by taking a long ocean voyage in a warm climate, so he travelled around southern Africa. On board ship he met a married couple who ran a Presbyterian mission near Lake Nyasa (now Lake Malawi), and they persuaded him to accompany them there. Despite a bout of malaria, he thoroughly enjoyed a long visit there. For five months he took a naive delight in the colonial encounter at the mission as well as Africa's exotic natural bounty.[12] Afterwards, he set sail for the South Pacific and visited New Zealand and Australia. On his return voyage home to England, he danced on deck every night. In his memoir, Douglas never mentions how these travels were financed, but the family must have paid all the bills.

In January 1889, he returned to London and his desk job at Lloyd's, but he soon resigned. Meantime, he resumed service in the Volunteer Force, improved his qualifications, and was promoted up the ranks of the officer corps. Later that year, his father was made Vicar of Saffron Walden, a Sussex town the family loved. Douglas's father bought a large, red-brick Georgian house called Walden Place.[13] Douglas remembers its delightful garden. He enjoyed life in Saffron Walden, spending time shooting, playing tennis, and performing in an amateur theatre company.[14]

For all of 1889 he searched for more suitable work in England – certainly not an office job – but without success. No family money was available to set him up in a career because his allotment remained tied up in Lloyd's.[15] He began to consider some prospect in "the colonies," an option pursued by many second sons who lacked large financial resources. He was familiar with attractive newspaper advertisements offering opportunities for "farm pupils" interested in going to Canada. In early December 1889 he answered Mellersh's advertisement in the *Standard*. Mellersh put Reginald Birchall in touch with him about outdoor work and an investment. In a letter, Birchall told Pelly that his brother, a partner in their farm in Canada, had just left him so he was looking for an educated man to go out to Canada with him and his wife and become an active partner in the farm.[16]

In the memoir, Pelly reproduces a letter that Birchall sent him, which Pelly tells his readers shows that Birchall was an "educated gentleman."[17] It appears that Birchall's Oxford education accounted at least in part for how he was able to gain Pelly's confidence. Certainly, the letter makes the proposition appear highly attractive. Moreover, Birchall played to Pelly's vanity as an English gentleman and a "University man."

In the same letter, Birchall described the horse farm as being of 120 acres near Niagara with two branch operations elsewhere. He said that he and his wife lived "in the English style with English servants." Pelly would not be expected to do any heavy work, such as ploughing, as that would be left to the labourers. Instead, he would superintend either the main farm or the two branch ones and attend to horse sales. If Pelly were to invest £500, he would get his board, lodging, expenses, and "a good salary." Alternatively, he could agree to take "a fair share" of the profits, which were substantial. The previous year, Birchall said, he had earned £800 in the horse business alone. Birchall closed the letter by suggesting they get together in London to discuss the matter further.

In the memoir there follow six more letters from Birchall to Pelly firming up their arrangement. In them, Birchall provides various specifics about his affairs that make the offer sound even more genuine. For instance, Birchall refers to his brother taking away four thoroughbreds, which now need replacing. Birchall writes that he has succeeded in buying two at £312, but he wants to find two more to bring to Canada.

6.1. Douglas Raymond Pelly, the Crown's star witness.
Source: *Sentinel-Review*, 14 March 1890.

His stock there stands at thirty-seven horses, which he will dispose of at the first sale of the new season. Birchall reassures Pelly that he has just succeeded in renewing his sales contract with the Canadian Pacific Railway for an additional two years.[18]

The correspondence, all of which came from Bainbridge, the London home of Birchall's in-laws, details the arrangements for their London meeting there on 7 January 1890. Included in one letter are the names, addresses, and positions of six references to whom Pelly is invited to inquire regarding Birchall's character. Apparently, Pelly checked two of the references, which reassured him.[19]

When Pelly met the Birchalls over tea, he was reassured by them. He was impressed with the appearance of Florence Birchall, whom he recalls "was a rather good looking woman." She and her husband were "good company, and he especially made himself exceedingly agreeable." Moreover, at their meeting Pelly met Florence's mother, the wife of David Stevenson. Pelly would have heard of Stevenson because he had the reputation of being one of England's foremost authorities on railways.[20]

Birchall and Pelly met on more occasions, both at Pelly's parents' home in Saffron Waldon and in London, and Birchall provided more details of his business in Canada. Douglas and his father met and agreed that the arrangement with Birchall was a good one and that Douglas should proceed with it. By registered mail, Douglas sent Birchall a cheque for £170, which he quickly cashed.

Off to Canada

Douglas Pelly grew annoyed that Birchall frequently changed plans for their departure for Canada. At last, it was settled they would meet at London's Euston Station on 4 February and travel together to Liverpool, where they would spend the night at the London and North Western Hotel.[21] Birchall and Pelly drank whiskies in the hotel bar that evening, and Birchall sent brandy and soda to Mrs. Birchall in her room. Pelly writes in the "Detailed Account": "This struck me at the time as a very curious thing for a so-called lady and made me wonder what sort of people they were that I had run against." It was that day that Birchall showed Pelly his revolver, which he said he always carried in his back pocket.

In the hotel bar Birchall mentioned for the first time that a young man named Fred Benwell would be going out to Canada with them. Birchall added that Benwell being "a most unattractive fellow," he planned to shake him off as soon as possible when they arrived in Canada. When Pelly met Benwell the next morning, Pelly "found him all that Birchall had described, and I felt at once that I would never be on very friendly terms with him." Pelly describes Benwell as being "short, very dark, very sallow," with "a most disagreeable manner." Benwell patronized Pelly, which naturally he found annoying.[22]

At this point in the memoir, Pelly talks about Benwell's origins. His father, the colonel, had met his Eurasian wife while serving in India. She was the well-educated daughter of an army officer (identified as the brother of Lord Braybrooke) and an Indian woman. The colonel and his wife had several children, Fred being the second son. Pelly adds that Benwell's origins explained his dark complexion. Pelly also remarks that he later met Mrs. Benwell and found her "very handsome."[23] (The 1891 census of England shows Col. Fredrick W. Benwell and his wife Marian living in their Cheltenham home "Iseultdene" with four remaining children, ranging in age from ten to twenty-four, and a cook, a parlour maid, and a housemaid.)

After Benwell's murder, Col. Benwell corresponded with Raymond Pelly, writing father to father about the experiences of their sons. By this point, the Colonel was aware that Douglas Pelly had not taken to his son, which surprised him. He writes: "With those who knew our beloved boy he was a favourite and was much liked. Generous and kind hearted to a degree, frank and open, and to strangers usually polite." He put it down to Birchall's manipulation of the two and the fact that the two young men were mutually suspicious of the competition the other's presence implied. The Colonel was surprised and disturbed that the two lads had not compared notes and protected each other from Birchall. Looking back, it must have troubled Col. Benwell that his son, who was the main victim and paid with his life, got little sympathy in public accounts of the murder and was reported to have been unpleasant and unlikeable.[24]

Pelly continues his story, writing about the ten-day voyage across the Atlantic aboard the White Star steamer *Britannic*, then known as "the Greyhound of the Atlantic" and "the last word in luxurious ocean travel."[25] Pelly says that his letters home were full of the beauty, comfort, and speed of the ship. For most of the voyage, Birchall was seasick. Pelly visited him in his cabin each day, and Birchall would warn him off Benwell. "I did not need much persuading," writes Pelly, "as I disliked the man and his swaggering ways." Nevertheless, Pelly did talk to Benwell enough to learn that he was in fact going out on much the same terms – as a potential investor and partner in Birchall's farm.[26] This was in sharp contradiction to what Birchall had told Pelly. (And it turned out that Birchall had told Benwell a parallel lie: that Pelly was a friend going out to Canada for his health.[27]) When Pelly confronted Birchall, he explained that he had in mind that Benwell would invest in a small, subsidiary farm Birchall owned, which would both satisfy Benwell and get rid of him.

While aboard the *Britannic*, Birchall spoke of his neighbours at the farm, mentioning an Englishman called Pickthall and "a French lady." He explained that they wouldn't see many horses at the farm, as most of his horses were being looked after in Toronto. Mrs. Birchall told Pelly that at one point when living in Canada, finding farm life dull, she and her husband had taken a home in Woodstock, a town they knew well.

The ship arrived in New York on 14 February, and the party spent the night at the Metropolitan Hotel. The city did not impress. It rained steadily all day, and as a result, the Statue of Liberty was all but hidden.

The hotel was second-rate, as was the farce, "Bluebird Junior," that they saw at Niblo's theatre that evening.[28]

The next evening the party left New York and went by train to Buffalo, where they stayed at the Stafford House, "a very poor hotel." Birchall said he thought they would soon move to Niagara Falls, Ont., and stay for a while because the weather was poor and the snow deep, making it difficult to access his farm. In any event, the caretakers needed time to vacate and the house would need cleaning before their arrival. Birchall spent the evening in the smoking room showing off his skill in altering his handwriting. He persuaded Benwell to work at copying his signature, while Birchall copied his. Soon Birchall had mastered Benwell's signature, and he proposed that Pelly join in the game. Pelly says he refused. He writes that this was when he first had an inkling that Birchall was not trustworthy.[29]

Birchall told Pelly that his plan was that on the following day he would take Benwell by train to see a property in Ontario and get him settled there as a farm pupil. The two departed at six in the morning, leaving Florence Birchall and Pelly behind in Buffalo. Birchall had said he would send them a telegram later that day telling them whether they should stay in Buffalo or go by train to Niagara Falls, Ont. Pelly found that throughout the day, Mrs. Birchall was in "an extraordinarily nervous state and quite unable to keep still." In the evening, the wire arrived instructing them to stay put in Buffalo. Soon afterwards, Birchall arrived at the hotel alone, his boots covered in mud. The two men had a few drinks in the hotel bar. Birchall said he had had a "worrying day" with Benwell, who didn't like what he had seen of the farm. Birchall had given him addresses of other farms he might look at, and expected that he would probably visit London, Ont., to see Mr. Hellmuth, who, with his wife, had travelled with them aboard the *Britannic*. Eventually Mrs. Birchall summoned her husband and Pelly too went to bed.[30]

The next day Pelly and the Birchalls, "who had become quite normal again," went to stay in Niagara Falls, Ont. After having difficulty finding any accommodation, they eventually took lodgings at a boarding house run by a Mr. and Mrs. John Baldwin, "typical lower class Americans, but extremely kind." Pelly recalls that they treated him well, like a son, and that the house "was clean and the food good." He was beginning to experience the different class relations in Canada. It was startling for him to find that the housemaid spent her evenings with the owners and guests in the drawing room. "Fortunately," he adds, "she was a clean wench and very quiet." Birchall played the piano, and there was singing, including of hymns. "Birchall knew hundreds by heart!" On Sunday, Pelly attended the local Anglican Church and was bemused by the "funny old parson [who] kept losing his place and using wrong words."[31]

Life at the boarding house was pleasant enough, but Pelly wondered when they would get down to business on the farm. "The Birchalls made themselves very agreeable to me and the time passed quickly," he writes. On frequent walks around town with Birchall, Pelly came to realize that, strangely, his companion was not very familiar with Niagara Falls, a town supposedly close to his farm. They got lost in the streets, and when questioned, Birchall couldn't identify who lived in various houses. Pelly noticed that now there was no mention of the English Club. Birchall did, however, introduce him to the Bampfields, who ran the Imperial Hotel, where the Birchalls had previously stayed. The introduction shocked Pelly a little. He writes: "Fancy being asked to be friends with a public house keeper!" Later, they accepted an invitation to a dance hosted by the Bampfields, "although they were hardly the sort of people one cared to know."

Pelly was becoming aware that many things Birchall said were not true. "My idea of his unsatisfactoriness," Pelly writes in his "Detailed Account," "had only been aroused by numerous small circumstances, each single one being too trivial to make a fuss about."[32]

At one point while in Niagara Falls, Birchall told Pelly he had had a wire from Benwell asking that his luggage be sent to the Fifth Avenue Hotel, New York. Pelly assumed Benwell was going home.

The Bombshell

In late February, Pelly became aware of the newspapers' fixation on the discovery of a body in a swamp near Princeton, Ont. Everyone was talking about it. "Then came a bombshell!" he writes. On Friday, 28 February, Birchall called Pelly into his room at the boarding-house and said: "What do you think I have seen in the papers about the man who was murdered up country? There has been a cigar box found near marked F. C. Benwell." Pelly replied, "You don't mean it?" He had not paid much attention to the newspapers but now closely read their reports of the murder.[33]

"At once all my suspicions of Burchell were certainties," writes Pelly, "and I realized that I was in a very difficult position indeed." He was convinced that Birchall had murdered Benwell, and he realized he was the only one who knew Birchall's movements since leaving England. If Birchall got rid of him, there would be little or no evidence against the man.[34]

At this point in the memoir, Pelly recounts the three occasions when he thought that Birchall was trying to murder him by pushing him into the Niagara River. He writes that when he told the police of those incidents later on, they surmised that he had been in great danger. The police also thought there had been a poisoning attempt on him. Pelly had mentioned to them that one time when he had begun to smoke a cigar, he noticed it tasted bad, so he stopped. He was soon ill. Had he smoked the whole of it, who knows what would have happened?[35]

Upon learning of the cigar-box with Benwell's name, the three decided that Birchall and his wife would go to Princeton and that Pelly would take the train to New York to look for Benwell there. The trip kept Pelly out of the way. Birchall promised that, when talking to the police, he would keep Pelly's name out of things. Pelly saw them board their train and later caught the train for New York.[36]

Pelly's sense of things when he got to New York is given immediacy by his inclusion in the memoir of a copy of a letter he wrote from there on 1 March to Arthur Durrant, his brother-in-law in England.[37] "I have struck one of the biggest difficulties I ever was in," begins the letter. Pelly goes on to explain that upon arrival at the Fifth Avenue Hotel he had found that no one there had heard of Benwell. Inquiries elsewhere in the city similarly came up empty. Pelly then relates his growing suspicion that Birchall had murdered Benwell. He notes that before leaving Niagara, Birchall had told him he had given Benwell his revolver. He believes that this may have been Birchall's way of preparing for news that the murder weapon was Birchall's pistol. At the boarding house, Pelly had confided in the Baldwins and found that they were equally concerned that Birchall was a murderer. Pelly said that if his suspicions were proven true, he would break with Birchall at once. He had already determined that Birchall was "one of the most shifting, lying brutes unhung." Almost all that Birchall told him in England had turned out to be only "partly true, although on the other hand nothing [was] quite false." Pelly feared that he had seen the last of the £170 he had paid Birchall, but was resolved to try to get the money back. The letter ends by revealing his ambivalence. "But for all this I'm very fairly happy and find the Burchells very pleasant people. Shan't I feel a fool if all this proves to be only imagination."

Early on Sunday, 2 March, Pelly returned to Niagara Falls by train and found a constable waiting for him. Pelly learned that the Birchalls had identified the murdered man as Benwell and was told that the Birchalls were suspects in the murder. Florence Birchall called Pelly up to their room, where her husband was still in bed. She asked whether the police were downstairs. Pelly replied evasively and quickly left the room. At Mr. Baldwin's suggestion, Pelly went with him to Magistrate Hill's home.

Hill told them that John Murray, the provincial detective, had got a warrant for Pelly's arrest because Birchall had told the detective that Pelly had "skipped off to the States." Magistrate Hill asked Pelly to tell him all the details of his time with the Birchalls, which he did. It turned out that Hill had Pelly's diary, seized from his room, and was following along as Pelly told his story. At the end, Hill said Pelly's oral account followed the diary exactly. Hill turned "extremely kind" and said to go back to the boarding house, where something would soon happen.[38]

Shortly after Pelly returned to the Baldwin house, police arrested Birchall there. He asked Pelly to wire Hellmuth to come immediately, which Pelly soon did. After Birchall said goodbye to his wife, police took him away.

Mrs. Birchall was very upset. For the first time she told Pelly that she and her husband had earlier been in Canada under the name of "Somerset," a name assumed for "business purposes." She asked him whether she thought her husband was mixed up in the murder. He replied disingenuously that he did not, but that he thought it "a great pity" that they had deceived him about the farm. She now admitted that, although they had once looked at a farm near the Falls, they had never owned one.

Pelly went to visit Birchall in his cell in the Niagara Falls lock-up, where he found him to be cheerful but unusually quiet. That same day, Det. Murray arrived in town and immediately insisted on having a fresh warrant for Pelly's arrest. Murray and two constables came to the boarding house with pistols and handcuffs. Pelly was outraged and of course told them that he had been cleared by the magistrate. Murray "was gruff and rude." However, one of the policemen took Pelly's side, and together they persuaded Murray to first question him. They all went to a hotel, where Murray grilled Pelly until 4:00 a.m. At that point, the detective said he was tired and wanted to go to bed. He placed Pelly in a locked room for the rest of the night. Pelly writes that he "was almost too tired to be angry." For the next two days, police guarded him closely everywhere he went. "It was a most uncomfortable position to be in," he observes.[39]

Pelly writes that he was unimpressed by Det. Murray, even after Murray was persuaded of his innocence and became "kind and polite." Pelly writes that he didn't like Murray or his methods, and thought that he showed no aptitude for his job. He was "a lower class American" and gave Pelly the impression of "being more like one of the criminal class than a detective." Pelly found him to be "very conceited" and thought that he "delighted at the notoriety the Birchall case brought him."[40]

Crown Witness

The day after his interrogation by Det. Murray, Pelly appeared as a witness at the police court. He was questioned from noon until 6:30 p.m. and then made to watch as police searched Birchall's room for hours. The next day, he was again in the witness box, this time for three hours. Pelly recalls that at this point he "was almost in tears with utter fatigue and nervousness." He had a sinking feeling that Birchall might get off because his evidence was increasingly mechanical and could not be corroborated.[41]

Then suddenly there was a dramatic development. One of the ushers of the court approached the magistrate, at which point Hill promptly dismissed Pelly from the witness box and a railway worker was sworn who recognized Birchall as one of the two men who had travelled to Eastwood on 17 February and as the man who had returned to Niagara alone. Pelly really appreciated this corroborating evidence. "I felt at once relieved of a great weight of responsibility," he writes. Yet more corroborating evidence then came from other witnesses, with the result that on 12 March, Birchall was committed for trial at the assizes in Woodstock.[42]

Mrs. Birchall, Pelly writes in a compressed version of events, was discharged a few days later. He observes that "a great deal of sentimental pity had been aroused for her." He doubts whether she would have gotten off in a court in England. Pelly balances that criticism with some positive remarks. When the inquiry was over, Mrs. Birchall thanked Pelly for his testimony, saying she realized he was bound to state the truth and that she had no complaint about what he said. Pelly writes: "I think this was nice of her."[43]

In the midst of the police-court hearing at Niagara Falls, Pelly and others had gone to Princeton for the coroner's inquiry. For Pelly, the most dramatic part of that experience came when he was required to identify the disinterred body of Benwell. Despite the cold, the temperature being fifteen degrees Fahrenheit below zero, some 500 people crowded the little cemetery. Pelly recalls how he dreaded viewing his first corpse, one he expected to be especially "nasty" given the extended time it had been in the ground. As it transpired, the cold weather had helped to preserve the body, and Benwell's face was easy to recognize. Pelly found it comical that the locals had chosen to dress the corpse in evening clothes – not something ever done in his own circles. Pelly recalls the kindness of the Woodstock chief of police who led him to the grave and did everything possible "to make the beastly job as easy as possible."[44]

During this period, Pelly received from his parents copies of letters sent to them about his predicament and Birchall's identity. A Mr. N.F. Robarts had written to Pelly's mother saying that Birchall had worked recently at Myall and Co. Ltd., a photography studio on Bond Street in London. He had been taken on with good references. His job had been to use his contacts in the theatre to persuade actors to visit the studio to have their photographs taken. He had been made to leave the firm at the end of December because of evidence that he had been lying. After that, Birchall had been at Morley's Hotel in London, where it appeared he had a business associate, an American "colonel."[45]

A Mr. Charles F. Emery wrote saying that he had worked with Birchall in a travelling theatre company in which Birchall served as manager. They had shared apartments together in various places. Birchall had swindled lodging keepers and theatre proprietors, and at one point he had threatened Emery with violence. Birchall parted the company leaving a trail of debt. Having read about Pelly's troubles in Canada, Emery had written Scotland Yard telling this story, and he had sent a photograph of Birchall to Toronto.[46]

There was also a note from Douglas Pelly's father saying that he had asked his friend Sir Robert Herbert, under-secretary of state for the colonies, to do what he could to help Douglas. Herbert telegraphed Lord Stanley, the Governor General of Canada, saying that Douglas Pelly was "a man of high character, thoroughly trustworthy, and deserving of every consideration." Douglas's father observed: "Is it not splendid."[47]

What with all the publicity the Birchall case had now gained, Pelly found that he himself had become something of a celebrity. When he travelled by train, a parade of passengers passed his seat, and at every station, a crowd gathered on the platform. He was pestered by the press and by people wanting to buy his photograph. (He had none to offer.) He was bombarded by letters with proposals of marriage. A servant girl, for instance, wrote from a farm: "I am always interested in romance in real life. I offer you my trusting little heart." At hotels he had many would-be visitors, including "the inevitable stream of prostitutes." He was offered a high salary by theatre managers who wanted him to stand for an hour or two at their shows. He visited a dime wax museum to view replicas of Birchall, Benwell, and himself. The curator told him it was a fine likeness of Pelly, without realizing he was standing next to the man![48]

Authorities believed Pelly was at risk because Birchall had many sympathizers who wanted to discredit Pelly and his evidence. To protect the Crown's star witness, a policeman followed Pelly everywhere he went for a month. Pelly says he thought the fears unwarranted.

On Sunday, 23 March, Florence Birchall's father, David Stevenson, and her married sister, Marion West-Jones, arrived from England. Pelly disliked the sister; he doesn't explain why. He talked with Stevenson, who had no idea about his daughter's actual behaviour. "My favourite daughter is quite incapable of the least deceit," he declared. Nor did he know that she was, in Pelly's view, "too fond of the bottle and was occasionally very drunk."[49]

Putting in Time

After a few weeks, life at the Falls settled into a routine. There was plenty to amuse him, including euchre parties and dances. A fellow boarder at the Baldwins' home worked on the railway, and he would call out a locomotive from the yards to take them for a ride on the cow-catcher at the front. Sometimes they helped with operating the train, which Pelly loved doing. A highlight of Falls life for him was teaching a troupe of sixteen "charming girls" stage dances for a charity entertainment they mounted.[50]

"This was all very nice," comments Pelly, "but I could not stand the prospect of months of this sort of life." (The trial was still five months away.) Moreover, the government compensation as he waited to be a Crown witness was just £10 a month, which made it difficult for him to live comfortably. Pelly needed to find work in Canada, both for the distraction and for the pay.

Fortunately, Pelly heard from T.C. Patterson, the well-known postmaster at Toronto and former politician, who took an interest in helping his fellow countrymen recently out from England. When they met, Patterson looked Pelly up and down and said, "Well you are a damn fool!" But then he offered his help. Eventually Patterson suggested that

Pelly might enjoy surveying in western Canada, a suggestion that thoroughly appealed to him. Patterson wrote his friend, Prime Minister Sir John A. Macdonald, and almost immediately, Pelly found himself on a train bound for Regina in the heart of the prairies. He had a letter of introduction to Hugh D. Lumsden, whom Pelly identifies as being the Canadian government's chief railway engineer, who was at the time overseeing the construction of the Regina, Long Lake, and Saskatchewan Railway.[51]

In Regina, Lumsden gave him a job at $1.50 a day "with grub," about the going rate for such work. His assignment began with laying out a chain from Regina the 140-mile length of the nearly completed line so as to mark the mile posts. In a letter home around this time, Pelly exclaims, "I am working jolly hard for my pay."[52] He was called upon to do all sorts of jobs, from scrubbing floors to drawing up plans of the surrounding lands. Pelly liked working for Lumsden, but he detested being supervised by another man on subsequent jobs he did in the North-West.[53]

Near the beginning of August, Pelly quit work to allow time for travel before his return to Woodstock and the trial. He headed farther west and greatly admired the mountain scenery of British Columbia and the Pacific Northwest. He then travelled across the United States, returning to Ontario in September.[54] Back in Toronto, he was interviewed more than once by Ontario's attorney general. (Unfortunately, the memoir does not record what was said.) As there was still time before the trial, Pelly visited Kingston and then followed the tourist itinerary by shooting the Lachine Rapids in the St. Lawrence before arriving in Montreal, a city he enjoyed. Back in Toronto, he had meetings with lawyers, who were busy preparing the case against Birchall. He also met Charles Benwell, Fred's brother, who had come to Canada to represent the family. He was very cool to Pelly, who got the impression that he resented that Pelly had survived while his brother was dead. In time for the trial, Pelly went to stay with T.C. Patterson at his house near Woodstock. He remained there until the trial was over, at which point he rushed back to England, eager to be home and put the ordeal behind him.[55]

Assessing the Memoir

Authorities and journalists regarded Pelly as a reliable witness when he was first questioned by Magistrate Hill and later when he testified at Birchall's preliminary hearing and trial. The account he provides in his memoir corroborates and expands a little on what he said as a Crown witness. Unlike his courtroom testimony, however, the memoir includes frank assessments of people. Naturally, Pelly's own background and personality affected his perceptions of people and events. His biases are clear. He more readily took to well-educated, white, British men like himself, and he was suspicious of and condescending towards Americans and people who in his mind ranked lower on the social scale. In Canada, he associated with people far outside his circle of well-born Britons, an experience that only reinforced his outlook as a gentleman. His rendering of the events he experienced in connection with the Birchalls nevertheless has a ring of authenticity, and in almost all respects it jives with statements made by other witnesses.

7

The Great Detective?

A familiar figure to readers of newspaper accounts of the Benwell–Birchall case was the Crown's detective, John Wilson Murray. His memoir about his career, immodestly titled *Memoirs of a Great Detective*, was first published in 1904.[1] One of its chapters deals with his investigation of the Benwell murder. Given the importance of Murray's role in the case, as well as the fact that some authors have treated it as a reliable rendition of the case, it bears scrutiny here.

The Man and His Memoir

John Wilson Murray was born in Scotland in about 1840 and came to North America with his family as a boy. Little is known about his early life. We do know that he served as a seaman in the US Navy during the American Civil War. He was a gunner aboard the *Michigan*, an armed steamer based at Erie, Pennsylvania.[2]

While in Erie, John Murray married and had two daughters who were recorded by the US census takers as being nine and five years old in 1870.[3] After being discharged from the Navy in 1866, Murray began working on the Erie police force and was soon made a detective. In Erie he became acquainted with the president of the Canada Southern Railway, who hired him to work as a private detective. Railway companies routinely employed detectives to combat labour trouble and to protect property. In his new position, Murray spent most of his time in Canada because the Canada Southern Railway linked Buffalo with Detroit through Canada. He was based in St. Thomas, Ont.[4]

The detecting abilities of Murray came to the attention of Ontario's attorney general, Oliver Mowat, who in 1874 hired him on contract to combat a counterfeiting operation in the province. He was successful. The attorney general's department then appointed him to the full-time but temporary position of "Government Detective Officer." Soon afterwards the position was made permanent. In 1877, he became one of several police officers given authority to act in any county and district of Ontario.

Murray's appointment as provincial detective came about because of the shortcomings of a system that had been relying on the work of local constables who were part the long-standing community-based administration of justice inherited from England. By the late nineteenth century in Ontario, the system's shortcomings were obvious. Especially in rural areas, local constables had at best limited experience in detecting crime, only meagre resources, and strictly local authority. Murray's appointment marked a shift towards a new emphasis on professional police. Attached to the attorney general's department, Murray remained Ontario's only provincial detective until 1884, when a second joined him. In 1887, the province hired one more, and these three men became the inspectorate (with Murray as chief) in the Criminal Investigation Branch when it was formed in 1897. That branch would become part of the Ontario Provincial Police Force when it was established in 1909.[5]

As government detective, Murray and his expertise were in demand from many local authorities outside the big cities. From the start, his instructions were to keep local authorities informed of his activities and to cooperate with them. Because many of his cases were sensational, he soon became a familiar figure to newspaper readers and something of a celebrity. He had the reputation for solving the biggest cases of his time. A search of the online *Globe* for the years 1870–1906 produces 255 hits for "Detective Murray." Headlines for the stories were glowing, as this sample shows: "Detective Murray Captures a Notorious Criminal"; "Detective Murray's Good Work"; "After a Long Chase across the Continent, Detective Murray Comes Up with Him"; and "Praise for Detective Murray."[6]

As far as the record reveals, his detective techniques were not notably innovative. He pontificated about the need for "conscientious work, the exercise of human intelligence, and efficient system of organization."

7.1. John Wilson Murray, the Ontario government detective assigned to investigate the swamp murder in February 1890.
Source: *Sentinel-Review*, 14 March 1890.

At the same time, however, he saw crime as a disease and declared that the ability to tell truth from lies was "largely a matter of instinct."[7]

A *Globe* obituary under the headline "A Fine Specimen of Manhood" describes Murray as being tall and sturdily built, and notes that he had exercised regularly to maintain his physique. His hair was fair, as was his bushy mustache, and his eyes were blue, almost grey. His eyelids drooped a little, which the writer thought gave him "a mild, almost benevolent appearance, which was apt to deceive." His eyes would twinkle with humour, but they were "keen, missing nothing that went on around him." The writer notes that Murray got on well with journalists, knowing exactly how much to reveal to them and when. Certainly, he could be remarkably forthcoming to journalists.[8]

Murray is best known today for his *Memoirs of a Great Detective*, which focuses on his most sensational cases, nineteen of them murders. The memoir was written with much help from Victor Speer, a journalist and ad agency worker, who is identified in some editions as compiler and editor. His voice takes over from Murray's at many points of the memoir. Speer based the memoir on newspaper accounts of the crimes and to a lesser extent on the detective's inaccurate recollections. The stories embellish the facts to enhance both the drama and Murray's role in solving the crimes. Murray's biographers acknowledge the exaggeration in each of the stories but maintain that "the main features of the story are usually correct."[9] As will be shown here, in Murray's chapter on the Birchall case there is much exaggeration and considerable distortion as well.

It appears that Murray wrote his memoir in part to combat the negative image of detectives among the public. From the time of their emergence in late eighteenth-century London, detectives had a mixed reception.[10] While valued for searching out criminals, recovering stolen property, and helping convict lawbreakers, their familiarity with the criminal underworld and their sometimes devious methods gained them opprobrium. An 1889 article in the *Globe* praising the work of the detectives employed by the Toronto Police Force observed: "They mix with the criminal classes and often become aware of plots before they can be executed."[11] The puff piece did not point out the risks to their reputation of such mixing, but when describing the individual detectives, the writer felt compelled to emphasize that the men were "upright" and had "unquestioned integrity." In late nineteenth-century Canada, the reputation of detectives took a battering because the enforcement of controversial liquor laws invited detectives to use deception, particularly undercover work, which undermined public trust.[12]

Phillips Thompson, the well-known left-wing Canadian journalist of the late nineteenth century, offered a critique of the collusion between detectives and newspapers that resulted in the courts becoming instruments of injustice. Newspaper reporters, he wrote, "anxious for items, often play into the hands of the detective, conceal their blunders, exalt their achievements, endorse their theories, and, in fact, bind themselves in every way to impressing the detectives' views upon the public."[13]

The growing popularity in the late nineteenth century of detective fiction only complicated the reputation of detectives. Fictional detectives were often stereotyped as unintelligent and morally lax, with a tendency to spy on innocent people or bend the laws. Even the brilliant Sherlock Holmes, who first appeared in print in 1887, showed a willingness to break the law when he found that it did not align with justice. Yet many fictional detectives were heroic. The detective work done by the Mounties in Canada's North-West only added to their portrayal as unassailable figures of rectitude.[14]

Murray's memoir both burnished his own reputation and countered negative images of the detective. In writing it, Murray joined a growing number of detectives whose stories of battling crime were eagerly sought by publishers wanting to take advantage of the popularity of crime stories. In England, a new genre was born in the 1890s when the growing number of retired detectives of the Metropolitan Police Force found publishers for their autobiographies. These writings focused on the careers of the detectives and, unlike other biographical genres, made little or no mention of family circumstances or issues other than crime. A study of English detectives' memoirs observes: "Undeniably the texts can be viewed as success stories of individuals and as accounts of personal triumphs," but also as defences of the Met. Certainly, Murray's memoir fits the genre perfectly with its self-celebration, but he has strikingly little to say about his place among other police.[15]

The memoir expresses an ideal of vigorous masculinity. Murray presents himself as a man of action, keen to take charge and discover the truth. Shrewd, but by no means intellectual, he has the determination and talent to get to the bottom of things.

"Occupation Murderer"

Murray's chapter on the Benwell murder is titled "Reginald Birchall: Occupation Murderer." It begins by painting an eerie picture of the Blenheim Swamp, where "thick grow the briars" and the "spirit of solitude broods." At its centre lies bottomless Pine Pond, a site that had given up "the bones of dead men." Murray reports that it was the Elvidge brothers who discovered the body. Out chopping wood, "one of them stepped on the body, slipped and almost fell upon it." (In fact, the Elvidges stayed clear of the corpse.) Once the body was removed from the swamp, a telegram was sent to the attorney general in Toronto requesting Murray's presence. He says he responded immediately.[16] In fact, the telegram that prompted his dispatch to Princeton was not sent for another week, when Const. W.J. Watson of Princeton requested a provincial detective on 1 March after Birchall identified the body.[17] In the meantime, it was Const. Watson who investigated the crime as best he could, given his lack of training and experience in detective work.

Murray in his memoir puts himself at the centre of the action from the start. He is the one who has the clever idea of having the body photographed and copies of the image sent to newspapers far and wide. "I hoped," he explains, "that some one somewhere in the world, seeing the face of the unknown dead, would recognize it and thus solve the mystery of his identity." Certainly, the body was photographed a day after its discovery and photos sent to newspapers, but this was accomplished a week before Murray arrived in Princeton.[18] Murray did arrange to have photographs taken of the body, which were the second set sent to newspapers.

Murray enhances his image as a detective by providing details of his meticulous and revealing crime scene investigation. At first, he had wondered whether the man had been killed elsewhere and the body brought to the woods and deposited on the pile of saplings at the swamp. However, he says that his investigation proved otherwise. "I crawled on hands and knees," he writes, "over the surrounding ground, and I found a crimson trail." It ended in a blotch of blood nor far away and went no farther. "Here the murder had been done, here the shot had been fired, here the victim had fallen." In fact, what little blood was discovered at the crime scene had been found by the Elvidges and Const. Watson well before Murray's arrival. Whether the man had been killed and fallen where discovered, or been shot nearby and moved to the pile of saplings, remained a point of contention throughout the trial.[19]

In the memoir, Murray says he undertook close examination of the crime scene on three occasions. Only on the third visit did he discover, half-hidden in the ground, as if stepped on, "a cigar-holder with an amber mouthpiece marked 'F.W.B.' It was the first clue." [20] In fact, the cigar-holder had been discovered before Murray's arrival. And it was not such a revealing clue because it had no initials on it. As we have seen, it was the discovery by one of the Elvidge brothers of the cigar-box marked "F. C. Benwell" that was the big clue and crucial to the body's identification. It brought the Birchalls to Princeton to identify the exhumed body, which in turn brought them under scrutiny. Oddly, the memoir makes no mention at all of the cigar-box and so significantly distorts how the investigation proceeded.

In Murray's rendering of the story, his decision to photograph the body provided the breakthrough as to the man's identity. He explains that on the sixth day following the body's discovery, a man and woman arrived at Princeton prompted by the photograph he had supposedly sent to newspapers, and they offered to make an identification of the deceased. "They said," writes Murray, "they had crossed from England recently, and on the same ship was a young man who resembled strongly the picture of the dead man." On Saturday, 1 March, the body was exhumed, and both of the visitors said the body was that of their fellow traveller. In fact, as other sources show, the Birchalls had come to Princeton to offer an identification for quite another reason: the name written on the cigar-box, which had been prominently and widely reported in the press. And it was only Rex Birchall who performed the identification.[21]

When the couple saw the body, they said, according to the memoir, "His name, we think was Benwell. He was merely a casual acquaintance aboard ship, and we knew nothing of him." As Murray admits, he was not actually there when the identification was taking place. Rather, he was questioning neighbours in the vicinity of the crime and missed the dramatic moment entirely.[22]

Murray did meet the Birchalls later that day (1 March), when he interviewed them in Paris, Ont., in an upstairs parlour of the hotel where they were staying. He describes Birchall in terms that could be read as homoerotic:

> The gentleman was dressed in perfect taste. He was handsome and easy in manner, with a certain grace of bearing that was quite attractive. He came toward me, and I saw he was about five feet nine inches tall, supple, clean cut, well built. His hair was dark and fashionably worn; his forehead was broad and low. He wore a light moustache. Two dark-brown eyes flashed at me a greeting. Clearly he was a man of the world, a gentleman, accustomed to the good things in life, a likeable chap, who had lived well and seen much and enjoyed it in his less than thirty years on earth.

Murray has much less to say about the wife: "The lady stood by the window looking out. She was a slender, pleasant-faced blonde, a bit weary about the eyes, evidently a woman of refinement."[23]

The memoir next proceeds to detail the back-and-forth of the interview with the man who introduced himself as Reginald Birchall of London, England. His wife remained in the room. Birchall said he was unsure of the dead man's name – Bentwell, Benswell, Benwell. (This hesitation over the name seems unlikely given that it was the Benwell name on the cigar-box that had actually brought the Birchalls to Princeton.) Birchall mentioned to Murray that the young man had left a lot of luggage at Niagara Falls. Murray expressed interest in having Birchall show it to him, which the Englishman agreed to do. Murray asked Birchall how the deceased had been dressed when last seen in Niagara Falls, and Birchall, with "his delicate hand," pointed to navy-blue cloth and said he had been wearing navy – whereas the body had on brown tweed.

According to the memoir, during the conversation Florence Birchall appeared nervous and paced up and down. However, she was visibly relieved when Murray said that the young man might have got into trouble by going to London, Ont. "They would kill a man for a five dollar note there," he had said. Birchall expressed his pity for the young man. They chatted "quite cordially."[24]

According to the memoir, when asked whether he had heard from Benwell since they had been together at Niagara Falls, Birchall replied that he had had just a line, asking him to take care of the luggage. Murray asked to see the note. Birchall searched his pockets but failed to produce it. He asked his wife about it, and she said she had seen the note but didn't know where it was now. Birchall said the note was signed "Fred." (If Benwell scarcely knew Birchall, this was a peculiar way for a gentleman to sign.)[25]

At the end of the interview, Birchall congenially proposed that Murray be their guest on Sunday at Niagara Falls. The detective replied that he would not be available then, but would like to meet Birchall there first thing Monday morning so they could go to see about Benwell's luggage. The men shook hands, and Florence Birchall bowed cordially.

As Murray tells the story, he learned nothing in the course of the interview about Douglas Pelly, the man whose story would blow the case wide open.

Murray writes that by the end of the interview with the Birchalls, he was sure that "the man was lying." He immediately telegraphed police at Niagara, telling them to shadow Birchall but not to arrest him unless he tried to cross into the States. There is no evidence to corroborate that such a message was sent.[26]

It is doubtful that the detective was really suspicious of the Birchalls at this point. Right after the interview, Murray took a train to London. In the memoir he says he was following up on the lead that Benwell might have gone there. Murray had been definite the day before he talked to the Birchalls that his suspicions were focused on the two men seen on a spree in the vicinity of the crime. In a long statement to the press, Murray said, "Suspicion points to two men who were seen driving round the district in a buggy on the night the corpse is supposed to have been left in the wood." He had questioned them, and because their account was unsatisfactory, he was going to London to pursue a clue about these men.[27]

In Niagara Falls

We know that while Murray was in London, Ont., Chief Tom Young and Magistrate Andrew Hill of Niagara Falls interviewed Pelly, who provided so many details about the Birchalls that the police arrested them. If Murray had instructed Young to wait to arrest him unless he was leaving for the States, then Young ignored Murray's directive. The "great detective" arrived at the Falls that evening, having missed these dramatic developments. None of this deters Murray from representing his detective work as the sole reason police succeeded in nabbing the chief suspect.

In the memoir, Murray says he "found" that the Birchalls were staying in Niagara Falls at the Baldwins'. (In fact, police at the Falls had traced where the Birchalls were staying well before Murray's appearance there.) He "found" that they were staying with a young man named Douglas Raymond Pelly. "He was a handsome young fellow," comments Murray, "about five feet nine inches tall, slight build, small light moustache, and a decided English accent." Pelly told him he was a cousin of beautiful Lady Pelly, who had been in the retinue of Lord Lansdowne when he was Governor General of Canada – a fact Murray uses to place Pelly high on the social hierarchy.[28]

Murray writes that upon his arrival in Niagara Falls on the evening of Sunday, 2 March, he sat down with Pelly and they talked for several hours. This is indeed the case, although Pelly describes it as an aggressive interrogation.[29] What Murray omits to say is that Pelly had been questioned earlier by police and Magistrate Hill. The information he presented to them led directly to the arrest of Birchall. What Pelly revealed to Murray was in fact already known to authorities and had been acted upon by them.

In the memoir, Pelly's story is told over the course of several pages, all in quotation marks to indicate that it came from the young Englishman.[30] And indeed, the story follows closely what Pelly said at the police court during Reginald Birchall's preliminary hearing.

At the end of the lengthy quotation, Murray writes that "Pelly was telling the truth from first to last." As proof, he reproduces letters he found that were sent between Birchall and Benwell as they made their financial and travel arrangements.[31]

In the memoir Murray says he attempted to verify Pelly's story about the stranger who interrupted Birchall's attempt to push him into the

Niagara River. He reports that his advertisements across North America for the stranger bore no result.[32]

Murray says that his requests of Scotland Yard to verify the identities of the Birchalls, Benwell, and Pelly produced detailed reports from them. This is very unlikely. A reporter in England interested in the Birchall case had interviewed the head of Scotland Yard's Criminal Investigation Division, who had declared that a killing in Canada was strictly Canadian business and no concern of the Yard's. He added that the story that he was sending out a man to Canada in connection with the case was untrue.[33]

At this point in the memoir, Murray provides details of the life of Birchall, an account probably lifted from the newspapers. He writes that he investigated the Birchalls' stay the previous year in Woodstock, and relates stories similar to the ones told in the press about the extravagance of "the Somersets."

Working Up the Case

"I took up the trail of Birchall and Benwell," writes Murray. He puts himself at the centre of all the news about the witnesses who placed the two Englishmen aboard the train for Eastwood, their arrival there, and Birchall's return alone to that railway station and onward to Niagara Falls. Many of his revelations begin, "I found." (Actually, several of the witnesses had come forward as soon as the news of the murder broke, and others had been tracked down by journalists.) "Thus I traced them," he writes, "step by step, to the swamp and to the very hour of the murder."[34]

In the memoir, Murray does not discuss his interactions with the witnesses, a subject of considerable controversy during the trial. The defence counsel accused him of having coached them so as to convict Birchall and to have arranged the identifications of Birchall in ways that assisted the Crown.[35]

To make its case, the Crown needed official verification of the movements of the Birchall party, and Murray writes that it fell to him to conduct those investigations. For instance, he went to the Metropolitan Hotel in New York to confirm the visitors' stay there, as well as to the Stafford House in Buffalo where they had stayed. Although necessary police work, his visits brought no revelations. Journalists had long before verified the party's movements.[36]

Murray explains that he "studied all the data ... on hand, and worked out the theory on which I was certain we could convict the clever murderer." In Murray's assessment, Birchall had chosen to become a "professional murderer." He did not kill in a moment of rage. The lives of Benwell and Pelly "represented so much ready money." He went about taking their money and Benwell's life in "a practical, quiet, methodical way." He planned to conceal the bodies of both victims so that neither would be found. Fate was against him, however. Because the way to bottomless Pine Pond was blocked, Benwell's body was left where it was soon found. Because strangers appeared on occasions when Birchall planned to dispose of Pelly in the Niagara River, he was not killed. In Murray's view, it had been a mistake for Birchall to have taken on two targets at once. The first he had disposed of, but the second had lived to incriminate him.[37]

In the memoir, Murray insists that he never believed the theory of some people who thought that Birchall was part of a conspiracy, whereby a group of villains was luring rich young Englishmen to Canada to fleece and kill them. He was always certain that Birchall acted alone. This is contradicted by statements he made to the press at the time. On 22 March, Murray told journalists, "I have very little doubt Birchall is one of a gang of conspirators who were in league to first rob and then murder their victims." He had described evidence he had about two men who had come to North America to be farm pupils and disappeared.[38] An advantage of the conspiracy story for Murray in March was that it supported his contention that the shooting had been premeditated so that the crime was murder. In the retrospective memoir, Murray preferred to stick to the Crown's theory of the crime that had led to Birchall's conviction: Birchall had acted alone.

Assessing Murray's Role

The Birchall case put Murray in the spotlight, which he relished. Reporters detailed his movements, and when he spoke to the press his words were recorded for all to read. Lengthy renditions of his observations were reported in the *Globe* on 1, 11, and 22 March.

The detective liked to tantalize reporters with statements such as that authorities "were on the eve of disclosing one of the most diabolical plots of wholesale fraud and robbery that had ever been placed on the criminal records."[39]

Murray's willingness in the midst of working up the case to share thoughts with the press became controversial, a development the memoir does not record. On 19 March, a front-page article in the *News* titled "Murray Speaks" quoted the detective as saying to the paper's reporter, "In all my experience in criminal business, and it has been a lengthy and varied one, I have never handled such an extraordinary case as the Benwell murder. At present the evidence points but in one direction, against the prisoner Birchall." He then laid out that evidence in some detail. In the Ontario legislature, a few days later, Opposition member William Meredith declared:

> It was unprecedented in the history of criminal justice in this Province and greatly to be deprecated. A gentleman occupying such a responsible position as Mr. Murray should not make the statement he has reported to have made, both in Ontario and on the other side, in regard to this case. It was manifestly unfair that a man not yet proven guilty should be spoken of by an officer of the Crown in the way Detective Murray was reported to have spoken.

In reply, Oliver Mowat, the premier and attorney general, both covered for Murray and admonished him:

> Detective Murray was a man of large experience, and had always shown himself efficient in the discharge of his duties. There might be some doubt as to the authenticity of the statements attributed to the detective, but he would have the facts inquired into. He certainly was of the opinion that a detective should not give publicity to prejudicial statements while a case was still under investigation.[40]

Murray must have been warned by his superiors in the office of the attorney general, for he gave no further lengthy statements about the case to the press.

Journalists continued to speak highly of Murray's handling of the case. As Birchall's trial approached, the *Globe* commented: "The working up of the details of the case is intrusted to Provincial Detective John Murray, a man of first-class ability and long experience. Mr. Murray has had valuable assistance from Chief Young of the Provincial police at Niagara Falls." And upon the trial's conclusion, the same newspaper observed that the Crown's case had been "worked up with consummate ability by Chief Detective Murray."[41]

By contrast, Birchall and his counsel were highly critical of Det. Murray, accusing him of dodgy, underhanded methods in handling Crown witnesses and persuading defence witnesses to reconsider their statements. It is revealing that in the long list of Crown witnesses appearing at the trial, Murray, with all his knowledge of the case, was not included. Perhaps the Crown feared the evidence he might have been forced to give when cross-examined under oath. Alternatively, the Crown attorney might have worried that the dodgy reputation of detectives would enable the defence to undermine whatever Murray said.[42]

In the memoir there appears a letter "Somerset" sent from England, soon after his return there in the spring of 1889, to William McDonald, the fellow he had met through the farm-pupil business in Woodstock. Presumably it had been among other correspondence in Birchall's possession seized by police in Niagara Falls. The letter apologizes for his sudden departure from Woodstock and debts he left unpaid. Birchall makes clear that he is engaged in the farm-pupil business when he says he will send McDonald several men in August. The letter might have been useful if Murray and the Crown had chosen to pursue the argument that Birchall was part of a conspiracy, entangled as he was with McDonald and the immigration scam. But Murray and/or the Crown attorney had not taken that route. The letter only became public years afterwards when Murray included it in his memoir. The existence of the letter in Murray's hands makes one wonder how many other documents he had that never saw the light of day.

Assessing the Memoir and Its Impact

The *Globe* reviewed the memoir in 1904, when it was first published. The unnamed reviewer admires the book and features the Birchall chapter. "One of the most striking things in the book," writes the reviewer, "is Mr. Murray's description of how he first met the murderer Birchall and his wife." There follows a long quotation about this topic from the memoir.[43]

Murray's account of the case, however, gets a negative review from Douglas Pelly, who witnessed Murray's activities first-hand. The detective "wrote a book about his work in the detection of notorious crime," says Pelly. "To judge from his description in this book of the Birchall case, his accounts of these crimes were greatly inaccurate. He was very conceited and appeared delighted at the notoriety the Birchall case brought him."[44] Pelly got it right.

Over the years, authors have relied on Murray's account of the case when writing about the Benwell–Birchall story, so his distortions have continued to shape readers' understandings of the case. Stewart Wallace's account of the case first published in *Maclean's* relies on the memoir. Not long ago, even a scientific journal, *American Journal of Forensic Medicine and Pathology*, published an assessment of the case that relies heavily on Murray's memoir as a source.[45] The availability of Murray's book online is likely to result in the publication of yet more poorly informed stories.[46]

An accurate and truthful account of the case from the perspective of the government detective would have enhanced understanding of the legal proceedings. It is a pity Murray's memoir is full of inaccuracies. Unfortunately, readers cannot rely on it, nor can they learn about how Murray interacted with other police and the rest of the Crown's legal team.

Comparing the memoir against the evidence from other sources brings into focus Murray's relationship with the press. Newspapers make it evident that contrary to what is said in the memoir, for a while Murray firmly believed that a conspiracy was responsible for the scam and possibly for Benwell's murder, too. It would be interesting to know how he came to drop that theory of the crime. For a few weeks in March 1890, Murray showed a readiness to talk to the press, no doubt because it put him in the limelight where he loved to be. Journalists eagerly interviewed him, expecting good copy would follow. However, Murray's readiness to point a finger at Birchall and call him a murderer well before the man had been put on trial overstepped the rules of fair and proper behaviour for public officials.

8

The Trial Begins

Nearly six months after Birchall's arrest, his trial began in Woodstock on Monday, 22 September 1890. In mid-September, with the fall assizes about to open in Woodstock, journalists from a great many newspapers arrived in town to provide original reports of Birchall's trial for their readers. Most of the newsmen stayed at the O'Neill House (later the Oxford Hotel), which faced the town square just across the street from the courthouse. During off-hours, their presence spilled from the barroom on the hotel's ground floor and into the town square.

On the eve of the trial, Woodstock was alive with excitement. It was reported that every scrap of gossip having anything to do with the Benwell murder was "canvassed and made the most of." In the eyes of the reporter from the *Empire*, there was far too much speculation about Florence Birchall and her sister, who were staying at the Commercial Hotel. People were circulating "all manner of pathetically unkind stories."[1] The *Empire* did not speculate as to why locals told mean stories about the ladies, but later comments indicate that the visitors behaved snobbishly and refused to mingle with even the women of the local elite.[2] Class trumped gender.

Preparations

Birchall's trial took place in the Woodstock Town Hall because the town's first courthouse, built in 1839 to serve the District of Brock, had been condemned as unsafe in 1882 and a new courthouse had not yet been

8.1. Old Town Hall, Woodstock, Ont., where Birchall's trial took place.
Source: Author's photograph, 2020.

completed by 1890.[3] The town hall had been constructed in the town square soon after Woodstock's 1851 incorporation. The two-storey brick building, which still stands proudly in the square, is a simple rectangular structure topped with a cupola. Architectural details are Italianate: strong vertical lines, arched windows and doors, and ornate stone trim. Originally the ground floor was leased to market vendors and the large, second-floor room, the "Grand Hall" where the council met, was frequently rented out for dances, concerts, plays, and meetings. About two decades after its opening, the market moved out, making room on the ground floor for a new council chamber and offices for the mayor and clerk. The Grand Hall remained the town's largest indoor space for public events. This was how the building was configured at the time of Birchall's trial. Today the Old Town Hall is a national historic site that preserves the late nineteenth-century layout and houses the Woodstock Museum.[4]

Shortly before the trial began, Woodstock's *Sentinel-Review* expressed its disgust that politicians had not responded sooner to the newspaper's goading to build a proper, up-to-date courthouse. Instead, while the whole world watched Woodstock, the trial would be taking place in "the old town hall, which bears the scars of many winters and more variety troupes, and which is far from a credit to the town."[5]

For the trial, the local building committee had done its best to spruce up the town hall with a coat of paint and other minor improvements. Upstairs, in the Grand Hall, the venue for the trial, workers shifted scenery to the wings of the stage. At centre stage they placed the judge's bench, which consisted of the mayor's chair, moved up from the council chamber below, and a simple four-legged table. The drop curtain hung rather threateningly above the judge's head. On a newly built dais just in front of the stage stood chairs for the sheriff, clerk, and crier. On the floor of the room to one side were chairs for the jurors, with the witness box standing between the jurors and the judge. Nearby was a table and chairs for reporters, with additional seating for them on the stage to the side of the judge. Behind the curtains on the sides of the stage, the dressing rooms were made to serve as retiring rooms for the judge and barristers. The prisoner's dock, a pine box recycled here from the town's former courthouse, stood between the lawyers' tables and those of the reporters. Altogether these arrangements took up about half the floor space, the remainder being occupied by rows of chairs divided by aisles newly carpeted. The ground floor and gallery had a seating capacity of 400, including officers of the court, reporters, and others. Jurors would use the downstairs council chamber as a retiring room.[6]

For the first time ever, a Woodstock courtroom was fitted out with telegraphic equipment. The Great North Western Telegraph Company obtained approval to install two instruments in the courtroom so that everything said could be directly transmitted to Toronto and New York. "A few minutes after words are said in [the] court room, they may be read on the streets of New York," boasted the *Sentinel-Review*, adding: "This is the fast age."[7]

It was extraordinary too that telephone lines were used to transmit minute-to-minute developments in the trial. For the benefit of a few privileged people, a telephone receiver had been suspended above the judge's chair with lines running off to listeners who paid to hear the proceedings. An enterprising hotelier had arranged for telephone lines to run to his establishment and rented telephones on an hourly basis to eager followers of the trial.[8]

All the preparations notwithstanding, however, the Grand Hall still looked like the theatre it usually was. Journalists couldn't resist referencing that fact. "Never in the history of the opera house," declared the *World*, "has a play been placed on the boards at all approaching the subtlety of plot, dramatic situations or nicety of detail [than] the drama in real life which will be enacted in the trial of Rex Birchall."[9]

The Legal Talent

The press treated the judge and lawyers in the trial respectfully. They were men who had risen to positions of responsibility, earned recognition in the profession, and showed talent in analysing what had happened. The lawyers were praised for their manly assertiveness in the courtroom and compelling oratorical styles.

Ontario's assize courts met generally twice a year, in spring and fall, in many centres throughout Ontario.[10] A roster of a dozen or so judges resident in Toronto travelled to county towns and other places to preside over trials of serious offences. Woodstock was on the "Oxford Circuit," which also included Guelph, Cayuga, Simcoe, and Hamilton. In the fall of 1890, the presiding judge in Woodstock was Justice Hugh MacMahon.

Called to the bar in 1864, MacMahon had practised in Brantford and then in London, where he built up a large and lucrative practice. He was made QC (Ontario) in 1876 and QC federally nine years later. The financial success of his law practice enabled him to become a respected collector and connoisseur of fine art. In 1880, MacMahon had gained public attention as a result of his role as defence counsel in the infamous Donnelly murder trial. In 1887, Sir John A. Macdonald selected him for appointment as Puisne Judge of the Common Pleas Division of Ontario's High Court of Justice. Just before Birchall's trial began, the *Globe* referred to MacMahon as being "one of the newer appointments to the bench, but a sound lawyer and a clear-headed, able man."[11]

In September, the lead attorneys on both sides arrived in Woodstock after spending their summers in England. The lead Crown attorney had been at work on the case before his trip overseas; his defence counterpart arrived back with little time to prepare.[12] Both men were part of the small, tight-knit Toronto establishment and had frequently shared a courtroom.

Britton Bath Osler, the lead attorney for the Crown, was not Oxford's usual Crown attorney, but a first-rate lawyer often used by the federal government as a troubleshooter. Osler had been called to the bar in 1862 and first practised in Dundas. Appointed Crown attorney for Wentworth

8.2. Justice Hugh MacMahon (top), George Tate Blackstock (left), Britton Bath Osler (right).
Source: *Sentinel-Review*, 22 and 24 September 1890.

County in 1874, he gained a reputation for his single-minded dedication to prosecutions. "Formidable in appearance," writes his biographer, "he frequently persuaded juries by leaning over their box ... and addressing them in a firm, logical manner." He was made QC (Ontario) in 1876 and QC federally four years later. In 1882, he ran in Windsor as a Liberal in the Canadian general election but was defeated. That same year, after leaving his Crown position, he joined D'Alton McCarthy's Toronto law firm, which became known as McCarthy, Osler, Hoskin, and Creelman. Frequently Osler represented railways, making good use of his exceptional expertise in engineering matters and earning substantial fees. National exposure came in 1885 when the government of Sir John A. Macdonald appointed him to lead the prosecution in Regina in the treason trial of Louis Riel, the Métis leader. According to his biographer, he gained notoriety in the 1890s for his prosecution of murder trials, beginning with the Birchall trial.[13]

Placing Osler "in a class by himself in Canada," Edwin Guillet, a historian writing in the early 1940s, when many people could remember

Osler, describes his courtroom style: "The way his small, black eyes pierced through a witness was fascinating to behold but unpleasant to experience. Sometimes he spoke in short, terse, crisp, incisive sentences; again he would lean in the jury box and talk in quiet – even confidential – manner; but on occasion, when he was deeply stirred, he would thunder forth in resounding and cogent phrases that seemed to rock the very courtroom."[14]

At Birchall's trial, Osler was assisted by Oxford County's Crown attorney, Francis Ramsay Ball, QC. From an old Loyalist family and a son of the manse, he had been called to the bar in 1850 and had practised in Woodstock. He had been Oxford County's Crown attorney since 1863.[15] In the Benwell–Birchall case, Ball's main role was to prepare the Crown's case during the six months between Birchall's arrest and the start of his trial. Preparation was assisted by Det. John Murray and Niagara Falls police chief Tom Young.

Birchall recalled that he was besieged by lawyers wanting to represent him because the case would bring them attention. For his defence, Birchall wanted a prominent lawyer from Toronto, and he chose George Tate Blackstock, who took the case both for his fee and for the publicity he expected from the case.[16] Coming from a well-connected family and another son of the manse, he had been called to the bar in 1879 and practised in Toronto, along with his brother, the pre-eminent lawyer Thomas Gibbs Blackstock. George Tate Blackstock specialized in handling civil cases, including ones for the powerful Canadian Pacific Railway.[17] He was appointed a federal QC in 1889. He ran as a Conservative candidate several times, unsuccessfully. Branching out as a criminal lawyer, he became renowned for his powerful courtroom presence. Guillet vividly describes Blackstock: "He was an orator and actor, and the court was full of pageantry whenever he appeared on a case. His long, silky-black hair helped create a sensational appearance, and his emotional style made him unforgettably impressive. He never stood still as he examined witnesses or addressed the jury, but swaggered up and down with pomp and ceremony, as if acting a part upon the stage."[18]

Blackstock was assisted by Isidore F. Hellmuth, the attorney whom the Birchall party had met on the Atlantic crossing aboard the *Britannic* and who had aided the Birchalls after their arrest. Called to the bar in 1877, Hellmuth was practising law in 1890 in London, Ont., where he had an excellent reputation for handling civil cases.[19] Also assisting the defence was the Woodstock law firm of Finkle, McKay, and McMullen, who prepared the case on the ground. Finkle had become a judge, and according to the *Sentinel-Review*, it was Samuel G. McKay, a young and energetic lawyer, who did most of the work on the Birchall case.[20] The defence attorneys were assisted by "Charley" Bluett, a private detective from Toronto who gathered evidence and checked out leads.[21] He stood out in a crowd because he was a big man and sported a flamboyant, broad-brimmed cowboy hat.

The Office of the Attorney General took the unusual step of placing a representative at the trial as a resource for the Crown attorneys. As a political matter, the government needed to ensure that the much-watched trial would be perceived to be utterly fair. John Robinson Cartwright, the deputy attorney general, sat in the Woodstock courtroom throughout the trial and occasionally asked a question of a witness. A member of the well-connected Cartwright family of Kingston, he had had a privileged English education at Rugby and Oxford.[22]

The Assizes Open

The fall assizes in Woodstock opened on Thursday, 18 September, a few days before the Birchall trial itself began. The first matter of business was the work of the grand jury, an institution no longer in place in Canada, but in the nineteenth century, its twelve to twenty-four jurors vetted the cases the Crown wished to pursue at the assizes. It determined whether there was sufficient evidence for the cases to be tried. Earlier in the century, it had had important investigative powers, too, but those had faded with time. It still reported on the condition of jails, asylums, and other public institutions, although increasingly government inspectors provided oversight.[23] In the late nineteenth century, the future of the grand jury was hotly disputed as a result of a concerted attack on it led by Ontario judge James Robert Gowan.[24]

Before hearing the Crown's evidence, Justice MacMahon used the platform provided by the convening of the grand jury to express his views on certain matters. He spoke at length in defence of the grand jury system. He also warned the jurors that secrecy must be upheld. He spoke about the various cases, highlighting the Benwell murder case because of the seriousness of the charge. He instructed the jury that while they had no doubt read a great deal about the case in the newspapers, they were to pay attention only to the evidence set before them in court. For the jurors' benefit, MacMahon defined murder as "an unlawful homicide with malice aforethought." He explained that in the Benwell case there could be no dispute whether it was a matter of murder and not manslaughter because Benwell had been killed by two shots fired into the back of his head. The question was who had fired the shots.[25]

The newspapers had nothing to say about the results of the grand jury's deliberations in the Benwell case. It was a foregone conclusion that, because the Crown had plenty of evidence against Birchall, the grand jury would return a "true bill," and he would stand trial.

The charge of accessory to murder against Florence Birchall came before the same grand jury. On 20 March, she had been released on bail of $1,000. As expected, the grand jury found "no bill" against her. She was now officially a free woman.[26]

The First Day

On Sunday, 21 September, the day before the trial began, Blackstock went out to see the swamp where the murder happened. Later he was joined in Woodstock by his wife, who had come from Toronto accompanied by Dugald MacMurchy, a young lawyer from Blackstock's office. Det. Murray and Chief Tom Young also went out to the swamp that day, where they encountered about 2,000 other visitors curious to see the scene of the crime. A thriving trade was being done in furniture and walking sticks made from timber cut in the swamp.[27]

Arriving in town in time for the start of the trial was the murdered man's younger brother, Charles Benwell of Cheltenham, England. Their father, Col. Benwell, had intended to cross the Atlantic for the trial, but he had a health setback in August, so the family delegated Charles to represent them. Journalists were frustrated by Charles's refusal to reveal the nature of the testimony he would give. On his way to Woodstock, he had remained tight-lipped when journalists accosted him in both New York and Toronto.[28]

Admission to the courtroom was managed by a ticket system, but it didn't prevent many people without tickets from clamouring for a seat. Altogether there were thirty journalists present in the courtroom. On the stage near the judge, as if to balance the all-male scene, were seated several "ladies," the women of the local elite and Blackstock's wife. To the regret of the audience, Florence Birchall and her sister Marion were not present.[29]

A last-minute preparation was the sprinkling of ample sawdust on the roads around the town square to deaden traffic noise. And to counteract the courtroom's poor acoustics, a thick layer of sawdust was spread on its floor for the benefit of the official court reporter, Mr. Nelson R. Butcher, who needed to catch every word.[30] Butcher, a Woodstock resident, had considerable experience in shorthand court reporting in western Ontario and was the reporter for the County of Oxford.[31]

At 10:50 on the morning of 22 September, a hack drove up smartly to the town hall, having traversed the three blocks from the jail. It carried Deputy Sheriff John Perry, Chief Tom Young, who had arrested Birchall, guard John Entwhistle, who had been specially hired to prevent Birchall's escape, and the man of the hour himself, John Reginald Birchall.

A crowd that had been waiting for two hours rushed up to the hack, but guards kept people back. The passengers proceeded on foot to the door of the hall. The reporter for the *News* thought Birchall appeared pale but showed no signs of nervousness. He was smartly dressed in a new suit he had ordered for the occasion. It was of black tweed with a cutaway coat. He sported a black Christy (bowler) hat and black bow tie. His face was freshly shaven and his black moustache looked elegant. Reporters agreed that since March the prisoner had gained weight, no doubt due to hotel meals and a lack of exercise. Courthouse staff ushered the prisoner to the upstairs courtroom, where all eyes were fixed upon him until he took his seat in the dock, the structure recycled from the demolished courtroom and so tall that only the top of his head could be seen. Shortly afterwards, Justice MacMahon took his place on the bench and the court opened.[32]

The prisoner was arraigned and pleaded not guilty. When asked by the judge, Blackstock expressed his readiness to proceed.

Jury selection followed. At the time, to be eligible to serve on a jury, one had to be a man, a resident of the county, over twenty-one years of age, the owner or tenant of property assessed at not less than $400 (or $600 in cities), "in the possession of his natural faculties, and not infirm or decrepid [*sic*]."[33] The explicit retention of a property qualification for jurors, notwithstanding the period's growing liberalism, signified the Ontario legislature's insistence that labourers and the landless be excluded from jury duty. Jurors were modestly compensated for their time and trouble, receiving $1.50 per day and travel expenses. A county board of selectors designated eligible jurors according to provincially specified procedures and called jury panels to the courts as needed.[34]

For Birchall's trial, a "double panel" of sixty-six men formed the pool from which the jurors were selected. The clerk of the court drew cards from a box, each card having a man's name, his occupation, and his address. Because it was a capital case, the defence had the right to challenge as many as twenty prospective jurors peremptorily, that is, without cause or explanation. The Crown could peremptorily challenge four men and had the right to cause a juror "to stand aside" until the rest of the panel had been gone through; if needed they could be called upon to stand. Both sides also had the right to challenge with cause, that is, to convince the court that the individual was biased or infirm. Challenges with cause were seldom exercised in Ontario courts because, unlike in the United States, prospective jurors could not be questioned, which made proving bias difficult. In Birchall's trial, the clerk called forty-one names altogether. The defence challenged nineteen men and the Crown four, with six made to stand aside. Those challenged and called aside came from places connected with the case. All the prospective jurors from Woodstock and from Blenheim Township were set aside. In the end, one of the twelve chosen was "a gentleman" from Ingersoll by the name of George Christopher, who served as chairman of the jury. The other eleven were all farmers from various Oxford townships. The *World* observed they were young and middle-aged men, and all "intelligent looking."[35] Upon these good men rested the fate of the accused.

Jury selection took about forty minutes, astonishingly little time compared to today or to American trials of the late nineteenth century. However, empanelling a jury usually took little time in Canadian trials of the nineteenth century, easily explained by the restriction on questioning jurors. Still, the brevity of the selection process in the Birchall trial gave rise to comment. The *World*'s headline was "Jury Chosen in 40 Minutes," and Hamilton's *Spectator* observed: "Contrary to expectations of everyone, a very short space of time was occupied in the very important matter of empanelling a jury."[36]

Once the jury was in place, Blackstock took the step of asking that the Crown witnesses be excluded from the courtroom. He was guarding against the possibility that witnesses would adjust their testimony to fit with that of others they heard. Osler agreed to the proposal, and the judge ordered the Crown witnesses to leave the room but remain nearby in a room prepared for them. ,

Justice MacMahon invited the Crown to make an opening statement.[37] Osler rose and spoke for nearly two hours. He began by urging the jurors not to be guided by newspaper reports or hearsay and instead to focus on the evidence. Osler then calmly and methodically outlined the Crown's case: the sequence of events leading up to the murder, including Birchall's first contacts with Benwell and Pelly in

England, their trip to Niagara Falls, the minute details of movements on 17 February, the day the Crown maintained Benwell had been murdered, and what followed. He also spoke of Birchall's previous stay in Oxford County and his familiarity with the neighbourhood of the swamp. Many newspapers both summarized what Osler said and printed every word of his long speech. In the courtroom, the audience listened in "a deathlike silence."[38]

Much of what Osler related had already been well covered by journalists, but there was one revelation. Osler read out the undated letter to Col. Benwell that Birchall had mailed from Niagara Falls on 20 February. Crucial to the Crown's case, its exact contents had never previously been revealed to the public. Even the defence got a copy of the letter only the day before the trial began. In it, Birchall urged Benwell's father to send a £500 bank draft to an account at the Bank of Montreal in Niagara Falls held by the partnership of Birchall and Benwell, saying that young Benwell approved of the transaction because he had found the business arrangements "all that he wished." The year's profits from the farm had been high. Birchall added that he preferred to use a typewriter when corresponding. He expected Col. Benwell would soon hear from his son endorsing the plan.

After reading the letter, Osler emphasized that there was no farm, nor were there any profits. Given that Birchall knew that Benwell was already dead, it had been his plan also to type a letter to the colonel over the imitated signature of Fred Benwell. Osler drew attention to evidence that would be presented showing that Birchall had practised Fred Benwell's signature. He also drew attention to the reference to the typewriter. (In 1890 it was just becoming widely used in business correspondence.) As the *Spectator* explained, "The use of the typewriter would obviate the danger which would arise from an attempt to imitate another's handwriting for a whole letter."[39] The letter read out was damning evidence that showed Birchall's duplicity as a con man and implied his motive in murdering Benwell.

When Osler completed his address, he called as his first witness William McDonald, who identified himself as a retired farmer.[40] Osler's purpose in calling this witness was to place in evidence how Birchall had come to Woodstock and vicinity in 1888. McDonald explained that as an agent for the London firm of Ford, Rathbone and Co., he had placed the prisoner, along with his wife, as a farm pupil with a farmer named Wilcox. They had stayed only one night and returned to

8.3. The Birchall trial under way in the upstairs theatre of the Town Hall.
Source: Woodstock Museum, image 1989.7–2.

Woodstock, boarding with him for a time and then elsewhere in town. Somerset had told him that he had not come to Canada to actually work on a farm but rather to assist with the management of a gentleman's farm. In Woodstock, McDonald explained, Birchall had spent most of his days driving out with hired horses.

Blackstock, the defence attorney, put McDonald through a long and severe cross-examination to show that the witness was not trustworthy and had had dealings with Birchall that he wasn't eager to make known to the public.[41] McDonald agreed that he often drank a good deal and had done considerable drinking with Somerset. Moreover, he reluctantly admitted to defrauding Ford, Rathbone by claiming a farm pupil had stayed long enough to earn payments from the firm when he had not. He said that Birchall still had an outstanding loan to him of $30.[42]

Blackstock probed the presence of McDonald in Princeton and Niagara Falls at times crucial to the case, implying that his role in the case was significant. McDonald admitted that he had gone to Princeton on 22 February and viewed the body. Blackstock asked who had told him to go there. McDonald insisted that no one had and that he had simply been curious about the deceased after learning from the *Sentinel-Review* that the body was that of an Englishman. Similarly, when asked about his appearance in Niagara Falls at the time of the preliminary hearing, McDonald maintained that he had gone because he had information that a man he wanted to see was at the Falls. Blackstock probed how it was that McDonald had come to testify at the hearing, making comments harmful to Birchall's case. McDonald admitted that he had been introduced to Det. Murray at the Falls and that he had gone to the courthouse with him. Blackstock asked what he and Murray had talked about, implying that Murray had coached McDonald, but the witness insisted they had only talked about the Falls. Blackstock sarcastically retorted, "They only talked about Niagara Falls, how pretty!"

Blackstock also asked about a visit McDonald admitted to having made five months previously to the Woodstock Jail to see Birchall. The lawyer suggested that the witness had gone there to apologize to Birchall for his testimony in Niagara Falls that had made the prisoner look bad, and that afterwards McDonald had been seen weeping. The witness insisted that in the jail, they had only had a brief encounter and McDonald had simply asked the prisoner how he was. There had been neither an apology nor weeping. Blackstock implied that the visit had been made secretively. McDonald did not agree, but he admitted that he had not had permission to visit and that he had been admitted by the turnkey because he had once been a turnkey there himself.

At the end of McDonald's testimony, it was evident that the defence had had some success in discrediting McDonald as a reliable witness by suggesting that Det. Murray had manipulated him, as well as by planting the idea that McDonald's role in the affair had been more significant that he was ready to admit.

All eyes were on Douglas Raymond Pelly as he entered the courtroom after being called as the next witness. The *World* reporter noted that Pelly was dressed in "a swell suit of light clothes very suggestive of spring." He had on a white wing collar and a white tie. The reporter quipped that Pelly looked "as if his six months of ease and travel at the expense of the Government thoroughly agreed with him."[43]

Just as Pelly began relating his familiar story, Blackstock objected to his reading from the correspondence of Mellersh and Birchall concerning the farm-pupil business, saying it was irrelevant to the case and would prejudice his client "cruelly." Justice MacMahon declared that certain quotations could be read into evidence and that he would reserve judgment on the principal objection. After explaining how he had been enticed into investing in Birchall's horse business and coming to Canada, Pelly described their travels. He remarked that on the train between London and Liverpool, Birchall showed Pelly his revolver. Pelly said it was smaller than his own, which he showed to the court. He told of the party's travels to New York and then to Buffalo where he had seen Birchall and Benwell copying each other's signature. On Monday, 17 February, the day that Birchall and Benwell left Buffalo together supposedly to see the farm, Pelly saw that Birchall was wearing a blue jacket, thick boots, and a black, imitation Astrakhan cap like the one produced in court. Pelly explained that upon Birchall's return alone, he had reported that Benwell did not like the farm, was sulky, and hadn't eaten anything. Pelly noticed that Birchall's boots were muddy, and the next day he had seen them being cleaned in front of the hotel. On 19 February, he and Birchall cleared all the luggage through customs in Niagara Falls, Ont. Birchall had the keys for Benwell's trunks and opened them. On 27 February, Birchall said he had had a telegram from Benwell asking him to send his luggage to the Fifth Avenue Hotel in New York.

Continuing, Pelly related how he had gone on his fruitless trip to New York in search of Benwell and how, prompted by the discovery of the cigar-box labelled "F. C. Benwell," Birchall and his wife had headed for Princeton to identify the body. Before he left, Birchall said that Benwell had taken his (Birchall's) pistol. (No pistol had been found either at the murder scene or in the possession of the prisoner.)

Osler showed the clothing from Benwell's body to Pelly, who identified the hat, the black-and-white checked coat, and the silk tie with spots as clothing he had seen Benwell wear.

At six o'clock, the court rose, leaving the remainder of Pelly's testimony for the morning. The judge cautioned the jury about forming an opinion in advance. Four constables escorted the jurors to the Royal Hotel where they were sequestered. The twelve men spent the night guarded by constables in an upstairs parlour converted for them into a sleeping apartment. Their meals were taken to them there. For exercise, first thing each morning guards ushered them on a vigorous walk.[44] Thus, the court showed care in keeping the jury from news and discussions of the case by others. It is likely, however, that the jurors had heard a great deal about the case before the trial began.

The *World* reporter noted that at lunchtime, Birchall had remained in his seat in the courtroom and his meal had been brought to him from a hotel. He had eaten with relish and joked with the tipstaffs, the minor officers of the court. At day's end, some 500 people stood waiting to see the prisoner as he left the courthouse. As he walked out, Birchall smiled familiarly to some of the young men and women in the crowd.[45]

Continuing with the Crown's Case

For nearly four more days the Crown continued to present its case.[46] Each day, a crowd met Birchall upon his arrival and departure from the courthouse. People clamoured for entry. A minor controversy arose over the many women who succeeded in gaining admittance to the courtroom thanks to the chivalry shown them by the guards at the door. Speaking against the backdrop of the movement for equal rights for women, some commentators complained that giving the women preference was denying equality for "the county's yeomen, the bone and sinew of Oxford."[47]

Birchall continued to appear confident and cheerful. When reporters interviewed him, he insisted that the evidence would prove his innocence of the murder charge. Fortunately for the spectators, after the first day a carpenter cut down the dock so he could be better seen. Early in the trial, Birchall appeared disinterested in the courtroom testimony and spent his time happily sketching the characters in the drama. As the evidence against him piled up, however, he paid more attention to the testimony and handed his lawyers many scribbled notes about what was being said.

Early on the second day, the Crown called Charles Benwell to the stand. The *News* reporter described him as closely resembling his late brother. An Englishman dark in complexion, with a small, dark moustache, he wore glasses. The witness answered the questions readily but tersely. Charles Benwell said he was a year and a half younger than Fred.[48] The two brothers had attended Cheltenham College and then gone together to school in Switzerland for about a year. Afterwards, Fred lived for a year at home, pondering a military career while enjoying football, hunting, and riding. Fred then went to New Zealand and lived on a farm for a year and a half. He had been living in England again when he left for Canada. Their father was in comfortable circumstances and able to settle his sons in life. The witness identified Fred Benwell's gold plate, eyeglasses, pencil case engraved "Connie, Sept.

15, 1869" (a birthday gift to wee Fred, known as "Connie" in the family, from his nurse at the time), and the cigar-case with the name written in Fred's handwriting. He also recognized the waterproof coat as one bought by their father at the Army and Navy Store.[49]

Next to testify was William F. Davis, a land surveyor employed by the Crown to map the routes between Eastwood and the swamp, measure the distances, and determine how much time it took to get from the Eastwood railway station to the crime scene. He gave the distance of the route supposedly taken by Birchall and Benwell as 4.61 miles and the return trip taken by Birchall as 4.88 miles. The witness walked the route and found he covered the trip there in one hour and twenty-five minutes, and the return trip in one hour and twenty-three minutes. (In July, Osler had done the same.) According to the Crown's theory, that left the murderer one hour and twenty-six minutes before the return train's departure from Eastwood, and thus enough time for the crime, rifling the pockets, and cutting off the marks on the clothing. On cross-examination, Blackstock expressed a keen interest in the fact that it had been Det. Murray who had shown the witness the routes and accompanied him on the walk. The defence would continue to point out Murray's guiding hand in the preparation of witnesses.[50]

A few witnesses testified briefly. A tax man from Niagara Falls, Ont., certified that no Birchall or Somerset owned property in the county. A banker from Niagara Falls, New York, presented records showing that on 22 February, Birchall had deposited $152, money the Crown implied had been taken from the deceased's pocket. A handwriting expert confirmed that various letters and notes were all in the same hand and that many had been signed by Birchall. A telegrapher from Buffalo testified that on the evening of 17 February, Birchall had paid for a telegram signed "Stafford" and directed that it be sent to himself at Niagara Falls, Ont. The telegram's contents appeared to give Birchall the authority to collect Benwell's trunks and send them to New York.

Richard McGuire of Blenheim Township testified that when he had been in the swamp where the body was found between ten and eleven o'clock on the morning of 17 February, he hadn't seen a body there. He had been peeling tamarack bark for horse feed just twelve feet from the site, which was in clear view. He would have seen a body had one been there. He remembered the date because on the evening of 17 February, there'd been a ball at Jerry Dake's hotel in Princeton. On cross, to weaken the testimony, Blackstock got McGuire to say that he couldn't absolutely swear whether there was a body on the spot where Benwell had been found; rather, he hadn't noticed one.

The Crown next presented witnesses who had seen the body on the day it had been discovered. Joseph and George Elvidge described how on 21 February they had found the body in the woods where they were cutting wood, stayed clear of it, and gone immediately to fetch the local justice of the peace. Magistrate Crosby had come out to the swamp with the Elvidges, and together they had looked closely at the body's location and condition. Joseph Elvidge said that the left foot of the deceased was frozen into the ice, which had to be cut to move the body. The coat and vest were open, exposing the front of the shirt, which was white and stiff with frost. The trousers were also open. They noticed a bullet hole in the back of the head and just a little blood.

Const. Watson of Princeton, who had also gone to the scene, swore that the blood found under where the head had rested was beneath a crust of snow. He found ice and frozen snow in the sleeve of the upright arm. No tracks went right up to the body, and there was no evidence that the body had been dragged. This evidence of ice and snow would assist the Crown in establishing when the murder took place.

As George Elvidge explained, it was the next day, when the brothers returned to the scene, that George had found the cigar-case, half-open, under a couple of inches of snow. Despite its exposure to foul weather, it appeared undamaged. The brothers also discovered eyeglasses and a cigar-holder with a stub under the snow where the victim's head had lain.

Presenting the Crown's Medical Evidence

At the inquest, Dr. Oliver Taylor and Dr. Charles R. Staples had testified about the autopsy they performed on the deceased. Since then, they had expanded their report and given it to the Crown but not to the defence. At the trial, Blackstock strongly criticized the physicians for favouring the Crown in this way. Clearly annoyed, he tangled in the courtroom with Osler about the fairness of it. Spectators enjoyed this dispute among legal greats. Justice MacMahon, however, put a stop to their disagreement.

First up was Dr. Taylor, whom reporters admiringly described as young, slim, dark, and intelligent-looking. He said he had seen the body for about fifteen minutes when it was on a sled in the swamp and then later at the undertaker's in Princeton. It was the body of a healthy young man. He reckoned that, when found, the body had been dead for four to seven days. He said that the right arm of the body was extended upright and that the sleeve contained a considerable accumulation of frozen water. There was much frozen snow and ice between the overcoat and vest. He remembered coming home on the evening of 17 February, when it rained for hours, after which freezing had set in. Next morning the ground was covered with ice. The testimony helped the Crown to establish that the body had lain in the swamp on 17 February during the rainstorm and before the frost.

Taylor described the two bullet wounds. He said that either bullet would have killed the man instantly and that there was no possibility he had inflicted both himself. He found bruises on the body, their colour indicating that they must have been caused either just before or within two hours of death. A body falling on an uneven surface would likely produce such marks. He found that a small piece of one ear was missing, probably gnawed off by an animal.[51]

Dr. Charles R. Staples of Princeton, who had assisted Taylor at the post-mortem, corroborated what Dr. Taylor had said, adding that from the condition of the stomach he didn't think the deceased had eaten anything for six hours before his death. On cross, Blackstock hammered Staples for expanding and altering the report first given at the inquest. Initially he had said the body had been where it was found for two or three days, but now he was saying longer. (The longer timeline fit better with the Crown's theory of the crime.) When asked why he had changed the report, he said he had reflected further on the evidence of the frozen clothes – a reasonable explanation but one that did not assist the defence.[52]

Next up was Dr. A.B. Welford, "the swell young physician of Woodstock." He had gone to the undertaker's with Miss Pickthall to see whether the body was that of her missing brother. He testified that even after the body had been thawing for several hours in the undertaker's establishment, the right sleeve was still frozen so solid that the clothing could not be separated from the body. He testified that because there was no swelling around the bruises, they had to have been made less than one and a half hours before or after death. On cross, he thought the man had been dead at least forty-eight hours when found. The cold air had slowed decomposition and had also caused the exposed flesh to darken. He had noticed an abrasion on the leg and a mark made by a charred stick on the man's drawers. He thought the body had been placed where found. In the view of the *Spectator*, the cross-examination had produced evidence that helped the defence. It was consistent with the defence's theory that the body was moved to where it was found and had lain there fewer days than the Crown alleged.[53]

The Crown called three Dominion meteorological observers in Woodstock to verify the claim of Dr. Taylor (and others) that heavy rain had fallen on the Monday evening and that freezing weather had set in on the Tuesday. While they did stress the heavy rain of Monday evening (unaccompanied by thunder), they also reported that rain and sleet had fallen on Wednesday evening and that there had been drifting snow on and off Thursday evening and Friday morning. The latter part of the testimony was useful to the defence, whose contention it was that Benwell's sleeve might have frozen on a day later than what the Crown alleged.

Identifying the Body

Several witnesses testified about Birchall's identification of the body. The first to do so was Const. Watson when asked about it by defence attorney Blackstock during cross-examination. Watson said that on the evening of 28 February, he spoke to the prisoner and his wife in Princeton and agreed to have the body exhumed the next morning. Among other things, the prisoner said that when he had last seen the deceased at Niagara Falls, Benwell had told him that he wanted to purchase a farm and that he was going to London, Ont., with stop-offs at Paris and Woodstock. After their talk, the prisoner and his wife had gone to Paris for the night. The next morning only the prisoner came to Princeton. Watson saw him lean over the body and say, "'It is him,' wiping his eyes with a handkerchief at the same time." At first the prisoner had said that he wanted to cable Benwell's family in England from Princeton, but then he had decided to do so when he returned to Niagara Falls. Watson said he had accompanied the prisoner back to Paris, and on the way the prisoner had said he was willing to pay considerable to have the case worked up, and he had asked Watson to take charge of it. It appeared that Birchall thought the amateur village constable could easily be misled.

James H. Swartz, the Princeton undertaker, testified that on 28 February, he had had a conversation with Birchall, who told him he had lost a friend with the name that was on the cigar-case. Swartz, who had wondered whether the man had been killed at a brothel, asked Birchall whether Benwell was in the habit of going to houses of ill fame, and

Birchall said that he was. Birchall had had to pay considerable to get him out of scrapes in such places. Birchall also told Swartz that he and Benwell were men of independent means. Swartz had asked how it was then that he had needed to pay for Benwell's scrapes, and Birchall had replied that Benwell always made it up to him. Swartz testified that Birchall told him that Benwell had sent a letter to him from London, Ont., about his luggage. It included the keys to his trunks. Swartz asked to see the letter, but after searching his pockets, Birchall had said he didn't have it but his wife did. When Swartz offered to go to Paris to get the letter from the wife, Birchall then said the letter was back in Niagara Falls. Swartz maintained that he had grown suspicious of Birchall's shifting story.

On cross-examination, Swartz said he had told this story to Det. Murray and to Const. Watson. (Murray later told the same story about the letter, but had himself in the role of the interrogator rather than Swartz.) Blackstock feigned surprise that Swartz told the story to the police officers. Next, Blackstock ridiculed the witness for what he called his "lively imagination." He pointed out that soon after the body was discovered, Swartz had said he had seen the deceased at Drumbo on Nomination Day and again at the Royal Hotel singing Indian war songs. Swartz explained that he thought he recognized the clothes and the ring. Blackstock observed that Swartz had said he had seen large footprints near the body, tracks made by moccasins. And he asked, "Tell us what under heaven made you ask Birchall whether the man was in the habit of going to houses of ill fame?" Swartz explained that there was a pedlar who was in the habit of playing euchre and going where he shouldn't. Blackstock said to the witness, "It must make you feel rather foolish now, doesn't it?" Swartz replied, "Not a bit."

John W. Gregg, sexton of the Princeton Cemetery, testified he was present when the body was exhumed on 1 March and Birchall made his identification. On cross, he said that Birchall had remained in the cemetery for about five minutes. Looking nervous and frightened, he had taken the constable's arm. He did not see Birchall cry or take out his handkerchief. Blackstock then asked, "How is it you were the only one who saw him frightened?" Gregg replied, "Quite a number there that day noticed it."

J.H. Hull, a lumberman of Princeton, recalled the conversation he had had with Birchall when Birchall came to identify the body. The prisoner told him stories similar to the ones he had told to Swartz, including about the letter Benwell had sent from London, Ont. Hull had asked him whether it was written on letterhead, and Birchall had then revised his story to say there was actually no letter, just the baggage checks and keys in an envelope. On cross, Hull said that from what the prisoner had said, he believed Birchall was genuinely concerned about his friend.[54]

A similar story was told by the next witness, Captain Peter H. Cox, a gentleman farmer living near Paris. He had talked to Birchall in Paris when the prisoner was there in connection with identifying the body. Cox had offered to assist Birchall in finding out what had happened. When asked about Benwell's letter, Birchall said it was not written on hotel stationery. He didn't know where Benwell had stayed in London, but probably with friends. He also said that he didn't know whether the deceased had much money with him.

Establishing Birchall's Familiarity with the Swamp

Three witnesses who farmed near the "Swamp of Death" testified about having seen Birchall nearby back in 1888–89. George Hersee, who owned the swamp, said he had seen the prisoner, or "Somerset," on three occasions at Pine Pond during that winter. He had usually been with others, including ladies. The witness described a number of little lakes in the area, including Mud Lake and Pine Pond located close to where the body was found. Birchall had asked him about the location of Mud Lake.

Joseph Piggott testified that he had also seen "Somerset" in 1888–89 riding out to Pine Pond. Piggott explained that in October 1889, a fire had burned down timber, causing saplings to blow down that blocked the trail to Mud Lake. The body was found on part of the old trail, near where it was blocked. On cross, Blackstock became unusually aggressive, apparently frustrated by the witness's failure to respond promptly. He quipped that he didn't want to bring in a stumping machine to pull out the answers!

James Ellis testified that during the hunting season in the winter of 1888–89, he had seen the prisoner with another Englishman in the swamp. Ellis described the trail where the body was found as a sleigh path used by hunters to reach Mud Lake. On cross, the witness said he had met the prisoner, he thought in October 1888, and they had passed the time of day. Blackstock pointed out that Birchall was not in Canada in October 1888. Crown attorney Ball re-examined the witness, who said he couldn't remember the exact month. It could have been a month or two later.

The Crown was gradually building up a chain of circumstantial evidence meant to drive home that Birchall had murdered Benwell on Monday, 17 February. As the trial progressed, the *Sentinel-Review* published a few reports giving details of Birchall's behaviour. At the end of the trial's second day, the prisoner had begun sketching a group of ladies in the gallery who were waiting for the crowd to disperse. One of them noticed what Birchall was doing and raised her parasol in front of her face. Birchall laughed heartily at her response. The reporter for the *Sentinel-Review* commented: "Such vivacity and pluck as his would carry many men through all the troubles of life with a triumphal success." The same paper observed: "Physcologists [sic] will find him an interesting study." By the end of the third day, however, the "nervy" prisoner was showing signs of anxiety. Nevertheless, when Birchall passed through a dense crowd of people as he left the courthouse, he didn't appear at all discomfited by the stares they gave him.[55]

Interest in the Birchall trial continued to grow as the Crown's case progressed. During the trial, the *Sentinel-Review* observed that its circulation had increased to 5,000, five times what it had been the previous week. As the days went on, Woodstock was thronged with even more visitors who hoped to gain entry to the courtroom. Thirty journalists kept the two telegraphers in the courtroom and ten more outside it busy sending out a massive number of words each day. News to England was being sent via Reuter and Dunlop's cable.[56] Each day, a crowd jammed the town square as the prisoner arrived at the courthouse, and demand remained strong for seats in the courtroom, especially from women.[57]

Placing Birchall and Benwell in the Vicinity of the Swamp

The Crown called several witnesses to show that on the morning of 17 February, Birchall and Benwell had travelled by train from Niagara Falls to Eastwood and then walked towards the swamp.[58]

Louis Drege, ticket agent for the GTR at Niagara, testified that he sold two, consecutively numbered tickets to Eastwood on 17 February and only two tickets. He had records to support his testimony, although not the tickets themselves, which the railway didn't retain. George Crumb, assistant ticket agent at Niagara Falls, produced the two ticket stubs.

Three witnesses placed Birchall and Benwell aboard the westbound train to Eastwood. Conductor W.H. Poole testified that he worked aboard the GTR trains running west from Hamilton. He explained how it was possible to take an express train from Niagara Falls first thing in the morning and connect with his westbound local train at Hamilton. On 17 February he had charge of the No. 7 train, which left Hamilton at 9:26 and arrived at Eastwood at 11:12. Only two passengers had boarded at Hamilton and gotten off at Eastwood. They were ticketed from Niagara Falls to Eastwood. He saw them on the Eastwood platform after they got off. He described the men and their clothing to the court. He said one of the men bore a very strong resemblance to the prisoner.

On cross, Blackstock asked Poole about dining facilities. Poole said there was no dining car on his train, but there was one on the express from Niagara Falls to Hamilton, and there were dining rooms and lunch counters at the stations in Niagara Falls and Hamilton. (The defence aimed to show that deceased's empty stomach did not make sense given the possibilities he had had for having breakfast.) Blackstock contrasted various statements the witness had just made with those made on previous occasions. For instance, he had earlier described one of the Englishmen on the train as light complexioned and wearing light-coloured clothes, but now he said the opposite.

The next witness was Miss Mary Lockhart, described by the *Sentinel-Review* as "an intelligent-looking spinster." She identified herself as working for Coldback's department store in Woodstock, where she supervised the mantle (cloak) department. She testified that on the morning of 17 February, she had taken the train from Paris to Princeton. She had seen two men aboard. One had worn a short dark coat and an Astrakhan cap similar to the one produced in court. "The prisoner in the dock is the man I saw that day," she declared emphatically. She continued, saying that he had gotten off with his companion at Eastwood. The other man wore a checked overcoat, cape, and faded brown hat similar to the one produced. The witness saw the exhumed body at Princeton cemetery and had sworn then that it was that of the other man whom she had seen on the train.

On cross, Lockhart said that upon seeing in the weekly *Sentinel-Review* of 28 February Matthew Virtue's brief description of the two men going up the road from Eastwood station, she had said at home, "Those are the two men I saw." She explained that Det. Murray had told her she would have to go to Princeton to identify the body. She insisted that she had seen no photograph of the deceased. She conceded that she had talked about the matter to her friends, but not more widely. No one had suggested what evidence she should give. Blackstock then asked her whether she had talked about the matter to Miss Bessie Francis of

Woodstock. Lockhart replied that she couldn't remember. He pressed her but her reply didn't change. He asked her whether she had told Miss Francis that the man she had recognized as Benwell was the light-complexioned man. "I couldn't have told her so," was the reply.

Blackstock next produced a copy of the weekly *Sentinel-Review* of 28 February and asked her to point out where she had seen Virtue's description. She could not. Blackstock said that Virtue had not given his description until 7 March. He asked her whether she had been mistaken, and she conceded that she may have been. The lawyer then broached what he referred to as "a delicate question," the witness's age. She demonstrated a reluctance to respond, and he abandoned the attempt. (The 1891 Canadian census reports her age as thirty-seven.) In sitting down, Blackstock remarked sarcastically that "he couldn't examine so infallible a witness." On redirect, Lockhart responded to Osler by saying she had no distinct recollection of the date of the newspaper where she saw Virtue's description of the men.

While it appeared that the defence had made some progress in undercutting the witness and her testimony, the *Sentinel-Review* nevertheless called her "a strong witness for the Crown" and said her testimony was "the most sensational incident of the trial so far." As she spoke, the audience had listened with "a thrilling hush of suspense and a general flutter."[59] For a male journalist of the period, this was a generous account of a woman and her importance in the trial.

Of course, the defence attorney's dynamic cross-examination also got praise. The *Spectator* called it "a masterpiece." Many of the reporters whispered, "Look at him now; that's Blake's style" – the reference being to Edward Blake, a distinguished Canadian barrister and former Canadian attorney general. Blackstock had his hands clasped behind his head and, "like a volley of fire, he extracted statements from the witness."[60]

Miss Carrie Choate, who lived near Ingersoll, testified that on the morning of 17 February she took the train that ran from Paris to Ingersoll. She saw two men who came aboard at Paris sitting with their backs to her two or three seats ahead of her. One of them was a little shorter than the other. One man had on an Astrakhan cap, which fell off at one point. When he turned to get it, she glimpsed his face. Looking at the prisoner in the dock, she said the man she saw was not as stout. The other man had on an overcoat with a cape, a brown, stiff hat, and glasses. She said that she heard one say, "They offered me five hundred." And she heard one say something about possibly being late reaching where they were going that night. They had gotten off the train between Princeton and Woodstock.

On cross, Blackstock asked how the witness had become connected to the case. She said a detective had come to see her about ten days before the trial. He asked how the detective would have learned about her as a possible Crown witness. She explained that about five weeks after her train trip, she was visiting in Brantford and someone told her about Miss Lockhart's evidence. Blackstock interrupted to say that Miss Lockhart had never given evidence until a few minutes earlier. (She had, however, been quoted in the newspapers.) Continuing, Choate explained that in hearing about what Miss Lockhart had said, it reminded her of what she had seen and heard aboard the train. She told friends and relatives about it, and one of them must have said something to the authorities. In response to Blackstock's asking how it was that the men had gotten on the train at Paris, Choate said she thought they must have gotten off the train there for a stroll and then gotten back on. Blackstock, appearing incredulous, wondered how she could remember such a thing. She insisted she could.

Two witnesses testified that they had seen Benwell and Birchall soon after they arrived in Eastwood.[61] Alfred Hayward, a miller living and working in Eastwood, said that on the morning of 17 February, just after the westbound train left Eastwood, between eleven and twelve o'clock, from a distance of 125 to 130 feet, he saw two gentlemen pass the mill gate. He noticed their clothing. One of the men was the prisoner.

On cross, Blackstock asked sarcastically if the witness's eyes improved with time. He said Hayward had been unable to identify the men when asked by a reporter in February. Blackstock then noted that Sutherland, the MP, and the lawyers McKay and Finkle had recently visited the witness, and he asked the witness what they had been wearing. Hayward said he couldn't remember. Blackstock, feigning surprise, said, "Yet you remember what the two men were wearing back in February!" The lawyer then asked the witness to identify a man he knew in the gallery (Const. Midgley), but Hayward couldn't see him well enough to identify him. Blackstock expressed amazement that he couldn't see that short distance, but had seen the two men in February who were much farther away. The cross-examination effectively undercut the witness's testimony.

John Crosby of Blenheim testified that on the morning of 17 February he had gone to Robinson's blacksmith shop in Eastwood. On the way, between eleven and twelve, he had met two men going east on

Governor's Road. One wore a dark coat and had a dark, fur cap. The other man had on a darkish overcoat with a cape, wore glasses, and was smoking a cigar. He had a stylish appearance. The man with the glasses was, he believed, the dead man he saw later in the Princeton cemetery. The other was the prisoner. He said the roads were frozen that morning and then later got muddy as a thaw set in. (The latter point would account for Birchall's muddy boots and Benwell's clean ones.)

On cross, Crosby said that he went to Princeton to see the body, but he didn't remember the date that he had done so. He agreed that he had seen the photograph of the dead man and hadn't recognized him from it. He said that Const. Watson asked him to attend the inquest, where he gave evidence. Blackstock asked whether the witness had told a *Sentinel-Review* reporter that the man with the fair complexion wore a felt hat. "I would not swear to that," replied Crosby. He was then asked whether he had previously said the other man was a little stout. "I may have," he replied. "If so, it was true." Crosby agreed that he had previously sworn that the man in the spectacles was carrying a parcel about a foot square. He also agreed that he had been asked to go to the jail to identify the prisoner, and that he had gone but been unable to identify him there.

Five witnesses who lived near the swamp said that on 17 February they had seen tracks of two people going northeast through a field. They remembered the date because of "a cheese meeting" (when local dairy farmers and makers of cheese met) and the ball at Dake's. After the discovery of the body, they started to think the tracks might have significance. Later Det. Murray had come to ask about what they had seen.

Five other witnesses recalled seeing two men walking in the direction of the swamp in the early afternoon of 17 February. John Cosby, identified as a young farmer, saw two men walking. Archibald Elmiston of Blandford Township said that on the day of the cheese meeting, he saw two men walking east on the Second Concession. One was a little ahead of the other. The man behind had on a light-coloured coat and a hat about the colour and style of the one produced. On cross, he admitted he had seen them only briefly before the woods blocked his view. He therefore couldn't identify either man.

William Oldham of Blenheim Township remembered bringing a load of barley to Eastwood on 17 February. At About 12:30, where the Second Concession crosses the town line, he saw two men walking towards the swamp. He saw only their backs and so couldn't describe their faces.

One wore a long coat and the other did not. On cross, he agreed that he had met "Lord Somerset" a year before but maintained that when he had passed the men on the road in February, he hadn't noticed them particularly.

Ruth Ferguson of the First Concession, East Oxford, saw two men near Eastwood walking through Mr. Perry's woods.

Ellen Fallon, about thirty, who lived with her mother in a house about 300 yards from the entrance to the swamp, recalled that on the day of the ball at Dake's, just after dinner at about one o'clock, she was knitting at a window and saw two men passing on the road. One wore a cape overcoat and one had on a short coat. In front of her house, they passed from the south side of the road to the north, moving closer to the swamp entrance.

At the Scene and Returning to Eastwood Alone

The Crown failed to produce any witnesses who had seen the two men at the swamp. However, witnesses testified about hearing shots fired there and seeing Birchall alone returning to Eastwood.

George Fredenburg, a cheesemaker who lived near the swamp, said that on 17 February he had been hunting with two friends in the swamp. At about 12:30 he had heard two shots, which he had taken to be from a rifle. They had been fired not very far apart. At the time, they were standing 200 to 300 yards from where the body was later found. His two companions told similar stories. One of them, George McDonald, testified on cross that he hadn't been able to tell just where the shots had come from, but he had supposed from the concession road. He agreed that he had told Det. Murray this but denied that afterwards he had had a drink with the detective. When asked whether he had told a newspaperman that the shots had been fired three minutes apart, he denied saying that. When asked whether, when he had gone to the newspaper office, he had pointed to a nearby telegraph pole and said the shots came from as near as that, he agreed that he had. He said that between the firing of the two shots, he had had time to speak about fifteen words. He said he fixed the time they heard the shots by when the train went by.

Alexander Logan, a fireman employed by the GTR, remembered that on 17 February, he had gone to Woodstock to get oysters for the ball at Dake's. Between 3:00 and 4:00, certainly before the 4:00 train came into Eastwood, he had seen a man walking west on the Second Concession at the town line. He wore a checked coat and his pants were rolled up. He had a round cap that looked like Persian lamb. When the hat of the deceased was produced in court, the witness said that it was not the cap. When the deceased's coat was shown, Logan said it was not the coat he had seen. (Thus, it was not Benwell he had seen returning from the swamp.) On cross, the witness explained that Det. Murray had asked him to go to the jail to identify the prisoner, and he had done so. He said that most of the prisoners at the time were wearing prison clothes, but there had been one other man, a horse thief, dressed in everyday clothes, as was Birchall.

Charles Beck, a Blenheim farmer and mason, said that between 2:00 and 3:00 on 17 February, he had been returning from Woodstock when he met a man walking near the Second Concession and the town line who asked him if he was on the road to Gobles. The man he saw was the prisoner in the box. He remembered the date because he paid for a one-year subscription to the *Sentinel-Review* that day, and he still had the dated receipt.

In Eastwood and Returning to Niagara Falls

Several witnesses placed Birchall at Eastwood Station in time to catch the eastbound train, and others saw him aboard the train on his return trip.

When Alice Smith was called, there was a great stir in the courtroom in anticipation of her testimony. The *World* described her as "a prepossessing young woman," small in stature and dressed in black.[62] She testified that on 17 February she had been living in Eastwood with her grandfather, George Hayward, but was now living in the house of Mr. Zybach in Niagara Falls. She said she had known the prisoner in 1888–89 as "Somerset" or "Lord Somerset" during his several visits to her grandfather's house when she was there. Sometimes he had come with Mr. Dudley. She said she had seen the prisoner near Eastwood Station on 17 February. Here is how the *World* presented her testimony:

> The prisoner came up to me, shook hands, and said, "How do you do?" He laughed and said, "Don't you know me?" I thought it was Somerset, but said, "Is it Somerset or Dudley?" and he said "Somerset." The prisoner then told me he was on some business with horses in the Northwest and was going to Hamilton for his luggage. He would return and see the "governor," (meaning my grandfather whom he used to call governor). The prisoner had a cigar in his fingers, but it was unlit. I accompanied the

prisoner into the station where he bought a ticket for Hamilton and walked out on the platform with me. I saw Ida Cromwell, Mary Swartz, Harry James, Stationmaster Dunn, and James Hayward at the station. I went to the station to send a letter. After the mailing I went to Mr. Hayward's store and left 4 ½ dozen eggs there.

In response to Osler, she said she had a passbook showing that she had left the eggs at the store. She said the prisoner's boots had been muddy and his trousers had been turned up.

In his cross-examination, Blackstock badgered the witness and sought to besmirch her character. He asked about her living arrangements and elicited that she worked for Zybach, the photographer, and lived in his house in Niagara Falls, Ont., along with a Miss Tucker, her roommate. Blackstock asked rhetorically whether she thought it all right to live with a man recently separated from his wife. He asked how old she was, and she replied seventeen.

Blackstock then took up the topic of her relations with Dudley. He asked wasn't it true that he had been her special friend. She denied it. He asked whether she had been alone with him, and she said never. He asked whether it was true that Dudley paid a great deal of attention to her.

At this point, Justice MacMahon interrupted, saying, "Unless there is something very important in the question, I don't think it should be asked." According to the *World* reporter, in response to the judge's remark, "The crowd showed a disposition to applaud." Any stomping was quickly suppressed, however.[63] Undeterred, Blackstock repeated the question about Dudley paying attention to her, and the witness replied, "No." "Were you not," asked Blackstock, "in the kitchen with Dudley?" She said others had always been present too.

Blackstock asked when she first thought of this story of the horses in the Northwest. She replied, "All along." He asked why then had she not mentioned it when giving evidence earlier, and she answered that she had not thought of it then.

Osler on redirect had Smith explain that she was staying at Zybach's with the consent of her betrothed, Night Policeman Blunt of Niagara Falls. When Mrs. Zybach left her husband and the house, the mother of the witness's roommate had come to see the situation, and she had approved of the girls' continuing to live in the house. A chivalrous Justice MacMahon commented: "There cannot be anything wrong with a young woman going to Toronto or Niagara Falls or elsewhere to secure honest employment."

When leaving the courtroom, Smith was repeatedly congratulated on the manner in which she had passed "a severe ordeal." The *World* thought that Blackstock had exhibited bad temper and harshness in dealing with the witness, "a girl of but 17." His aspersions on her character had been "extremely cruel." Some of the women in the crowd shed tears for her. Nevertheless, her testimony was important for the Crown's case because she had talked to Birchall in Eastwood on the afternoon of 17 February. Throughout the day and after the adjournment, there was "an enormous increase of interest" in the trial, according to the *Sentinel-Review*.

Other young women also testified. Miss Ida Cromwell who lived near Eastwood said that on 17 February, she had been at Eastwood Station. She remembered the date because she had met some friends there and seen the prisoner. She first saw Birchall in the lane leading off the Brantford Road to the station. He had on a short, navy-blue coat and a black cap similar to the one produced. He wore light pants, rolled up at the bottom, and very muddy boots. She had known the prisoner the year before. That morning, she heard Stationmaster Dunn sell Birchall a ticket to Hamilton. Soon after the prisoner's arrest, she had identified him at the jail. She pointed to the prisoner in the dock, saying he was the man she had seen.

On cross, Blackstock elicited from Cromwell that she was unable to remember the dates of other visits she had made to Eastwood Station. The lawyer observed sarcastically that her recollections had gotten better with time. At the inquest, where she had been a witness, she had said something different, that she had first seen the prisoner coming up the Brantford Road. Cromwell denied saying that. Blackstock asked her how she had described the cap at the inquest. She said she had testified that it was a black cap. The lawyer corrected her, saying she had said it was a curly cap. The witness agreed. Blackstock pointed out that she had just testified that the prisoner had had a cigar in hand, but that was something new. When asked whether she had said anything about a blue coat before, she said she hadn't. "Now, Miss Cromwell," said Blackstock, "I want to know on your oath what explanation you can give to the jury for these new statements today?" There was a long pause and no reply. "Very well," he said, "if you can't explain it that will do."

Miss Mary Swayzie testified that she had been at the Eastwood Station on 17 February and at about three o'clock had seen a stranger there. She had noticed that he wasn't tall, that he wore heavy clothes with pants rolled up, and that his shoes very muddy. She had thought he looked to be "a very shrewd, sharp-looking man," and had wondered who he was. Later, Det. Murray had taken her to the jail and she had picked out the man. When asked by Blackstock, she agreed that she had given evidence previously but couldn't remember whether she had previously said the man was medium tall. She denied that she had seen Det. Murray shake hands with the prisoner at the jail. The detective had only said to the prisoner, "Look this way." There had been no other prisoners with him.

The Crown called James Hayward, who kept a store and ran the post office at Eastwood and remembered being at the station on 17 February. He fixed the date by a draft due that day that he had paid to the station agent. He saw Mr. Dunn, as well as a man talking to Alice Smith. He knew he had seen the man before and had known him as Somerset. On that day, Somerset was wearing a dark cap and dark blue coat. His trousers were rolled up. He didn't notice his boots. He had a cigar in his mouth. He identified the prisoner in the dock as the man he had seen.

On cross, Blackstock pointed out discrepancies between what the witness had said at the inquest and what he had just said. When queried, the witness could not account for the greater detail he had just given. It was suggested that Hayward had spoken about the matter to a lot of people since the inquest. Next Blackstock asked the witness about a time when he had been at the Woodstock races and had said that a man there looked as much like Birchall as the man he had seen at Eastwood. But at that time Birchall was in jail. The witness denied that he had said exactly that and maintained he merely pointed out a resemblance. Blackstock kept pressing him, but he stuck to his position.

Henry James of Drumbo said that in February he had been a porter at the station in Eastwood. He remembered 17 February because it was the day the station agent had returned to work after an illness. At about 2:30 he had seen a man there who they had said was Lord Somerset. He was standing on the platform with Miss Smith. The witness said he had talked with them, but he couldn't remember what was said. Det. Murray later took him to the jail to identify the man. He recognized him among about thirty prisoners. No one had pointed him out. He had no doubt that it was the man he now saw in the dock.

On cross, Blackstock asked when the station agent had gone off sick, but the witness couldn't remember exactly, but thought it was about a week before. He said that for the purpose of testifying he had gotten a memo from the company stating the day the agent came back, but it didn't say when he had booked off. When asked, he said he couldn't remember when the identification had taken place at the jail, but it was some time in February, March, or April. Blackstock pointed out that it was odd his memory was so much sharper about 17 February. He elicited from the witness that at the jail all the prisoners had been wearing jail clothing except Birchall.

George Hay, brakeman on the eastbound (No. 10) train on 17 February, testified that he had seen the prisoner on the train that day. He had gotten on at Eastwood and off at Hamilton, and then got on again with a ticket to Niagara Falls. He had also seen him later that night in Niagara Falls. He had identified the prisoner at the jail in Niagara Falls soon after the arrest. The witness said that in 1888 he had seen a man his father had told him was Lord Somerset with a man called Dudley, but he hadn't been on speaking terms with Somerset.

Blackstock again contrasted the specifics of what the witness had just said with what he had testified to on an earlier occasion and admonished him for the discrepancies. He elicited that it was Det. Murray who took the witness to the jail for purposes of identification. On redirect, the witness said that he remembered the man on the train because the man had opened a conversation.

James Duffy testified that he had been news agent on the eastbound GTR train in February. On the seventeenth, he had seen the prisoner in the smoking car as the train left Eastwood. He had sold him a copy of *A Tramp Abroad*, some cigars, and some fruit. The prisoner had given the witness a cigar and they had had about a half hour's conversation after the train left Hamilton. The man had offered him a drink from a flask, but the witness had told him he didn't drink. "Smith" was the name the man had given. He had said he had a brother who would be meeting him at Buffalo. The man had worn dark clothes and a dark round cap like the one produced. His shoes had been muddy and his pants had been rolled up. He had gotten off at Niagara Falls.

George Phemister, a telegrapher in the Great Western Telegraph office at the Falls, testified that about ten minutes after the No. 10 train had arrived from the west on 17 February, a man had hurriedly given him a message addressed to "Pelly, Stafford House, Buffalo." It read: "Arrive at Buffalo 9 to-night. Must remain there to-night. Signed Bastell." Phemister was unable to identify the man who had sent the telegram. Another telegram, this one sent on 27 February and addressed to "Burchell, Imperial Hotel," read: "Telegram and letter were sent on to you yesterday to ship heavy baggage to Fifth-Avenue Hotel, New York.

Signed Stafford." Phemister was unable to identify the man who had sent the telegrams.

At exactly noon on the Friday, Osler declared, "That is the case, my lord, for the Crown." Blackstock said he would be able to proceed with the defence at 2:00 p.m. Justice MacMahon adjourned the court until then.

Newspapers judged that the Crown had made a strong case to convict the prisoner. Yet uncertainty remained. The *News* pointed out that the evidence was circumstantial and that the Crown was relying on Birchall's previous bad character. It warned that there might not be enough evidence to safely convict and send a man to the gallows.[64]

9

The Defence and Conclusion

Knowing that the defence would begin its case at 2 p.m. on 27 September, the crowd outside the courthouse grew larger than ever before. While the public had had a good idea of the Crown's case ahead of time, the defence's case was as yet unknown, which heightened the curiosity.

"When the doors were opened," reported the *World*, "the constable had literally to fight with the surging mass which would not be kept out. It was the most aggressive, eager crowd ... they had had to deal with." Once again, in the crowd were many "ladies" who were "pretty roughly handled on the outside steps and in the hallway." The hall was even more packed than before; the numbers struggling to enter would have filled it several times over.[1]

The Defence Gets Under Way

As if to disparage the defence by its unmanly display, journalists reported that Blackstock was assisted by Dugald MacMurchy, who appeared in court wearing carpet slippers because his boots had just been stolen.[2] Blackstock began by stating for the record that the defence found the Crown's case insufficient.[3] As he called the defence witnesses, it became apparent that a main objective was to establish that other possible suspects had been in the vicinity of the swamp on the days before the body had been discovered and that the murder could have occurred after Monday, 17 February, the day the Crown maintained it took place and the only day when Birchall had been in the vicinity.

As first witness for the defence, Blackstock called John R. Rabb, who the *World* identified as the old German farmer living in the little house on the west side of the entrance to Blenheim Swamp. In the summer, he had been conducting tours in broken English of the murder site and earning "not a few coins for the trouble." Rabb testified that from his home a half mile from the swamp, in wintertime he could see clearly the place where the body was found. Det. Bluett had conducted a test with a boy, and Rabb could also see him plainly in the road nearest where the body was found. He further testified that he had seen no strangers around during the week of the murder. On 18 February he had heard two shots fired in the swamp at about 6 p.m. He noticed the shots because hunters would shoot twice when they got lost in the swamp, and he would holler or fire his gun to help them find their way out. That evening, he watched as two men came out of the swamp immediately after the shots. When asked how much time there was between the two shots, the witness replied a half mile. The audience erupted in laughter, and Justice MacMahon threated to clear the room. Rabb clarified that the shots were fired almost on top of one another.

On cross, Osler elicited that Rabb had heard the shots at about six o'clock, just before dusk, the time when hunters generally left the swamp and signalled to him that they were leaving by firing shots. He said he knew it was 18 February because that evening he tended his stock and Mrs. Schutz was over to his place. Osler asked whether he tended his stock every night and whether Mrs. Shultz frequently came over. Rabb agreed that was the case. Blackstock re-examined the witness, who sought to clarify matters by saying that he remembered the date because that evening he and Mrs. Schultz had had a conversation about the shots.

The court's focus was on Rabb's testimony about the shots, but he had also made the point that where the Crown maintained Benwell had been killed – either where the body was found or nearby on the road – was a risky place to commit murder because both locations were in plain view of anyone at Rabb's house.

Rachel Schultz, described by the *World* as "an elderly German lady," testified that she lived across the road from the Rabbs. She said she remembered hearing the sound of a firearm at about 7 p.m. on the Tuesday before the body was found. When asked about her clock, she said it was an hour too fast. She said she hadn't seen anyone. On cross, Osler elicited that when the firearm sounded it was getting dark and about the time hunters generally left the wood. The implication was that the shots were insignificant. He asked whether her memory was poor and she had difficulty recollecting one day from the next, and she agreed that was so. She said that about every day her family and the Rabbs visited back and forth and chatted in German.

Blackstock asked her how she fixed the day. She replied that it was the night after the thunderstorm. (The Crown had shown that the thunderstorm came Wednesday night and that the rain of Monday was unaccompanied by thunder.)

John Stroud, age thirteen, said he had gone with Det. Bluett and had stood on the Second Concession in front of the swamp near where the body was found. He could see Bluett standing in front of Rabb's home. On cross, he said he had gone there for the purpose of determining whether Rabb's house could be seen from the spot, but it could not. The Crown was suggesting that Birchall could have committed the murder there without being aware that a house was so close or that he might be seen.

James Atkinson, a hotelkeeper of Drumbo, said that on Thursday, 20 February, at about 4 p.m., two men came to his hotel in a muddy buggy and he served them beer, crackers, and cheese. One of the men, Robert Caldwell, he knew well, and the other he later learned was Baker. Baker wore felt boots with rubbers over them. Caldwell wore common overshoes and a common boot. The men were "worse for liquor."

On cross, Osler suggested they were two men on a spree, and Atkinson agreed. "Only that and nothing more," said Osler. "Exactly," the witness replied. Osler pointed out that at the inquest, Atkinson had said that Caldwell wore leather boots and no overshoes. The witness conceded that he must have got it wrong either one time or the other. (The point of dwelling on the footwear had to do with the tracks seen near the body, tracks that showed no heel marks, which might be the appearance of ones left by moccasins or by rubbers.)

Adam Oliver, a farmer living one and a half miles north of Princeton, said two men called at his door wanting to get back to Princeton. He told them to keep going down the road. He said he had known the swamp for twenty years as a hunter and had never seen anything of a trail leading from the spot where the body was found. On cross, Osler elicited that the incident with the pair of men had occurred at about 3 a.m. on either the Wednesday or Thursday.

Andrew Young, a farmer living across the road from Oliver, remembered that at 3 a.m. on Thursday, 20 February, strangers had asked him the way to Princeton, and he directed them. They wore rubbers and overshoes and made no noise when they entered his house through the unlocked door and made their way across the kitchen to the hallway. On cross, Osler asked how he fixed the date, and the witness replied that there had been a cheese meeting the day before.

Samuel Stroud, son of the owner of Stroud's Hotel in Princeton, testified that at about 10 a.m. on the day prior to the discovery of the body, two men named Baker and Caldwell had arrived at the hotel, saying they had come from Drumbo. He said that on the day after the discovery of the body, he and two other members of the coroner's jury had visited the swamp and seen the tracks of two persons leading from the spot where the body was found. The tracks looked as though they had been made with moccasins. He didn't think the deceased's boots would have made a similar track.

On cross, Osler asked whether by signing the report of the coroner's jury the witness had signalled that the tracks were insignificant to the murder and had been made by the Elvidge boys. The witness agreed. He said he hadn't spoken or thought of the tracks until Det. Bluett came and inquired about them. Osler asked him a number of questions about why he thought the tracks had been made by moccasins. The main response was that there'd been no sign of a heel. Blackstock elicited that Det. Bluett had merely asked the witness to tell his story to the prisoner's lawyers.

Joseph Martin, who had been on the coroner's jury, said that the day after the body was found, along with other jurors he had examined tracks at the swamp. He had seen that two sets were larger than the others and looked as if they had been there longer. He admitted he had looked for items that might have fallen at the site but had found none. Osler brought out that the witness had found no frozen water in the large tracks and that they had not gone within six feet of where the body was found. It did not appear that those who made the tracks had sought to go around a body. Under pressure, he admitted that at the time he had been unimpressed with the tracks and that the coroner's jury had not found them important. He conceded that the tracks might have been made by the Elvidge brothers when they had gone on the Monday to do some logging.

Blackstock re-examined Martin and asked him whether he was a retired farmer. The witness said, no, he was just "a tired farmer," which brought laughter from the spectators. Blackstock drew from the witness that he thought the tracks might have been made by someone carrying the body to the swamp and that the tracks did not go up to where the body had been because of the brush that was in the way.

William Lancaster testified that George Baker and a companion called at his place at Gobles Corners and that Baker asked how to find the road to Drumbo. The witness told him he knew the road as well as he did himself. Baker and his companion had then scuffled.

Up to this point, the defence had been attempting to persuade the jury that Birchall was not the only suspect. Blackstock next questioned whether the body was Benwell's.

James Oliver, a bartender of Woodstock who had been a witness at the inquest, testified that he had seen the body. He had sworn at the time that to the best of his knowledge, he recognized it as that of the man he had seen at the North American Hotel selling a silver polish. Osler asked about the moustache on the man seen at the hotel, and the witness said he had sworn at the inquest that the man had a light moustache. (The body did not.) Osler said that the witness could not then or now firmly identify the body as that of the man with the polish. The witness agreed. When asked whether he had only a hazy idea of what the man with the polish looked like, the reply was, "That is about it."

J.W. McKay, proprietor of the North American Hotel, said when he saw the body, he thought it bore a resemblance to the man with the polish only that man had had a moustache.

George Fowler, a farmer near Drumbo, thought that when he saw the body, it reminded him of a young man he had seen peddling cheap clothing at Waterford. Osler simply asked, "You know you were mistaken now?" "Yes," he replied.

Alfred Laycock, who lived near Gobles, thought when he saw Benwell's body that it was that of a man he had seen selling jewellery in Drumbo and Woodstock. Osler asked whether he had seen the salesman sometime before 1890, and the witness agreed.

William Burgess, known as "Old Knuck," said he had been hunting in the swamp for not less than fifty years and had never heard of a trail leading from where the body was found to Mud Lake. Two other hunters said they knew of no such path. On cross, all the witnesses conceded that they hadn't been hunting there in a few years.

Frederick Millman, a young grocer of Woodstock, said he had known the prisoner well by sight in 1888–89, having lived next door to him. He had then seen him in February 1890 between ten and eleven o'clock one morning about two weeks before he learned of the prisoner's arrest. On cross, the witness said the encounter had occurred on Dundas Street (Woodstock's main street). The man wore clothes similar to the ones he had always worn: a brown sealskin cap and breeches with red stockings tied with white bows. "Rather a startling appearance on the streets of Woodstock," commented Osler. The witness did not reply but said he had not stopped to speak to the prisoner. Osler, who sought to discredit the story by implying that the man had been drinking, asked the witness facetiously whether he had been feeling well, adding, "Nothing wrong with your liver?"

James Hood, liveryman, swore that George McDonald, who had given evidence the day before, had told him that the shots he had heard were fired between 2:30 and 3:00 p.m. and came four or five minutes apart. Osler elicited that MacDonald had said it just in a casual sort of way.

Blackstock now stood and explained to Justice MacMahon that his next witness would take considerable time to complete his evidence. The judge agreed to let the defence present its next witness on the following day (Saturday). It was now clear to MacMahon that the case couldn't be wrapped up on the Saturday. He told the court that, while he didn't like to have the jury sequestered for all of Sunday, there was no choice. The court adjourned for the day.

After hearing the day's testimony, people were disappointed that the defence appeared so weak. The *World* called it "simply a fiasco." The lawyers had strained hard to save their client, but they had failed in the face of "one of the strongest chains of circumstances that ever was welded against an accused man in a Canadian court." Calling the defence "extremely weak," the *News* summarized the points the defence had attempted to make: that Baker and Caldwell were connected to the tragedy; that there was doubt as to the identification of the body; that there was no trail to the swamp from near where the body was found; and that other tracks were in the snow. Even if the points had been proven – and they were not – it didn't add up to a powerful argument.[4]

The press reported that throughout the day the prisoner had shown little interest in the proceedings of the court. "No one knows what to make of him," declared the *News*. "It is hard to imagine any person with such wonderful nerve, and many people believe him to be utterly without feeling."[5] Amazement at Birchall's sang-froid was giving way to doubts about his humanity.

When the trial resumed, the defence called medical men to the stand.[6] The defence had brought a few physicians to listen to the Crown's medical witnesses in the hope that a least some of them would agree to testify for the defence. Blackstock hoped to show that death could have occurred later than 17 February and that the evidence from the autopsy could be interpreted in various ways. Dr. J. Mearns of Woodstock, described as being "a fine-looking, portly gentleman," agreed to testify. As did Dr. James H. Richardson, whose professional credentials were noted. He had a long-standing practice in Toronto and was an ex-president of the Ontario Medical Association, surgeon of the Toronto Jail, and a professor of anatomy in the Toronto School of Medicine.

Dr. Mearns said he disagreed with Dr. Welford that rigor mortis comes two to two and three quarters hours after death. It comes on much later after death in the case of a healthy young person suddenly killed. It would have taken eight, ten, or twelve hours in this instance. The witness said the bruises were not consistent with the man simply falling forward. A body falling forward would not have bruising to the extent described. It would have taken much more violence to cause the bruises. Given their bluish-green colour, the bruises must have been received from one to two days before death. He referenced Tidy as his medical authority. (Some of Dr. Mearns's testimony was difficult to follow as he qualified statements in several ways.)

In response to Osler, Mearns declared that some authors say that bruises received in life may not appear until after death, although the point was disputed. He also said it was impossible to tell whether a wound received less than three hours before death was received before or after death. Inflammation usually sets in twelve to twenty-four hours after the injury occurs.

Justice MacMahon asked for clarification. Supposing, he said, the deceased lived twenty-four hours after the blow was inflicted, would it have appeared at the autopsy that inflammation had set in? "Not necessarily," was the reply.

Dr. Richardson testified that in the case of a healthy young man, rigor mortis would set in from four to eight to ten hours after death. He thought, while not impossible, it was improbable that the bruises were caused by falling forward. If the bruises were bluish-green then they would have been caused at least twenty-four hours before death. On cross, Richardson replied to Osler, saying that there are bruises that are difficult to tell whether caused before or after death.

Justice MacMahon asked what the appearance of the body would have been forty-eight hours after death if the deceased had fallen forward, bruising himself. Richardson replied that the bruises would have retained their original appearance, the effusion of blood would be apparent, and the colour darkish purple.

Blackstock asked the significance of the testimony of one of the surgeons who said one bruise was bronze in colour. The witness replied that that would indicate more time had elapsed than if it were bluish-green.

That concluded the defence's medical testimony. The defence had attempted to have its medical men show that the deceased had not fallen immediately after being shot. Their testimony at least had muddied the waters on that point. It suggested that Benwell had had an altercation or accident that caused the bruising well before his death. The significance of the rigor mortis testimony is unclear, but the point may have been simply to demonstrate that the expert knowledge of the Crown's medical men was limited.

The defence then moved on to other witnesses.[7] Norman McQueen testified that he had seen the prisoner in Woodstock in February. He fixed the date by the fact that for three weeks he had been sick, but he wanted to go to a ball on 18 February. He went to the doctor the day before and that is when he had seen Birchall in Woodstock. He nodded to him in the street.

In reply to Osler, McQueen said he had known Birchall well the year before. Osler then implied that it was odd McQueen only nodded to a friend he hadn't seen in a year. He asked the witness what the man had been wearing. The witness said knickerbockers with bows, as he had usually done the year before. Osler asked whether he really had seen knickerbockers rather than the man, but the witness insisted it was Birchall he had seen. In reply to Blackstock, the witness said he didn't like Birchall because he had called him a name, which explained why he had merely nodded to him.

S.G. McKay, one of the lawyers assisting the defence, was called to the stand about two matters. First, he testified about having visited Alfred Hayward, the miller, in August with three other men. Of the four, three had worn capes.

Hayward, who had not heard McKay's testimony, appeared on the stand again and was asked about the visit of the four men in August. He said he remembered the visit, but when asked about the clothing he could not remember it. He remembered nothing about capes. Blackstock commented that it was strange he could remember a cape from February but not three from much more recently.

Second, McKay testified about being at George McDonald's with Det. Bluett when McDonald had said that the gunshots he heard came three or four minutes apart, and he had pointed to a telegraph pole about forty feet away and said he had been that close to where the shots were fired when he heard them. That is where the defence left matters.

Justice MacMahon addressed the jury, saying all the evidence was now in. The court was not moving directly to the barristers' addresses because he was giving them time to prepare them. The court could not meet until Monday because of the Sabbath. He regretted keeping the jury over until Monday, but it had to be so. He asked the jurors not to form a firm opinion about guilt until they had heard the addresses and his own charge to them. There would be time enough for reflection once all was complete.

Press opinion judged the defence had been weak and that Birchall's chances of getting off were poor. The defence's main objective was a verdict of not guilty, but failing that, it hoped that the jury would recommend mercy and the judge would write a report to Ottawa authorities that dealt favourably with the prisoner.

An Anxious Wait

Everyone waited anxiously for the trial to resume on the Monday. People involved in the trial and reporting it spent Sunday in various ways. Justice MacMahon and his wife took the opportunity Sunday afternoon to go see the swamp and the area around Eastwood.[8]

That same afternoon, a number of reporters went out to the swamp to resolve in their own minds whether there really was a trail leading from near where the body was found, a point of dispute among the witnesses. By this point, however, the site where the body had been found had been stripped of all saplings by relic hunters. Possibly no obvious trail had been there in February, but after visits by countless curious visitors there was a well-worn path leading from the site into the swamp. That Sunday, the trail was crowded with people collecting cedar and tamarack branches as souvenirs. About a quarter of an hour walk along the trail was Mud Lake, sometimes known as "Spruce Lake." The spring-fed pond was obviously shallow in places, although local knowledge asserted that it was bottomless in parts, too. It stood in the middle of the woods and all around its shores grew pitcher plants, those strange plants that feed on insects.[9]

Even Birchall appeared anxious, and was uncharacteristically pensive throughout the day. He spent much of it talking with the turnkey, Forbes, about whether there was a chance of a disagreement among the jurors. It was reported that he had given up hope of a verdict of not guilty, but, depending on the judge's charge, he had hope that it would be a hung jury. A rumour was circulating that Birchall had prepared a long statement to deliver in court in the event of a guilty verdict. On the Sunday morning a Baptist pastor had held a service in the jail, which Birchall did not attend. Still, he couldn't help but hear the carefully selected hymn: "Oh! What will the answer be?"[10]

Sunday allowed time to ponder the financial implications of the trial. Some people guessed that it had cost the public $10,000, but the *Sentinel-Review* believed it probably cost more in the range of $7,000 to $8,000. People wondered how Birchall had afforded his lawyers. Some held to the belief that he was part of a wide conspiracy and that his co-conspirators had put up the cash. The *Sentinel-Review* dismissed that idea, saying that no doubt Mr. David Stevenson, Birchall's wealthy father-in-law, out of concern for his daughter, was bankrolling the defence.[11] The *News* reported that Woodstock merchants were eagerly awaiting the end of the trial because business had ground to a stop. However, the hotels were doing a booming business and had jacked up their rates by one third.[12]

The jury was closely guarded throughout the interval and mostly confined to their space in the Royal Hotel. When members of the public got too close to the jurors on their morning march, guards shooed them away. Authorities refused to allow a barber to shave the jurors even though he had agreed to sign a document swearing he would not speak to them.[13]

On the Monday morning, several constables at the courthouse had to rough-handle determined individuals who blocked the entry of officials and the jury. For a time, it looked as if a stampede of men and women would break down the doors. "The gallantry of the men was down to zero," declared the *Sentinel-Review*. "They crowded and hustled the women with scarce courtesy. The men as a rule made it clear they believed in equal rights, nothing more."[14]

Birchall appeared as well-groomed as ever, but more serious. Florence Birchall and her sister chose to attend the court that day. As they took their seats, all eyes were on the prisoner's wife.[15]

Justice MacMahon opened the proceedings on time at ten o'clock. It turned out that before Blackstock could begin his much-anticipated address, there were a few witnesses still to testify.[16]

Blackstock had called James Costin, but he had arrived to give his evidence on Saturday just as the court adjourned. Blackstock got the judge's permission to enter the witness's sworn statement. Costin did not appear in court even though Canadian law required witnesses to do so.[17] Costin said he was a farmer living a half mile from Princeton. On Tuesday, 18 February, a well-dressed stranger came to his door asking to stay the night. He said he was from Brantford and going to Woodstock. The witness refused him, saying he was just leaving for a tea meeting in Princeton. The man grew angry and asked if there were woods nearby. The witness thought that that the man was slightly intoxicated. When later Costin looked at the body from the swamp, he knew it wasn't the man he had seen, but had thought that perhaps he had seen the killer. Because Costin was not present in the courtroom, the Crown had no opportunity to cross-examine him. MacMahon's willingness to permit the testimony without the possibility of cross-examination is unusual. Presumably he wanted to avoid criticism that he had dealt unfairly with the defence.

George W. Patterson testified that he had been the shorthand reporter at the inquest. He had not taken down the questions and answers, but rather had written down the story of each witness in narrative form. Witnesses at the inquest signed the shorthand notes. Few, if any, could have read them.

The register of the Metropolitan Hotel, New York, was entered into evidence, and Birchall's signature was declared to be in his hand.

Blackstock's Address

At last, the business of the day got fully under way when Blackstock rose to address the jury.[18] The defence attorney reminded the jurors of their onerous responsibility, where a conviction meant the death penalty. He noted that a vast majority of the evidence might have been effectively challenged by the prisoner, but the law did not allow him to speak in his defence.

Murder trials, he said, were always a challenge, but this one presented particular ones. He spoke at length about the press's role in the case. Good work had been done by the reporters. "In his opinion," he said with a dig at Det. Murray, "all the honest detective work had been done by the newspapers." He said he opposed circumscribing the liberties of the press. Yet he feared that a verdict of guilty would not be because of the court evidence but because "the drag net of the newspaper had been abroad airing insinuations and innuendos." The judge had correctly instructed the jury to pay no attention to what they had heard outside the courtroom, but in this case "it was impossible to ignore what the press had been saying. The human mind is not so constituted." He only asked the jury "to do their best to set aside false impressions received early in the case."

"I find my mind filled with dismay and terror," declared Blackstock, "because I stand charged with the responsibility of defending a man pilloried for a crime of which he is innocent." He emphasized that the prisoner was not on trial for dishonest dealings with Benwell, in the course of which he had certainly told untruths. Rather, as the judge would no doubt remind the jury, it was a question of his guilt on the charge of murder, for which he had been indicted.

Blackstock spoke of the many inconsistencies in the evidence. It was not his belief that the witnesses had lied, rather that the human memory is unreliable. But he urged the jury not to dwell on these inconsistencies. Instead, he wanted them to focus on two points. "Was the prisoner at Eastwood? Even supposing he was at Eastwood, what then?"

Blackstock sought to discredit the Crown's evidence that put Birchall and Benwell aboard the train to Eastwood. He observed that while the Crown had shown that two tickets were purchased, it had failed to show that they had been used. Det. Murray had been unable to come up with them. The conductor who remembered a man saying he was Smith with a brother at Niagara sees so many passengers every day and can't keep track of every conversation. Why would Birchall say his name was Smith?

Witnesses Poole, Hay, and Duffy, without meaning to lie, wanted a conviction and testified so as to assist in reaching that objective. There were problems with their evidence. Conductor Poole said one man was taller than the other, but Birchall and Benwell were actually the same height. In earlier testimony Poole said one was fair, but there was no such man. Earlier, he said one man wore a suit of a light colour but now, having seen the waterproof, says it was worn by the light-complexioned man. Formerly he saw a case handed at the baggage room and checked there, but now that the Crown has failed to trace a baggage check, his testimony is that there was no check. "This is how things grow up on people," declared Blackstock. "They talk and talk and talk until finally they come to believe what they are talking about."

As for Miss Lockhart and Miss Choate, he couldn't help but criticize women who would swear away the life of a fellow human being. Miss Lockhart swore events were brought to her recollection by Mr. Virtue's evidence printed in the *Sentinel-Review* of 28 February, but she had been compelled to admit there was no such statement in it. Miss Choate said it was Miss Lockhart's evidence in the newspapers that brought the matter to her attention, whereas at the time Miss Lockhart hadn't given her evidence. If the witnesses were mistaken on matters that could be proved, what of the rest of their evidence? Blackstock added rhetorically: "The meanness of human nature; the greatness of human vanity."

Turning to the evidence about Eastwood Station, Blackstock said that Miss Smith had testified that she asked the man at the station whether he was Dudley or Somerset. He asked whether the jurors could believe that if the prisoner was the man she saw, she would not have known him from Dudley. She knew they didn't resemble each other. Ida Cromwell previously had sworn she knew nothing about the man's coat, but at trial she said it was navy-blue and short. She also said before that the man was light-complexioned, which could not be Birchall. Miss Swayzie formerly said the man was medium-tall, but in fact the prisoner was short.

Blackstock next pilloried Det. Murray for the way he had conducted the identifications of Birchall in the jail. The barrister opined that Murray should have used an outsider to conduct them, but instead he himself had "snuck off" to the jail with the witnesses. He took them past twenty-five to thirty men in prison clothes and then showed them a man isolated from the rest and not wearing prison clothing. The witnesses knew that Birchall would not be wearing prison clothing. The detective asked the man to turn his way. Why, Blackstock declared, "the identification was done about as well as some of those human hell hounds can do and just as well as the man Murray knows." Blackstock then told the jurors that he could show them dozens of law books telling them to beware of the evidence of detectives.

James Hayward's testimony also changed between the inquest and the trial regarding the clothing, the cigar, and the man he had seen in the crowd at the races. Blackstock declared: "If that man had soon been arrested, the whole blessed crowd would have gone like a swarm of bees into the witness box to swear they had seen him at Eastwood on the 17th!"

Blackstock then referred to the testimony of Swartz, the undertaker, who had such an extraordinary imagination. He called attention to it only to show that an honest man might be mistaken. The Crown had not dared to bring in some of the witnesses who had appeared at the inquest before Birchall was arrested because they had said all kinds of things to which the Crown did not want to draw attention.

Blackwood asked the jury to suppose that Birchall *was* at Eastwood. There was no harm in being there. Birchall told Pelly he was in Niagara Falls rather than at Woodstock because that is where he had said the farm was that the men were going to see.

Blackstock attacked the testimony of Alfred Hayward, whom he called "an old man" and a "pitiable spectacle." (This characterization appears unduly harsh today, but at a time when the manly ideal featured strength and vigour, it gave less offence.) At the inquest Hayward said only that he saw two men pass by and told his wife they were Englishmen going to Mr. Patterson's, but at the trial he said he had recognized one of the men as Birchall from a distance of 135 feet and that he had worn a cape.

Witness John Crosby said it was the fair-complexioned man who wore the cape, but neither Birchall nor Benwell was fair. Crosby said one of them was carrying a parcel. What became of it? Where was it?

The Crown wanted the jury to believe that witnesses Millman and McQueen were mistaken when they said they saw Birchall in Woodstock. But were they? How were we to tell which witnesses were mistaken?

Blackstock spelled out all the inconsistencies in the testimony of Crosby, Edmiston, Oldham, Ferguson, and Fallon, all of whom said they saw two men walking near the swamp, as well as the witnesses who said they heard shots. He also pointed out witnesses' contradictions regarding the existence of the path.

Blackstock said that the Crown's theory was that Benwell was killed on Monday, which was proven by the ice found in his sleeve, which had to have come from Monday night's rain, but it could have come from the rain storm on Wednesday.

How could it be that if the two men were together at the swamp, Birchall's boots were muddy, as testified to by Crown witness after Crown witness, when Benwell's were not?

The post-mortem showed that Benwell's stomach contained only a few split peas. How could it be that two Englishmen with money in their pockets passed three restaurants and never had breakfast?

Blackstock asked the jury to ponder many questions. Why did Birchall select a spot for the murder that could be seen from Rabb's house? How did he convey the body to where it was found without getting any blood on his clothes? Where was the evidence of a scuffle? Why not kill at night or at Niagara Falls with its many convenient places? Why talk to every person he met and court recognition at Eastwood? Given that Birchall knew there were police at his boarding house before his arrest, why didn't he dispose of the gold pencil and keys?

Blackstock then asked the jury to consider Birchall's letter to Col. Benwell. Given there was no possibility of the prisoner getting the £500 unless Fred Benwell wrote to his father, what use to Birchall was killing Fred Benwell?

The defence attorney reminded the jury that if they had a reasonable doubt as to the prisoner's guilt, then they must give him that benefit. He told them they should not deceive themselves – if the verdict be guilty, there would not be a pardon. It was up to them to decide whether the prisoner should go to the gallows or be handed back to his wife, "who with a womanly grace and womanly dignity such as been rarely exhibited, has hung like a beautiful garland about his neck during these times of trial." Finally, he asked the jurors to think what they would say to her after he was hanged and the actual murderer surfaced, as he surely would.

The Crown's Reply

Osler rose to give his reply shortly after 3:30 p.m. He began by saying that although the Crown sought no man's life, it had an obligation to the community to find out who committed this crime. It was the jury's duty to find a verdict according to the evidence presented. Should it turn out subsequently that the testimony was incorrect, it was not upon the jury but upon the witnesses that the responsibility rested. He pointed out that convictions must be possible where there is only circumstantial evidence. "The educated criminal, the clever criminal, the man who takes advantage of his condition to commit the crime would otherwise escape unless caught red-handed in the act."

As for the motive for this murder, Osler referred to Birchall's first letter to Col. Benwell dated 28 December 1889 where it spoke of engaging a partner in the business of which he was the principal. It was a business that did not exist. How then did he plan to get the £500 investment? In a later letter, Birchall prepared the mind of Col. Benwell for the fact that *he*, not young Benwell, would be the corresponding member of the firm. "What was the object of that scheme, what termination could it have except the Blenheim Swamp?" The situation with Pelly differed insofar as Birchall had already got £170 from him, all that he was to get.

Osler then referred to the letter Birchall posted to Col. Benwell two or three days after the death. The man who wrote that letter knew there was no risk that a subsequent letter would be sent from young Benwell saying the farm was a fraud. "The word you read between the lines is MURDER," declared Osler. He continued, saying the prisoner maintained Benwell was going west to look for farms. Would a young stranger wander a country he did not know? No. He would have cabled his father to say the representations were false. But there was no trace of such a cable, or a letter, nor any trace of him at all since that fateful 17 February.

Osler challenged Blackstock's argument that Birchall would not have access to money the Colonel sent if young Benwell were dead, saying that the money was to go to the firm and that Birchall had full access to the account as a partner.

The defence had presented no evidence to show what the prisoner was doing the afternoon and early evening of 17 February. With whom did he dine? In all of Niagara country, the defence could not find a man to come forward and say, "I saw him." The prisoner's whereabouts that day were no mystery, however. Twenty witnesses for the Crown explained where he was, and thirteen positively identified him.

Osler argued that the defence had focused on petty discrepancies in the witnesses' statements. These were only natural to find when parties gave different stories of events. One of the best tests of truthfulness is that the witnesses differ in details but agree in the main. There was a thread of truth running through it all that fit with the acknowledged fraud with the object of murder in view.

Osler reminded the jury that the Crown had produced the railway clerk's vouchers for the sale of the two tickets to Eastwood. The tickets themselves could not be produced because the company never kept them for long. When the prisoner returned to Niagara, he told Pelly that Benwell had been sulky and would not eat. The post-mortem showed he did not eat anything. The evidence of Birchall's boots showed that he did not confine his journey to sidewalks. The telegram "Bastell" sent from George Phemister's office at 7:44 showed the prisoner must have come into Niagara on the train that arrived at 7:24. Why did Birchall sign it "Bastell"? He wanted to conceal his identity in case of inquiries about who had arrived and sent a telegram. But he knew that Pelly, expecting a telegram only from him, would assume "Bastell" was just a miscopy.

Osler next turned to the identifications. He said that if any one of them was believed, then it covered the whole journey. Blackstock, who was especially hard on Alfred Hayward, rejected his testimony because he could not pick out a nondescript face from the gallery rendered indistinct by a cross-light. Could the jurors, he asked, reject the oaths of Miss Smith and Miss Choate? Why should they be disbelieved? Did Miss Smith quail under the vigorous attack of the defence attorney? Her testimony indicated that she knew the man she saw, but that she forgot the names. Osler called it "just one of the little things by which it could be told the witness is telling the truth." And then there were the identifications of Duffy the newsagent who sat beside Birchall on the train, and of the telegraph operator Phemister who sent the Bastell telegram.

Osler insisted that there was no evidence to contradict the hunters who heard two shots fired close together. Rabb did hear shots, but the men came out of the swamp so quickly there was no time for cutting the clothes. The crime was conducted in daylight because only then could the labels be cut from the clothing. The man was not known locally, and the only means of identifying him would have been by his name sewn into his clothing. It was imperative that Birchall, the only man in Ontario who knew Benwell, remove the names.

"Amid a deathlike silence," said the reporter from the *Spectator*, Osler recited how the body looked when found. The glasses were found underneath the head and the cigar stub and holder nearby. The defence argued that the man was shot elsewhere and the body moved to where it was found, but the evidence of the glasses and cigar showed otherwise. The man was coaxed into the swamp, shot twice in the back of the head, and fell. The bruises came from the fall. The defence claimed that the wounds were inflicted twenty-four hours before death. If Benwell was attacked from the front, why was he not shot from the front? "No, gentlemen," exclaimed Osler, "the man who murdered poor Benwell gave him no alarm, but shot him down in cold blood without warning."

Osler called the Baker–Caldwell phase of the defence's case "really pitiable." "Fancy the men befuddled with liquor skilfully cutting off the marks on the clothing!"

The record written by nature showed the day when the murder took place. First came the rain, which washed away the blood. Then came the frost that froze the rainwater in the sleeve. The rain on the Wednesday was not enough even to register on the measuring instrument at the college in Woodstock. The state of the collar showed that it had been subjected to a cold rain. If it had been a warm rain the starch would have been washed out. But when the collar thawed, it was still stiff with starch.

A point had been made that the prisoner's boots were muddy but not those of the deceased. But remember Crosby's evidence, said Osler. The roads were frozen in the morning and only got muddy in the afternoon when there was a thaw.

All the business about the luggage and telegrams was evidence of Birchall's desire to conceal what he had done. It was all absurd. If Benwell had really been in western Ontario he could only have got to New York by going through Buffalo, where he could have picked up his luggage himself. Yet Birchall claimed that Benwell had instructed him to send the luggage through to New York. The letter telling him to do so had never been found. The keys and luggage checks he had taken when he emptied the deceased's pockets.

Birchall objected to dealing with Det. Murray because he preferred a county constable to handle the case. The hatred of the detective was reflected in the harsh words of the counsel for the defence, which were totally unwarranted. They were said in anger because Murray had done the work of the Crown so well.

The fact that when arrested the prisoner had the dead man's gold pencil was evidence of his guilt.

The evidence of Millman and McQueen about seeing Birchall in Woodstock was simply a case of mistaken identity. A passing glance on the street was not like a meeting on the train or in the country.

In concluding, Osler came back to his main point. The defence had offered no statement or explanation regarding where the prisoner was on 17 February. From the day of his arrest Birchall had been silent about it. The defence was right in saying there was more at stake than the prisoner's life. There was the safety of the whole community. His closing remark: "Gentlemen, I leave the case to you."

Justice MacMahon's Charge

The judge began his charge by saying that in this "great and important case" neither he nor the jury had anything to do with the punishment.[19] (He was alluding to the fact that in a murder trial a guilty verdict came with a mandatory punishment of hanging.) He explained at some length the difference between direct and circumstantial evidence and pointed out that in this case there was only circumstantial evidence. Such evidence was in fact the more reliable, he maintained. A witness offering direct evidence might lie, but when several witnesses pointed to a pattern of behaviour it would be convincing.

The first matter for the jury to consider was the object of Birchall and Benwell leaving Niagara together on 17 February. Pelly's evidence showed that they left early, at 6 a.m., and that they had said they were going to look at a farm near Niagara. In fact, there was no farm. What then was really the objective?

The Crown had presented evidence to show that the two men had gone that day to Eastwood and then to the swamp. It is known that two tickets were sold to Eastwood and that Poole collected them. The conductor thought he saw two men get off at Eastwood. Miss Lockhart said there were two men on the train who got off at Eastwood and that one of them was the prisoner. Miss Choate also recognized the prisoner on the train that morning. Alfred Hayward gave a description of two men passing his yard. If the jury believed this evidence, it was powerful circumstantial evidence.

The defence attempted to break the force of Hayward's evidence, pointing out that he could not remember much about Lawyer McKay calling on him, nor could he recognize Const. Midgley in the gallery. Crosby's evidence went to show that one of the men had a parcel under his arm. The jury would have to take this point into consideration.

Three witnesses gave a description of the tracks in the field after these men had passed near the swamp. It was for the jury to decide whether they were made by the men seen on the train. Miss Fallon was positive that she had seen two men walking near the swamp, one with a short coat and one with a coat with a cape. If the jury believed her evidence, then they were the same men. McGuire early in the morning passed the spot where the body was found, and there were not tracks then.

The judge referred to the three men who heard shots between two and three o'clock, and to the statements made by Hersee and others about the prisoner's knowledge of the swamp. Then there was the evidence about Baker and Caldwell going through that part of the country that week.

As for the evidence of Miss Smith, who was the only one who spoke with the man at the Eastwood Station, she said she spoke with Birchall. It was powerful evidence, if believed. Was her statement pure fabrication? Miss Cromwell also said she saw Birchall at Eastwood. Altogether five persons saw him there. The jury would have to decide whether they told the truth, or had together concocted a story, or were mistaken in the identification of Birchall.

The evidence of newsagent Duffy and telegrapher Phemister was also to be considered. "If you believe these witnesses," said the judge, "then the case against the prisoner presents very serious aspects."

As for the letter to Col. Benwell, if £500 had been sent to the firm, Birchall would have had access to it. Justice MacMahon said he was bound to tell them this as a matter of law. In the letter, the prisoner spoke of the purchase of another property etc. and that the prisoner was writing by the next mail. All was deception, so the prisoner must have known that young Benwell would never write such a letter to his father.

The judge then spoke of the bank account opened in Niagara Falls, New York, and the money deposited. The question suggested itself: was this the money the deceased had?

Witnesses agreed that the body had been lifted to the brush pile.

The prisoner had made statements to Watson, Hull, and Cox, none of which agreed in detail. Birchall was telling these stories to show how he came to have the baggage checks. The variations showed in the judge's mind that the prisoner had come into possession of them by some improper means. Justice MacMahon said that if the jury was satisfied that Birchall had sent a telegram at Buffalo to himself at Niagara, then it was of the gravest moment to the prisoner.

When it became known that the cigar case was found, the judge found the prisoner's conduct to have been very strong presumptive evidence of guilt.

According to the reporter for the *News*, the judge had tears in his eyes when he reminded them of the solemn duty of the jury to pass judgment on the murder.[20] Justice MacMahon's charge certainly favoured the prosecution and thus made clear his own opinion of the evidence. In the present day, a jury charge that leans too far in one direction may result in a successful appeal; in the nineteenth century, by contrast, jury charges were not subject to appellate review. Thus, judges had much latitude in composing their charges.[21]

At the end of his charge, MacMahon told the jurors that when circumstantial evidence is strong, they can be comfortable basing their verdict on it. The trial transcript containing MacMahon's charge makes no mention of "the rule in *Hodge's Case*": that the evidence must not only be consistent with the guilt of the accused, but also must be inconsistent with any other rational inference.[22] The rule had been established by Baron Alderson in an 1838 murder case in Liverpool, England, and thereafter it became the usual practice of judges to so instruct juries in England and Canada.[23] Oddly, in the Birchall case, neither the defence nor public commentators brought attention to the absence of a reference to the rule in *Hodge's Case*.

The Verdict

Justice MacMahon concluded his address at 9:50 p.m. and then called for a recess of an hour and a half. The jury promptly retired for their deliberations. It was reported that before the prisoner was removed from the courtroom, he spoke to Det. Murray, saying he was sorry for what his counsel had said about him because he had always treated him with the greatest consideration.[24]

The jurors were out of the courtroom for nearly an hour and a half. They had returned by the time Justice MacMahon resumed his seat on the bench at 11:37. Soon the crowd poured back into the courtroom, packing it completely. The barristers resumed their seats, and the prisoner was brought to the dock. In the estimation of the reporter from the *News*, several of the jurors wore self-satisfied grins. One of them whispered the verdict to a reporter, and instantly England was cabled with the result even before the verdict was announced in court.[25] The newsmen were not just on top of the story, but running ahead of it.

In response to the court clerk's question whether the jurors had come to a decision, foreman George Christopher rose and said in low voice. "Yes, we have. We find the prisoner Birchall guilty." According to the *Empire*, "a shudder passed over the entire audience." Birchall seemed to choke, but then he clenched his teeth "and recovered himself in a remarkably short space of time."[26]

Hellmuth then rose and explained to the court that his colleague Mr. Blackstock could not be present because of illness. Hellmuth asked that the jurors be polled, which showed they were unanimous. He then asked that the case be reserved until the Mellersh letters could be considered. In law, there was no right of appeal against murder convictions or sentences of death, it being widely believed that appeals would result in unnecessary cost and delay and that they would undermine the deterrent effect of convictions.[27] However, a case could be reserved if the judge believed that a difficult point of law had been raised by the case. If so, a panel of judges would consider the point.[28] Justice MacMahon said he did not see a reserve case.

The judge instructed the prisoner to rise and then asked whether he had anything to say. [29] Birchall replied in a clear, strong voice: "Simply that I am not guilty of the crime, my lord."

Before passing the death sentence, Justice MacMahon told Birchall that he had been defended with "great ability" and that all the defence's points had been fully brought to the attention of the jury. He said he agreed with the jury's verdict. He then admonished Birchall for failing in his duty to look after the young man in his charge and instead conspiring to take his life for the £500 expected from England. He continued, nearly choking:

> It is a melancholy circumstance to think that a young man with your education and opportunities should have followed the course you did, and dip your hand in the blood of your fellowman. It is melancholy to think that with your honourable connections, and other connections that you have formed, you should have brought disgrace upon your respected relatives. I can hold out no hope of commutation of your sentence. My advice to you is to use every hour in supplicating the throne of grace for the forgiveness of your sins.

The judge then passed the death sentence and declared that the hanging would take place at the jail in Woodstock on Friday, 14 November.

Upon hearing the sentencing, John Entwhistle, Birchall's guard, lowered his head and wept. "Great sobs shook his strong frame," reported the *News*, "and tears flowed freely." One of Birchall's lawyers asked him whether he was satisfied with their efforts on his behalf, and as he shook hands, he replied, "Yes, sir, quite satisfied." Several other men came up and shook his hand.

10
Aftermath of the Trial

News of the verdict in the Birchall trial sped everywhere thanks to telegraphers. "It is not exaggeration," observed Montreal's *Gazette*, "to say that millions of people were watching for the end of the murder trial that ended last night."[1] A great many newspapers in Canada, Britain, and the United States reported on the verdict and commented at least briefly. Some newspapers published editorials that were lengthy and thoughtful. Many editors who had avoided commenting on ongoing legal proceedings at last felt ready to express themselves freely on the quality of the trial and its verdict.

Assessing the Trial

Editorial writers were unanimous in endorsing what Woodstock's *Evening Standard* called "a righteous verdict." London's *Daily News* declared unequivocally, "The jury only did their duty in convicting a cruel and hardened villain of the very foulest of crimes." Edinburgh's *Scotsman* opined, "Bluster and brag have not blinded the Woodstock jury to the baseness and brutality of the prisoner John Reginald Birchall." The press found the circumstantial evidence presented by the Crown utterly persuasive. In its long editorial, *The Times* expressed what everyone appeared to think: "Although the evidence against the prisoner is wholly circumstantial and he persists in protesting his innocence, no reasonable mind can doubt the juror's decision is just." In the words of Toronto's *News*, "Although there was no evidence he actually fired the shots, the circumstances connecting the prisoner with the shooting were so strong as to justify the jury inferring that his hand and no other committed the crime."[2]

Only one letter to the editor has surfaced objecting to the verdict. Sent from the small town of Kingsville, Ont., and appearing in the *Sentinel-Review*, it was from "Justice." (Pseudonyms like this one were often used in letters to the editor in nineteenth-century Canada.) The writer accused the Crown and especially Det. Murray of resorting to "every artifice in order to prejudice the entire world against Birchall." The writer also charged that the jury had made up their minds before hearing the evidence and that some of the jurors became biased once Blackstock treated Det. Murray and a female witness harshly. "Justice" hoped that Birchall would escape from jail rather than hang. Finally, the writer objected to capital punishment, concluding: "Shame upon the intelligence of our fair Dominion that it perpetuates that relic of barbarism – the gallows." The *Sentinel-Review* observed that quite a few people shared some or all of these sentiments, but it offered no specific evidence in support of that observation.[3]

It is likely that editors received other similar letters that they chose not to publish. The *Mail* admitted that it had received a great many letters supportive of Birchall and arguing that justice had committed an error, but that the editor decided not to print them. Possibly the *Mail* feared arousing widespread opposition to the verdict and thus undermining public faith in the justice system.[4]

A number of newspapers assessed the performances of the lawyers and the judge, particularly with regard to their addresses on the last day of the trial. Osler was lauded for his reply to the defence both for what he said and for how he said it. "Osler's address is the talk of the town," said the *Spectator*. "He was awfully forcible in his presentation of the case. It is known he was moved by the sense of duty." The special correspondent for the *Philadelphia Inquirer* who witnessed the performance said that at the end of Osler's speech the feeling against Birchall "was more bitter than at any time since his arrest."[5]

Blackstock garnered less enthusiastic reviews for his address, but commentators agreed that, given the evidence, he had the more difficult challenge. "It is admitted that Blackstock made the best possible of a desperate case," conceded the *Spectator*. "Counsel for the defence," observed the *The Times*, "succeeded in pointing out several small discrepancies in the evidence of the Crown witnesses, but although done with considerable ingenuity, they were not in fact wider or more numerous than are usually found in descriptions given by different truthful persons of the same event." There was a consensus that Blackstock's inability to present alibi evidence for Birchall on 17 February had been a decisive factor in the failure of his case. The *Globe* found fault with Blackstock's decision to call as a witness McQueen, who testified that he had seen Birchall in Woodstock on the afternoon of 17 February. The paper judged it impossible that if Birchall spent that afternoon in Woodstock, no one else noticed him "sporting his red stockings and all the rest of his caddish notions of aristocratic dress." In the end, the testimony "simply emphasized the poverty and despair of the defence."[6]

Comparatively little was said about Justice MacMahon's charge to the jury, although there was agreement that Birchall had had a fair trial. The *Spectator* reported that "Judge MacMahon's charge was plain and clear, but did not attract special attention on the part of those who heard it." The *World* was warmer, declaring that the "impartial summing up of the Judge left nothing to be desired." In a letter to the editor of the *Sentinel-Review*, E. Topping referred admiringly to the "tender emotion of Judge MacMahon when passing sentence."[7]

Most newspapers remarked on the enormous interest in the trial, and a few offered explanations for why that was so. The *Globe* argued that it had much to do with the way family members of both the accused and the victim had entered the narrative. The pathetic plight of Florence Birchall had gained the public's sympathy, even though people realized that she must have known her husband was swindling Benwell and Pelly. "It was this portion of the story which led the public on both sides of the Atlantic to watch the proceedings with acute and painful interest," opined the *Globe*. "Fathers', sisters', brothers' hearts were bleeding."[8]

Atlanta's *Constitution*, in its long editorial on the verdict, maintained that the public's fascination with the case had to do with the murderer himself. "What surprised one most in the trial was the coolness of the prisoner. He never lost his composure," it observed. "But his indifference was not that of an innocent man; his idea was to brave his way to an acquittal." From the fascinating story, were Edgar Allan Poe still alive, he "could weave a thrilling romance." The *Philadelphia Inquirer* similarly drew attention to the personality of the murderer. "J. Reginald Birchall is an extraordinary man," it declared. "He is a study for the psychologists." The *New York Tribune* agreed. "The Benwell case is a curious psychological study," said the metropolitan paper. "It discloses abnormal depravity and constructive talent for conspiracy and crime, and in connection with these qualities a singular credulity and lack of personal discernment."[9]

Several newspapers maintained that it had been Birchall's propensity for tangling himself in his own lies that had resulted in his downfall. "Murderers usually display a weakness of some sort," commented the *Globe*. "Birchall's was his mania for fibbing where silence would have better served his purpose." The *New York Tribune* declared: "His lies were certain to find him out and to brand him as the only possible murderer." London's *Standard*, after recounting his lies and deceptions, concluded: "It was a scheme of which the stupidity almost equalled the wickedness."[10]

Birchall's demise was also attributed first to his greed that led to his attempt to con two men at once, and then to his miscalculation regarding Pelly, who became a key Crown witness. "It is evident [Birchall] counted upon the removal of the evidence of the crime," observed the *Chicago Tribune*. "But he failed to take Pelly into account ... Pelly's evidence laid bare the animus and all the steps leading up to the murder from the time they left England."[11]

Several newspapers assessed various aspects of the legal proceedings. The trial was held at a time when the law barring the accused from testifying was being debated, and some thought that Birchall might have benefited from the opportunity to testify at his trial. In his address to the jury, Blackstock had made that point. The *News* agreed, saying that had Birchall been able to testify, he might have "put a different complexion on the case."[12] The *Mail* disagreed, maintaining that there was no reason to believe that the inability of the accused to testify had led to any "gross injustices." Birchall's testimony would only have had heft if it were part of chain of evidence presenting an alibi; the other links were missing.[13] Not long after the trial, in 1893, the Canadian law was changed to make it possible for the accused to testify on his own behalf.[14] Defence lawyers, however, were often leery of the risks of putting their client on the stand.[15]

On another matter concerning the legal process, the *Sentinel-Review* drew attention to the frequent practice in Canadian trials of defence barristers badgering witnesses. It suggested that the legal profession consider whether the dignity of the profession and the interests of justice might be better promoted if the practice were abandoned.[16] It was a chivalrous response to the treatment of female witnesses.

The jury system drew several comments. The *Gazette* expressed appreciation for the fact that the verdict was unanimous and hoped that it would give support to those opposed to a proposed law reform that would eliminate the need for unanimity.[17] The *Scotsman* observed that the unanimous verdict had put to rest the rumour that Birchall's supporters had tampered with the jury.[18]

The press in general showed an interest in the quickness of the jury's decision. The jurors had retired for only an hour and a half and were out that long only because the judge had called a recess. Several newspapers reported that jurors afterwards told journalists they were ready much sooner. "A juryman says," reported the *Scotsman*, "that if the Judge had not adjourned the Court for an hour and a half, the verdict would have been returned in ten minutes." The *Spectator* reported a statement of Hamilton's chief of police, just returned from the trial: "I believe that the jury could have come to a verdict without leaving the box, but they retired as a matter of form."[19]

American journalists expressed surprise and appreciation for the efficiency of the Canadian trial and compared it favourably to practices in the United States. By the time of the verdict, a trial that had started in New York on the same day as the Birchall trial had still not succeeded in selecting a jury. (The contrasting rules about questioning prospective jurors explained the difference.) "You do these things well in Canada," said a newsman from a New York paper. On the other side of the line, "it would have taken three weeks to complete that trial, and would have been appealed and the sentence stood off as long as the money lasted." The *Philadelphia Inquirer* judged the Birchall verdict to have been "fully as satisfactory to the community as an American trial that would have taken probably six times as long and cost six times as much." It added: "We might profitably take a leaf from the Canadian practice in trying our great criminal trials."[20] Similar remarks were made in the *Buffalo Times* and *Buffalo News,* New York's *Evening Sun*, and Detroit's *Free Press*.[21]

Leading newspapers in England expressed the hope that lessons might be learned from the trial. Their preoccupation was with the vulnerability of young Englishmen of means. *The Times* hoped that fathers would in future take more trouble to evaluate persons proposing to set their sons up in faraway places. Birchall, who turned out to be a swindler and murderer, had impressed Englishmen because his manner and appearance were good and he "had the education of a gentleman and passed some time at the University." These were credentials good enough to make his young victims "easy prey to his designs." *The Times* expressed the hope that in future, "a little care and pains on the part of their seniors would in most cases suffice to preserve them from such dangers." The *Standard* opined: "The friends of young Englishmen can hardly be too cautious and precise in the inquiries they make before they entrust him to the care of specious agriculturalists in distant parts of the world." Manchester's *Weekly Times and Examiner* concluded its editorial by declaring: "What is perfectly clear is that young Englishmen of means who decide to seek their fortune in Canada should act with the greatest caution."[22] In the hands of a designing English gentleman, Canada had proved to be a dangerous place. However proud imperialists might have seen the appeal of character-building sojourns in the Dominion, the risks could be enormous.

About Town

Besides printing editorials on the trial and verdict, newspapers treated their readers to coverage of the doings in Woodstock. Throughout the day after the verdict, the streets were crowded with people discussing, as the *World* put it, "the last act but one to the great drama." According to the reporter from the *Philadelphia Inquirer*, the verdict was discussed in subdued tones because of the gravity of the sentence. Oddly, there was also "sorrow for Birchall in a certain way, though no one would have the result otherwise."[23]

Grassroots Ontario had shown interest in what the verdict would be by waging bets on the result. It was reported that a particularly large number of people had wagered that there would be disagreement among the jurors. They, of course, were disappointed, financially speaking at least.[24]

Commentary focused on how Birchall was doing. It was widely reported that the day after the verdict he rose at the usual time and had a hearty breakfast. He spent the morning reading, writing letters to England, and talking with his guard and the jailer, both of whom felt acutely his situation. At noon he enjoyed a dinner from the Commercial Hotel of roast duck, potatoes, plum pudding, and pumpkin pie. He was moved to temporary quarters while his jail rooms were thoroughly cleaned. His cell still retained many images drawn from the press and artfully coloured by the prisoner, but his own drawings were gone because souvenir hunters had snapped them up.

Long afterwards, turnkey James Forbes recalled how the jail authorities had been "worried to death by reporters." Large numbers of journalists persisted in trying to interview Birchall. At one point, to keep reporters at bay, the jailers posted placards at the entrance warning "SMALLPOX," but hoteliers insisted that the placards come down because they were bad for business.[25]

Birchall was placed on suicide watch so as not to cheat the gallows. Authorities assigned County Const. John McGee, a man unknown to the prisoner, to stay with him in his cell, and detailed John Entwhistle to remain just outside his sleeping cell at night. Birchall's daily airing in the yard was cancelled. Ontario's new inspector of prisons, Robert Christie, visited the jail and expressed his satisfaction with the new arrangements.[26]

At one point in the day, far down the jail corridor could be heard Birchall's laughter as he watched the competition in the courtyard between turnkey John Forbes' Newfoundland dog Carlo and the "lunatic" prisoner as they scrambled for the meat scraps that Birchall threw from his cell window. The prisoner evidently thought them tastier than what he was routinely served. This widely reproduced report, which many readers today would find disturbing, was presented to amuse and to underscore the prisoner's remarkable nonchalance in the face of his grim sentence.[27]

That afternoon the prisoner was visited by a large group of reporters. For many, it was their last day in town, and they wanted to say goodbye. Birchall greeted them eagerly at the gate of his corridor. He had little to say about the trial. "Birchall takes everything connected with the trial and sentence as philosophically as he would a horse race or any sporting event," observed the *Telegram*. He said he thought the trial fair, but was a little disappointed by the evidence brought to his defence. He found the judge a little too severe in his comments. Then the conversation moved on to other topics.[28] Birchall and the newsmen discussed journalism, the prisoner flattering the reporters by saying how American journals were much brighter and more readable than English ones. They discussed Canadian politics. Birchall said he was in favour of Imperial Federation, then a hotly debated proposal that the Dominions, including Canada, send representatives to a central Imperial Parliament in London. Becoming more subdued when he mentioned his wife, Birchall said he thought she should be allowed one more visit and then promptly return to England.[29]

Newspapers made sure to include updates on Florence Birchall's fragile condition. Readers were obviously interested. Moreover, the contrast newspapers drew between her emotional response to the verdict and her husband's manly fortitude comfortingly confirmed the Victorian gentry's gender norms. The Anglican divine whom Florence had come to know locally, the Rev. Mr. J.C. Farthing, was designated to take the news of the verdict to her and comfort her. It was reported that when he told her the result, she had swooned. According to the *News*, her condition by the evening was "extremely pitiful, although a physician [had] been in constant attention."[30]

Coverage that day dealt with the main figures in the story. It was reported that at the Woodstock Jail, Charles Benwell remained solemn as he sorted through his brother's effects, selecting items to take back with him to England. Det. Murray passed through Toronto on his way to New York "to enjoy a well-earned vacation." Osler arrived back in Toronto and said he was "completely fagged out, not so much by the work in the case as by the anxiety." So exhausted was his counterpart Blackstock that he failed to show for the verdict and stayed on in the home of Judge Finkle at Woodstock, where a physician attended him. It was said he was "completely used up." Like Blackstock, Douglas Pelly had not been present in the court to hear the verdict. He had rushed to New York to catch the *Majestic* before she sailed for England. A reporter nabbed him along the way and learned that he was pleased with the verdict. Pelly added, however, that although his experience with Birchall had been "a terrible one," he could not help being sorry for him.[31]

The *Telegram* printed a story from England maintaining that at some time prior to his marriage, Birchall had been engaged to a Miss Sallie Reid of Crewe, Cheshire, and had postponed the wedding twice before walking out on her. She died of a broken heart and was buried in her wedding gown. The report contained a letter Birchall had addressed to a friend in which he wrote: "Death was the kindest thing that could happen. I was most certainly glad of the turn things took. I shall, I dare say, be blamed too much, but at the same time I am innocent."[32] In the wake of the verdict, this report could have done nothing to increase public sympathy for the man.

Enterprising local photographers, in conjunction with the *Sentinel-Review*, capitalized on the celebrity status of both the jury and those close to the story. The day after the verdict the photographers C.E. Perry and A.G. Westlake, the ones who had photographed Benwell's corpse,

10.1. The jury in the Birchall trial, photographed the day after the verdict by Woodstock photographers C.E. Perry and A.G. Westlake.
Source: Library and Archives Canada, item 3257825.

invited the jurymen to reassemble for a group shot. Later the photographers made a composite of portraits of the "celebrities of the trial." To boost circulation, both Woodstock newspapers offered copies of the photographs to people bringing in new subscriptions.[33]

After being convicted, Birchall was given the privilege of not wearing prison garb – no doubt a matter of importance to a clothes horse, which he was. A few days after the trial, Inspector of Prisons Robert Christie imposed new jail regulations for Birchall. Hotel meals were forbidden because of the risk of poisoning. Food was to be prepared in the jail under the supervision of the jailer. However, on the advice of the jail surgeon that the prisoner would suffer unduly if provided only with jail food, authorities opted to purchase better food prepared for him by a special cook, the tab picked up by the provincial Department of the Attorney General. Florence Birchall's visits were to be limited to no more than one a week, and the prisoner was not to be allowed a pocket knife or any other kind of knife. The inspector urged vigilance on the part of his jailer.

In an editorial, the *World* objected to the special treatment given Birchall in jail what with his special meals, civilian clothing, and carpeted cell. It suggested that other prisoners, some of them less responsible for their crimes, might well take exception to the favours shown him. The big-city newspaper blamed small-town county officials, whose lack of sophistication made them prey to "the cheap swagger of the semi-educated cut-throat."[34]

The press drew attention to the enormous use of the telegraph during the trial, which demonstrated both the unprecedented interest in the case and the efficiency of modern technology. Companies had sent out a staggering 300,000 words. A report from London, Eng., described the competition between the cable companies to get the news to England first. The jury's verdict was delivered to London at 3:05 a.m. local time by the Commercial Cable Co. and at 4:36 a.m. by Western Union. The date for Birchall's execution was received via Commercial Cable at 5:03 a.m. and via Anglo Cable by 5:15. British morning newspapers were able to include the results in the second editions that day.[35]

On the first Sunday after the trial concluded, clergy preached sermons on the topic. For instance, the *News* noted two delivered in Toronto. At Knox Presbyterian, the Rev. Dr. McMullen told the congregation that the trial had been creditable to British justice. The condemned man was unfit for this world, and unless he repented and sought the forgiveness of God, he would not be fit for heaven. At Central Methodist Church, the biblical text was "The years of the wicked shall be shortened." The minister spoke of the wickedness exposed during the trial, but also of the wonderful legal talent on display, and said he had never before understood the great importance of the press to human society.[36]

Further Evidence?

After the trial, people came forward saying they had information that was relevant to the case. It was widely reported that a few days after the trial, Miss Choate's harshly attacked evidence given at the trial was corroborated. John Cooper, a travelling salesman from Hamilton, came forward to say that on 17 February, he and two other salesmen had been aboard the same train as Miss Choate and the two Englishmen. He and his companions had noticed the gentlemen because of their English accents and English clothes. Cooper said that when the train reached Paris, the Englishman with the cape got off the train ahead of him and stood on the platform. The other man changed seats.[37] The *Sentinel-Review* observed that it sustained Miss Choate's view that he had gotten out for a stretch on the platform. The news would give her satisfaction that the public now knew that the evidence she gave, which was "so mercilessly criticized," was now supported by three new and creditable witnesses.[38]

Two letters gained press attention because they alleged to be able to divulge the whole story of the murder. B.B. Osler received a letter from "Mabel Morton" of Massachusetts, who maintained that she had been in Woodstock and shot Benwell. A report from North Adams, Mass., said the writer was likely Mrs. Marina Le Baron of Hancock, Mass., a respectable farmer's wife who had been talking a lot about the murder and was seen mailing a letter.[39] It was treated as a crank communication, and in any event, it arrived too late to have any effect on the proceedings. Likewise, a man by the name of Miller from western New York state gained much coverage in Buffalo; it was reported that he had confessed to the crime, which was part of a conspiracy to con well-to-do Englishmen who had come to America to take up farming.[40]

Florence Birchall

Florence Birchall is an illusive character in the drama. She avoided reporters, preferring to protect her privacy. When she was arrested and appeared in police court, she let her lawyer speak on her behalf. Almost every mention of her in the press is somewhat hazy; journalists, having so little to go on, ascribed to her the stereotypical behaviour of an upper-middle-class woman.

What little is known about the woman can be briefly summarized. Florence Stevenson, the daughter of David and Elizabeth Stevenson, was born in 1862 and grew up sheltered in an upper-middle-class London home. Her father's wealth and sterling reputation as an authority on railways set the family off as privileged. She had an older sister and

10.2. Florence Birchall (right) and her elder sister, Marion West-Jones, elegantly clad for a studio portrait.
Source: Woodstock Museum, image 1989.7.6.

a younger one. When she was twenty-six she met Reginald Birchall at a social event. Within three months of meeting, Reginald and Florence eloped for Canada, where she left little trace for reporters to pursue later. When she and Rex returned to England, they lived with her parents near the Crystal Palace. When Fred Benwell, a discerning young gentleman, visited the Stevenson family at their fine home, he found "everything as it should be."[41]

During the period of close public scrutiny after police laid charges against Florence and Rex, reporters learned little about her. Because of her silence, they could describe what she looked like when the Crown required her appearances in court, but they had little or no access to her feelings or to how she behaved in private. Journalists resorted to stereotypical portrayals of the English gentlewoman. The prevalent image of the sheltered lady was of "a creature of leisure, enclosed within a private circle of family and friends and completely supported by father or husband."[42] Indeed, Florence had spent most of her adult life as a single daughter in her parents' home. There, she would have been educated to "the accomplishments – needlework, a smattering of French, a bit of painting, and piano." Even once married, the ideal Victorian lady was expected to be "an acquiescent, passive, unintellectual creature, whose life revolved around social engagements, domestic management, and religion."[43]

Florence's lived experience did not fully conform to this ideal. Her short married life took unusual directions, first with travel to Canada and life in Woodstock, a small town lacking English women of her class, and then with the legal turmoil and all the press attention. People suspected that Florence, far from being a passive wife, had played a highly active role in hooking the two men her husband was swindling. She had gone so far as to lie to Douglas Pelly about her first-hand familiarity with the non-existent Niagara farm and house. Pelly wrote with shock that, contrary to the image of the ideal lady that Florence superficially projected, she drank, sometimes to the point of drunkenness.

In early October 1890, Florence Birchall broke her silence to reveal a little about herself to a reporter for the *News*.[44] She was probably prompted to do so by her concern that the press was reporting she had been her husband's collaborator in the swindle. Even on this occasion, however, Florence did not speak directly but rather through her married older sister, Marion West-Jones. In the interview, Marion reassured readers that what she was now saying had Florence's approval. The interview emphasized that Florence had long been deceived by her husband. According to the article, before the Birchalls left for Canada the first time, in 1888, Birchall told his betrothed's father that he had been called to America on urgent business and had to leave at once – hence the elopement. There had been no opportunity to provide reassurance about the suitability of the marriage because with such pressing business matters, there had been no time to present his high-ranked friends. Once in Woodstock, Florence believed Rex when he told her he had a lot of capital invested in farms. "Wherever he got it," Florence explained through her sister, "he always appeared to have plenty of money."

Back in England, where they stayed in the Stevenson home, Rex Birchall showed the family many photographs of farms he said he owned in Canada. He had explained that because his money was tied up in them and in the horse-buying business, he had been left short. (That explained the threats made by his creditors, which Florence's father was aware of.) Once back in Canada, however – so he told them – he would have his profits. While the couple was living in England, neither she nor her sister ever heard a word against Rex. He was good and affectionate. He kept regular hours. Each day he went out as if to a business. (At this point in the narrative, the *News* commented that the sisters had been brought up at home and were "innocent and guileless, not to say credulous.")

When Florence Birchall met Pelly and Benwell, she repeated her husband's stories about the farms "like a parrot." Sometimes she noticed discrepancies in what he told everyone, but he always had a plausible explanation. In her luggage when coming to Canada the second time, she brought decorative pieces for the farmhouse that she truly believed she would soon see.

Florence Birchall maintained that from his arrest onward, Rex Birchall always professed his innocence to her. He would tell her about a piece of evidence Det. Bluett had found, or a witness they had. It was mainly the letter he had written to Col. Benwell that convinced her of the swindle, but even with that, she believed Rex might be innocent of the murder. Because she was his wife, she vowed dutifully to remain in Woodstock and stand by him to the end.

The reporter for the *News* said that after interviewing Florence he spoke to Birchall about his wife. When the reporter mentioned the widespread public feeling that she had been aware of the swindle, Birchall became visibly upset. "'My wife,' he said with much warmth, 'is a perfectly honorable woman. She knew nothing of what was going on. I deceived her. I lied to her. She believed all I said.'" The prisoner hoped that the public would do her justice and believe she was absolutely without blame.

The *News* reporter commented that those who knew Florence Birchall best were also certain of her innocence. They said she was infatuated with Rex. Moreover, "he had a stronger will than she, and dominated her completely, besides lying to her with all the profuseness and clumsy art of which he is capable." Of course, there remains the possibility that she manipulated the journalist and the public by opting to project the Victorian stereotype of the vulnerable wife easily led by her husband.

Certainly, Florence Birchall puzzled journalists because of the apparent contradiction – the refined lady who had helped her husband carry out his dastardly schemes. She and her husband unsettled understandings of gentility. She had every appearance of the refined lady but seemed to have assisted her husband, a debonaire, Oxford-educated gentleman swindler convicted of murder.

A Psychologist's Report

Puzzlement with Rex Birchall and his personality continued while he awaited execution. Jailer Cameron told a reporter that "we know the mean villainous thing he did. Yet we like him. You can't help liking him. Your heart warms to him in spite of you. You feel like giving him a cigar or something before you've talked to him for a minute. I understand how he humbugged people. He is a charmer – a snake charmer."[45]

The public was keenly interested in insights into why Birchall had committed the fraud and murder. In response to this interest, on 3 October, the *Globe* and the *Sentinel-Review* published a long statement written by Dr. W.G. Bessey of Toronto, identified as "a specialist in character and an eminent psychologist."[46] He had talked to Birchall at the jail and studied "his peculiarities." In keeping with many late Victorian psychologists, Bessey had much to say about Birchall's appearance, from which he leapt to evaluative remarks about his character. "His eyes are full, quick and furtive," declared the doctor. His lower lip was thick and projecting, which indicated "selfishness and sensuality" – both shortcomings in the doctor's view. He was "vainglorious as any peacock." A few remarks could be taken as flattering his masculinity, such as: "his body is the greatest part of the man and would show well on horseback." But the gist of the report was that Birchall's villainy derived from his low-born ancestry.

In the doctor's view, Birchall was of plebeian origin, whatever the outward appearance of him and his parents, and it was this inherited fact that did most to account for his depravity and lack of morality. "He is not a monster in human form," argued the doctor, "but a moral deformity, the result of being not well but badly begotten and low-born – no matter who his parents were." Because Bessey thought that his inherited shortcomings went a long way to excusing his crimes, he didn't think he should be hanged. He called him "a moral idiot," attributing that deficiency to his "being the offspring of a line of ancestors who placed pride, vanity and self-gratification above everything, and only conformed outwardly to what is expected from persons of good society." Bessey, it seemed, found it impossible to believe that a swindler and murderer could come from gentle stock.

There were critical reactions to Bessey's analysis. The minister of Toronto's Central Methodist Church objected to Bessey's characterization of Birchall as "a moral idiot." He found the idea "contrary to the revelation of God, which contemplated the redemption of all men."

With understatement, a *Globe* report said that when Birchall read Bessey's statement, "naturally he did not consent in all that the doctor had said." Birchall maintained that, given Bessey had spent only a couple of minutes with him, he had not sufficient observations to make all his claims. A letter to the editor of the *Sentinel-Review* from a resident of Flint, Mich., dismissed Bessey's report as "the silliest twaddle." Purporting to know something of Bessey's life, he insisted he was "not 'eminent' in anything."[47]

John Frances Waters, M.A., "a well-known literary man" who worked in the Department of Justice in Ottawa, accompanied by a reporter from Ottawa's *Journal,* interviewed Birchall probably with the purpose of countering Bessey's report. Waters and the reporter spoke with the prisoner through the bars of his day cell, which was decorated with many sketches. "No English gentleman in a pleasant home could have received two visitors with more graceful ease," declared Waters. His first impression of the prisoner was favourable. "Birchall's features are very good and he might almost be called handsome," said Waters, adding, "He has good eyes and he looked me straight in the face, as the most honest man might do." They discussed a wide range of topics, and Birchall became excited when Waters mentioned Dr. Bessey's psychological report. Birchall begged his guest to reiterate that he repudiated the report, that Bessey and he had never spoken, and that the doctor had simply looked at him for a couple of minutes. Waters noted that the report was based on erroneous premises and faulty deductions and contained several contradictions. He also countered some of Bessey's assertions. "Dr. Bessey thought Birchall's eyes were furtive, [but] I thought them singularly honest," declared Waters. Moreover, he thought "the deplorable fate which has overtaken [Birchall] might overtake any young man who would emancipate himself from moral and religious restraints."[48]

Weighing in was a truly eminent psychologist, Dr. Daniel Clarke, the medical superintendent of the Toronto Asylum, who dismissed some of Bessey's remarks. "There is no such thing as a moral idiot who is not of weak intellect altogether," Clarke declared unequivocally. He disagreed with Bessey's blaming heredity for Rex Birchall's failings. Clarke asserted that there was no law of transmission. Deformed parents may produce perfect children and imperfect ones.[49]

Experts in the then fashionable pseudoscience of phrenology chimed in with their assessments of Birchall. (Phrenologists study the conformation of the skull in the belief that it is indicative of mental faculties and character.) The *Phrenological Journal and Science of Health* out of Philadelphia regretted that its experts were unable to make an assessment of Birchall because they had no plaster cast of his head nor even useful photographs. In the only photograph they had, Birchall was wearing a hat. However, the journal included the results of an examination of him by Prof. F. Cavanagh of Toronto. Birchall scored his only seven out of seven on "firmness (will power)," and he scored sixes in several categories: language ("a good talker"), agreeableness, imitation, mirthfulness ("active, jovial"), individuality ("very shrewd observer"), form ("excellent memory for faces and forms"), and size. He did less well for veneration, benevolence, and conscientiousness.[50] Birchall himself admitted to having been assessed by phrenologists, but also to his scepticism about phrenology.[51]

The *Globe*'s "Partial Confession" and "Interesting Documents"

On 6 October, the *Globe* published a long, front-page story headlined "Statement Made by the Doomed Man: A Partial Confession." Edward Farrer, the *Globe*'s lead editorial writer, had interviewed Birchall, and the newspaper grabbed public attention with what at first glance appeared to be revelations the prisoner had made to him. In fact, Birchall had been tight-lipped. The material was actually pieced together from things he had said to various people (or things people imagined he had said to them). Since the time of the verdict, Birchall had been talking almost non-stop about the case. Much of the *Globe* account was no revelation at all, but matters previously reported in the press. Other newspapers expressed extreme scepticism about the *Globe*'s story.

One of the "revelations" concerned the original plan Birchall had supposedly devised for fleecing Benwell. It implicated as an accomplice his old friend from Woodstock, Neville Pickthall. According to the *Globe*, Birchall confessed that after he had returned to England in 1889, he had kept in touch by letter with Pickthall. When Birchall snared Benwell as a mark, he informed Pickthall. Their plan was for Pickhall to raise money and meet Birchall in New York, but to keep clear of Benwell and Pelly. Pickthall was to return to his Oxford farm, where Benwell would be sent, having been told that the farm was Birchall's and Pickthall the manager of it. After a day or two, Pickthall was to ask Benwell to take a good deal of money, said to be two months' profits, to Birchall at Niagara or Buffalo. In this way Benwell would be induced to get the £500 from home and turn it over to Birchall. Pickthall was to share with Birchall in the takings. The story gybed with the known facts: that Pickthall had suddenly left his Oxford farm and had taken substantial cash with him to New York. The *Globe* noted that it did not guarantee the story's veracity but was simply reporting what Birchall had said.

"What a lot of rubbish," was how it was reported Birchall responded to the story. The Conservative *Mail*, a rival Toronto paper of the Liberal *Globe*, sniped that the "partial confession" had been "manufactured out of whole cloth." The *Sentinel-Review* dismissed the *Globe*'s report as a misguided attempt to revive flagging public interest in the case. Its account of Pickthall as accomplice was not to be believed.[52]

Pickthall dropped into the *Sentinel-Review* office and denied emphatically any involvement with Birchall. "I never had any communication with him since he left Woodstock [in 1889]," said Pickthall. "I never heard of Pelly until after the murder; I was never asked to go to New York to meet Birchall. I did not see him in New York or any of his party, and I had no thought of taking Benwell to my farm. I cannot understand why Birchall should tell such lies."[53] Of course, Pickthall's stance was self-serving, and it's possible that his denial was fabricated to hide his involvement in the fraud and murder.

Another story told in the *Globe*'s account of the "partial confession" pointed to an accomplice in the murder. Birchall had allegedly said that at the swamp he was with another man by the name of Graham, who had been living at Pickthall's house. It was Graham who shot Benwell. The *Globe* report is dismissive of the story, pointing out there was no evidence that Graham had been present at the swamp. Friends of Graham (or Graeme), a young Englishman, said that Birchall, who had known him in Woodstock in 1888–89, had it in for him.[54] The *Sentinel-Review* said that when Birchall presented "Graeme" as his accomplice, he was "probably lying as wickedly as ever." Graeme had not been around Woodstock for a long time. He was "a kind-hearted, gentlemanly Englishman, with no guile in his nature, but with an uncontrollable appetite for drink." It added that his brother was an English baron with a seat on the Isle of Wight.[55]

About a week later, Grosvenor Hood Graeme filed suit against the *Globe* for $50,000, alleging that the story about Birchall's accomplice, Graham, being the real murderer had seriously damaged his reputation. Graeme was working as a delivery-wagon driver in Toronto, but the *News* reported that he was a young Englishman, well-spoken, and the son of the late Sir Hammond Graeme of the Isle of Wight and Lady

Dowager Graeme. Graeme had retained the characteristics of a gentleman, his descent to delivery driving notwithstanding. The plaintiff had come to Canada in 1884 as a farm pupil through the auspices of Ford, Rathbone & Co., but his farm training and career did not go as planned. Thus began the degradation of his high-born status. While living in town and working as a deliveryman, he married an "attractive little wife." In November, the court dismissed the case as frivolous and ordered the plaintiff to pay costs. The *Globe* had argued that in the article it had said that no one would believe that the statements about Graham were true. Graeme nevertheless persisted, but on appeal the judge declared that it was clear that the man referred to by the *Globe* was not plaintiff Grosvenor Graeme, and it was impossible to conceive how he could have imagined that he was. The court dismissed the appeal with costs.[56]

The *Globe* maintained public interest in the Birchall trial when in late October it published what it contended were excerpts from "interesting documents" that Birchall had written for the benefit of his defence team when they were preparing the case.[57] Particularly sensational were notes he had made about his movements on 17 February. In the notes, Birchall wrote that he had planned to spend the day keeping Pelly busy in Buffalo and to send Benwell alone to Eastwood where he was to meet McDonald, the farm manager, at 11 a.m. Benwell, however, had refused to go alone, so Birchall had accompanied him. Once in Eastwood, Birchall had sent Benwell off to find McDonald, who had good connections with many farmers and could have found Benwell a placement or investment opportunity. Birchall had planned that meantime, while at Eastwood, he would meet with Pickthall, his good friend, who might help him fleece Benwell and Pelly, but he had sent his letter to Pickthall to the wrong address. As a result, he had not succeeded in meeting with Pickthall that day.

Birchall also speculated in the notes about what had happened to Benwell. They had agreed to meet back at Eastwood after Benwell had gone off to find McDonald. But they had not connected. Birchall thought that Benwell might have turned up late and missed him. Perhaps Benwell had then gone off in search of him, or encountered someone who had sent Benwell looking for a person mistakenly said to be himself. Or possibly Benwell had taken a ride with someone. The notion that the two would meet up that afternoon is undermined by the tight timeline. Benwell had little time to meet with McDonald and get back to Eastwood for the afternoon train.

It is significant that, if genuine, the notes were not used by the defence attorneys to probe McDonald on the stand regarding his meeting with Benwell. Perhaps the lawyers doubted the veracity of Birchall's story and didn't want to have McDonald deny the plan in court.

Several newspapers were uncertain what to make of the *Globe*'s extracts. The *Sentinel-Review* accepted them as genuine but also noted Birchall's difficulty in presenting a persuasive account of his actions on 17 February. The *Telegram* doubted the authenticity of the extracts. The *Globe* responded by publishing a facsimile of handwriting from the extract so that readers could see that it matched other examples of Birchall's handwriting.[58]

People asked about the source of the extracts, which the *Globe* was unwilling to divulge. It was thought that Birchall's lawyers would not have risked their high professional reputations by leaking the documents. His lawyers suspected that Det. Bluett was the culprit, a suspicion that would have had resonance because detectives generally lacked the public's trust. Writing from his Toronto home, Bluett asked the *Sentinel-Review* to publish his assertion of innocence: "I most emphatically deny furnishing the *Globe* with material for its article on Birchall." The *Sentinel-Review* published Bluett's statement but expressed doubt about the detective's reliability.[59]

The Colonel

In late October, Birchall received a letter from "the Colonel" dated 8 October and postmarked 28 October in Jackson, Mich. The *Mail* promptly printed the letter, and other newspapers followed suit. Written in a breezy style, the letter provided an account of what had happened at the swamp back in February. The author largely kept to the facts of the Crown's case, except for the crucial time near the swamp.[60]

"Well, Rex, my dear boy," it begins, "I have been watching you ever since that fateful 17th of February." The Colonel explains how he (and he alone) had gone with Benwell to the house by the swamp, where arrangements were to be made for Benwell's stay there. When that didn't pan out, they had decided to see whether they could find any game to shoot in the swamp itself. While in there, the writer says, "the devil seemed to come over me, and I told him straight out it was a clear case of a swindle, like the whole farm pupil business." Benwell had reacted in anger and had threated to expose everybody.

"Great Scot! Didn't he get up a steam," says the author. "Threatened to shoot me on the spot." Knowing that exposure would be disastrous, the Colonel says he "settled it then and there." He expresses regret for having killed Benwell, but puts some of the blame on Birchall, who had failed to tell him that Benwell carried a revolver. The Colonel closes by wishing Birchall the best. He explains that he would keep the letter until ready to leave Jackson and then mail it. By the time it arrived in Woodstock, he would be in a place where neither Canadian nor American law could reach him.

A postscript reminds Birchall about "'Smarty'" of Montreal, whom they had met in London, Eng., back in January. The writer threatens to give him a different "box" than the one Birchall had given him at the theatre that night.

The *Sentinel-Review* reported that when Birchall read the letter, which was four pages of closely penned writing on linen notepaper, he was delighted by its account, which exonerated him. He contacted his lawyers in the hope that his execution would be immediately delayed to allow for an investigation. He said that the Colonel was on old friend, but he did not say what his name was.[61]

Newspapers differed sharply regarding the letter's authenticity. "From beginning to end," opined the *Sentinel-Review*, "the letter bears the stamp of having been concocted by some one who never saw Birchall." (The newspaper does not elaborate.) According to the *Sentinel-Review*, "the Colonel" appeared to allude to a story circulating at the time of the murder about a man calling himself "the Colonel" who had stopped for the night at the Thompson House in Woodstock back in February. He had left the next morning and had never been traced. Birchall said he knew the Colonel, sometimes calling him "Graham" and sometimes "Jones."[62]

The *Mail*, which claimed to have broken the story, maintained that the letter provided valuable missing links in the Crown's version of events, and that as a result, public opinion was shifting fast. Many people who had been uncertain about Birchall's guilt were now fully persuaded that he was not the murderer. It was reported that when Florence Birchall saw the contents of the letter printed in the *Mail*, "she burst into tears and said that the letter was only further confirmation of her faith in her husband." Even her sister, who had been sceptical about Birchall's innocence, was now thinking otherwise.[63]

Some people speculated that Birchall was the author of the letter, but his jailers insisted he could not possibly have written it or got it out of the jail without their knowledge. A rumour circulated that Birchall's guard, John Entwhistle, had relatives in Jackson, Mich., and that he had something to do with the letter, but of course he denied it.[64] The press did not report any attempt to compare the letter's handwriting with Birchall's. Most commentators worked from the printed version in newspapers, and it remains unclear who had the original handwritten letter. Given that the *Mail* broke the story, it is possible the newspaper had the original but chose not to share it or question its authenticity because doing so would have undercut the import of the story. Eventually, the original letter found its way into an archival collection. A comparison of the handwriting with other letters written by Birchall indicates that it was likely written by him.[65]

As soon as the letter was printed, the press sought to discover the identity of the Colonel. George Stevens of Montreal, the owner of the Hope Coffee Shop, told the Montreal press that in the winter he had been staying at Morley's Hotel in Trafalgar Square, London, when at breakfast in the dining room one day he had met Birchall, Benwell, and a man calling himself "the Colonel." The three men were drinking beer and talking loudly, especially the Colonel. Stevens described him as being a thick-set man of forty-five or fifty, with a heavy jaw and a dark moustache. On his coat he wore a medal, apparently from the Grand Army of the Republic (the northern force in the American Civil War). On other occasions, too, Stevens had met Birchall and his wife at Morley's. Apparently, Stevens was the "Smarty" of the postscript.[66] A Crown attorney took down Stevens's sworn statement and forwarded it to the Department of Justice.[67]

Using their imperial network, the Canadian newsmen arranged for reporters in England to check out the story. They reported that the name "Colonel Lewis" was on the register of Morley's Hotel in January at the same time that Stevens was staying at the hotel. Hotel staff were said to remember Lewis well as pompous and a heavy drinker. The press divided as to whether this information lent credence to the letter's authenticity.[68]

A little later, a "Colonel" who had stayed at Morley's Hotel was tracked down in New York. He was a railway financier who had stayed at the hotel with his wife and daughter for six months, including during February. He had met the Birchalls and dined with them at the hotel. Of course, he had been far from the murder scene and had had nothing to do with it. The Colonel of the letter was never found.[69]

"Birchallism"

Newspapers sought to keep alive the story that had been so rewarding to the press by publishing tidbits on a near daily basis about Birchall and his now tiny world. The *Sentinel-Review* dubbed such coverage "Birchallism."[70] It is extraordinary to have evidence of the stories that circulated at the time, some of them mere snippets of gossip. Only because of the enormous interest in the case were these trivialities recorded.

The press generally continued to report that Birchall's mood remained chipper even as the gallows loomed ever nearer. Hellmuth, his lawyer, was less certain. He found it difficult to judge how the prisoner really felt, "as he would naturally want to keep up appearances." A reporter with the *Telegram* who interviewed Birchall disagreed with the headlines everywhere that reported on the prisoner's indifference to his fate as though it were extraordinary. The reporter maintained that Birchall was only displaying the manly behaviour expected of a gentleman of his position in similar circumstances. During the interview, Birchall mostly discussed the sporting news, showing special enthusiasm for reports of horse races involving his blue-blooded friends. He complimented the Canadian press, even though it had been instrumental in his conviction. "He dearly loves notoriety," explained the reporter. "To him the fact that the whole world was watching his trial was a balm which took the sting from the judge's words consigning him to the gallows."[71]

With time, Birchall grew less complimentary about his lawyers. By the end of October, it was reported that he had harsh words for them and accused them of selling him out.[72] A friend of Birchall's living in Montreal made available to the press letters the prisoner had written to him. In them he blames his lawyers for being unprepared for all the lying witnesses, who, he writes, "were doubtless procured by Murray, the detective whose conduct throughout was atrocious." Birchall shows more frankly here his frame of mind in jail. "I am comfortable, as far as I can be, and well cared for," he writes, "but it is a miserable existence altogether. I shall keep up to the end."[73]

The jail was inundated with letters addressed to Birchall. Jailer Cameron, who inspected them all, said that some were expressions of concern and pity, but others were "maudlin trash" from people with "weak intellects, morbid imaginations or criminal instincts." The *Sentinel-Review* added: "Poor Birchall! And never Poor Benwell!"[74]

Indeed, comparatively little was said about Benwell. However, one lengthy report related stories told by an unnamed school chum of his. The two had met at a junior academy in Cheltenham. The chum recalls vividly Benwell's impulsive temperament, athletic prowess, and his "punctiliousness about dress and appearance even to the point of fastidiousness." Quick to resent an insult, young Benwell would get into fights and refuse to concede even when obviously overpowered by his opponent. The friendship had continued at Cheltenham College, where Benwell had excelled at sculling, gymnastics, and football. When engaged in athletic endeavours, Benwell showed his particularity about dress. "On the river his 'flannels' were spotless, and seemed more immaculate than any others," says the friend. "Even after a hard football match, when the other players were carrying pounds of mud away with them on their faces, hands and clothes, he presented a better appearance than any."[75] Although the depiction is couched in a complimentary way, readers would likely have been put off by the man's departure from a prevalent masculine ideal, what with his overattention to his clothing.

Newspapers published follow-up reports about the changes in Birchall's regime introduced by the jail inspector. Relations between Birchall and John McGee, his extra guard, were poor. From the start Birchall was disappointed in him because he was a silent, older man with whom he found it impossible to chat. McGee annoyed the prisoner by complaining about all the cigar smoke and the presence of a black cat that Birchall had in his cell and refused to give up. McGee found tiresome the many jokes Birchall delighted in playing. Once when McGee returned home to his wife, she found attached to his coattail a placard announcing "3 for 25 cents, eggs are very fine today." That was the last straw. McGee resigned his position. He was replaced by a much younger man, George Perry, the sheriff's grandson, whose company Birchall enjoyed. They played leapfrog together in the jail corridor.[76]

Birchall found amusements to relieve the monotony of jail life. Much of his time was taken up with writing his autobiography and doing sketches with which to illustrate it. He also enjoyed reading the sporting news and pitching coppers with anyone who would take him on. And he loved his jokes. On one occasion, from his second-floor cell window he shouted to a prisoner in the yard below offering some of his special meal. Instead of the throwing down the food, Birchall dumped a pail of water on the fellow's head. It was reported that prisoners who had seen him play this joke on other newcomers laughed uproariously.[77]

Birchall spent much time reading letters sent to him by well-wishers and others, and he replied to some of them. The prisoner was touched by kind words sent from Douglas Pelly's father. In Birchall's reply to the Rev. Pelly, he praised "the manly & Christian spirit which prompted you to write in such a noble manner."[78]

The condemned prisoner had visits from pastors and clergymen offering comfort and encouraging him to confess his sins, particularly those relating to Benwell's murder. Birchall had little patience with these visitors, particularly the Roman Catholic ones, although he appreciated the ministrations of Rural Dean William H. Wade, the Anglican divine who was his spiritual adviser. Like the prisoner, Dean Wade had been born and educated in England, which probably helped him establish the rapport he had with the doomed man.[79]

In October, Birchall had jewellery made in Montreal. He planned to give inscribed rings to three people: his guard, John Entwhistle, his local lawyer, S.G. McKay, and his sister-in-law, Marion West-Jones. Two lockets were fashioned. One for his wife, which would hold a lock of his hair and his portrait, and another holding a lock of her hair that he planned to wear on the scaffold and in the grave.[80]

On 20 October, the *World* reported that the shorthand reporter at the trial (Nelson R. Butcher) had completed the trial transcript. It included all evidence, Osler's opening statement, Justice MacMahon's charge to the jury, the verdict, all legal points raised, and decisions about them. The report ran to 867 legal-size pages in two volumes, or about 270,000 words. The record was required by the Department of Justice in Ottawa and would form part of the Birchall file to be reviewed by cabinet ministers before the final decision was made about whether to carry out Birchall's sentence.[81]

It was reported that the cost of the trial to taxpayers was actually less than predicted. Oxford County's bill was $2,500, and the province covered the $5,000 cost of the Crown's prosecution.[82]

It is remarkable how many articles newspapers succeeded in publishing about Birchall and the crime. Newspapers gave far more attention to Birchall and his trial than to most murder trials of the period. Journalists and publishers showed determination to make the most of a story that sold newspapers.

11

Birchall's Own Story

Shortly after Reginald Birchall's conviction, it was widely reported that he was writing his autobiography. He had six weeks until his scheduled hanging. Working on it would give him a project while he waited for the dreadful finale. His declared purpose in writing it was to raise money that would go to support his soon-to-be widow, Florence. He expected, correctly as it turned out, that newspapers would pay well because the public anticipated that the autobiography would shed new light on the man and his crimes. Perhaps, even, it would bring a confession.

Reports were that in his jail cell Birchall was applying himself with dedication to the completion of his autobiography. It became his routine to begin writing at 10 p.m. and continue until 4 or 5 a.m., and then he would sleep until noon. He wrote carefully with a pencil in his flowing script on foolscap, turning out ten or fifteen pages a night. He took care to rewrite portions that didn't satisfy him and to draw illustrations.

Various newspapers made offers on the rights to publish Birchall's memoir. On 24 October, C.W. Bunting of the *Mail* and John Habberton of the *New York Herald* obtained the copyright for the autobiography before Birchall completed it. Together they paid $1,700, half down with half to go directly to Florence Birchall upon its completion. The *Mail* held the Canadian rights and the *Herald* the American and international ones.[1]

Various attempts were made to purloin parts of the autobiography and get the scoop on its purchasers. Some newspapermen attempted to bribe officers of the jail, but, as the *Mail* put it, "they were too loyal to allow any such dastardly proceeding." One of them had even allegedly rejected a $700 offer from an American publisher.

A few days after its purchase, journalists got hold of the incomplete manuscript. They freely commented on it, but editors resisted the temptation to infringe the copyright and publish any of it. The *Globe* printed a long article, titled "Birchall's Book," that was highly dismissive of the manuscript purchased by its rival, the *Mail*. "There is of course nothing of literary merit in the book," observed the *Globe*. Birchall had mainly jotted down "the trivialities of a misspent life." So far, the manuscript didn't deal at all with the Benwell murder, although Birchall had let it be known that he was working up to it and would eventually "touch on the incident." It was pathetic to see a man spend his last days satisfying his "insane love of notoriety and a desire to make a noise in the world, no matter how." The *Globe* conceded, however, that running through the manuscript was evidence of his wish to show kindness to his wife, "whose life he has ruined with his own."[2]

In contrast, of course, the *Mail* heartily promoted the autobiography, making exaggerated claims that now appear amusing. It called his style "singularly clear and distinct for a man who did not follow letters as a profession." Comparisons were even made to Victor Hugo and Tolstoy! Indeed, claimed the *Mail*, Birchall's "writing is as brisk and fresh as that of a literary man just after returning from a holiday." The *Mail* assured its readers that especially the people of Woodstock and western Ontario were eager for the first instalment.[3]

On 6 November the *Mail* began publishing the autobiography. It was given pride of place, taking up the newspaper's front page and continuing on inside pages. The headline read: "BIRCHALL – Story of His Life – Told by Himself – The Only True and Authentic Version." Instalments would appear daily through 18 November.

A Start

Birchall begins his story with a preface that explains that his purpose in recording his reminiscences is, through its sale, "to add somewhat to the slender provision that I am otherwise able to make for my wife." He hopes too that in recounting his university days he might provide a warning to others embarking on university studies who are "naturally inclined to follow the paths of idleness and folly."[4]

Birchall's university experience crucially shaped his sense of self, as was intended by the elite universities of Oxford and Cambridge in the late nineteenth century. Birchall absorbed the essential values promoted at Oxford – a sense of the superiority of university men over everyone else, and a gentlemanly ideal – even as he shared with many undergraduates a rebelliousness that thrived on defying university regulations and their enforcers.[5]

In choosing to address his memoir to young men destined for an education at Oxford or Cambridge, Birchall displays a peculiar conception of his audience. Among the many thousands of people likely to read his serialized autobiography, precious few would have been lads destined for England's elite universities. It is likely that he chose to address this particular audience because he knew well the advice literature to undergraduates that appeared in the many undergraduate periodicals produced and read by young men like him at Oxford.[6] That familiarity made him comfortable writing in the genre. Possibly too he thought the idea of giving a moral purpose to his writing would appeal to readers and earn him their respect. It was also an act of self-indulgence because he had thoroughly enjoyed his Oxford days and looked back nostalgically on them from a short distance.

The autobiography continues with a section titled "A Personal Explanation," where Birchall relates that the reminiscence would correct mistakes about him that had appeared in the press since his arrest. He admits that the press does much good, but "the knights of the pencil" respond to the public's desire for "the sensational." He points out that journalists make mistakes, which he attributes to the competition among newspapers to give the fullest possible accounts. That explains, he says with a dig, the tendency for journalists to yield to their "powerful faculties of genius and imagination." As an example of press distortions, he refers to repeated charges that while at Oxford he desired notoriety. In fact, he says, all through his escapades at university, he never sought notoriety. Rather, it was thrust upon him in response to his desire to enjoy life and step "flagrantly out of the beaten path."[7]

Having dispensed with the preliminaries, the account shifts to "Home, School, and College."[8] Birchall notes that he was born on 25 May 1866 and proudly writes that his father, the Rev. Joseph Birchall, the late rector of Church-Kirk near Accrington, Lancashire, was an authority on ecclesiastical law and very well-known in the North of England. Rex does not mention the other members of his family. We know that in 1838 his father had married Maria Anne Gray and they had had four children, three daughters and a son, Oswald. In 1855, Maria died, and nine years later Joseph married Mary Eleanor Parker.

They had two children, Reginald and Maude, a sister two years' his senior.[9] All the children of both mothers were then living at home in the rectory of Church-Kirk.[10]

Birchall writes that as a lad he had few cares and "was naturally jolly." At age ten, under his father's stern regime, he began studying Latin and Greek. Two years later he was deemed ready for school. He was sent to Rossall, a public (independent) school of 300 boys, near Blackpool in Lancashire. His father was on its board. Rex was placed in the first form, one up from the bottom.

Rossall School had been founded in 1844 "to provide, at a moderate cost, for the sons of Clergymen and others, a classical, mathematical and general education of the highest class." Housed in Rossall Hall on the Lancashire coast, it withstood the winds and storms that were said to strengthen and brace students for the challenges of life. Queen Victoria granted the school a royal charter in the very month that Birchall was writing his memoir. By the end of the century, the school enjoyed the reputation of being "the Eton of the North." It continues today as an independent boarding school.[11]

Birchall writes that his integration into the population of schoolboys at Rossall was helped by his being able to boast to them that his father was a life governor of the school. After being at school only a little while, however, Rex learned of the sudden death of his father. The lad was grief-stricken. He remembers his father as "the best and kindest of fathers." Rex attended the funeral, a large, public one, and the reading of the will, which left the family well provided for.

Back at school, Reginald had difficulty overcoming his despondency. He did poorly at his studies in Greek and Latin but was soon excelling at science, topping his class. He enjoyed singing in the school choir with his fine treble voice and took solo parts in concerts, his nerve never failing him. He also excelled at football and became captain of his club. He recalls that during this period at Rossall he got into scrapes. "I was pursued," he writes, "by farmers when in search of birds' eggs, chased by irate gamekeepers in the most flagrant acts of trespass, and though constantly suspected for various untimely events that happened, I escaped many times without my desserts."

Just when Rex had truly found his feet at Rossall, his guardians, who lived in the south of England, decided he should attend a school near them. With great regret and bad grace, he says, he left Rossall for Reading School in Reading, Berkshire. One of the oldest schools in England, it has been teaching boys since 1125.

Soon after Birchall began at Reading he realized that the standard of discipline was far lower than at Rossall, and he was quick to take advantage of the laxness. Academically the standards were also lower, which enabled him to coast with plenty of time on his hands. As one of the privileged boys to have a private room, Birchall hosted evening parties, where food and alcohol were served during "carousals."

Because he excelled at sports, Birchall was made secretary of the school's Games Committee, which enabled him to arrange for students from nearby Oxford and Sandhurst (the military academy) to compete with Reading students. Of the Sandhurst lads, he writes that "their style, loud and horsey; their assumption of bogus authority, and their practical jokes, carried sometimes to startling reality, were very much to my taste." The Reading boys became confident enough to rebel against the masters. The "spirit of insubordination" grew to such an extent that the trustees undertook an inquiry that resulted in a major shake-up of the school.

Birchall presents his three years at Reading as preparation for the life he would lead at Oxford. He won prizes in science and athletics that helped his university career. But the real preparation Reading gave him was a taste for "whatsoever was against the rules and whatsoever was redolent of lawlessness and disorder." He thrived on being part of a coterie of bad boys.

At Oxford

The bulk of the autobiography concerns Birchall's time at Oxford.[12] It begins with Birchall's warning to young men about to enter upon a university career to follow two rules: "First, never get into debt. Second, never borrow money." At Oxford, he explains, the temptations for getting into debt are many. A new arrival finds in his rooms advertisements and letters from tradesmen offering all manner of things. As the debts pile up, the student is embarrassed to reveal things to his parents and so borrows money from lenders who charge extortionate rates of interest. Although Birchall writes from the vantage point of one who knew the problem of debt personally, he was addressing a topic commonly found in the undergraduate periodicals of his day and confronted by many students.[13]

As the autobiography relates, in the late winter of 1885, after having to take the entrance exam twice, he was admitted to Lincoln College.

He had fine rooms there, which he recalls fitting up "handsomely in a sporting style – foxes' brushes, sporting prints, whips and spurs being prominent." Clearly, he made the space robustly masculine, with an upper-class ambiance that reflected his interest in horses. Decorating and furnishing one's rooms according to personal tastes was expected of undergraduates, who, upon their initiation into manhood, were asserting their individuality and independence.[14]

The autobiography correctly explains that Oxford undergraduates self-divided into sets: the readers, the aesthetes, the sportsmen, and so on. Birchall soon became part of the sporting set. He was elected to a place on the football team and invited to join in the hunt, whose rituals he lovingly recalls: smart attire, boots polished to brilliance by an old Oxford servant, and the hunt breakfast of cold roast beef, game pies, and college ale. He writes of the abundance of foxes and fine hounds near Oxford.

As a freshman, Birchall took great pleasure in perfecting "the art of driving." He was already familiar with driving in all its forms, "whether single, double, four-in-hand, tandem." At Oxford he took instruction from renowned whips and became expert and well-known for his ability to race coaches four-in-hand, which was a craze at the time.

As the press had reported, Birchall had started the Black and Tan Club and was its first president. He explains that it was all about driving and carousing. Every week club members would drive to some "unsuspecting town" and spend the day partying. Local newspapers frequently would complain about their incursions. Afterwards, the clubmen would return to Oxford very late for an all-night dinner. Birchall corrects some of the stories the press had told about him and the club, saying for instance that a horse badly injured in a race had not been driven by him; rather, he was the one who had found a veterinarian to attend it.

From animals the autobiography turns to the topic of women at Oxford. "The fair sex are," Birchall writes almost dismissively, "necessary and pleasant adjuncts to picnics, balls, dinners, parties, and on all occasions when on pleasure bent." Such a viewpoint put him squarely in the mainstream of undergraduate culture at Oxford, which was overwhelmingly male-centred and male-oriented. He writes that most of the women he encountered were "other fellows' sisters." Birchall speaks of the different types of women and illustrates them with his sketches: the boating girl, the girl one sees at the seaside, the dancing girl, the girl one meets out at dinner, the girl who studies and is very learned. He mocks

11.1. Pen-and-ink drawing by Birchall made to illustrate his autobiography.
Source: *Birchall: The Story of His Life, Trial and Imprisonment, as Told by Himself* (1890), p. 20.

the ignorance of women when it comes to cricket and football, but says he appreciated women on the dance floor.

Birchall seeks to correct an impression circulated in the press that he spent much time playing cards. He says that he preferred pastimes with "more movement and 'go.'" And like most undergraduates, he enjoyed hosting his parties in his rooms. Although Birchall doesn't mention it, university authorities permitted only gatherings of small numbers.[15] He defied the rule, hosting larger, more costly entertainments. He had a good piano and could play it well, which added to the attraction of his gatherings. Men with musical talents would attend, playing an instrument such as a banjo to accompany a comic song. He would also invite theatrical artists who would sing a ballad or operatic song.

The author emphatically protests press reports that painted him as being mean and selfish. On the contrary, he maintains that he never refused someone in want and often gave friends in financial difficulties money he himself needed. He insists that he was generous, too, in providing drink and dinners. Nothing gave him more pleasure than to see the guests in his rooms thoroughly enjoying themselves.

The autobiography relates stories of Oxford students who became attached to young, local women beneath their station. A friend of his fell for a barmaid who was of course working class. He and other university chaps attended the wedding. He mocks the bride's mother, who appeared the worse for whiskey and arrayed in "violent contrasts of colours." When asked to speak at the wedding breakfast, the woman said "'Lor blimey, if this get-up won't fetch 'em I'd like to know wot will!'" The father passed out at the table before the gathering broke up in an uproar. Still, the marriage turned out all right in the end, Birchall concedes.

In addition to enjoying his "Canadian canoe," Birchall sometimes went with a couple of friends in a canal boat for a month or so "camping out." He remembers the best trips being up to the source of the Thames. One fellow would cook, one would look after the boat and tent, and the third would do a little hunting. Rabbits and partridges were easily got, and sometimes the crew did some poaching. They would bathe early in the morning, sleep most of the day, and proceed along the river at night. He had great fun and enjoyed "our rural and simple life." Perhaps this pastime later made Canada seem appealing to him.

Birchall devotes many pages to pranks played by him and his Oxford friends, who delighted in defying the rules of the colleges and outwitting the proctors ("progs"). One example suffices. At midnight one evening Birchall and a friend put a ladder up to a student's rooms, climbed up, broke the window, and entered the room. They set a fire with some papers and showed them at the window while shouting "fire!" They tossed down items of furniture from the room. Many young men gathered at the bottom of the ladder and some climbed up. Birchall and his friend then doused them with pails of water. "The place was a perfect pandemonium," he writes. They repeated the joke in other parts of the university that night. The following day the dean called them in. He didn't buy their story that they had been conducting a fire drill. Birchall was evicted from his college rooms and told to rent a place nearby, which he says he didn't mind doing at all.

The autobiography comments on the many welcome and supportive letters he received in jail from true friends at Oxford, now in many walks of life. Birchall mentions especially letters from Arthur R. Leatham, formerly of Queen's College but currently living in Montreal. He wrote encouragingly many times and was unshaken by the verdict. Birchall writes: "He is a true type of an Oxford man, a fine fellow in every way, and thoroughly English in his ways."

The autobiography next turns to pursuits that he began while at Oxford and followed after his departure.[16] Birchall recounts his days in the theatre. At Oxford he and friends founded the Oxford University Histrionics Club. The young men toured around putting on amateur performances of plays for charitable purposes, which met with varying degrees of success. The high cost of mounting the plays led them to abandon the tour, but he says that the experience left him even more keenly interested in theatre.

During the long vacation of 1887, he became acting manager of a theatre company travelling the country. He was subsequently appointed as its paid manager and then bought the lease the company had on a theatre in Burton-on-Trent, Staffordshire. Mostly the shows satisfied public tastes by mounting music hall entertainments. Birchall boasts that he met many actors, some of whom went on to prominence. He writes that "a better-hearted, more generous-minded, brotherly class of men I have never chanced to meet." Nevertheless, he advises against pursuing a stage career. "Either sterling merit or influence is required to enable a young actor to rise," he writes, adding that "the profession is entirely overcrowded."

Birchall had a second passion, horse racing, which he wryly observes "offers the best means of being able to lose a very large amount of money in the very shortest time." Oxford had its time-honoured races at Aylesbury, which Birchall and friends enjoyed. He also travelled by rail to races held in major cities. Occasionally he himself raced. To bet on the races, it wasn't necessary to leave town, thanks to bookies in Oxford. He says he had good and bad luck betting, but didn't do badly overall, whereas some of his friends lost heavily. His advice to young men was don't bet at all but if drawn to betting, avoid systems for betting, all of which are rubbish.

Both while at Oxford and later on he would join "a select party" attending Ascot, the most fashionable races in England. They would drive out in a well-appointed coach, four-in-hand, wearing the regulation dress of grey frock coats, white plug hats, lavender gloves, and so forth. The pomp clearly appealed to him. He concludes the discussion by remarking that over the course of four or five years, his fascination with horse racing grew ever greater.

"A good deal has been said about my 'want of education,'" he writes. He defends himself. To enter Oxford, he needed "a moderate acquaintance" with Latin and Greek authors, and he read many classical authors for pleasure. He also read ancient and modern history, and passed an examination in the Holy Scriptures. He mentions many novelists whose works he has read with pleasure.

The Canadian Sojourn

The autobiography explains that in fall of 1888, Birchall had some money on hand after his wedding and opted to become a farm pupil in Canada.[17] He says he had corresponded several times with the London firm Ford & Rathbone, which he prefers to call "Fraud & Rathbone." When he called upon the firm, they assured him of the comfort and ease of a farmer's life and showed him a photograph of a grand house. He signed a contract with the firm, deposited £500 with them, and sailed for Woodstock on 21 November 1888. (We know that his bride was with him, although he makes no mention of her.)

Upon arrival in Woodstock, he spent a few days with William ("Billy") McDonald, the representative of Ford & Rathbone, who placed him on the Wilcox farm in Durham Township. Conditions shocked him: "A dirty house, dirty children, a filthy bedroom, a bed that even the commonest gaol bed would give points to." The farmer was only interested in the $125 he was to receive for taking him on as a farm pupil. The very next day, Birchall left the "human pigsty." He pressed Ford & Rathbone to return his payment, but got only a little from them. As he had the time until May on his hands, he decided to stay in Woodstock and make the best of it. Probably, he was actually keeping a distance from his English creditors.

The autobiography gives a less than full account of why in Woodstock he styled himself "Somerset." He says it was a name he took sometimes in England. He did so for "a private reason and connection which [he] was not at liberty to make public." The assumed name probably had to do with escaping debt collectors in England, whom his father-in-law reported had placed announcements in the press with threats to sue. He maintains that some people called him "Lord Somerset" but that whenever anyone asked him whether he was Lord Somerset, he told them no.

In Woodstock, Birchall had rooms in the home of Mrs. John McKay on Brock Street, where two young Englishmen also lived, Dudley and Overweg, "both gentlemanly fellows" and protégés of Ford & Rathbone. He says he spent most of his time riding out to different places. He went hunting and fishing. While it is true, he writes, that with friends he sometimes visited Pine Pond, he had no knowledge of the swamp.

In his brief account of his Woodstock sojourn, Birchall makes no mention of his wife, the parties it was said they hosted, or indeed carousing of any kind. He says that in May 1889 he left Woodstock for England, convinced that he would never return to Canada.

Home Again

The autobiography explains that upon returning to England, Birchall and his wife lived in a part of the home of her father, Mr. David Stevenson, in London.[18], Birchall writes that contrary to press reports, he and his father-in-law were on the best of terms. He calls the old man "somewhat eccentric and erratic" but also notes his long career with the London and North Western Railway Company and his reputation as one of the foremost authorities on railways.

For the first month back, Birchall spent his time at the races. Then, growing tired of doing nothing, he accepted a position as advertising agent for a fashionable firm of photographers, Mayall & Co., of New Bond Street in London's West End. The firm maintained an elite clientele, including Queen Victoria and members of the royal family, nobility, gentry, "and first-class artistes." It was Birchall's job to seek out people in the news and arrange appointments for sittings, which resulted in photographs the firm sold in West End shops. Appointments were made with actors, married couples from high society, financiers, debutantes, and more. Birchall mentions the names of some of the famous people he dealt with, including William Gladstone. He enjoyed the fact that his position often took him to the theatre to judge whose images would sell best. Birchall was sorry when, as a result of a depression in trade, his contract expired at the end of 1889.

"The Great Scheme"

At last, Birchall turns to the much-anticipated topic of the swindle.[19] The scheme, he writes, was to make "a great pile of money" out of the English Derby to be run in 1890. He planned to fleece young men interested in investing in a Canadian farm, place the money on the Derby, and with the winnings reimburse them while still having plenty remaining for himself. He says that he had "certain information" about the upcoming race, meaning that he had had a tip that the race would be rigged so that the favourite would lose.

When the race was run on 4 June, the lead horse went mad, biting another, and the outcome led *Sporting Life* to conclude that "the race was falsely run." It has been calculated that had Birchall been in a position to bet £500 on Sainfoin at the beginning of April as he says he had planned to do prior to his arrest, he would have realized £12,500.[20] There is plenty of room to doubt whether the betting story has any validity. By the time Birchall was writing the memoir, the race had been run and the scandal had been aired in the sporting press, which he read in jail; thus, he would have been able to incorporate the story into his account. By claiming that his plan had been to repay Benwell and Pelly, he hoped to make himself and the swindle look more benign. Birchall goes on to say vaguely that because he couldn't work the swindle single-handedly, he arranged with (unnamed) others to take part.

The memoir continues, reporting that after placing his advertisement in London's *Daily Telegraph* for a "university man" wishing to invest in a Canadian farm, he received a reply from a T.G. Mellersh of Cheltenham. When the two met, Mellersh proposed that Birchall give him £50 and he would give him a list of names he had collected of would-be investors in overseas enterprises. Mellersh said that he advertised constantly and had often got replies. According to Birchall, for whatever reason, Mellersh gave him the list without the £50 up front. Birchall chose about four men, including Benwell and Pelly. He wrote to these two men and got replies from both.

Birchall went to call on Col. Benwell at his London club, the Army and Navy in Pall Mall. He says that he knew immediately that the colonel, being an army officer, had little business sense. After telling him "many lies," Birchall soon gleaned that the colonel was eager to invest £500 in the farm. Birchall then met young Benwell at his London club, the National Conservative Club, and found him keen to participate. Benwell wanted to get away quickly. Birchall surmised that Fred Benwell feared his father, who frequently rebuked him even in Birchall's presence.

Birchall also went to meet Pelly at his father's home in Saffron Walden, "a somewhat antiquated little village in Essex." The Pelly family entertained him hospitably in their house, which was "redolent of affluence and prosperity." The Rev. Pelly kept "a butler and footman, carriage and pair, hacks and hunters, men and dogs." Birchall was told that the Rev. Pelly had recently inherited some money, which he was eager to invest. Birchall says that he found the man, "like most country clergymen, simple and confiding." It was soon agreed that they would pay Birchall £170 for certain terms in return.

During a subsequent meeting with Col. Benwell at his London townhouse, the colonel insisted that the £500 investment would only be made after Fred Benwell had seen the farm property and approved of it. Birchall underscores that it was of course necessary to be able to show Benwell some farm property and a fraudulent deed indicating that Birchall owned it. The plan was that to avoid having to stay at a farm, Benwell and Birchall's manager would go here and there to horse sales, where nothing would suit Birchall so no money would need to be spent. "We were after the money by fraudulent means," writes Birchall, "but not by foul means, and there is a great and wide distinction here." The scheme was well set out and "was only entirely frustrated by the untimely death of F.C. Benwell."

Birchall emphasizes that his wife was entirely innocent of the fraud. Before they first came to Canada in 1888, he had told her he owned a farm near Niagara that was being managed by someone. When in Canada, he told her the payments he got from Ford & Rathbone were profits from the farm. She believed him. When questions came up, he managed to "put her off in some way or another successfully."

He gave his wife elaborate descriptions of the fine farm and house he had, and she shared the information with Pelly and explained to him how she planned to fix up the house to her tastes. Because of this, Pelly later said she must have been involved in the fraud, although Birchall insists that that was not the case. Birchall refers to Pelly's "base and cowardly insinuations." It was despicable that "a totally innocent and good woman" was accused of helping perpetrate the fraud. Without help from him, she was unable to fight her own battle against "such shameful slander."

Birchall says that aboard the *Britannic* it was to his advantage to keep Benwell and Pelly apart. Fortunately for him, they developed a strong dislike for each other. Pelly later said bad things about Benwell, but in fact Benwell was "studiously polite in manner and bearing, and a gentleman all the way through." The writer objects to accusations in the press that he himself avoided the other passengers. Rather, he was seasick and in his cabin until the last few days, when he befriended Mr. Isidore Hellmuth of London, Ont., who later would serve as his lawyer.

At one point while Birchall's party was staying in their Buffalo hotel, Benwell told the other two men that his signature was difficult to copy, and both Birchall and Pelly had tried. Pelly had utterly failed. At the trial Pelly would call it their "silly" occupation. In sharing the exercise, he had ended up with Benwell's gold pen marked "Conny."

He dismisses with contempt the Crown's claim during the trial that he had stolen the pen from Benwell's dead body.

At this point in the narrative, Birchall has nothing to say at all about 17 February or about his time at Niagara Falls. He jumps ahead to his time in the Woodstock Jail.

In Jail

Birchall recounts that on 13 March 1890, Magistrate Hill of Niagara Falls committed him to trial, which resulted in his taking up residence in the west wing of the jail at Woodstock.[21] Birchall referred to this "strange and weird institution" by the familiar name "Castle Cameron." He jokes about its origins, one theory being that the ancient place was accidentally discovered by Christopher Columbus while he was racoon hunting with friends in the bush! Another was that it was the result of a violent earthquake: "the confused mass of brick, stone, and mortar would lend colour to this theory."

In his autobiography, Birchall writes that the jail at the time had twenty-four cells, full only in winter, when it was a popular resort for men seeking a place for the benefit of their health! Birchall expresses outrage that Oxford County has no poor house, hence the aged poor are jailed with the prisoners. "Shame on the authorities who allow this state of things to continue! Shame on the mock economy and cringing meanness of those who oppose a poorhouse!" A few of the inmates are "off base," and he describes them unsympathetically as "extremely funny." They stay until sent to the asylum in London. Most of the inmates are there on a charge of "drunk and disorderly," a catch-all used when police "can't get a man convicted of anything else." A few "ladies" are in residence, he notes, but they are "far removed from the curious eye of man," so he knows nothing about them. (The Woodstock Jail Register confirms that in the winter of 1890, twenty-five "labourers" were incarcerated for vagrancy and a one man labelled "insane" was transferred after a month to the asylum in London, Ont.[22])

Birchall quips that unlike hotel residents, who lock their own doors at night from the inside, here it is "kindly done for them from the outside to prevent anyone intruding." He says that the rooms, although not luxurious, are comfortable. He adds: "A strange idea prevails here that too much exercise has a deterrent effect upon the body; consequently the area is limited by four walls, built sufficiently high to keep out the biting winds which occasionally howl around this pile of rock."

The jail has no appointed chaplain, Birchall explains, so on Sundays it is attacked by "a strong force of the Salvation Army" in scarlet jersey and glittering dress, firing "a strong salvo of Gospel shots." They are met with ridicule by the prisoners, he remarks, adding that "their ministrations within the gaol are quite ineffectual."

Birchall turns to the topic of the jail's officers. Mr. John Cameron, governor of the jail, is described as an elderly gentleman of long experience and "eminently fitted for the post he occupies." His keen powers of discipline, Birchall says, are allied with "a kind heart and considerate nature." Birchall rages at the revised "idiotic" rules imposed on him from Toronto, but observes that Cameron, in applying the regulations, lets common sense and humanity prevail. Birchall praises Cameron's lieutenant, Mr. James Forbes, if anything even more. A former farmer and cheesemaker in Zorra Township, he and Birchall had become friends back in 1888–89. In the jail, Forbes treats Birchall in a generous-hearted way and always has a kind word. He and Mrs. Forbes show unbounded kindness to Florence.

Similarly, Birchall pays tribute to others in attendance at the jail. Dr. Andrew T. Rice, the jail surgeon, he calls "a sound practical man," always "genial and courteous." Sheriff Perry, although elderly, is nevertheless prompt and efficient in the discharge of his many duties. He shows Birchall kindness, as does his son, John Perry, always jolly and widely regarded as "'a good sort.'" The grandson, George Perry, one of Birchall's guards, is similarly kind and deserving of "the warmest praise." John Entwhistle, for several months his night guard, is "a genial and amusing companion, full of wit and with a keen sense of humour." They have become trusted friends. Colour-Sergeant Midgely of the Oxford Rifles has taken over from him and proved to be "cheerful, with an inexhaustible fund of anecdotes and humour." From him he has learned much about the military life of Canada. Only his guard, McGee, comes in for criticism. Because his forte is "grumbling and growling at everybody save himself," Birchall is glad when he leaves in a huff.

Birchall remarks on his many visitors, some welcome, some not. He rails against Dr. Bessey, whose analysis of Birchall's personality resulted in so many negative assessments. By contrast, he enjoyed the visit of Mr. John Francis Waters of Ottawa, the essayist and scientist who took Bessey to task in "a very able article." Since then he has written to Birchall "freely and feelingly" from time to time and sent him books and papers, but not the preaching epistles he gets from others. Birchall deals harshly with a Roman Catholic priest, "sleek and catlike in appearance," who has tried but failed to cast his net around Birchall. By contrast, the Rev. Rural Dean Wade, an Anglican and his spiritual adviser, is always welcome.

Birchall writes that during his time in jail, he has received 700 letters from England, along with many newspapers, sometimes twenty in a single day. His mother has written to him every mail a "loving letter of comfort which only a mother's tenderest love can give." He has received many letters from Canada and the United States, nearly all from people he doesn't know. Many ask for autographs, and many come from women concerned about his spiritual welfare. (He finds Canadians' spelling "atrocious.") There are also many letters from cranks, some of them claiming to know how Benwell was shot or to have done the deed. Countless tracts have also arrived, which he gives to Jailer Cameron to distribute on Sundays so that prisoners will have something to accompany the weekly issues of the Salvation Army's *War Cry*.

The Trial

Many lawyers approached Birchall wanting to represent him, always claiming to be "the very best," or "the most eminent," "the foremost," or "the greatest" criminal lawyer in Canada.[23] One Toronto newspaperman (unidentified but probably from the *Empire*) pestered him relentlessly, trying to get him to engage a certain Toronto lawyer. Birchall says that Det. Bluett, after being paid $100 by another lawyer, pressed hard to get that lawyer hired.

Birchall recalls that early on he retained as his counsel his acquaintance from the *Britannic*, Mr. Hellmuth of London. Because Hellmuth felt that he couldn't give the case enough time and that he lacked criminal experience, Birchall hired Finkle, McKay & McMullen to work on his behalf in Woodstock. For the trial itself, Hellmuth recommended he retain Mr. Edmund Meredith of London, Ont., but Birchall wanted either Edward Blake or George Tate Blackstock, both of Toronto. Eventually arrangements were made with Blackstock at the last minute.

Hellmuth engaged Det. Bluett of Toronto to join the defence team. "Although he came well recommended," writes Birchall, "I never had any faith in him, and my opinion that I formed was afterward fully justified." By Birchall's account, he did a poor job of working up the defence's case; not only that, but he took money and "flagrantly committed" a "breach of confidence" by selling the *Globe* private notes written by the defendant.

There had been much speculation in the press about where Birchall found the money to pay his lawyers. In his autobiography, Birchall presents the details. His brother gave him £100, his sister £210, an uncle £50, Mr. Stevenson £45, an old Oxford friend (Mr. Lynch) £45, and an old Lancashire friend £30; there were other small amounts besides. His brother sent a further £30 to defray the costs of the petition for mercy. As for expenses, after Blackstock took his modest fee of £100, the remainder was paid to Hellmuth & Ivey to settle the bill with Finkle, McKay & McMullen, which had not yet come in by the time of writing. Hellmuth & Ivey paid Det. Bluett $250.

Birchall is critical of the courtroom and what occurred there. Because the trial was held in a space that was usually a theatre, it was "very grotesque to anyone who has been used to the judicial majesty of the English courts of justice." The motley crew of constables in "their withered garb" showed their incapacity to take orders. The scramble at the doors, and the favouritism the constables showed to women and even children, amounted to an insult to the yeomen of Oxford County and "a disgrace to any civilized country."

Birchall discusses how witnesses proved to be a serious problem for the defence. He complains about Const. Watson of Princeton, who insisted the defence pay him $10 for valuable information, which was paid, after which he withdrew his statement. He also complains that Det. Bluett would come up with wonderful reports, but then "the evidence exploded when touched." Meantime, after several visits from the Crown's Det. Murray, the imaginations of witnesses grew. To make matters worse, the Crown prevaricated, repeatedly refusing to share the written evidence with the defence up to the brink of the trial. With understatement, Birchall writes that when witnesses at the trial told "fairy-like tales," he found it "somewhat galling." Birchall takes exception to the uneven payments the Crown made to witnesses. Pelly got $255, as did Charles Benwell. Yet many of the witnesses subpoenaed by the Crown got nothing.

"I thought Mr. Blackstock's speech in my behalf a wonderful effort," Birchall writes. "And I truly appreciated his touching allusions to my dear wife, which were more than fully deserved." Indeed, he praises Blackstock for all that he did, especially given that he had joined the defence team so late. Birchall even acknowledges that Osler handled the Crown's case "in a wonderful manner, and his address to the jury was a very fine effort indeed." Birchall appears magnanimous here, but possibly he fell comfortably into the role of theatre reviewer.

As for the jury, Birchall observes that of the seventy-two in the pool, fully forty declared their prejudice beforehand, an indication of the state of things. He had felt confident about the verdict before the trial. It was not until he heard the embellished evidence from the array of witnesses that he came to realize the trial was going against him. He writes – needlessly – that he did not agree with the verdict.

"The Fatal Journey"

Oddly placed in the narrative is Birchall's discussion of the events of 17 February and his involvement in identifying Benwell's body.[24] It comes not in sequence, but as the penultimate instalment. Perhaps it was added late because of pressure from the publishers, who knew readers wanted, if not a confession, then at least his version of his time with Benwell.

Birchall writes that it was decided in New York that on 17 February he and Benwell would go to see the farm near Woodstock. Birchall had arranged with unnamed friends there to be ready to show his protégé a farm that they would say was Birchall's. These friends were waiting in the vicinity of Woodstock on the fateful day. He says that en route to Woodstock from Buffalo, he and Benwell had breakfast in the Hamilton refreshment room. (This detail confirms that Benwell did not die that day because the autopsy showed his stomach was empty.) On the slow train to Eastwood, he saw Mr. Matthew Virtue (a Crown witness) for a moment in the smoking car where he and Benwell were sitting. Miss Lockhart and Miss Choate were certainly mistaken when at the trial they told stories of sitting near them and hearing them. (Women would not have been in the smoking car.) Birchall thinks he remembers seeing Conductor Poole on the train.

After getting off the train at Eastwood, he and Benwell proceeded to the Governor's Road without seeing anyone. Old man Hayward could not possibly have seen them. About a mile out of town they saw a man driving a team and a younger man driving a sulky, but they never appeared as witnesses. He walked with Benwell to where the road to Pine Pond begins. Benwell was to proceed towards Pine Pond to meet the men who would show him the farm. Birchall turned back, wanting to catch the afternoon's eastbound train at Eastwood. He doesn't believe the evidence of witnesses who say they saw him returning alone along the muddy road. At Eastwood Station he saw Miss Smith some way off and went up to her, and they conversed. He saw some of the other young women there who testified at the trial, and he had a long conversation with the stationmaster, Dunn.

Birchall says that once in Niagara Falls, he sent Pelly the telegram signed "Bastell," which was the mistake of the boy who wrote it down. He made no attempt to conceal his name. Upon arriving at the Stafford House in Buffalo, he went up directly to talk with his wife and Pelly, without changing his clothes or muddy boots. Because Pelly had been told previously that he and Benwell were going to the horse farm near Niagara Falls, he prevaricated in explaining to Pelly about the day's activities. He told Pelly that Benwell was dissatisfied with the farm and had said he was going to London, Ont., to see other properties and people. Birchall led Pelly to believe that he would be Birchall's sole partner.

Birchall told Pelly that Benwell wanted Birchall to bring his baggage to the Falls and pass it through Canadian customs. Benwell had sent him by mail a cheque for his bonded cases and sent a telegram asking him "to get all of his goods out of my possession." The telegram had never been produced. Birchall implies that the Crown had it but suppressed the evidence. Later Birchall had Benwell's cases brought to Baldwins' boarding house, where Pelly and the Birchalls were staying in Niagara Falls. After not hearing from Benwell for a couple of days, they wondered what had happened. Eventually Birchall went to Buffalo, where he found a letter explaining that Benwell was dead. Birchall was at a loss as to what to do. He sent a telegram signed "Stafford" so that he could show Pelly he had the authority to send away all of Benwell's things. Birchall arranged for the Customs people to collect Benwell's trunks and send them to New York, and they did collect them from Baldwins's the next day.

Birchall says that the previous week he had written the famous letter to Col. Benwell. He fully expected that Benwell, after visiting the farm near Woodstock, would be sending a letter to his father telling him to send the £500. That price was "dirt cheap" for such a fine farm. Birchall expected the letters to arrive in England at the same time. He never had any intention of writing a letter with the forged signature of Benwell. He mentioned the typewriter only because he, Benwell, and Pelly had been impressed by one of the new machines when they tried it out in New York. He could not have written a convincing letter to the colonel because he had no idea how Fred would have addressed his father or signed off.

Birchall had read about the body found near Princeton but had paid little attention. When he read about the labelled cigar-box, he decided he needed to go to Princeton to identify the body. Meanwhile, Pelly went off to New York in search of Benwell. In Princeton, Birchall spoke with Swartz, the undertaker, and asked him about the buried man's clothing. When it was described, Birchall said he believed he could identify the body, and it was arranged for him to do so the next day. He spoke to Const. Watson, who was eager to pursue the case in hope of a reward. Birchall writes that he thought about confessing his role in the fraud, but decided he would tell him lies and "let the numbskull flounder." After making the identification, he spoke with Drs. Staples and Taylor, who had performed the autopsy. At that time, they were certain the body had been placed where it was found on the Wednesday, but they changed their story at the trial. Similarly, a man by the name of Maguire who was at the swamp Monday afternoon said no body was there then, but at the trial he changed the time of his swamp visit to the morning.

Birchall returned to his wife in Paris, Ont., and found her distraught, fearing that he would be blamed for the murder. He points out that she still did not know that he had travelled to Eastwood on the Monday. After talking with his wife, Birchall was introduced to Det. Murray, who also told him that the body was placed there Wednesday. The Crown did not dare to put Murray on the stand, so the substance of their talk was never entered into evidence.

Birchall says he threw away his gun because, not knowing the calibre of the bullets that killed Benwell, he was afraid authorities might use it as evidence showing he had shot him.

When the Birchalls returned to Niagara Falls, it was evident that Chief Young had put a watch on their premises. Birchall expected he would soon be arrested. He had in his possession the baggage check, keys, and gold pencil. Had he been "the cunning villain that the Crown would have people believe," he would not have held on to them. He was placed in the filthy lock-up at the Falls, where Murray and Young questioned him. Neither cautioned him, and they badgered him again and again. But he would only say that his lawyer instructed him to say nothing. In anger and frustration, Murray kicked the bars of the cell.

The police went away to arrest Florence Birchall. "Their treatment of her was brutal," Birchall writes. They drugged her with morphine to stupefy her. She was "grossly insulted by the officers ... The way she suffered at their hands is a blot on the administration of Canadian justice."

Meanwhile, Pelly told the public a "cock-and-bull story" about Birchall trying to push him over the Falls "and sundry other idiotic and childish ideas, which, of course, were without a shadow of the truth."

Hellmuth was supposed to appear to represent Birchall on the first day of the police court hearing, but he failed to turn up. "I was left," writes Birchall, "to the tender mercies of the prosecution – a fatal mistake for which I all through suffered." Murray told the witnesses what to say.

This concludes Birchall's account of his involvement in the events surrounding Benwell's death – "the fatal journey." He adds that he had been offered by various people large sums of money to write a sensational confession for publication. He would not do so because he meant what he said at the start of the trial when he declared that he was "not guilty!" As for the "Colonel's letters," he denies having had anything to do with them or knowing their origin.

Approaching Death

Birchall ends his narrative by thanking all those who have sent him a kind word or contributed to the comfort of his dear wife.[25] He forgives all the many people who have wronged him. He praises the Rev. Rural Dean Wade, a dear friend and welcome visitor.

The final paragraph of the autobiography begins: "And now I say, Farewell." He thanks once again the *Mail* and the *Herald* for making the publication possible. The last line reads: "If this little work has done no good it cannot do any harm, and at any those who have read it may warn their children in time and season to beware of the follies and sin that led to the writing of this book and the untimely fate of the writer."

Observations

Birchall's autobiography highlights his experiences at Oxford, vividly revealing how thoroughly he imbibed and valued the undergraduate culture that flourished there. In his book, *Oxbridge Men*, historian Paul Deslandes describes the values and practices of exclusivity, superiority, and dominance Oxbridge men of the Victorian period developed when self-fashioning a male identity as Britons and future imperial leaders. In Canada, Birchall's extraordinary self-confidence in the face of his murder trial and grim sentence was surely nurtured by this Oxford experience. Deslandes goes on to show how undergraduates used student clubs and their college rooms to indulge in the pleasures of male sociability that gave shape to their various masculine identities. Birchall put himself in the thick of such activity when, for instance, he entertained lavishly in his rooms, which he had decorated to indicate his embrace of the sporting set, founded the Black and Tan Club for carousing, and attended the races with friends. The flamboyant clothing he wore on Woodstock's streets emphasized his exceptional presence and his confidence in his elite masculinity. He was a dandy, but his high-class status and his skill in driving four-in-hand countered the effeminacy often said to characterize the dandy.

While revealing in many ways, Birchall's autobiography also contains significant silences, one being his relationship with his wife, Florence. He relates nothing about the circumstances of their first meeting, engagement, or wedding. The autobiography divulges nothing about their married life. Similarly, Birchall says little about Florence in his depictions of both their first stay in Woodstock and their trip to Canada with Pelly and Benwell. Florence appears fleetingly as a concerned wife at the time of her husband's identification of Benwell's body, as a victim of police harassment at Niagara, and as a loyal wife who frequently visited him in the Woodstock Jail. In these passages Birchall expresses extravagant sympathy or praise for her but gives no indication of her feelings. She remains a one-dimensional figure, a Victorian stereotype: the loyal wife, the respectable lady. His depiction of her is not out of line with how he views women more generally, revealed in his treatment of the topic of women at Oxford, whom he presents as "necessary and pleasant adjuncts." The intensely male-centred experience of Birchall's schooling shaped what he thought important to write down.

Birchall reveals more about his affection for and involvement with the many men in his life. He shows how he thrived on their company at university. He has quite a bit to say, some warmly positive, some definitely negative, about Benwell and Pelly, Det. Murray and Det. Bluett, the lawyers, and the male staff of the Woodstock Jail. He speaks especially warmly of his university chum, Leatham. However, there is never a hint in the autobiography about sexual relationships with the men in his life, and perhaps there were none. In any event, the silence is to be expected in a narrative written for public consumption in 1890.

In the autobiography, Birchall explicitly sets out to explain his downfall and thus provide a warning to other young men, especially ones headed for university. In doing so, however, he reveals the enormous enjoyment he derived from wine and song, if not women. He presents himself as being eager to involve himself in his male community and to be the life of the party. He takes pleasure in showing how he got away with his misdemeanours by outwitting college authorities. The failings he sets out to explore, it turns out, are actually represented as being good fun and the result of boys being boys. By contrast, Birchall gives no explanation for his failure to complete his degree, a topic he must have found embarrassing.

Unattractive to today's reader of the autobiography are Birchall's prejudices, ones his Oxford experience can only have nurtured. He has nothing good to say about Roman Catholic priests or their Church, a prejudice widely shared in 1890 among non-Catholics in both England and Canada. His class prejudices are even more amply shown, again reflecting the undergraduate culture of Oxford. He takes his wealth for granted throughout, even though the Canadian caper was prompted by his need for funds. He sneers at the behaviour of some people from modest backgrounds, whom he depicts as vulgar, notably when he tells the story of his Oxford chum who married beneath his station. He boasts of his lifelong involvement with noblemen, and he derides the snobbish elite of Woodstock, whom he believes stand far beneath his own lofty position.

As for the autobiography's account of Birchall's movements on 17 February and the identification of the body, his account has some plausibility. Everything he says makes sense, and the account deals effectively with several points that the Crown exploited at the trial. The letter to Col. Benwell that was used to great effect by the Crown is here given a context. As Birchall admits, it is proof of the fraud, but it does not explicitly show that Birchall shot Benwell. Some of the contradictory statements Birchall made to various people, he effectively dismisses as nonsense he had said to confuse them – as not so much the words of a compulsive liar, then, but certainly devious. Plausible too is his depiction of Det. Murray as the presence behind the scenes who coached witnesses to alter their testimony and suppressed certain evidence so that the Crown's theory of the crime would be compelling in court.

Curiously, however, this version of the day's events differs from the "extract" printed in the *Globe*. In it, Birchall says he planned to meet Pickthall at Eastwood, but there is no mention of him in the memoir's account of the day. Certainly, at least one of Birchall's accounts is either wrong or incomplete.

Still, the autobiography does not present an alibi for Birchall on 17 February, which reduces its persuasiveness. As he presents the story, no one saw him bid Benwell farewell at the road to the farm. His account would be much more persuasive if he identified the farm Benwell was supposedly going to see and the men who were ready to show it to him. The omission is explained in the account as his gentlemanly erasure aimed at protecting his friends. It is doubtful whether he would have been so gallant, given how, if presented at trial, their testimony could have saved his neck and reassured his wife.

12

Pleading for Mercy

From the time of Reginald Birchall's sentencing, it was expected that petition campaigns would be launched to urge Ottawa authorities to commute the death sentence to life in prison. The Dominion government in Ottawa was responsible for the criminal law, including clemency decisions, even though the Ontario government administered the criminal law in the province.

State machinery was in place for the Crown to consider petitions and letters urging clemency, and it was customary in capital cases for attempts to be made to persuade officials to stay executions. Officially, the governor general made decisions about whether or not to commute sentences, but in practice he took the advice of the Dominion cabinet. Given Canada's considerable autonomy within the Empire, the governor general was expected to follow cabinet's advice, whatever his personal views. In 1890 the governor general was Lord Stanley, whose lasting gift to Canada was the cup given annually to hockey champions. The Conservative government of Sir John A. Macdonald held power. The Department of the Secretary of State, headed in 1890 by Sir Joseph-Adolphe Chapleau, collected the petitions for the governor general and sent them along to the Department of Justice. Officials in that department and its minister, in 1890 the future prime minister, Sir John Thompson, considered them and made a recommendation to cabinet.

The lawmakers and officials who devised the post-Confederation procedures for making commutation decisions were reluctant to set them down.[1] The process was highly discretionary and opaque. In theory, each case was to be handled with fairness and on its own merits. Authorities never assumed that all people convicted of capital crimes would hang. The Crown's ancient prerogative of mercy came into play. When deciding who should die and who should live, "mercy was to offset rigour," writes historian Carolyn Strange, "so that the deserving subject might be accorded the privilege of commutation." Between Confederation and Canada's last hanging in 1962, one half of convicted murderers escaped the hangman thanks to executive clemency. Clemency was more likely to be granted in cases where the jury recommended mercy. In Birchall's case, there had been no such recommendation. Other factors besides legal ones came into play, including the health of the prisoner and political considerations. The justice minister and other cabinet ministers were politicians and thus sensitive to public opinion and the implications for their re-election.[2]

Petitions

In October and early November 1890, petitions in support of saving Birchall's life were circulated in both England and Canada so that people might sign them. A vigorous petitioning campaign was conducted in Ontario, but reluctance to sign was a powerful factor in this because of the widespread belief that Birchall was a murderer who deserved his sentence. Florence Birchall served as the titular head of the campaign because she continued to be certain (at least in public) that her husband was innocent and because the campaigners hoped that widespread sympathy for her might help his cause. Quebec, too, saw a spirited petition campaign. In England, the public generally was less engaged with the issue, but campaigners found less opposition to their cause and greater sympathy for an English gentleman who had encountered trouble far away.

Campaigns in Ontario were carried out mainly in Toronto as well as in southwestern Ontario near where the Birchall drama had unfolded. Florence Birchall, following the norms of her class and gender, did not take to the podium to drum up support for clemency. Instead, she did what was then the appropriate thing: she politely asked members of the public to sign the petitions. Newspaper offices received her request written in her own fine hand on quality notepaper. The petitions were available for signing, usually in newspaper offices – yet another indication of the press's importance in the case.

Florence Birchall also worked behind the scenes – again, the appropriate place at the time for a woman to attempt to influence public officials. At the end of October, she went with her sister to see Ontario's deputy attorney general, John Cartwright, at his Toronto office. The ladies did not go there unaccompanied. Jail governor John Cameron did the chivalrous thing and escorted them on the train to the provincial capital. The *News* expressed surprise that his duties as a servant of the Crown had not prevented him from acting as "friend, advisor, and escort." What took place at the meeting was not reported, but it was noted that the women accepted Cartwright's invitation to his home for lunch.[3] (It's possible that the invitation had less to do with the women's influence than with the desire of Cartwright's family to meet the renowned Mrs. Birchall.) After the visit, the attorney general's office approved Florence Birchall's having more frequent visits with her jailed husband. The *Mail* reported that the decision had raised Attorney General Oliver Mowat in the estimation of those Woodstock women who were sympathetic to the prisoner's wife.[4]

There were critics of both the petitions and Florence Birchall. One person wrote to the *Sentinel-Review* fuming that one of the petitions reflected unjustly on Oxford County, in that its preamble stated that it was impossible to get an impartial jury there and that the newspapers worked up the case against the unfortunate young man so that he didn't get a fair trial. "Whatever people may think of Birchall," said the letter, "surely no man in the county would sign the petition." In fact, some did. Another letter writer asked the *Sentinel-Review* to divulge the first ten or fifteen names of those who signed the Woodstock petitions – presumably to embarrass them in public. The editor replied that as he had not seen the petitions, the paper could not comply, but added: "We are told that a good many business men and esteemed citizens signed them."[5]

The justice minister received a letter at the end of October from a W. Street that cast doubt on Florence Birchall's motives in mounting the clemency petitions. It argued that she must have known about the swindle of Pelly and Benwell ever since the days spent crossing the ocean with them. Street suspected that Birchall had threatened that if she didn't "lend her fascinating ways to save his neck, then his postmortem confession would expose her rogueries." The *Sentinel-Review* had more sympathy for Florence Birchall, saying that people understood why, as a wife, she would feel she must do what she could for her husband, but then it added, "Surely her feelings are not a sufficient basis for executive action" – that is to say, for staying the execution.[6]

Some Canadian newspapers lamented the popularity of Birchall during the petition phase. In Montreal, the *Gazette* echoed the concern of the *Ottawa Citizen* regarding published statements about the condemned man that went "perilously near making him a hero." The man's "good humor, the favor in which he was held by former acquaintances, and his conduct in prison," declared the *Gazette*, should not obscure the fact that he was "the perpetrator of a notorious crime."[7]

The press published comments by people who doubted the likely effectiveness of the petitions. "Nobody," declared the *New York Tribune*, "excepting the unfortunate woman herself, expected the petition his wife is circulating could sway the Minister of Justice in Birchall's favor."[8]

A petition signed by thousands of people from many places in Ontario (and referred to as "the Ontario petition") highlighted the role the press had played in bringing about a guilty verdict against Birchall: "The Press of Canada, and particularly the Province of Ontario, had prior to the trial, by their articles, comments and accounts, influenced and prejudiced the mind of the public of Ontario against the said John Reginald Birchall."[9] In a similar vein, J.B. Warren, editor of Montreal's *Patriot*, urged Ottawa to at least delay Birchall's execution, accusing Warren's own profession of "prejudic[ing] the mind of the public against him."[10] Given that thousands of people signed petitions in support of Birchall, a significant portion of the public blamed the press for the guilty verdict. Clearly, there was a widely held view that news coverage had significantly affected the trial, with a disastrous result for the accused.

A petition made available for signing in Toronto's newspaper offices argued that Birchall's sentence ought not to be carried out, for several reasons: a murderer should be given the chance to reform; hanging defied the divine commandment "Thou shalt not kill"; in the past, circumstantial evidence had often hung the wrong person; hanging violated the covenant "Vengeance is mine, sayeth the Lord"; hanging did not prevent crime, as shown by Birchall, who knew the penalty for the murder he had committed. It urged that instead of being hanged, Birchall should spend the rest of his life behind prison walls at hard labour.[11] This petition reflected the minority view, held especially by some clergy, that executions in general were wrong on moral and religious grounds.

By 4 November, the number of signatures was mounting. The Ontario petition circulated in Woodstock had 300 supporters, and it was said there were 3,564 signatures altogether on the petitions collected in Toronto. A day later the total was reported as 5,200, and when petitions from elsewhere were added, it was 10,000. The *Mail* declared it to be "the largest petition asking for Executive clemency yet presented to the Dominion Government."[12] According to the *Mail*, a turning point came after it published a letter, signed simply "the Colonel," in which the writer admitted to the murder. That letter raised about Birchall's guilt in the minds of many people and persuaded fence sitters to sign.[13]

It was reported that Florence Birchall was "much gratified" by the growing support for clemency. A reporter for the *Mail* who said he had spoken to her wrote sympathetically, "Though still care worn and sad-eyed under the strain of anxiety she bears with such courage and fortitude, her refined features are lit up at times by an expression that shows hope to be strong within her."[14]

From Montreal came the news that that city's petition campaign and the one in Quebec City were both going well. Two boosters of the Quebec campaign were Arthur Leatham, Birchall's steadfast friend from university days, and Dugald MacMurchy, the Toronto lawyer who had been involved in Birchall's defence as Blackstock's junior.[15] A petition arrived in Ottawa from Montreal signed by, among others, Anglican Bishop William Bennett Bond, Mayor Jacques Grenier, and business leaders Sir Donald A. Smith, Sir Joseph Hickson, and the Hon. Henry Starnes.[16] It was reported that a mass meeting would be held at the skating rink to protest the execution of Birchall. The *Sentinel-Review*, always happy to take a swipe at Quebec, sarcastically observed that these Quebeckers "must know infinitely more of the evidence and the circumstances than a judge and jury in a court at Woodstock."[17]

The petitions with signatures, still extant in the Department of Justice records, show that a remarkably large number of Quebeckers signed petitions urging clemency.[18] Men and women, anglophones and francophones, the affluent and the working class all signed in significant numbers. It is apparent from the occupations listed by the signatories that typically a petition was passed around an industrial workplace owned by a sympathizer, and all the workers would sign one after the other.

A rumour circulated in Ontario that dignitaries of the Roman Catholic Church in Quebec were directly lobbying the justice minister, Sir John Thompson, who was a Roman Catholic.[19] This unsubstantiated claim reflected what many Protestant Ontarians likely suspected in the then-current context of inflamed French–English and Catholic–Protestant relations. Recent years had seen bitter disputes over the execution of Louis Riel, the handling of the Jesuit Estates, and the 1887 assumption of power in Quebec by the Parti National. More plausibly, it was reported that the Catholic bishop of Montreal had signed a petition.[20]

Meantime, news arrived of support for Birchall in England, where supposedly he had "powerful friends" who would induce the British government to ask the Canadian government for clemency. Birchall's half-brother, the Rev. Oswald Birchall, claimed he had collected 3,000 signatures of prominent men.[21] The *Globe*, however, received a cable saying it was not true. There were only a handful of petitions from some of Birchall's Lancashire friends.[22] The Department of Justice records contain several petitions that reached Ottawa from England, one with just two signatures and others with several dozen.[23]

The *New York Tribune* reproduced the preamble of the English petition dated 21 October. It urged the commutation of Birchall's sentence of several grounds: Birchall's own strenuous denials of his complicity in the murder; the absence of direct evidence at the trial; and the unsatisfactory evidence of witnesses at the trial who contradicted one another or who changed their testimony from the inquest. The whole case, maintained the petitioners, was unduly prejudiced by Birchall's behaviour regarding the fraud, which had to be admitted but was no proof of murder. The top signatures were those of Birchall's mother, Mrs. Mary Eleanor Birchall, and his half-brother, Oswald Birchall. There was no mention of his sister Maude having signed.[24]

An English petition that took another tack was circulated by the Rev. Mr. Walker, rector of East Hastings, and the Rev. George Spooner, vicar of Ingelsham, Wilt. It argued that the Canadian government should not hang Birchall because it had not inquired into reports that Birchall was part of a conspiracy, an inquiry that might show that others may have been more responsible for the murder.[25] Another English petition, this one from Leamington, Warwickshire, referred to the circumstantial evidence and asserted that "no English Jury would have convicted upon it."[26]

In November, it was reported that Birchall wasn't confident the petitions would succeed. One report said he had discussed with his wife what kind of a man justice minister Sir John Thompson was and what effect the petitions would likely have on him.[27] Prime Minister John A. Macdonald had brought Thompson, a Nova Scotia judge, into his cabinet in 1885 as justice minister. By 1890 he had a well-earned reputation as a kingpin in Macdonald's cabinets and as an exceptionally hard-working manager of his department. He carefully examined capital case files on a case-by-case basis, and at least twice, overriding the advice of his own department, he had approved reprieves because he felt the evidence against the men justified conviction but not execution. Had the Birchalls known this, they might have been encouraged. However, the public's perception of Thompson's views on capital punishment derived mainly from his having been justice minister when the Macdonald government made the highly controversial decision to hang Métis leader Louis Riel for treason, and from his having led the voices in Parliament in opposition to a motion of regret for Riel's execution.[28]

Florence Birchall Presents the Petitions and the Crown Responds

On 5 November, Florence Birchall, her sister Marion West-Jones, and Dugald MacMurchy travelled by train to Ottawa to present the petitions to Sir John Thompson. The main petition was said to have been signed by 5,000 people, including thirty or forty clergymen, as well as bankers and medical men. According to the Associated Press report from Ottawa, the minister "received Mrs. Birchall most kindly, she being visibly affected."

In the minister's office, it fell to a man, MacMurchy, to present the case for commutation. He dwelt on the salient arguments made by Blackstock in his concluding address at the trial. Florence Birchall spoke too, emphasizing that she fully believed in her husband's innocence. If he were hanged, her life would be "blighted and two honorable families ruined." She choked up, "tears gathering in her eyes as she sank into a chair, covering her face with her hands." There may have been some creativity used in making this report because no reporter was in the room at the time. The *Globe*'s reporter in Ottawa imagined "a very affecting scene, recalling some historical pictures of a woman pleading before a sovereign power."[29] Indeed, there was a long tradition of women petitioning the Crown, best exemplified in Ontario by the Loyalist women who had struggled through the American Revolutionary War.[30]

The minister said he would give careful attention to the petition. That statement was, of course, a polite formality, and offered no real hope to the woman.

Ottawa Authorities and the Decision

At the time, an important task for the judge in a capital case that ended in a conviction was to provide a post-trial report to Ottawa authorities. Cabinet decisions regarding mercy relied heavily on what the trial judge had to say.[31] Justice MacMahon's report, dated 16 October 1890, and directed to Secretary of State Joseph-Adolphe Chapleau, was a handwritten document of fourteen pages, still extant. It relates the Crown's case in succinct fashion. The only evidence quoted is Birchall's letter to Colonel Benwell, which is reproduced in full. Nothing of the defence's case is included, the only comment being that "the prisoner did not at the trial account or attempt to account for his whereabouts on the 17th of February." Where MacMahon referred to a specific witness and the gist of the testimony, the justice department staff annotated the report to provide page references to the trial transcript.

The judge's report was pored over by bureaucrats in the Remissions Branch of the Department of Justice, overseen at the time by its long-standing chief officer, Augustus Power.[32] A memorandum by a Remissions Branch official remarks that the judge's report was "a compendious statement of the case" and notes that, although it lacked an express statement of the judge's opinion of the verdict, his charge to the jury made clear that he fully concurred with it. It added comments on the defence: "The prisoner's defence, though conducted with a scrutiny of the great mass of evidence presented by the Crown, did not offer any affirmative theory of the defence. No attempt was made to account for his movements on the 17th February, nor to establish the truth of any of his statements as to the circumstances of his parting with Benwell on that day." The memorandum appended a list of the evidence the Crown presented regarding Birchall's movements on 17 February, the shots heard, and the fact that he was familiar with the locality where Benwell's body was found. Also appended was a list of twelve petitions and letters urging commutation, as well as a sketch map of Blandford and Blenheim townships, showing Eastwood and routes to and from the swamp. No evaluation was made of the petitions or correspondence by supporters of commutation.

The various documents – Justice MacMahon's report, the memorandum of the Department of Justice official, the petitions, and letters from members of the public – were presented to cabinet. On 7 November, the meeting of the governor general in council took place that made the final determination. In addition to Lord Stanley, several members of cabinet were present: Sir John A. Macdonald, Sir Hector-Louis Langevin, Sir Adolphe-Phillipe Caron, Sir Joseph-Adolphe Chapleau, Sir John Thompson, and Sir Charles Tupper. At the conclusion of the meeting, Stanley gave royal assent to an Order in Council allowing the law to take its course.[33] The cabinet treated the case as open and shut; political considerations were not nearly as significant in this case as in some others.[34]

Two days after seeing the justice minister, Florence Birchall and her sister were back in Woodstock. There, she was shown despatches from Ottawa stating that the governor general had signed the Privy Council order declaring the government would not interfere in the sentence. She did not believe the despatches, partly because she had understood that no decision would be made for a few days. She went to see her husband at the jail but said nothing to him about the matter. Nevertheless, the press described it as an interview "full of pain."

Later that afternoon, her trusted legal adviser, Dugald MacMurchy, telegraphed her saying that it was indeed official. The deputy justice minister had telegraphed saying: "the governor general was pleased to order the law be allowed to take its course in re Birchall." The sheriff of Oxford County would be informed by mail.[35] In the Birchall case, as in nearly all cases, authorities never revealed the rationale for the decision.

It was said that Florence Birchall and her sister both returned to the jail in tears and that the turnkey, Forbes, could not hold back tears either. Birchall immediately sensed that the news was in and that it was bad. The reporter for the *Sentinel-Review* observed that, although relating the sad news was "an awful task," Mrs. Birchall "bravely faced it." In response, her husband replied simply, "Then, I suppose I must go."

Reports described Birchall's demeanour upon hearing the decision in different ways. The *Sentinel-Review* said Birchall was "completely unmanned" (a revealing expression) and that it took nearly an hour for him to regain "his marvellous sense of composure." The reporter for the *World* wrote: "He did not break down, yet he showed signs of great emotion as the last ray of hope vanished." The report in the *News* said that the "prisoner was quite calm, and did not show the slightest tremor or fear or dread." Mrs. Birchall returned to her hotel, said the *Sentinel-Review*, "the incarnation of despair and misery."[36] Reporters had gone to the jail in hope of witnessing the scene, but given the jail rules imposed by then, it is unlikely that they had actually done so. Their varied descriptions may simply have reflected how they imagined the encounter, or what they gleaned from jail officers who had been present. It was reported that evening that Birchall said he had been hoping for a respite that would give him time to prove his innocence. The *Sentinel-Review* pointed out to readers that he had had eight months to do so.[37]

Newspaper editorials approved the official decision to allow the death sentence to be carried out. "The Dominion Government has done its duty," said the *Sentinel-Review*. "The fountain of justice in Canada remains pure." It maintained that the decision enhanced Canada's national reputation. "English people now know that Canadian justice, like Canadian sentiment, cannot be influenced from abroad." The Canadian press cared how the case would be seen in England, the heart of the Empire. Moreover, such a comment from a Liberal newspaper reflected a position in political discourse at the time, one that backed up the Liberal view in support of asserting Canadian autonomy within the Empire.

Montreal's *Gazette* praised the tough-minded decision of the authorities. Given that the temptation of the Government ... would naturally be to take the side of leniency," it was certain that "only a sense of duty to the obligation of their office led to a different result." The public was solidly in favour of the verdict; the petitioners represented the views of comparatively few.[38]

Opponents of capital punishment spoke out, however. Prompted by the Birchall case, the Rev. W.B. Booth preached a sermon in the Don Mills Methodist Church that called hanging "a brutal act" and "a relic of a coarse past age." He maintained that the law hanged men to avenge itself, contrary to the spirit of the Gospel. "If prisons became schools for education and salvation," Booth declared, "even bad Birchalls might be reformed and go forth to the ends of the earth as mighty for truth as they had been for wrong."[39] The *Globe* devoted three columns to the objections to capital punishment raised by the Rev. Dr. Stafford of Toronto's Sherbourne Street Methodist Church. In his oration to his congregation, Stafford argued that capital punishment had no adequate support in the Scriptures; furthermore, it reflected the spirit of vengeance, was carried out in a brutal way, and caused malice in the human heart.[40] Although for decades a few voices would call for the abolition of capital punishment, support for state executions was overwhelming. What had been firmly resolved in November 1890 was that Reginald Birchall would hang that month.

13

The Hanging

Newspapers lavished attention on Reginald Birchall's hanging, both the lead-up to it and the event itself. Journalists sensed the public's thirst for a story presented dramatically and with all the ghastly details. The reporters' prose at times turned deeply purple as they sentimentalized the scene, drawing out its maudlin aspects.

Between Confederation in 1867 and 1976, when capital punishment was eliminated, Canada executed 697 men and 13 women.

Birchall's Hangman

At the time of the Birchall case, county sheriffs were responsible for overseeing executions. It was customary for them to contract the job to a hangman.[1] As 14 November approached – the date set for Birchall's execution – some people expressed concern both about this process and about the kind of person likely to get the job. At the Toronto Presbytery meeting on 4 November, the Rev. Dr. William Caven, a prominent Presbyterian minister, deplored the system for selecting hangmen: "What a shocking thing it was to tempt with money a man who has no fear of God and whose qualification in most cases is lack of human feeling." The meeting resolved that the government should have in place as executioners "reputable public officials." As the Rev. D. J. MacDonald explained, it was essential that "this most awful act that can ever be done by the community should be done in the most solemn way by the official representative of the community."[2]

Several men applied for the job of hanging Birchall. The successful applicant was John Robert Radclive, who had experience with the work and claimed to have the support of Attorney General Oliver Mowat.[3] In November 1890, Radclive told reporters he had assisted with fourteen hangings in England before his recent arrival in Canada, where he had been the principal hangman of three convicts prior to Birchall. He claimed to have trained in England under the great William Marwood, who served as London's executioner from 1874 to 1883.[4] Because of his experience and the pride he took in his work, Radclive called himself a "professional, public executioner" and styled himself "John Radclive, P.E." He longed to become Canada's full-time, salaried executioner. In 1890, however, it was part-time, occasional work. His day job was as steward of the Sunnyside Boating Club in Toronto's west end. When he was chosen for the much-publicized Birchall hanging, a few club members found it appalling and called for his resignation as steward, but the majority supported his continued employment at the posh club. He never hid his calling as an executioner from his friends in his Parkdale neighbourhood. "Many of those who take a glass of beer with him occasionally at Johnny Scholes' are aware of his identity," reported the *World*.[5]

The press took an interest in a man who was willing, even eager, to undertake such a gruesome task and more than willing to talk to reporters. The *Sentinel-Review* described Radclive as "a middle-aged, fairly good-looking Englishman." (He was thirty-four.) Of medium height, he was said to have large, piercing eyes. It was regarded as being a good thing that he bore a look of determination, for the job needed to be carried out unflinchingly. Hamilton's *Spectator* described him a bit differently, saying he was "a short, florid-faced Englishman, with blonde moustache and bustling cheerful manner."[6] A reporter in Toronto who interviewed Radclive reported in flowery prose that "on a trio of previous occasions have his services been called into requisition when the gory and ill-Crowned Juggernaut of justice has been dragged forth to crush out a guilty life beneath its wheels."[7]

Reporters asked Radclive whether he would wear a mask when he executed Birchall. "Why would I?" he replied. "The execution is legitimate. It is sanctioned by law." Radclive mused that because Birchall had not been a working man, his neck would not be muscular and thus the job would be an easy one.

There was considerable curiosity about the unusual technique Radclive proposed to use for Birchall's hanging. The conventional method was to build a scaffold for the condemned individual to climb; then, when the noose was in place, he would fall through a released trap door to open space below. Instead, Radclive relied on a 350-pound weight suspended by a rope from a wooden structure. When it was time, Radclive would release the weight and it would fall, jerking the convict upwards by the attached noose. Radclive argued in favour of the system, sometimes referred to as the "jerk-em up" technique, because it eliminated the need to conduct the prisoner up steps to a height, a procedure that caused some condemned men to quake and need assistance. Birchall could simply stand on the ground until jerked up.[8]

A challenge for hangmen was to ensure that the neck snapped, while avoiding both the gruesome mistake of decapitating the convict and the undue suffering of a slow death by strangulation. The convict's weight had to be taken into account, as well as the scaffold's height and the length of the rope. Botched hangings were frequent, especially when inexperienced and incompetent hangmen were deployed. Decapitations and partial decapitations shocked spectators and newspaper readers alike. Bungled hangings were an important impetus to the Canadian government's eventual decision to hire a professional hangman.[9]

On Friday, 13 November, the day before Birchall's execution, Radclive arrived in Woodstock in time to observe the construction of the unusual scaffold. That day, Birchall was moved to another cell to spare him the view from his cell of the northeast corner of the jail yard where the structure was being built. He could, however, hear the sawing and hammering. Birchall was intrigued by how the thing worked, and he asked a guard to go into the yard and make a drawing of the device so he could understand it better. When he saw the sketch, he was disappointed and called it crude in design. Still, he expressed the hope that it would be effective and get the job done quickly.[10]

Executioner and condemned man checked each other out. From his cell window, Birchall could see his executioner down in the yard below. Always interested in men's apparel, Birchall noticed Radclive's brown corduroy coat and said he was "a smart-looking fellow." Later, when Birchall was asleep in his cell, the hangman came to size him up. A reporter said that it looked as though he were measuring a suit. He was in fact confirming his calculations for the success of the hanging. Earlier he had told a reporter that he liked to look at the condemned man "to judge as accurately as possible, his build and other points in advance as everything must be taken into account when arranging the rope."[11]

On the day before the execution, Radclive drew attention to himself in Woodstock. Many executioners took steps to obscure their identity, but not Radclive.[12] He spent his time walking the streets and several times dropped into a saloon, where he told people about the "jerk" he had planned for Birchall. "This invariably created as sensation," wrote a reporter for Hamilton's *Spectator*. Eager to be interviewed that day, Radclive sought out reporters. The *Spectator's* reporter believed that the way Radlive "put himself on exhibition through the town was most offensive to people of old-fashioned ways of thinking." By the evening, Radclive was very drunk and making a nuisance of himself in saloons. The deputy sheriff prudently removed him to the jail office, where Radclive continued to make trouble until he passed out.[13] This experience was not nearly as bad as on a subsequent occasion, when after boasting publicly about his occupation on the night before an execution, he was attacked by a crowd. Police rescued him and put him in jail for his own protection.[14]

Preparing for the End

Newspapers detailed how Birchall spent his last full day on earth. Because he had been up most of the night before, he slept late. His breakfast of cold chicken, toast, and tea went untasted. Even when the noise of the scaffold builders began, he remained in bed until after the noon hour. At 1:50 he ate his dinner of venison steak from a deer killed at Long Point by a Woodstock hunter, Joe Thompson. It disappointed him because, the gourmet judged, the game had not been sufficiently aged. After eating his meal, he changed and felt better. Sitting up all night had knocked him out, he said.[15]

The day before, Birchall had made a list of clothing he wanted. For the hanging, he planned to wear a white flannel shirt with its collar turned down – he feared that a stiff collar on a dress shirt would get in the way of the rope. No white flannel shirt could be found in local stores, so one had to be ordered from London, Ont. The plan was that once he was cut down, the flannel shirt would be removed and he would be dressed for burial in a linen shirt with a stiff collar. "You should call in an auctioneer tomorrow and see what this flannel shirt will bring," Birchall quipped to the deputy sheriff. "The reporters will make the bidding brisk."[16] The prisoner had already got $150 for the clothing he had worn on 17 February. Wonderland, an amusement business with premises in Toronto and Buffalo, had bought his outfit for display. In a contract between M.J. Robinson of Wonderland and Birchall, the prisoner gave Robinson the exclusive right to display an effigy of him made from a plaster cast of his face (made before and after execution) and dressed in his outfit from February. Whether the casts were taken is unclear.[17]

Birchall wasn't the only one thinking about the relic hunters. That afternoon, a *World* reporter interviewed Radclive, who boasted that after the hanging he could get a dollar a foot for the rope. Madame Tussaud's had already ordered a foot for her exhibition in London, England, where she had been displaying a portrait model of "Birchall, the Benwell Murderer."[18]

On the last afternoon of his life, Birchall wrote to friends and read some letters that well-wishers had sent him. He autographed photographs of himself and chatted with his guards.

At 7:30 p.m., Florence Birchall was admitted to the jail, accompanied by her sister Marion and by Birchall's friend, Arthur Leatham. Her escorts stayed in the jail office, until Marion spied the rope and tackle stored there, which moved her deeply. Florence Birchall's final visit lasted into the wee hours, as she dreaded parting from her beloved. By midnight, the town was asleep, but a group of reporters still kept watch at the entrance of the jail. Finally, at 1:30 a.m., the visit ended and Florence was met by her sister and Leatham, who accompanied her to her hotel. Waiting there was her doctor, who had opiates ready to administer to her.

Upon his retirement as turnkey, James Forbes recalled being with the couple during their final visit, then allowing them some private time to talk, and finally observing Birchall when, just after his wife left, he "broke down completely, and went all to pieces." The prisoner's remarkable self-control gave out at last, but only in a private setting.[19]

Birchall's spiritual adviser, Rural Dean Wade, sat up with the prisoner throughout what remained of the night. His role was to provide comfort at an extraordinarily anxious time, and it was speculated that at last the prisoner might confess to his crime. For the public, Birchall maintained his innocence to the end. It is possible that Wade had heard his confession privately, perhaps a day or two earlier, but the spiritual adviser refused to say anything publicly about the matter.

At a time when most people in Ontario were religious, many folks were shocked by stories of Birchall's irreverence and refusal to confess his sins. One report was that when Rural Dean Wade was praying intensely with Birchall that last night, he glanced up to find the prisoner making shadow puppets on the cell wall with his hands. It was also reported that earlier Dr. Andrew Rice, the jail doctor who had been attending him for months, had challenged Birchall's lack of Christian views. "Surely you know whether you would rather go to heaven or hell," suggested the physician. Birchall joked irreverently that he wasn't sure – he had friends in both places.[20]

By contrast, Dean Wade spoke admiringly of Birchall's adherence to the tenets of his Anglican faith. He was quoted as saying that Birchall's "deportment is everything that could be desired. He joins in religious exercises, being as devout as could be wished."[21]

The Execution

The day of the execution dawned bright and crisp with a frost on the ground that soon melted in the sunshine. The sheriff had issued 200 tickets for admission to the jail yard where the hanging was to take place. About half of them went to reporters, who represented newspapers from across the United States and Canada.

Hangings in Canada had at one time been open public events, the theory being that the terrible sight would deter crime. As popular events they often became occasions for drunkenness and horseplay, which disappointed authorities bent on teaching moral lessons. In 1869, Canadian law, in step with a change in law in England, dispensed with public hangings and required that they be private. They were henceforth to take place out of the public eye at jails. Especially in small jails, it was not possible to comply with the law. The height of the jail wall also determined the visibility of hangings. And in any event, journalists were permitted to attend hangings so that they could confirm to the public what had happened and draw moral lessons for readers. The Birchall hanging, with its 200 ticketed spectators and 100 newspapermen, stretched the notion of the private hanging, but the same was true for many other executions around that time.[22]

That morning Birchall's special cook prepared his breakfast of poached eggs and toast with canned peaches and blackberries. The prisoner touched only the eggs. It was reported that he laughed and joked with his guards. He took great care with his appearance for the big day. His black jacket and vest and checked trousers fitted him perfectly, and his hair, smartly parted in the centre, and grand moustache were carefully groomed.[23]

At 8 a.m. the sheriff and police admitted the swarm of the ticketholders into the yard. Police Chief Willis ensured that the crowd was pushed back from the scaffold so that the onlookers formed a hollow square around it. Many men and boys without tickets climbed the leafless trees near the jail. Police chased them down, but they immediately reappeared on their perches, which provided a view of the proceedings. A half century later, a former newsboy still remembered the excitement of the time when he defied his mother by playing hooky and climbing a tree to view the hanging.[24]

The hangman inspected the scaffold and made adjustments to his rope and pulleys. It took three men to lift the 350-pound weight to its raised position. Radclive, who appeared to be suffering no signs of his previous night's spree, had replaced his corduroy coat with a tight-fitting black one.

A procession formed inside the jail. Slipping in behind Birchall, the hangman pinioned Birchall's arms with a leather strap, routinely done to limit the condemned man's resistance but allow his forearms freedom to shake hands.[25] Rural Dean Wade, in his vestments, led the way into the yard and towards the scaffold, reciting passages from the Anglican Book of Common Prayer in a voice described as being "manly and musical." Birchall followed, accompanied by Perry on one side and Leatham on the other. Bringing up the rear were Jail Governor Cameron and newly appointed inspector of prisons, Dr. Theodore F. Chamberlain. When Birchall stepped into the doorway where the crowd could see him, he paused. "It is a dramatic touch," wrote the reporter from the *Spectator*. "He is evidently posing." The reporter cynically observed that Birchall had made "an extremely effective tableau – creditable to his art as a stage manager."

The journalists all agreed that Birchall was putting on a brave face, a demeanour much preferred to that of convicts who broke down pathetically, detracting from the climactic moment.[26] The reporter from the *News* described how he walked erect, looking ahead, and appeared "composed and calm." The *Sentinel-Review* said: "There was a look of determination about him. His eyes were steady. He was very pale, but showed no symptoms of nervousness. His step was firm and elastic." The *Spectator* said: "He draws himself up to his full height and faces the crowd defiantly and with a half-amused smile." The reporter added with a flourish: "It seems hard that one so young, so comely and so brave should die on this bright sweet morning." Birchall's manly, self-controlled demeanor, seen as exceptional at such a moment, was much admired.

At the scaffold, Birchall said his final farewells. As his friend Arthur Leatham stepped up, wrote the reporter from the *Spectator*, "a really beautiful smile lights up Birchall's face. 'Kiss me again, old fellow,' said the condemned man. They kissed on the lips. 'Now good-bye and God bless you,' said Birchall. Leatham turned away weeping. Dean Wade approached him and Birchall kissed him too on the lips. Birchall asked to shake hands with his executioner, and as they did so Birchall said, 'Well, good-bye, old fellow.'"[27]

The hangman put the noose around Birchall's neck and the black cap over his eyes. Rural Dean Wade began the Lord's Prayer with tears streaming down his face. It had been arranged that at the phrase, "Deliver us from evil," Radclive would pull on the cord to release the weight. However, the cord had become twisted and it took a few moments for the weight to fall. It was 8:27 a.m.

Birchall shot up "like a rocket." He hung suspended slowly spinning around. Radclive tried to steady the turning. For a full three-and-a-half minutes the body jerked about. Reporters counted fifty-two convulsions. A little later, a physician checked Birchall's pulse and found that it was still beating at sixty beats per minute. After six minutes, he checked again and pronounced Birchall dead. At 8:44 the body was cut down as Rural Dean Wade, Leatham, and Perry sobbed.

It was as a Victorian gentleman that Birchall approached his death. In England, the gentlemanly code had been long established, having been derived from eighteenth-century English conceptions of the ideal male aristocrat. As historian Donna T. Andrew explains, key to that ideal were courage, self-direction and self-control, and an easiness of demeanour.[28] Even at the end, Birchall displayed these qualities impeccably.

The story of the execution was wired instantly by two Great North Western telegraphers in the jail yard via wires strung for the occasion. "The public was known to be anxiously eager to hear 'how Birchall stood it,'" observed Toronto's *Telegram*. It noted that just six minutes after the hanging the news was known "all over America." Seven minutes after his death, the *Telegram*'s presses were churning out a special edition. Many publishers enjoyed unprecedented sales that day. The *Telegram* boasted that 38,866 copies of the paper were issued and sold that day, with newsboys continuing busy until mid-evening.[29] A report from London, Eng., said that crowds had gathered outside newspaper offices there waiting for news of the hanging. Just three minutes after Birchall died, the news had reached the metropolis. Eager readers were soon snapping up newspapers carrying the story.[30]

"It was the neatest job I ever attempted," Radclive boasted of his handiwork. "It ought to secure me the position of public executioner."

He also remarked that he had never seen a prisoner display such "a wonderful exhibition of nerve and backbone." It was, he declared, "a great pity to hang a man of such nerve, but there is the law."[31] Jail officials and Inspector Chamberlain, as well as physicians, announced that in their view the hanging was well done.[32]

Not everyone agreed that the hanging had gone well, however. One reporter estimated that witnesses divided about half and half over the question.[33] Certainly the long period of convulsions had been disturbing. A snapped neck brought instant death, but Birchall's death had taken long, agonizing minutes. Mishandled executions, however, were not uncommon.[34] The report of the autopsy added to concerns that Birchall had suffered.

Immediately after the execution, coroner Archibald McLay, who had led the inquest into the Benwell murder, convened a jury to investigate Birchall's death as required by law, and Drs. Oldham and Mearns conducted the autopsy. It showed that Birchall had died of strangulation. His windpipe had been crushed completely, but his neck had not broken. Even though the hanging had been inefficient and cruel, Canadian authorities in 1892 granted Radclive his wish of a permanent appointment as public executioner.[35]

The physicians performing the autopsy took a special interest in the condition of Birchall's brain. It weighed 50¾ ounces, heavier than the average brain, they reckoned. Dr. Meares said it showed that Birchall was a man "of no ordinary ability." One of the doctors mused that while the brain was healthy, "he would not call it an intellectual brain." He did not explain his reasoning.[36]

Workmen soon dismantled the scaffold. A local retailer who was eager to attract customers bought it to display along with the carpet from Birchall's cell.[37]

Birchall had made his will a few days before with the assistance of the Woodstock lawyer H.J. Finkle. Nearly everything went to his wife, but it was doubtful whether that amounted to anything at all. Items of jewellery went to Leatham and to Deputy Sheriff Perry.[38]

Florence Birchall and her sister had not attended the execution. They had remained at their hotel, Florence Birchall under the influence of opiates given her by her physician. Marion West-Jones, who had appeared over the weeks to be "almost indifferent" to Rex's fate, broke down completely on the day of the hanging. Woodstock people sympathized with the women, said the *News*. But as the sisters never mixed with the society of the town, the sympathy was "left unexpressed."[39]

It was reported that when the trousers Birchall was wearing were removed, a receipt was found from purchases he had made in Liverpool just before sailing for New York. The receipt was for an office stamp with the name "Birchall & Benwell" and for a cheap revolver at a total cost of £1 16s.[40] The story is likely apocryphal. It is hard to believe that the receipt wasn't found in police searches of him. Moreover, Birchall almost certainly had the revolver in hand before ever reaching Liverpool; Pelly testified that Birchall showed him his revolver on the train on their way to Liverpool.

Birchall was immediately embalmed (on instructions from Florence Birchall) and quickly buried in a metal coffin in the jail yard with no marker of any kind. The law prescribed jail yard burials for executed capital offenders.[41] Pleas from Florence Birchall and friends had gone to the office of the attorney general requesting that an exception be made in Birchall's case so that his body could be taken home to England. Attorney General Mowat rejected that proposal. No doubt with an eye on the electorate, Mowat declared publicly that the Englishman had already been extended more than enough privileges. Nevertheless, the coffin chosen was of metal in the hope that at some point it could be disinterred and buried elsewhere. Florence Birchall's lawyer, Dugald MacMurchy, had drafted a motion that went before the Woodstock town council maintaining that the body should not be buried in the jail yard near the town's centre for sanitary reasons. Although passed, the resolution had no effect.[42] Birchall's body remained unmarked in the jail yard. He lies there still.

Prof. Goldwin Smith, Ontario's foremost public intellectual of the late nineteenth century, expressed in a *Globe* article his elitist disapproval of some aspects of the Birchall hanging. He chided members of the public who worried that the man had been hanged on circumstantial evidence. Moreover, he was disgusted by the intrusiveness of the press, which resulted in the execution losing "its character as a solemn act of justice" and becoming "a butchery." He hoped that in future condemned men would escape having their last days "turned into a hideous pastime for the multitude." Nevertheless, as a gentleman, Prof. Smith could not help but admire Birchall's demeanour: "Birchall was bred a gentleman, and his breeding sustained him all those weeks under the gaze of the whole community, and at last upon the scaffold."[43]

It was reported in December that on the day before Birchall was hanged, he had written to Miss Mary Ann Page of Lancaster, Lancashire, who had nursed him as a child. He had asked her in the letter to place a wreath on his father's grave with these words attached:

> These few flowers were placed upon the grave by the youngest son of the loving father who lies beneath this stone. Though buried apart, father and son lay heart to heart, and before long will meet above, where there shall be no more pain and strife, free from this wretched world below and all its sorrows and cares.[44]

14

A Compelling Story

The Benwell–Birchall murder case became a news sensation around the English-speaking world for many reasons: the initial mystery surrounding the victim's identity; the revelation that both he and the accused came from highly respectable, wealthy families in England; the journalistic moment when newspaper readers delighted in sensational stories, which the dailies eagerly provided; and the communications technologies capable of quickly reporting on incidents in rural and small-town Ontario to readers throughout the English-speaking world and beyond. The alarming possibility that the murder was but one of many committed in the colonies by designing cads engaged in swindles of well-to-do Englishmen added to the concern the case aroused, especially in Britain. Adding to the fascination was the widespread assumption that gentlemen did not commit serious crimes such as murder. How could Birchall have done what he did? Public scrutiny of Birchall put the very idea of class on trial.

Attention was riveted on the story in part because of the demeanour of the debonaire accused, whose charm, self-control, and jaunty unconcern for his predicament appeared so extraordinary. Birchall's education in England's elite boarding schools and at Oxford University inculcated in him the behavioural code of the gentleman, the ability to rise above turmoil and maintain his dignity at all costs. In the face of the charge against him, he remained nonchalant and cheerful, his sturdy but genteel masculinity standing in sharp contrast to representations of his genteel but fragile wife, Florence. Rex Birchall denied to the very end that he was a murderer. Of course, admitting to the cowardly crime of shooting someone from behind would have been humiliating and almost impossible for a man imbued with the gentlemanly code.

Journalists at the time wondered about Birchall's psychological make-up, but psychologists in 1890 were ill-equipped to make sense of him. Today he might be called a "sociopath" or someone exhibiting "anti-social personality disorder."[1] One authority explains that "sociopath" refers to "a pattern of antisocial behaviour and attitudes, including manipulation, deceit, aggression, and a lack of empathy for others ... The defining characteristic is a profound lack of conscience."[2] Unlike psychopaths, who are unable to maintain genuine bonds, sociopaths can form an attachment to a particular individual or group. Another authority adds that the sociopath may be perceived as "charismatic or charming," a depiction that fits Birchall perfectly.[3] "Sociopath" describes Birchall to a tee. Perhaps, then, Birchall's self-confidence derived as much from a personality disorder as from his upbringing and Oxford education.

The Birchalls first came to Canada when Reginald signed on as a "farm pupil," a business that would later draw enormous public condemnation because of the case. Many Canadian farmers and the Dominion government had long recognized the farm-pupil business as dodgy and unnecessary. Birchall's swindle, so widely publicized, brought much greater awareness of the business's risks to Englishmen pondering a farming career in Canada. It was driven home to well-to-do and middle-class families in Britain that they were vulnerable to sharks in the business who could take them for substantial sums – a frightening enough prospect. Benwell's murder deepened anxieties enormously. People wondered whether the many young Britons who had previously gone to Canada and never been heard from again had met with the same tragic fate as Benwell. The case tarnished Canada's image in Britain, deepening fears that colonial adventures were too costly. Romantic notions of Empire were thus undermined for a moment at least. Even Birchall expressed a Briton's indignation about Canada when in his autobiography he expressed disappointment that in providing for the poor, Canada failed to enforce standards of civility.

The Benwell–Birchall case reveals the workings of Canadian criminal law in late-Victorian Ontario. As in other cases of the time,[4] a transition is evident from a long-standing, amateur tradition of community justice to a growing reliance on professional expertise. In its earliest phase, community figures had sprung into action to investigate the death, the local constable of Princeton and the justice of the peace of Blenheim Township being the first officials on the scene. A jury of ordinary men from the area had assessed the evidence at the request of the Woodstock coroner. When arrests were made in Niagara Falls, a justice of the peace there heard evidence and determined that the case against Reginald Birchall would go to trial. Yet the newer reliance on expertise was apparent too: the investigations by Ontario detective John Murray and by the medical experts who conducted the autopsy and who contested the scientific evidence during the trial. Legal expertise was on display during the trial as Crown and defence lawyers presented their arguments before both a learned judge and a jury composed of ordinary men of the community. A broad public signed clemency petitions that, along with the judge's expert report on the trial, were assessed by officials of the justice department as well as cabinet ministers, all of whom quickly rejected a change in punishment. A self-proclaimed expert – really no expert at all – hanged Birchall clumsily, which prevented neither praise for his expertise nor his appointment as Canada's first official hangman.

For the most part, the legal proceedings followed familiar lines, with no significant precedents being set. Two developments deserve notice, however. First, the premier and attorney general, Oliver Mowat, intervened in the preliminary hearing of Florence Birchall at Niagara Falls, an instance of meddling by a politician in a legal proceeding that now appears extraordinary, although it brought no comment at the time. Second, the back-and-forth arrangements of the preliminary hearing and the coroner's inquest were also exceptional. The fact that the hearing took place in Niagara Falls and the inquest in Princeton meant that the officials in charge were unfamiliar with one another and tussled to see whose authority would prevail. The result disturbed Det. Murray, who had found the proceedings "foreign" to anything he had ever seen.[5] It does not appear that this unusual feature of the case affected the course of justice, however. Predictably, the inquest found that Reginald Birchall had shot the deceased, and the magistrate at Birchall's hearing sent him to trial.

The trial put the period's gender conventions on show. In the Woodstock courtroom, masculine privilege and power were boldly displayed by the presiding judge, the jury, the lawyers on both sides, the medical experts, the reporters, and the constables at the door – all of them men. Women appeared in positions of less authority, many as eager spectators admitted to the courtroom by officials criticized for showing too much chivalry, and others as witnesses, whom some journalists sympathized with because of the badgering the women received from the overzealous, male, defence attorney.

Once the jury convicted Birchall of murder, thousands of people signed petitions for clemency, fearing that he had been wrongfully convicted – that he might have been a swindler but he had not committed the murder. Certainly, the overpowering evidence of the swindle shaped the pursuit and trial of Birchall. Douglas Pelly's early revelations about the hoax led directly to Birchall's arrest. After hearing from Pelly, the Crown quickly developed a theory of the crime, one it pursued unwaveringly thereafter. Newspapers reported early and extensively on the considerable evidence of Birchall's swindle, which surely prejudiced nearly everyone against the man, including men of the jury. The pleas of the barristers and the judge for jurors to put aside what they had heard could have done little to offset their prejudices, as Blackstock regretfully acknowledged in his address to the jury.

As noted above, within three years of the trial, Canadian law reversed on the possibility of the accused testifying in their own defence. In 1890, however, Birchall was muzzled. What if he had been permitted to testify and had told a version of events closely resembling the account of 17 February that he gave in his autobiography? The sightings of him going by train to and from Eastwood would have been explained and perhaps have appeared less damaging to him. The account in the autobiography was, however, less than compelling because it did not provide the names of the men that Birchall alleged had shown Benwell farm properties after Birchall and Benwell had gone their separate ways. What Birchall really needed was witnesses to come forward saying they had seen Benwell alive after Birchall had left the swamp. None did so.

Newspapers in 1890 acknowledged the concern that some people had about the guilty verdict and the press's role in that result. To an overwhelming extent, however, journalists had found Birchall just too tempting a culprit in the stories they told – a perfect villain for the Victorian melodrama that had played out in the backwoods of Ontario. Privileged, and having no scruples about fleecing other young men of his class, Birchall was an easy target for condemnation. His villainy made good copy for journalists in the business of attracting a large readership. So it was, then, that the story went viral.

15

Epilogue

This epilogue explores two questions. What happened to the characters in the Benwell–Birchall case after Birchall was hanged? And how has the case been remembered?

Lives Lived

Immediately after Rex Birchall's execution, Florence Birchall left for England, where she resumed living in her parents' house on Maberley Road, London. She, her parents, her elder sister, Marion West-Jones, and Marion's daughter were all still living there at the time of the 1901 census. Ten years later, the census catches Florence running a boarding house in a grand terrace in Notting Hill, London. At age fifty-seven, in October 1919, Florence married James Bowen, described in the marriage record as a bachelor and a merchant. Florence died in 1945 at the age of eighty-three in the London suburb of Hampstead.[1]

Charles Benwell, the brother of Fred Benwell, returned to England soon after the trial ended. In May 1892 he followed his father into the army, enlisting as a second lieutenant in the West Yorkshire Regiment.[2] After the First World War, he was attached to "F" Co. of the Royal Corps of Signallers. In 1921 he pleaded guilty to being an absentee from the company, and later that year he was court-martialled, probably as a result of his alcoholism.[3] In 1924 he died at age fifty-seven in a London nursing home. An inquest into his death determined that he died of "chronic alcoholism."[4]

As the trial was ending, Douglas Pelly rushed back to England, where he enjoyed a hero's welcome in Saffron Walden. A widely reprinted newspaper report noted that at the station he and his father were met by the Excelsior Band and many torch-carrying residents. "Amid a scene of great enthusiasm," and while church bells rang, men drew the Pelly carriage through streets elaborately decorated with flags and fairy lamps. The vicarage had an evergreen arch displaying the motto "Welcome Home." The report of the homecoming concluded: "Everyone in the parish seemed delighted to welcome Mr. Pelly on his safe return home after the many perilous episodes in which he has had a share."[5] Not long after his triumphal return, Douglas followed his father into the Church. He was ordained a deacon in 1895 and a priest a year later. Perhaps inspired by his travels before going to Canada, he served in the late 1890s as a missionary in Mashonaland in central Africa (now part of Zimbabwe) and later in Cape Town in what is now South Africa. In 1898 he married Verena Nellie Herbert, a clergyman's daughter. They had three daughters and four sons. Apart from a stint as a chaplain during the First World War, he spent his career as rector of a series of parishes in England. In 1943, he died at the age of seventy-eight in Somerset.[6]

Crown attorney Britton Bath Osler continued through the 1890s to gain prominence as a powerful courtroom lawyer. Several times he was offered the position of justice minister; each time he refused it. In 1900 his health failed, and he died the following year. Twenty years later, he was remembered as having been a criminal lawyer "in a class all by himself." The Birchall case was a high point in his illustrious career.[7]

Lead defence attorney George Tate Blackstock maintained a thriving legal practice for many years and enjoyed public renown as a witty speaker at banquets and political rallies in Canada, England, and the United States. He suffered throughout his life from occasional debilitating depressions and was institutionalized several times. When well, he was a society favourite in Toronto, New York, and London. His wife's decision to abandon him made the estranged couple the talk of the town, as they were again when she sued him for divorce, citing lack of financial support. Shortly before the First World War, Blackstock's health failed, and he never recovered. In 1921 he died in Toronto. At the time of his death, the *Globe* remarked that he had "gained fame over a whole continent for the defense of Birchall in the long and sensational murder trial at Woodstock 30 years ago."[8]

Defence attorney Isidore Hellmuth had a long and highly distinguished legal career in Toronto until shortly before his death at eighty-nine in 1944. Obituaries called his involvement in Birchall's defence a career highlight.[9] An early Canadian tennis star, in 1991 Hellmuth was an inaugural inductee into the Tennis Canada Hall of Fame. [10]

Justice Hugh MacMahon continued on the bench until 1911, when he died of a heart attack.[11]

Det. John Murray investigated a great many more cases after the Birchall trial. In 1906, he was still on the job – investigating a cattle-poisoning case – when he had a stroke, dying soon afterwards in his Toronto home on Brunswick Avenue. He was sixty-five. He left an estate valued at an impressive $40,000. His published memoirs were author Maureen Jennings's chief inspiration for the clever hero of her Detective Murdoch series of novels and its internationally popular offshoot, the long-running Canadian television series *Murdoch Mysteries* (*The Artful Detective* in the United States).[12]

Soon after hanging Birchall, John Radclive rushed back to Toronto to preside over a posh reception at the Sunnyside Boat Club. In 1892, on the advice of Ontario Premier Oliver Mowat, Attorney General John Thompson appointed Radclive to a permanent position as the country's executioner. It is said he hanged sixty-nine people in Canada. Radclive's heavy drinking eventually caught up with him, causing his death in 1911 at the age of fifty-five. In 2022, *Hangman* was published, providing an imaginative true-crime life of Radclive.[13]

Rural Dean William H. Wade, Birchall's spiritual adviser while in jail, later became rector of Hamilton's Church of the Ascension. In April 1913, when he died in Hamilton as Canon Wade, the short announcement in the *Globe* observed: "Though Birchall made a public statement proclaiming his innocence, it is believed that he made a confession to Canon Wade, which, however, the latter never divulged." When Wade's will was opened a couple of weeks later, people thought it might at last reveal Birchall's confession, but to their disappointment, the will was silent on the matter.[14]

Remembering

The Birchall story lived on. As noted in the introduction, several accounts of the case have been published. In addition, an especially interesting article about the case appeared in the Canadian national magazine *Maclean's* in 1943, written by Isidore Hellmuth. The magazine touted it as "the inside story," and it is true that by the time it was written, Hellmuth was willing to be frank, unrestrained by his long-ago role as defence attorney. A revelation of sorts comes at the end of the story when Hellmuth recalls a conversation he had a few months after Birchall's execution when on a train he encountered Osler, the Crown attorney. Osler asked Hellmuth what he thought of the Crown's handling of the Birchall case. Hellmuth replied that he thought it had been conducted in "a vindictive spirit." Osler implied he agreed. He explained that during the summer before the trial he had interviewed a woman in England, the mother of a son, who had responded to Birchall's advertisement about investing in his farm. Birchall told them they would need to pay $2,500. They said that was far beyond their means. The woman showed Osler a letter she later received from Birchall, saying that, because he had been so taken with her son, he would dispense with his usual rate and charge her only $500. Disgusted, Osler decided he was dealing with "'a reptile,'" and he became "'determined to crush Birchall.'"[15] It is significant that Osler was powerfully motivated to convict Birchall of murder because he was a swindler.

The Benwell–Birchall case has been commemorated in various ways in Oxford County. An impressive vault-like stone monument completely covering the grave marks Fred Benwell's final resting place in the cemetery at Princeton. The inscription reads: "In loving memory of Frederick Cornwallis Benwell, born 15th September, 1865; murdered in the Township of Blenheim, Feb. 17th, 1890. Oldest son of Lt.-Cl. Benwell of Cheltenham, England. Formerly Captain 100th Regiment. 'What I do thou knowest not now, but thou shalt know hereafter.'" The quotation is from the Bible, KJV John 13:7, and are Jesus's words. At the cemetery in 2003 a stone monument outlining the story was raised by a group calling itself the Birchall–Benwell Committee. Following Det. Murray's self-aggrandizing and misleading account, the monument erroneously attributes the arrest of Birchall to the photographs the detective had published in newspapers.

When the Woodstock Town Hall was declared a national historic site in 1956, the Historic Sites and Monuments Board placed a plaque beside the front door that noted the building's hall was the site of the famous Birchall murder trial. (In 1972, the plaque was replaced by a new one with different content.)[16]

The Woodstock Museum, housed in the old town hall, has a permanent display about the case. The backdrop of the glass cabinet features a blown-up photographic print of the trial under way. Displayed in the

14.1. Footstool crafted out of wood from where the body was found in the swamp and from the gallows on which Birchall was hanged.

Source: Woodstock Museum, image 1971.5.2–1.

cabinet are various items, including Birchall's boots and the wooden staff carried by a court official during the trial. In recognition of the trial's significance to the town, the large room where it took place has been restored to how it looked in 1890.

The Woodstock Museum has many items relating to Birchall and Benwell. Original exhibits presented as evidence at Birchall's trial include the receipt of Birchall's deposit into the Bank of Niagara soon after the murder, the handwritten financial agreement between Pelly and Birchall, and the much-discussed telegram from Birchall to the proprietor of the Stafford House, Buffalo. There are original pen-and-ink drawings by Birchall, and old photographic prints of the location of the body in the swamp, the courtroom during the trial, and the jury.

Local relic hunters active on the scene in 1890 collected items treasured by their descendants and eventually donated to the Woodstock

Museum. There is a red bentwood chair said to be the one Birchall sat on throughout the trial, and part of a purse thought to have been Florence Birchall's. Rather macabre are a footstool and a wooden box fashioned from the gallows on which Birchall was hanged and from the stump on which Benwell's body was found. A rusted single-action revolver discovered in the vicinity of the swamp in 1961 is thought to have been the murder weapon.[17]

High school students in Oxford County have access to archival kits about the trial. In partial fulfilment of the curriculum requirement in the law program for grades eleven and twelve, students are invited to assess the archival documents in the kit and produce a mock trial. The resource is titled "On Trial: The Crown vs. Reginald Birchall."[18]

Woodstock tourism promoters advertise opportunities for visitors to learn about the Birchall case. Walking tours of town include on the itinerary a visit to the Woodstock Jail, where visitors are told about famous trials, including Birchall's. Other websites encourage tourists to pay attention to local ghost stories, notably ones connected with hangings at the Woodstock Jail.[19] The infamous swamp, now known as the "Benwell Swamp," is a destination for intrepid travellers.[20] In 2016, when Woodstock was the site of the ghastly murder of a young girl, a story that got national media attention, news reports referenced the 1890 murder trial. A headline in Toronto's *National Post* asserted: "Murder put Woodstock on the map, and now its citizens are asking, 'why us?'"[21]

Notes

1 Introduction

1 *Gazette*, 12 March 1890; *The Times*, 1 October 1890; *Daily Post*, 1 October 1890.
2 *World*, 22 February 1890.
3 Paul Rutherford, *A Victorian Authority: The Daily Press in Late Nineteenth-Century Canada* (Toronto: University of Toronto Press, 1982); Minko Sotiron, *From Politics to Profits: The Commercialization of Canadian Daily Newspapers, 1890–1920* (Montreal and Kingston: McGill–Queen's University Press, 1997).
4 L. Perry Curtis, Jr., *Jack the Ripper and the London Press* (New Haven: Yale University Press, 2008), 67. See also Joel Wiener, *Papers for the Millions: The New Journalism in Britain, 1850s to 1914* (Westport: Greenwood Press, 1988).
5 P.F.W. Rutherford, "The People's Press: The Emergence of the New Journalism in Canada, 1866–99," *Canadian Historical Review* 61, no. 2 (June 1975), 173.
6 These searches were done on 26 January 2023. Hits for Canada appeared in fifteen newspapers, none of them being ones heavily used in the research for this book.
7 Rutherford, *A Victorian Authority*, 113–14; Jonathan Silberstein-Loeb, *The International Distribution of News: The Associated press, Press Association, and Reuters, 1848–1947* (New York: Cambridge University Press, 2014),

esp. ch. 2; Donald Read, *The Power of News: The History of Reuters* (Oxford: Oxford University Press, 1999), ch. 4.
8 *Telegram*, 1 October 1890.
9 Curtis, *Jack the Ripper*, 59.
10 Circulation estimates for 1891 are given for some Canadian newspapers in Rutherford, *A Victorian Authority*, 236–9: Hamilton's *Spectator*, 17,500; London's *Free Press*, 23,750; Montreal's *Gazette*, 12,171. The estimates for Toronto papers in 1891 are: *Empire*, 29,000; *Globe*, 46,450, *Mail*, 62,010; *News*, 31,500; *Telegram*, 21,695; *World*, 11,500. By comparison, the *New York Herald* had a reported circulation of 84,000 as of early 1861.
11 http://www.biographi.ca/en/bio/maclean_william_findlay_15E.html
12 Online searches for "Birchall" and "Benwell" in the World Newspaper Archive produced articles in newspapers from these far-flung places. The *Pioneer* (Allahabad, India) published articles on the case on fifteen occasions in 1890.
13 I consulted the *Sentinel-Review* on microfilm at the Archives of Ontario and the *Evening Standard* on microfilm at Library and Archives Canada.
14 J. Castell Hopkins, *A Historical Sketch of Canadian Literature and Journalism* (Toronto: Linscott, 1898), 230.
15 *The Canadian Men and Women of the Time: A Handbook of Canadian Biography*, edited by Henry James Morgan (Toronto: W. Briggs 1898), 809,
16 *The Benwell Murder: A Tragedy That Startled Two Continents; The Story of a Crime Conceived in England and Consummated in America* (New York: Richard K. Fox Publisher, 1890).
17 *The Swamp of Death or, The Benwell Murder* (Toronto: Rose Publishing Co., 1890).
18 John Wilson Murray, *Memoirs of a Great Detective: Incidents in the Life of John Wilson Murray* (London: Heinemann, 1904).
19 W. Stewart Wallace, "Murder in a Swamp," *Maclean's*, 15 May 1931. The story is part of a collection, W. Stewart Wallace, *Murders and Mysteries: A Canadian Series* (Toronto: Macmillan 1931), ch. 9. See also the pamphlet by Irene Crawford and Mary Evan, *The Trial of a Man: Reginald Birchall* (Privately published, c. 1978).
20 *The Cultured Criminal*, dir. Florin Marksteiner, Productionmark, 2014.
21 Rebecca Gowers, *The Swamp of Death: A True Tale of Victorian Lies and Murder* (London: Hamish Hamilton, 2004); Alan Bytheway, *Murder as a Fine Art: A Story of Fraud, Betrayal, and Murder across Two Continents* (Gloucestershire: Choir Press 2015), vii.

22 Natalie Zemon Davis, *The Return of Martin Guerre* (Cambridge, MA: Harvard University Press, 1983).
23 On the development of micro-history as a genre, see Steven Bednarski, "On Microhistory and Pedagogy," ch. 1 of his *A Poisoned Past: The Life and Times of Margarida de Portu, a Fourteenth-Century Accused Prisoner* (Toronto: University of Toronto Press, 2014).
24 Robert Sharpe, *The Lazier Murder: Prince Edward County, 1884* (Osgoode Society for Canadian Legal History and University of Toronto Press, 2011).
25 Martin L. Friedland, *The Case of Valentine Shortis: A True Story of Crime and Politics in Canada* (Toronto: University of Toronto Press, 1986); Rheinhold Kramer and Tom Mitchell, *Walk towards the Gallows: The Tragedy of Hilda Blake, Hanged 1899* (Oxford and New York: Oxford University Press, 2002); Jim Phillips and Rosemary Gartner, *Murdering Holiness: The Trials of Franz Creffield and George Mitchell* (Vancouver: UBC Press, 2003).
26 The Criminal Indictment Files of Ontario's Department of Justice, so often a rich vein for historians to mine, are for this case very thin indeed. See Archives of Ontario (AO), RG 22–392, Criminal Indictment Files, Oxford, 1890, Birchall, John Reginald, and Birchall, Florence. More useful is the fat Capital Case File at Library and Archives Canada, but sadly even it is missing half the official trial transcript. See Library and Archives Canada (LAC), RG 13–1, vol. 1559, file 350, Birchall, John Reginald (henceforth: LAC, CCF, Birchall, John Reginald).
27 Joseph Frank, *The Beginnings of the English Newspaper* (Cambridge, MA: Harvard University Press, 1961), 202–37.
28 James L. Crouthamel and Andrew Jackson, "James Gordon Bennett, the *New York Herald*, and the Development of Newspaper Sensationalism," *New York History* 54, no. 3 (July 1973), 294–316. See also James L. Crouthamel, *Bennett's New York Herald and the Rise of the Popular Press* (Syracuse: Syracuse University Press, 1989); and David B. Sachaman and David W. Bulla, eds., *Sensationalism: Murder, Mayhem, Mudslinging, Scandals, and Disaster in 19th-Century Reporting* (New York: Routledge, 2013).
29 Curtis, *Jack the Ripper*, citing Richard D. Altick, *Deadly Encounters: Two Victorian Sensations* (Philadelphia: University of Pennsylvania Press, 1986).
30 Steve Box, *Deviance, Reality, and Society* (London and Toronto: Holt, Rinehart and Winston, 1971), 40, cited by Curtis, *Jack the Ripper*, 289.
31 For the text of Treaty Three, "Between the Lakes Treaty," see https://www.rcaanc-cirnac.gc.ca/eng/1370372152585/1581293792285#ucls5.

248 Notes to pages 11–15

32 An Act to provide ... for the erection of Municipal Corporations; (1849) 12 Vict. C. 82; https://en.wikipedia.org/wiki/Oxford_County,_Ontario.
33 *Census of Canada, 1890–1891*, vol. 1, (Ottawa, 1892), 168.
34 Joyce A. Pettigrew, *A Safe Haven: The Story of Black Settlers of Oxford County* (South Norwich Historical Society, 2006); *Census of Canada, 1880–1881*, vol. 1 (Ottawa, 1882), 286; Rebecca Beausaert, "Not Guilty, but Guilty: Race, Rumour, and Respectability in the Abortion Trial of Letitia Munson," *Ontario History* 106, no. 2 (Fall 2014), 165–90.
35 *Census of Canada, 1890–1891*, vol. 1, 276–7, 346–7.
36 George Emery, *Elections in Oxford County, 1837–1875* (Toronto: University of Toronto Press, 2012, 18, 184.
37 Nancy B. Bouchier, *For the Love of the Game: Amateur Sport in Small-Town Ontario, 1838–1895* (Montreal and Kingston: McGill–Queen's University Press, 2003), 10–21; Art Williams and Edward Baker, *Woodstock: Bits and Pieces* (Erin: Boston Mills Press, [1967]1990).
38 Ernest Heaton, *Canada's Problem* (Toronto: The Week Publishing Co., 1895); *Canadian Breeder and Agricultural Review*, 6 March 1885; *Mail* (Toronto), 10 March 1890.
39 Reginald Birchall, *Birchall: The Story of His Life, Trial, and Imprisonment as Told by Himself* (Toronto: National Publishing, 1890); Western University, D.B. Weldon Library, Archives and Special Collections, Douglas Raymond Pelly, "His Memoir of 1933 ... plus letters surviving in the possession of the Pelly Family Relative to the Birchall/Benwell Murder" (hereafter Pelly, "His Memoir"); Murray, *Memoirs of a Great Detective*.

2 The Murder Mystery

1 *History of Princeton, 1795–1967* (Princeton, ON, 1967). Today Highway #2 closely follows the route of the Governor's Road (surveyed in 1793) between Paris and Woodstock. Near the swamp, Blenheim's second concession road runs parallel with and close to the Governor's Road.
2 Justices of the Peace Act, C.S.C. 1859, c. 100, ss. 1 and 3.
3 Ancestry.ca; *Sentinel-Review*, 25 September 1890.
4 Paul Romney, *Mr. Attorney: The Attorney General for Ontario in Court, Cabinet, and Legislature, 1791–1899* (Toronto: Osgoode Society and University of Toronto Press, 1986), 231–9; Robert J. Sharpe, *The Lazier Murder: Prince Edward County, 1884* (Toronto: Osgoode Society for Canadian Legal History and University of Toronto Press, 2011), 22–6; Greg Marquis, *Policing Canada's Century: A History of the Canadian Association of Chiefs of Police* (Toronto: Osgoode Society and University of Toronto Press, 1993), ch. 1.

5 Watson's biographical details are uncertain, but he may have been the William Watson who died in Ingersoll in 1911 at the age of fifty-eight (Ancestry.ca). The weathered gravestone in the Princeton cemetery for a William Watson is otherwise illegible.
6 See ch. 7.
7 *Gazette*, 25 September 1890.
8 *Evening Standard*, 22 February 1890.
9 *Sentinel-Review*, 24 February 1890.
10 *Sentinel-Review*, 24 February 1890.
11 *Evening Standard*, 26 February 1890.
12 Joseph Elvidge's recollections were printed in Myrtle E. Home, "Recalls Famous Murder Case of 47 Years Ago," *Sentinel-Review*, 9 February 1937.
13 *Sentinel-Review*, 24 February 1890.
14 *Sentinel-Review*, 25 February 1890.
15 *Sentinel-Review*, 25 February 1890.
16 *Sentinel-Review*, 25 February 1890.
17 *Evening Standard*, 24 February 1890.
18 *Sentinel-Review*, 26 February 1890.
19 *World*, 27 February 1890.
20 *World*, 27 February 1890; *Sentinel-Review*, 27 February 1890. Fred Cheeswright appears in the 1901 census of Canada, Blenheim Township, Oxford County, as an English-born tailor, age eighty-two (Ancestry.ca).
21 *Evening Standard*, 27 February 1890.
22 *Sentinel-Review*, 27 February 1890.
23 Coroner's Act, R.S.O, 1877, c. 79.
24 W.F. Boys, *A Practical Treatise on the Office and Duties of Coroners in Ontario*, 3rd ed. (Toronto: Carswell, 1893), 13.
25 Myles Leslie, "Reforming the Coroner: Death Investigation Manuals in Ontario, 1863–1894," *Ontario History* 100, no. 2 (2008).
26 Sharpe, *The Lazier Murder*, 43.
27 See trial testimony, ch. 8.
28 *World*, 1 March 1890.

3 Arrests at Niagara

1 *1891 Census of Canada*, vol. 1, 176.
2 *Sentinel-Review* and *World*, 3 March 1890.
3 *World*, 3 March 1890.
4 See Chief Young's testimony in ch. 8.
5 *Free Press*, 3 March 1890; https://en.wikipedia.org/wiki/I._F._Hellmuth.

6 *Canadian Men and Women of the Time: A Handbook of Canadian Biography*, edited by Henry J. Morgan (Toronto: W. Briggs, 1898), 454.
7 Ancestry.ca.
8 Ancestry.ca.
9 *Sentinel-Review*, 3 March 1890; *Evening Standard*, 3 March 1890; *Mail*, 7 March 1890.
10 *Evening Standard*, 3 March 1890.
11 *World*, 4 March 1890.
12 David Stevenson, *Fifty Years of the London and North Western Railway* (London: McCorquodale, 1891).
13 *Evening Standard*, 4 and 11 March 1890.
14 *Empire*, 4 March 1890.
15 *Herald*, 6 March 1890; *Gazette*, 7 March 1890.
16 Letter to the *New York Morning Journal*, cited in *Evening Standard*, 10 October 1890.
17 On 5 May 2020, a search for "Benwell" produced the results, which were checked to eliminate non-US newspapers.

4 The Net Tightens

1 Newspapers called him Andrew George Hill, but his gravestone and other sources make it clear his middle name was Gregory.
2 Ancestry.ca
3 An Act to provide for the better Government of that part of Ontario situated in the vicinity of the Falls of Niagara, 37 Vic. Cap. 18 S.O. (1874).
4 Young's obituary in the *British Whig*, 7 March 1901.
5 https://www.heritagetrust.on.ca/properties/niagara-district-court-house
6 The most detailed coverage of the hearing's first day appears in the *Sentinel-Review*, 4 March 1890. John Markey, age twenty-three, had been born in Ireland; by 1900, he was editor of Woodstock's *Express* (Ancestry.ca).
7 *Sentinel-Review*, 6 March 1890.
8 *Buffalo Times*, 6 March 1890.
9 *Standard*, 6 December 1889.
10 $800 is the equivalent given by newspapers in 1890. $33,000 CDN or £20,000 was calculated using www.measuringworth.com.
11 *Sentinel-Review*, 5 March 1890.
12 *World*, 6 March 1890.
13 Photocopies of Birchall's handwritten letters to the Rev. Raymond Pelly regarding arrangements (and stamped with exhibit numbers from

Birchall's trial) are in Western University, D.B. Weldon Library, Archives and Special Collections, Pelly, "His Memoir."
14 *Sentinel-Review*, 12 March 1890.
15 *Sentinel-Review*, 7 March 1890.
16 *Sentinel-Review*, 6 and 7 March 1890.
17 *Buffalo Evening News*, 7 May 1890.
18 *Sentinel-Review*, 6 March 1890.
19 Providing comparisons and context for the attorney general's intervention is not possible, given the inattention to the matter in the literature.
20 Paul Romney, *Mr. Attorney: The Attorney General for Ontario in Court, Cabinet, and Legislature, 1791–1899* (Toronto: Osgoode Society and University of Toronto Press, 1986).
21 *Sentinel-Review*, 7 March 1890.
22 *Sentinel-Review*, 4 March 1890.
23 *World*, 6 March 1890.
24 *Sentinel-Review*, 6 March 1890.
25 *Sentinel-Review*, 7 March 1890.
26 *Empire*, 8 March 1890.
27 *Sentinel-Review*, 8 March 1890.
28 Searches of the *Graphic* turn up news of the Benwell murder case, but no illustrations of it.
29 *World*, 8 March 1890.
30 This summary of the testimony of 7 March is based mainly on the *World*, 8 March 1890.
31 *Sentinel-Review*, 7 March 1890; *World*, 8 March 1890.
32 This summary of the second day's testimony is based on the report in the *World*, 10 March 1890.
33 *Brockville Illustrated, 1894* (Brockville: J.H. Godkin and A.G. Davie, 1894), 23.
34 *Sentinel-Review*, 8 March 1890; *World*, 10 March 1890; *News*, 10 March 1890.
35 *Sentinel-Review*, 6 March 1890.
36 *Standard*, 17 March 1890. Oddly, Canadian newspapers did not report the contents of this letter.
37 *Empire*, 12 and 13 March 1890.
38 *Buffalo Times*, 13 March 1890.
39 *World*, 13 March 1890.
40 *Mail*, 13 March 1890; *World*, 6 March 1890.
41 *Buffalo Times*, 13 March 1890.
42 *Buffalo Times,*, 13 March 1890.

43 *World*, 13 March 1890; *Mail*, 13 March 1890.
44 AO, RG 22–392, Criminal Indictment Case Files, Oxford County, 1890, Birchall, Florence.
45 This summary of the evidence given at the hearing is from the *World*, 13 March 1890.
46 *Buffalo Times*, 13 March 1890.
47 *Buffalo Times*, 13 March 1890.

5 In Woodstock Jail

1 *Empire*, 14 March 1890.
2 *Sentinel-Review*, 13 March 1890.
3 Ron Brown, *Behind Bars: Inside Ontario's Heritage Gaols* (Toronto: Natural Heritage Books, 2006), 70–1; www.city of Woodstock.ca; *Sentinel-Review*, 7 January 2020.
4 *Sentinel-Review*, 13 March 1890.
5 *Mail*, 14 March 1890; AO, RG 20, 104–1–5, Woodstock Jail Register, prisoner no. 108.
6 *Empire*, 14 March 1890.
7 *Telegram*, 14 March 1890.
8 *Telegram*, 17 and 18 March 1890.
9 *Empire*, 15 March 1890.
10 The details come from an interview with Birchall published in the *Mail*, 14 March 1890. More details of the business are given by the *Mail*'s own reporter in Woodstock; see *Mail*, 10 March 1890.
11 LAC, CCF, Birchall, John Reginald, handwritten trial transcript, McDonald testimony.
12 *Mail*, 14 March 1890.
13 Somerset to Ford, Rathbone & Co., 21 Finsbury Park, London, no date, printed in the *Mail*, 10 March 1890. See also stories of swindled farm pupils in *Evening Standard*, 11 March 1890.
14 Ernest Heaton, *Canada's Problem* (Toronto: The Week Publishing Co., 1895), 48–9.
15 *Canadian Breeder and Agricultural Review*, 6 March 1885, 146.
16 *Globe*, 10 March 1890.
17 *Times*, 1 October 1890; *Standard*, 14 March 1890.
18 James G. Snell, *In the Shadow of the Law: Divorce in Canada, 1900–1939* (Toronto: University of Toronto Press, 1991), ch. 9, "Divorce outside the System."
19 *Sentinel-Review*, 8 March 1890

Notes to pages 70–9   253

20 *News*, 11 March 1890.
21 *News*, 11 March 1890.
22 Quoted from an unidentified newspaper source by Rebecca Gowers, *The Swamp of Death: A True Tale of Victorian Lies and Murder* (London: Hamish Hamilton, 2004), 166–7.
23 The *World* had the same story the next day, 15 March, with a few extra details included.
24 *Chronicle*, 25 March 1890.
25 *Sentinel-Review*, 1 April 1890.
26 *Evening Standard*, 5 April 1890.
27 *World*, 3 March 1890.
28 *World*, 8 March 1890.
29 www.measuringworth.com
30 Col. Benwell to the Rev. Raymond Pelly, 7 March 1890; photocopy of original is at Western University, D.B. Weldon Library, Archives and Special Collections, Douglas Pelly, "His Memoir."
31 Notice reprinted in the *Sentinel-Review*, 9 March 1890; and the *News*, 12 March 1890.
32 *Sentinel-Review*, 6 March 1890; *Telegram*, 8 March 1890.
33 *World*, 9 March 1890. It wasn't Birchall's Lancashire accent that misled Canadians, because it was reported he had lost that accent while at Oxford (*Telegram*, 31 March 1890).
34 *World*, 12 March 1890.
35 *Weekly Standard and Express*, 8 and 15 March 1890; *Lloyd's Weekly Newspaper*, 18 March 1890.
36 *Gazette*, 13 March 1890.
37 *Telegram*, 11 & 12 March 1890.
38 *Herald*, 12 March 1890.
39 *Jackson's Oxford Journal*, 4 October 1890
40 Gowers, *Swamp of Death*, 122–3, quotes rector Dr. Merry and includes a reproduction of the College Order Book where the decision was noted to remove him from the college books.
41 *Sentinel-Review*, 17 March 1890.
42 *Empire*, 5 March 1890; *Telegram*, 11 March 1890.
43 *Sentinel-Review*, 15 March 1890; *World*, 5 March 1890.
44 *World*, 6 March 1890.
45 *Sentinel-Review*, 16 April 1890; *Globe*, 17 March 1890; *News*, 24 March 1890; *Lloyd's Weekly Newspaper*, 18 May 1890.
46 *Sentinel-Review*, 15 March 1890. The young man's name was variously spelled as "Rance," "Rants," and "Rantz."

47 *Globe*, 3 June 1890.
48 *Gazette*, advertisement, 24 March 1890. On dime museums, see Robert Bogdan, *Freak Show: Presenting Human Oddities for Amusement and Profit* (New York: St. Martin's Press, 1896).
49 *News*, 11 March 1890; Western University, D.B. Weldon Library, Archives and Special Collections, Pelly, "His Memoir of 1933," 132–3.
50 *Sentinel-Review*, 9 and 10 April 1890.
51 *Globe*, 25 June 1890; Upper Canada Reports, *R. v. Birchall* [1890] O.J. No. 202

6 Pelly's Story

1 Western University, D.B. Weldon Library, Archives and Special Collections, Douglas Pelly, "His Memoir of 1933." For the notes to this chapter, I have shortened the reference to Pelly, "His Memoir."
2 Pelly, "His Memoir," 1.
3 Pelly, "His Memoir," 2.
4 Pelly, "His Memoir," 9–10.
5 Pelly, "His Memoir," 10–11.
6 Pelly, "His Memoir," 13–15.
7 Pelly, "His Memoir," 15.
8 Pelly, "His Memoir," 15–16.
9 Pelly, "His Memoir," 15–18.
10 At the time, Lloyd's required that prospective underwriters pass an interview, pay a £200 entrance fee, and make a £5,000 deposit with the firm. See Charles Wright and C. Ernest Fayle, *A History of Lloyd's from the Founding of Lloyd's Coffee House to the Present Day* (London: Macmillan, 1928). See also Rebecca Gowers, *The Swamp of Death: A True Tale of Victorian Lies and Murder* (London: Hamish Hamilton, 2004), 2.
11 Pelly, "His Memoir," 17–20.
12 Gowers, *Swamp of Death*, 3–4.
13 https://britishlistedbuildings.co.uk/101196232-walden-place-saffron-walden#.XtGGqcB7nIU
14 Pelly, "His Memoir," 55–7.
15 Gowers, *Swamp of Death*, 6.
16 Pelly, "His Memoir," 58–60.
17 Pelly, "His Memoir," 61–3.
18 Pelly, "His Memoir," 63–6.
19 This assertion appears to derive from a letter held privately in the Pelly family. See Gowers, *Swamp of Death*, 14.

20 Pelly, "His Memoir," 67.
21 Pelly, "His Memoir," 68.
22 Pelly, "His Memoir," 68–9.
23 Pelly, "His Memoir," 69.
24 Col. Benwell to Raymond Pelly, 7 March and 7 April 1890, Pelly, "His Memoir," 130–2.
25 The SS *Britannic* was completed in 1874 for the immigrant traffic between Liverpool and New York. It accommodated 220 saloon and 1,500 steerage passengers. Scrapped in 1903, it is not to be confused with a later *Britannic*, a sister ship of the *Titanic*. https://en.wikipedia.org/wiki/SS_Britannic_%281874%29.
26 Archives and Special Collections, Weldon Library, Western University, London, Ont., Douglas Pelly, "Detailed Account to 23 March 1890," (hereafter "Detailed Account"), 102.
27 Col. Benwell to Raymond Pelly, 7 March 1890.
28 Pelly, "His Memoir," 70–1.
29 Pelly, "His Memoir," 71.
30 Pelly, "His Memoir," 72–3.
31 Pelly, "His Memoir," 72–5.
32 "Detailed Account," 113.
33 Pelly, "His Memoir," 73.
34 Pelly, "His Memoir," 75.
35 Pelly, "His Memoir," 75–6.
36 Pelly, "His Memoir," 76–7.
37 Pelly, "His Memoir," 79–80.
38 Pelly, "His Memoir," 81–2.
39 Pelly, "His Memoir," 86–7.
40 Pelly, "His Memoir," 87.
41 Pelly, "His Memoir," 88–9.
42 Pelly, "His Memoir," 90.
43 Pelly, "His Memoir," 90.
44 Pelly, "His Memoir," 90–1.
45 Pelly, "His Memoir," 83–4.
46 Pelly, "His Memoir," 85–6.
47 Pelly, "His Memoir," 86.
48 Pelly, "His Memoir," 92–3.
49 Pelly, "His Memoir," 93.
50 Pelly, "His Memoir," 95–6.
51 Pelly, "His Memoir," 133.
52 Pelly to _____, Saskatoon, 2 June 1890, Pelly, "His Memoir," 136.

53 Pelly, "His Memoir," 135–42.
54 Pelly, "His Memoir," 143–9.
55 Pelly, "His Memoir," 149.

7 The Great Detective?

1 John Wilson Murray, *Memoirs of a Great Detective*. The first edition was published in 1904 by Heinemann Ltd., London, England.
2 Ancestry.com, 1841 Census of Scotland, has John Murray, two, son of David and Christian Murray, living in North Middleton, Midlothian; US Civil War Draft Registrations Records, 1863–65, records John Murray entering service in May 1861 and being discharged in March 1866, having served as a seaman aboard the SS *Michigan*, and residing in Toronto. Jim Phillips and Joel Fortune, "Murray, John Wilson," in *Dictionary of Canadian Biography*, vol. 13, http://www.biographi.ca/en/bio/murray_john_wilson_13E.html.
3 Ancestry.com. The 1870 US census record for Erie, PA, gives John's age as thirty-seven and his birthplace as Ireland. His wife is listed as Mary Murray, age thirty-seven, born in Switzerland. Their daughters are Mary, nine, and Katy, five, both born in Pennsylvania. The 1881 Census of Canada for Toronto has John Murray, detective, age forty-two, born in the US of Irish descent. His wife is Lizzie Murray, thirty-nine, English-born; daughter Mary is now twenty and Katie fifteen. John Murray's gravestone in Mount Hope Cemetery, Toronto, gives his birth date as 25 June 1840.
4 http://www.biographi.ca/en/bio/murray_john_wilson_13E.html
5 http://www.biographi.ca/en/bio/murray_john_wilson_13E.html
6 Proquest search, 4 May 2020.
7 http://www.biographi.ca/en/bio/murray_john_wilson_13E.html
8 *Globe*, 13 June 1906.
9 http://www.biographi.ca/en/bio/murray_john_wilson_13E.html
10 J.M. Beattie, *The First English Detectives: The Bow Street Runners and the Policing of London, 1750–1840* (Oxford: Oxford University Press, 2012).
11 *Globe*, 6 April 1889.
12 Richard Manning, "Undercover Investigation, Liquor Laws, and 'Disreputable' Detectives in Late Nineteenth-Century Canada," *Canadian Historical Review* 103, no. 4 (December 2022), 516–37.
13 Phillips Thompson, "Letter on Behalf of Mrs. Sternaman," *Globe*, 11 December 1897.
14 David Skene-Melvin, "Canadian Crime Writing in English," in *Detecting Canada: Essays on Crime Fiction, Television, and Film*, edited by Marilyn

Rose and Jeannette Sloniowski (Waterloo: Wilfrid Laurier University Press, 2014), 19–54; Keith Walden, *Visions of Order: The Canadian Mounties in Symbol and Myth* (Toronto: Butterworths, 1982).
15 Haia Shpayer-Makov, "Explaining the Rise and Success of Detective Memoirs in Britain," in *Police Detectives in History, 1750–1850*, edited by Clive Emsley and Haia Shpayer-Makov (London: Routledge, 2006), 103–34.
16 Murray, *Memoirs*, 165.
17 *Sentinel-Review*, 1 March 1890. The *Evening Standard* reported on 22 February that the coroner had made a request and then reported another request on 1 March.
18 Murray, *Memoirs*, 142. On 25 February, the *World* placed a photograph of the body in its office window (*World*, 26 February 1890).
19 Murray, *Memoirs*, 142–3.
20 Murray, *Memoirs*, 143.
21 Murray, *Memoirs*, 143.
22 *Sentinel-Review*, 1 March 1890.
23 Murray, *Memoirs*, 143–6.
24 Murray, *Memoirs*, 146.
25 Murray, *Memoirs*, 146.
26 Murray, *Memoirs*, 147.
27 *Globe*, 1 March 1890.
28 Murray, *Memoirs*, 147.
29 Western University, Weldon Library Special Collections, Douglas Pelly, "His Memoir of 1933," 87.
30 Murray, *Memoirs*, 148–58.
31 Murray, *Memoirs*, 154–5.
32 Murray, *Memoirs*, 155. I have been unable to verify that these advertisements appeared in newspapers.
33 *Herald* (New York), 8 March 1890.
34 Murray, *Memoirs*, 158.
35 See ch. 9.
36 Murray, *Memoirs*, 158.
37 Murray, *Memoirs*, 162–3.
38 *Globe*, 22 March 1890.
39 *Buffalo Times*, 6 March 1890.
40 *Globe*, 25 March 1890.
41 *Globe*, 21 August and 30 September 1890.
42 See chs. 9 and 12.
43 *Globe*, 29 October 1904.
44 Western University, Weldon Library Special Collections," Douglas Pelly, "His Memoir of 1933," 87–88.

258 Notes to pages 109–15

45 W. Stewart Wallace, "Murder in a Swamp," *Maclean's*, 15 May 1931; W. Stewart Wallace, *Murders and Mysteries*, ch. 9; Gordon K. Murphy, "Birchall and Benwell: Murder in a Canadian Swamp," *American Journal of Forensic Medicine and Pathology* 9, no. 3 (September 1988), 255–7.
46 https://openlibrary.org/works/OL6620890W/Memoirs_of_a_great_detective

8 The Trial Begins

1 *Empire*, 22 September 1890.
2 *News*, 15 November 1890.
3 https://arcg.is/OGmGH
4 https://www.cityofwoodstock.ca/en/live-and-play/old-town-hall-history.aspx
5 *Sentinel-Review*, 18 September 1890. https://en.wikipedia.org/wiki/Woodstock,_Ontario#Oxford_County_Court_House.
6 *Sentinel-Review*, 18 September 1890; *World*, 19 September 1890.
7 *Sentinel-Review*, 22 September 1890.
8 *World*, 23 September 1890.
9 *World*, 18 September 1890.
10 Formally, Birchall appeared in the Court of Oyer and Terminer and General Gaol Delivery, the criminal court of the High Court of Justice (Ontario Judicature Act, S.O., 1881, c. 5).
11 *Globe*, 21 August 1890.
12 *Globe*, 22 August 1890.
13 Patrick Brode, "Osler, Britton Bath," in *Dictionary of Canadian Biography*, vol. 13, http://www.biographi.ca/en/bio/osler_britton_bath_13E.html.
14 Edwin C. Guillet, "The Swamp of Death: A Study of the Evidence in *The Queen versus John Reginald Birchall*, 1890," vol. 3 of his "Famous Canadian Trials," unpublished manuscript, 1944, a copy of which is in the Toronto Reference Library, Special Collections.
15 *The Canadian Women and Men of the Time: A Handbook of Canadian Biography*, edited by Henry J. Morgan (Toronto: W. Briggs, 1898), 46. The province's system of salaried full-time legally trained Crown attorneys dated from 1857. See Jim Phillips, Philip Girard, and R. Blake Brown, *A History of Law in Canada*, vol. 2 (Toronto: University of Toronto Press, 2022), 422.
16 Reginald Birchall, *Birchall: The Story of His Life, Trial, and Imprisonment as Told by Himself* (Toronto: National Publishing, 1890), 40, 48–50. In this memoir

Notes to pages 115–19 259

at page 50, Birchall says Blackstock's fee was £100, but in a private letter he refers to $700 paid to Blackstock (Woodstock Museum and Historic Site, Item X2012.66.1, Birchall to Samuel [McKay], 20 October 1890).

17 C. Ian Kyer, *Lawyers, Families, and Businesses: The Shaping of a Bay Street Law Firm, Faskin, 1863–1963* (Toronto: Osgoode Society and Irwin Lay, 2013), 93–112; C.M. Blackstock, *All the Journey Through* (Toronto: University of Toronto Press, 1997).
18 Guillet, "The Swamp of Death," ch. 16.
19 *Canadian Women and Men of the Time*, 2nd ed. (Toronto: William Briggs, 1912), 520–1.
20 *Sentinel-Review*, 22 September 1890.
21 Bluett first gained public attention when as a night watchman he was a key Crown witness at the sensational murder trial of Toronto abortionists Arthur and Alice Davis. See Ian Radforth, *Jeannie's Demise: Abortion on Trial in Victorian Toronto* (Toronto: BTL Books, 2020), 18–19.
22 Morgan, *Canadian Men and Women*, 164.
23 Blake Brown, *A Trying Question: The Jury in Nineteenth-Century Canada* (Toronto: Osgoode Society and University of Toronto Press, 2009), 206–10; Robert Sharpe, *The Lazier Murder: Prince Edward County, 1884* (Osgoode Society for Canadian Legal History and University of Toronto Press, 2011), 59–61; Mary Stokes, "Grand Juries and 'Proper Authorities': Low Law, Soft Law, and Local Governance in Canada West/Ontario, 1850–1880," in *Essays in the History of Canadian Law: Quebec and the Canadas*, edited by G. Blain Baker (Toronto: Osgoode Society and University of Toronto Press, 2013), 538–70.
24 *A History of Law in Canada*, vol. 2, 434–6.
25 *World*, 19 September 1890.
26 AO, CIF, Oxford, 1890, Birchall, Florence, Recognizance of bail in the case of *R. v. Florence Birchall*, 20 March 1890; "no bill" signed by J.W. Farrington, foreman grand jury, Oxford Fall assize, 1890.
27 *World*, 22 September 1890. *News*, 22 September 1890.
28 *World*, 15 September 1890.
29 *World*, 23 September 1890.
30 *News*, 22 September 1890; *Empire*, 22 September 1890.
31 *Sentinel-Review*, 19 September 1890.
32 *News*, 22 September 1890; *World*, 23 September 1890.
33 The Consolidated Jurors Act (1883), S.O. 46 Vict., c. 7.
34 Brown, *A Trying Question*, 211–13.
35 *World*, 23 September 1890; *Sentinel-Review*, 22 September 1890; *Spectator*, 23 September 1890.

36 *World*, 23 September 1890; *Spectator*, 23 September 1890.
37 This account is based on newspaper reports of the trial, but where possible the reports have been checked against the surviving parts of the trial transcript in LAC, CCF, Birchall, John Reginald.
38 *World*, 23 September 1890.
39 *Spectator*, 23 September 1890.
40 *Free Press*, 23 September 1890, gives the full testimony in a question/answer format. This account is based on the *Spectator* and *World* summaries.
41 Newspapers condensed McDonald's testimony, but it appears fully in the trial transcript in LAC, CCF, Birchall, John Reginald.
42 *Spectator*, 23 September 1890; *World*, 23 September 1890.
43 *World*, 23 September 1890.
44 *Sentinel-Review*, 24 September 1890.
45 *World*, 23 September 1890.
46 Unless otherwise noted, the discussion is base on *World*, 24–7 September 1890.
47 *Sentinel-Review*, 26 September 1890.
48 Ancestry.com. The 1891 Census of England, Cheltenham, shows Charles as twenty-four, having no occupation, and having been born in Cheltenham. In his home are his father, Frederick W. Benwell, fifty-six, born in India, mother, Florence F. Benwell, fifty-one, born in Cape of Good Hope, sister Florence, twenty, and brothers Reginald, twenty, and Percy, ten.
49 *Free Press*, 24 September 1890; LAC, CCF, Birchall, John Reginald, trial transcript.
50 *Free Press*, 24 September 1890.
51 *World*, 25 September 1890.
52 *Free Press*, 25 September 1890.
53 *Spectator*, 25 September 1890.
54 Last sentence from *Sentinel-Review*, 25 September 1890.
55 *World*, 25 September 1890; *Sentinel-Review*, 25 September 1890.
56 *Sentinel-Review*, 24 September 1890.
57 *Spectator*, 26 September 1890.
58 Unless otherwise noted, the testimony comes from the *Sentinel-Review*, 25 and 26 September 1890.
59 *Sentinel-Review*, 25 September 1890.
60 *Spectator*, 26 September 1890.
61 *Sentinel-Review*, 25 and 26 September 1890.
62 *World*, 26 September 1890.

63 *World*, 26 September 1890.
64 *News*, 26 September 1890.

9 The Defence and Conclusion

1 *World*, 27 September 1890.
2 *Sentinel-Review*, 27 September 1890.
3 The following discussion of the witnesses presented by the defence is based on the report in the *World*, 27 September 1890. Its account has been cross-checked with reports in other newspapers.
4 *News*, 27 September 1890.
5 *News*, 27 September 1890.
6 Medical testimony is based on accounts in *World*, 29 September 1890, and *Sentinel-Review*, 27 September 1890.
7 The testimony is based on *World*, 29 September 1890.
8 *World*, 29 September 1890.
9 *World*, 29 September 1890; *Sentinel-Review*, 29 September 1890.
10 *World*, 29 September 1890.
11 *Sentinel-Review*, 29 September 1890.
12 *News*, 29 September 1890.
13 *News*, 29 September 1890.
14 *Sentinel-Review*, 29 September 1890.
15 *Sentinel-Review*, 29 September 1890.
16 The following is based on the *Sentinel-Review*, 29 September 1890.
17 SC 1876, c.13, strengthened that requirement. See Jim Phillips, Philip Girard, and R. Blake Brown, *A History of Law in Canada*, vol. 2 (Toronto: University of Toronto Press, 2022), 440.
18 This summary of the addresses and judge's charge is based on the *Spectator*, 30 September 1890, but many newspapers carried very similar reports.
19 LAC, CCF, Birchall, John Reginald, vol. 3, trial transcript, 825–65.
20 *News*, 30 September 1890.
21 James Fitzjames Stephen, *A History of the Criminal Law in England*, vol. 1 (London: Macmillan, 1883), 455–6; Sharpe, *The Lazier Murder*, 112.
22 (1838), 2 Lewin 227, 168 E.R. 1136.
23 Benjamin L. Berger, "The Rule in Hodge's Case: Rumours of Its Death Are Greatly Exaggerated," *Canadian Bar Review* 84, no. 1 (2005), 47–74. The Canadian courts followed the rule until the decision in *R. v. Cooper* [1978] 1 S.C.R. 860.
24 *Spectator*, 30 September 1890.

25 *News*, 30 September 1890.
26 *Empire*, 30 September 1890
27 Sharpe, *The Lazier Murder*, 6.
28 Sharpe, *The Lazier Murder*, 115.
29 The following is based on *Spectator*, 30 September 1890.

10 Aftermath of the Trial

1 *Gazette*, 20 September 1890.
2 *Evening Standard*, 30 September 1890; *Scotsman*, 1 October 1890; *The Times*, 1 October 1890; *News*, 30 September 1890.
3 *Sentinel-Review*, 6 and 7 October 1890.
4 Rebecca Gowers, *The Swamp of Death: A True Tale of Victorian Lies and Murder* (London: Hamish Hamilton, 2004), 307.
5 *Spectator*, 1 October 1890; *Philadelphia Inquirer*, 1 October 1890.
6 *Spectator*, 1 October 1890; *The Times*, 1 October 1890; *Globe*, 30 September 1890.
7 *Spectator*, 1 October 1890; *World*, 2 October 1890; E. Topping to the *Sentinel-Review*, 24 October 1890.
8 *Globe*, 30 September 1890.
9 *Constitution*, 1 October 1890; *Philadelphia Inquirer*, 1 October 1890; *New York Tribune*, 1 October 1890.
10 *Globe*, 30 September 1890; *New York Tribune*, 1 October 1890; *Standard* (London), 1 October 1890.
11 *Chicago Tribune*, 1 October 1890.
12 *News*, 30 September 1890. Supporters of the law as it stood maintained that were the law to change, "fundamental common-law principles of the right to silence and the presumption of innocence would be undermined and the trial process would be overwhelmed with [the] tainted and unreliable evidence [of the accused]" (Robert Sharpe, *The Lazier Murder: Prince Edward County, 1884* (Osgoode Society for Canadian Legal History and University of Toronto Press, 2011), 84).
13 *Mail*, 1 October 1890.
14 Canada Evidence Act, 1893, S.C. 1893, c. 31. See Phillips, Girard, and Brown, *A History of Law in Canada*, vol. 2, 440–1.
15 Sharpe, *The Lazier Murder*, 85.
16 *Sentinel-Review*, 30 September 1890.
17 *Gazette*, 1 October 1890. On the debate over unanimity, see Blake Brown, *A Trying Question: The Jury in Nineteenth-Century Canada* (Toronto: Osgoode Society and University of Toronto Press, 2009), 204–6.

Notes to pages 169–79 263

18 *Scotsman*, 1 October 1890.
19 *Scotsman*, 1 October 1890; *Spectator*, 1 October 1890.
20 *Scotsman*, 1 October 1890; *Spectator*, 1 October 1890.
21 The *Sentinel-Review* reprinted the remarks from the US press on 3 October 1890.
22 *The Times*, 1 October 1890; *Spectator*, 1 October 1890; *Weekly Times and Examiner*, 3 October, 1890.
23 *World*, 1 October 1890; *Philadelphia Inquirer*, 1 October 1890.
24 *World*, 1 October 1890.
25 *Sentinel-Review*, 7 November 1907.
26 *World*, 2 October 1890; *Sentinel-Review*, 3 October 1890.
27 *Globe*, 2 October 1890.
28 *Telegram*, 1 October 1890.
29 *News*, 1 October 1890; *Telegram*, 1 October 1890.
30 *News*, 1 October 1890; *Telegram*, 1 October 1890.
31 *Spectator*, 30 September 1890; *World*, 1 October 1890; *Pall Mall Gazette*, 2 October 1890.
32 *Telegram*, 1 October 1890.
33 *Evening Standard*, 14 October 1890; *Sentinel-Review*, 27 October 1890.
34 *World* editorial reprinted in *Sentinel-Review*, 24 October 1890.
35 *Telegram*, 1 October 1890; *Spectator*, 1 October 1890.
36 *News*, 6 October 1890.
37 *News*, 6 October 1890; *Sentinel-Review*, 5 October 1890.
38 *Sentinel-Review*, 5 October 1890.
39 *Sentinel-Review*, 10 November 1890.
40 *World*, 11 November 1890.
41 Col. Benwell's letter to the editor appearing in the *Standard*, 17 March 1890.
42 Martha Vicinus, "Introduction," in *Suffer and Be Still: Women in the Victorian Age*, edited by Martha Vicinus (London, Methuen, 1972), 6. See also Deborah Gorham, *The Victorian Girl and the Feminine Ideal* (London: Croom Helm, 1982).
43 M. Jeanne Peterson, "'No Angels in the Home': The Victorian Myth and the Paget Women," *American Historical Review* 89, no. 3 (June 1984), 677–708. The historiography generally refutes the angel-in-the-home stereotype.
44 *News*, 6 October 1890.
45 *Philadelphia Inquirer*, 1 October 1890.
46 I have found a Dr. W.E. Bessey in Toronto city directories in 1888–89 and 1893. He was charged with murder in connection with an abortion

he was alleged to have performed in 1897. In 1898 he was removed for unprofessional conduct from the list of licensed physicians by the College of Physicians and Surgeons of Ontario. See Radforth, *Jeannie's Demise*, 58–9.
47 *Globe*, 4 and 6 October 1890; *Sentinel-Review*, 18 October 1890.
48 *Journal*, 22 October 1890 reprinted in *Mail*, 23 October 1890.
49 *Telegram*, 31 October 1890
50 "Reginald Birchall," *Phrenological Journal and Science of Health* 91, no. 2 (February 1891): 78–9. See also Francis Joseph Cavanagh, *Cavanagh's Phrenological Chart* (Toronto: n.p., 1903), 10.
51 Reginald Birchall, *Birchall: The Story of His Life, Trial, and Imprisonment as Told by Himself* (Toronto: National Publishing, 1890), 20–21.
52 *Sentinel-Review*, 6 October 1890; *Mail*, 7 October 1890.
53 *Sentinel-Review*, 6 October 1890.
54 *Globe*, 6 October 1890.
55 *Sentinel-Review*, 6 October 1890.
56 *News*, 14 and 15 October 1890; *Upper Canada Reports, Graeme v. Globe Printing Co.* [1890], O.J. No. 279.
57 *Globe*, 22 October 1890; the extracts were also printed in the *Telegram* and *Sentinel-Review*, 22 October 1890.
58 *Globe*, 25 October 1890.
59 *Evening Standard*, 23 October 1890; *Sentinel-Review*, 24 October 1890.
60 The letter is reproduced in full in the *Sentinel-Review*, 28 October 1890.
61 *Sentinel-Review*, 28 October 1890.
62 *Sentinel-Review*, 28 October 1890.
63 *Mail*, 28, 29, and 31 October 1890.
64 *Sentinel-Review*, 1 November 1890.
65 The original letter is in Western University, Weldon Library Special Collections, Hill Family Collection. Nora Louise Hill, a local historian of Woodstock and Oxford and founder of the Woodstock Museum, collected various letters, images, and so on connected with Reginald Birchall. The handwriting comparison is my own.
66 *Sentinel-Review*, 28 October 1890.
67 LAC, CCF, Birchall, John Reginald.
68 *Sentinel-Review*, 29 October 1890; *Mail*, 30 October 1890.
69 *News*, 30 October & 1 November 1890.
70 *Sentinel-Review*, 25 October 1890.
71 *Telegram*, 3 and 16 October 1890.
72 *Sentinel-Review*, 27 October 1890.
73 *Globe*, 24 October 1890.

74 *Sentinel-Review*, 27 October 1890.
75 *Telegram*, 4 October 1890.
76 *News*, 6 and 22 October 1890
77 *News*, 30 October 1890.
78 Western University, D.B. Weldon Library, Archives and Special Collections, Pelly, "His Memoir of 1933," Reginald Birchall to the Rev. Raymond Pelly, 18 October 1890.
79 Birchall, *Birchall: The Story of His Life*, 58. Wade's obituary gives a few details of his background; see *Globe*, 25 April 1913.
80 *News*, 24 October 1890.
81 *World*, 20 October 1890. Vol. 2 of the typed transcript is in LAC, CCF, Birchall, John Reginald. Volume 1 is missing, but a handwritten version of parts of the missing final transcript is in the file.
82 *News*, 25 October 1890.

11 Birchall's Own Story

1 *News*, 25 October 1890.
2 *Globe*, 27 October 1890; reprinted the same day in the *Sentinel-Review*.
3 *Mail*, 29 and 30 October 1890.
4 This reading is based on a compilation of the newspaper instalments titled *Birchall: The Story of His Life*. This paragraph refers to page 1.
5 Paul R. Deslandes, *Oxbridge Men: British Masculinity and the Undergraduate Experience, 1850–1920* (Bloomington: Indiana University Press, 2005).
6 Deslandes, *Oxbridge Men*, 11–14.
7 Birchall, 2–4.
8 Birchall, 4–7.
9 Penglase Factor & Gray Family Tree, Ancestry.com.
10 St. James's Church-Kirk, Wikipedia.com.
11 www.rossall.org.uk/about-rossall/history-rossall-school
12 Birchall, 7–27.
13 Deslandes, *Oxbridge Men*, 69–70.
14 Deslandes, *Oxbridge Men*, 71–82.
15 Deslandes, *Oxbridge Men*, 79–80.
16 Birchall, 27–31.
17 Birchall, 31–2.
18 Birchall, 32–4.
19 Birchall, 43–8.
20 Rebecca Gowers, *The Swamp of Death: A True Tale of Victorian Lies and Murder* (London: Hamish Hamilton, 2004), 323.

21 *Birchall*, 34–43.
22 AO, RG 20–104–1–5, Woodstock Jail Register, 21 January–18 March 1890.
23 *Birchall*, 40, 48–50.
24 *Birchall*, 50–8.
25 *Birchall*, 58–9.

12 Pleading for Mercy

1 Carolyn Strange, "Comment: Capital Case Procedures Manual," *Criminal Law Quarterly* 41 (1998), 184–98.
2 Carolyn Strange, "The Lottery of Death: Capital Punishment, 1876–1976," *Manitoba Law Journal* 23 (1995), 594–619 at 618. See also Jim Phillips, Philip Girard, and R. Blake Brown, *A History of Law in Canada*, vol. 2 (Toronto: University of Toronto Press, 2022), 450–2; Jonathan Scott Swainger, *The Canadian Department of Justice and the Completion of Confederation, 1867–1878* (Vancouver: UBC Press), ch. 4; and Robert Sharpe, *The Lazier Murder: Prince Edward County, 1884* (Osgoode Society for Canadian Legal History and University of Toronto Press, 2011), 117–20.
3 *News*, 31 October 1890.
4 *Mail*, 4 November 1890.
5 E. Topping to the editor, *Sentinel-Review*, 27 October 1890; E. Cory to the editor, *Sentinel-Review*, 4 November 1890.
6 W. Street to the editor, *Sentinel-Review*, 4 November 1890.
7 *Gazette*, 25 October 1890.
8 *New York Tribune*, 4 November 1890.
9 LAC, CCF, Birchall, John Reginald.
10 LAC, CCF, Birchall, John Reginald, J.B. Warren to Lord Stanley, 12 November 1890.
11 *News*, 3 November 1890.
12 *Mail*, 4 November 1890.
13 *Mail*, 29 October 1890.
14 *Mail*, 5 November 1890.
15 Toronto City Directory, 1892, records MacMurchy as being with the firm R.M. Wells and Angus MacMurchy with offices in the same building on King Street West as Blackstock.
16 *Sentinel-Review*, 4 November 1890.
17 *Sentinel-Review*, 3 November 1890.
18 LAC, CCF, Birchall, John Reginald.
19 *News*, 24 October and 3 November 1890.
20 *Mail*, 1 November 1890.

Notes to pages 219–24   267

21 The Rev. Oswald Birchall was an outspoken socialist and friend and neighbour of William Morris (Rebecca Gowers, *The Swamp of Death: A True Tale of Victorian Lies and Murder* (London: Hamish Hamilton, 2004), 124.)
22 *Sentinel-Review*, 29 October and 3 November 1890.
23 LAC, CCF, Birchall, John Reginald.
24 *New York Tribune*, 2 November 1890; reprinted in *Sentinel-Review*, 4 November 1890.
25 *New York Tribune*, 2 November 1890.
26 LAC, CCF, Birchall, John Reginald, petition dated 28 October 1890.
27 *Sentinel-Review*, 5 November 1890; *News*, 6 November 1890.
28 P.B. Waite, "Thompson, Sir John David Sparrow," in *Dictionary of Canadian Biography*, vol. 12, http://www.biographi.ca/en/bio/thompson_john_sparrow_david_12E.html.
29 *Globe*, 6 November 1890.
30 Janice Potter-MacKInnon, *While the Women Only Wept: Loyalist Refugee Women in Eastern Ontario* (Montreal and Kingston: McGill–Queen's University Press, 1993).
31 Strange, "Comment: Capital Case Procedure Manual," 184–.
32 Strange, "Comment: Capital Case Procedure Manual," 184 –.
33 The official document, dated 7 November 1890, is in LAC, CCF, Birchall, John Reginald.
34 By contrast with Birchall case, cabinet met four times in December 1895 to consider commutation in the politically sensitive murder case of Valentine Shortis, and in the end, the governor general had to make the decision. See Martin L. Friedland, *The Case of Valentine Shortis: A True Story of Crime and Politics in Canada* (Toronto: University of Toronto Press, 1986), 147–61.
35 The telegrams and correspondence relating to the decision are in LAC, CCF, Birchall, John Reginald.
36 *Sentinel-Review*, 8 November 1890; *World*, 8 November 1890; *News*, 6 November 1890.
37 *Sentinel-Review*, 8 November 1890.
38 *Gazette*, 8 November 1890.
39 *Globe*, 11 November 1890.
40 *Globe*, 17 November 1890.

13 The Hanging

1 Kenneth Leyton-Brown, *The Practice of Execution in Canada* (Vancouver: UBC, 2010), 88–90.

2 *Globe*, 5 November 1890.
3 John Radclive (sometimes Radcliff) was also known as Thomas Ratley. It was explained that Radclive was his professional name, and Ratley his social one.
4 Howard Engel, *Lord High Executioner: An Unashamed Look at Hangmen, Headsmen, and Their Kind* (Toronto: Key Porter Books, 1996) 67–8.
5 *World*, 13 November 1890.
6 *Globe*, 14 November, 1890; *Sentinel-Review*, 13 November 1890; *Spectator*, 14 November 1890.
7 *Sentinel-Review*, 13 November 1890.
8 *Globe*, 14 November 1890. For context, see Leyton-Brown, *The Practice of Execution*, 82–88.
9 Leyton-Brown, *The Practice of Execution*, 95–8.
10 *Globe*, 14 November 1890.
11 *Sentinel-Review*, 14 November 1890.
12 Leighton-Brown, *The Practice of Execution*, 88.
13 *Spectator*, 15 November 1890; *Telegram*, 14 November 1890.
14 Leighton-Brown, *The Practice of Execution*, 95.
15 *Sentinel-Review*, 13 November 1890; *Globe*, 14 November 1890; *Mail*, 14 November 1890.
16 *Globe*, 14 November 1890.
17 Toronto Reference Library, Special Collections, Edwin C. Guillet, "The Swamp of Death: A Study of the Evidence in *The Queen versus John Reginald Birchall*," vol. 3 of his "Famous Canadian Trials," unpublished manuscript, 1944 manuscript chapter titled "55 Years After," unpaginated.
18 *World*, 13 November 1890; *Standard* (London), 6 October 1890.
19 *Sentinel-Review*, 2 November 1907.
20 *Spectator*, 14 November 1890.
21 *Evening Standard*, 20 September 1890.
22 Leyton-Brown, *The Practice of Execution*, 104–17; *History of Law in Canada*, vol. 2, 452.
23 *News*, 14 November 1890.
24 Mason Manser's story is told in Guillet, "The Swamp of Death," chapter titled "55 Years After," unpaginated.
25 *Mail*, 15 November 1890; Leyton-Brown, *The Practice of Execution*, 71–2.
26 Leyton-Brown, *The Practice of Execution*, 89–90.
27 *Spectator*, 14 November 1890; *Mail*, 15 November 1890.
28 Donna T. Andrew, *Aristocratic Vice: The Attack on Duelling, Suicide, Adultery, and Gambling in Eighteenth-Century England* (New Haven: Yale University Press, 2013), 11, 35. See also Henry French and Mark Rothery, *Man's Estate: Landed Gentry Masculinities, 1660–1900* (Oxford: Oxford

University Press, 2012), 3; James Eli Adams, *Dandies and Desert Saints: Styles of Victorian Manhood* (Ithaca: Cornell University Press, 1995); Robin Gilmour, *The Idea of the Gentleman in the Nineteenth-Century Novel* (London: Allen and Irwin, 1981); and Mark Girouard, *The Return to Camelot: Chivalry and the English Gentleman* (New Haven: Yale University Press, 1981).

29 *Telegram*, 17 November 1890.
30 *News*, 15 November 1890.
31 *Sentinel-Review*, 17 November 1890 citing an article from the *Telegram*.
32 *News*, 14 November 1890. Radclive boasted to the press of his success, and the *Globe*, 19 May 1891, reports that he used the drop technique at least one more time – to hang James Kane in Belleville, Ontario.
33 *Telegram*, 14 November 1890.
34 Leyton-Brown, *The Practice of Execution*, 98.
35 Radclive died on 12 February 1911 at age fifty-five in Toronto, reportedly from excessive drinking. www.ebrandon.ca
36 *Telegram*, 14 November 1890; *Spectator*, 14 November 1890.
37 *Sentinel-Review*, 17 November 1890.
38 *Sentinel-Review*, 12 November 1890.
39 *News*, 15 November 1890.
40 *Weekly Standard and Express*, 15 November 1890.
41 The law changed not long afterwards. Canada's new Criminal Code of 1892, s. 395, empowered the lieutenant governor to allow for burial outside prison walls. On the introduction of the 1892 code, see Jim Phillips, Philip Girard, and R. Blake Brown, *A History of Law in Canada*, vol. 2 (Toronto: University of Toronto Press, 2022), 425–8.
42 *World*, 12 November 1890.
43 *Globe*, 25 November 1890.
44 *Gazette*, 20 December 1890. The 1871 census of England lists Mary Ann Page as the youngest (at nineteen) of four female servants living in the Birchall home.

14 A Compelling Story

1 The American Psychiatric Association no longer lists "sociopath" as a diagnostic term and prefers "anti-social personality disorder."
2 www.psychologytoday.com/us/basics/*sociopathy*
3 www.healthline.com/health/mental-health/sociopath
4 Robert Sharpe, *The Lazier Murder: Prince Edward County, 1884* (Osgoode Society for Canadian Legal History and University of Toronto Press, 2011).
5 *Buffalo Times*, 13 March 1890.

Epilogue

1. Ancestry.com, 1891, Census of England, Croydon, Surrey; 1901 Census of England, Hampstead; 1911 Census of England, Belsize Park; Marriages, Florence Birchall (Stevenson), 1 October 1919; Deaths, Florence Bowen, Hampstead, 1945.
2. Ancestry.com, Enlistment Record, Charles Benwell, 20 May 1892.
3. *Kent and Sussex Courier*, 25 February 1921; Ancestry.ca, court marshal record, 15 March 1921.
4. *West London Press*, 12 December 1924.
5. *Essex County Standard*, 11 October 1890.
6. 1891 Census of England, Saffron Walden; Marriages, Douglas Raymond Pelly, 14 April 1898; Death notice, Cambridge University Alumni, 1261–1900.
7. Patrick Brode, "Osler, Britton Bath," http://www.biographi.ca/en/bio/osler_britton_bath_13E.html; Albert R. Hassard, "Great Canadian Orators: Britton Bath Osler," *The Canadian Magazine* 54, no. 4 (February 1920), 353–60.
8. Blackstock, George Tate," http://www.biographi.ca/en/bio/blackstock_george_tate_15E.html; C.M. Blackstock, *All the Journey Through* (Toronto: University of Toronto Press, 1997), 242–89; *Globe*, 28 December 1921.
9. *Globe*, obituary, 19 February 1944; *Windsor Star*, obituary, 18 February 1944.
10. www.tenniscanada.com
11. *Globe*, obituary, 19 January 1911.
12. *Globe*, 13 and 23 June 1906; www.bookseriesinorder.com/detective-murdoch.
13. Martin L. Friedland, *The Case of Valentine Shortis: A True Story of Crime and Politics in Canada* (Toronto: University of Toronto Press, 1986), 135–43; Howard Engel, *Lord High Executioner: An Unashamed Look at Hangmen, Headsmen, and Their Kind* (Toronto: Key Porter Books, 1996); Julie Buttinshaw, *Hangman: The True Story of Canada's First Official Hangman* (New Westminster: Tidewater, 2022).
14. *Globe*, 25 April & 13 May 1913.
15. I.F. Hellmuth, "New Light on Old Murder," *Maclean's*, 1 October 1943.
16. https://woodstockmuseum.pastperfectonline.com/webobject/B1C856EA-EE5D-4396-8390-579545320997
17. https://woodstockmuseum.pastperfectonline.com/search?page=1&search_criteria=birchall&utf8=%E2%9C%93

18 www.oxfordcounty.ca'Explore-Oxford/Librarians-museums-and
-archives/Teachers
19 www.oxfordhistoricalsociety.ca/historic-walking-tours; https://*woodstock newsgroup*.weebly.com/*ghost*.html
20 www.travelingluck.com/North+America/Canada/Ontario/_5898637_Benwell+Swamp.html
21 *National Post*, 2 November 2016.

Newspapers Cited

British Whig, Kingston, ON
Buffalo Evening News, Buffalo, NY
Buffalo Times, Buffalo, NY
Chicago Tribune, Chicago, IL
Constitution, Atlanta, GA
Daily News, London, UK
Daily Post, Birmingham, UK
Daily Telegraph, London, UK
Empire, Toronto, ON
Essex County Standard, Colchester, UK
Evening Standard, Woodstock, ON
Evening Sun, New York, NY
Fireside Weekly, Woodstock, ON
Free Press, London, ON
Gazette, Montreal, PQ
Globe, Toronto, ON
Graphic, London, UK
Herald, New York, NY
Jackson's Oxford Journal, Oxford, UK
Journal, Ottawa, ON
Kent and Sussex Courier, Tunbridge Wells, UK
Lancaster Gazette, Lancaster, UK
Mail, Toronto, ON

Morning Post, London, UK
National Post, Toronto, ON
News, Toronto, ON
New York Tribune, New York, NY
New York Times, New York, NY
Pall Mall Gazette, London, UK
Philadelphia Inquirer, Philadelphia, PA
Scotsman, Edinburgh, UK
Sentinel-Review, Woodstock, ON
Spectator, Hamilton, ON
Standard, London, UK
Telegram, Toronto, ON
The Times, London, UK
Weekly Standard and Express, Blackburn, UK
Weekly Times and Examiner, Manchester, UK
West London Press, London, UK
World, Toronto, ON

Index

Accrington, Lancashire, 75
accused person's right to testify, 168, 238
Alderson, Baron, 162
Allahabad, India, 7
amateur tradition of justice, 9, 15, 51, 236–7
American Journal of Forensic Medicine and Pathology, 109
American newspapers, 4–6, 41, 165, 169. *See also* Buffalo Evening News; Buffalo Times; Chicago Tribune; Constitution; New York Evening World; New York Herald; New York Times; New York Tribune; New York World; Philadelphia Inquirer
American trials, 169
Andrew, Donna T., 231
appeals, 162, 163, 169
appellate review, 162
archives, 80
arrests: of Florence Birchall, 37; of Reginald Birchall, 33–5

assize courts, 78, 110, 113, 116–17
Associated Press, 6, 30, 48, 52, 220
asylums, 116, 180, 203
Atkinson, A.L., 26
Atkinson, James, 25, 145
Atkinson House, 26
Atlantic cable, 6
Attawandaron (Indigenous) people, 11
Attorney General, Office of, 116, 174, 216
attorney general (Ontario), 28, 51, 77, 94, 97, 100, 107, 233. *See also* Mowat, Oliver
Australia, 44, 45, 82
autobiography of Birchall. *See* Birchall's autobiography
autopsy – Benwell, 4, 17, 24, 149, 237. *See also* Staples, Dr. Charles R.; Taylor, Dr. Oliver
autopsy – Birchall, 232, 237. *See also* Mearns, Dr. J.; Oldham, William

bail, 15, 51, 59, 117
bailiff of Woodstock, 54
Baker, George, 25–6, 66, 145–8, 159, 161
Baldwin, John, 87
Baldwin Act (1849), 11
Baldwin hotel, 32, 33, 47, 87, 90, 94
Ball, Francis Ramsay, 115, 130
Bampfield, owner of Imperial Hotel, 60
bank deposits, 125, 162, 243
Bank of Niagara (Niagara Falls Bank), 49, 243
Beck, Charles, 137
Bennett, James Gordon, 10
Benwell, Charles, 94, 117, 1245, 172, 206, 239–40
Benwell, Col. Frederick W.: contacted by Det. Murray, 37; defends actions, 57, 75; defends son's character, 86; letter from Birchall, 73–4, 120, 157–8, 162, 178, 208, 212; opportunity for son, 68, 73, 201–2; unable to attend trial, 117
Benwell, Frederick Cornwallis ("Fred"): absence explained by Birchall, 46; character of, 40–1, 187–8; clothing of, 48, 74, 188; disappearance of, 87; as "the Dude," 78; grave of, 242; identity of dead man, 31; money in possession, 74; nicknamed "Connie," 124–5; photograph of, 32f3.1. *See also* trunks/luggage (Benwell)
Benwell, James W., 19
Benwell, Marian, 85
The Benwell Murder: A Tragedy That Startled Two Continents (*Police Gazette*), 7

Benwell–Birchall case: abnormal procedures, 237; additional evidence, 174–5; historical literature on, 7–11; as international news sensation, 7, 189, 235; local commemoration of, 242–4; locale of murder, 11–12; media's assessment of jury, 169; news coverage of, 4, 6, 10, 41, 168, 238; published accounts of, 241–2; sermons on, 174. *See also* Birchall's autobiography; coroner's inquest; guilty verdict; preliminary hearing; trial of Birchall
Bessey, Dr. W.G., 179–80, 204
Birchall, Florence: accessory after the fact, 55, 56, 59, 117; alcohol consumption, 85, 177; appears in court, 50, 58; arrest of, 37; attends final day of trial, 152; bail denied, 51; bail posted, 59; description of, 40; early life of, 175; freed by grand jury, 117; gossip about, 110; and husband's arrest, 34; innocence of, 178; insufficient evidence, 51; later life of, 239; marriage to Rex Birchall, 176–8; meets Pelly, 84; news of clemency denied, 222; news stories of, 36, 37, 51, 172; photograph of, 35f3.2, 176f10.2; and Pickthall, 69; pleads not guilty, 50; privacy and silence of, 175–6; provides interview to *News*, 177–8; remanded, 59; role in husband's swindles, 177–8; social status of, 37; as stereotypical Victorian lady, 176–7, 211; sympathy for, 167; visits to husband in jail, 174, 216, 228
Birchall, John Reginald: alleged innocence, 220; appears anxious by trial end, 152; arrested for murder,

33–5; brain size and weight, 232; burial of, 233; choice of defence lawyer, 115; college days, 76–7; court appearance, preliminary hearing, 48, 60, 61; criticizes defence lawyers, 187; debts, 38, 47, 75, 76, 108; deemed guilty at inquest, 56–7; descriptions of, 34, 47–8, 48, 59; dislike of Murray, 187; execution of, 229–34; as a "farm pupil," 12, 68, 120, 199, 236; as gentleman, 4, 233, 235–6; guilty verdict, 163; history of swindles, 92; identifies body, 28, 128; identity of, 75–7; impresses Col. Benwell, 57–8; inheritance, 76; interviews sought with, 171; irreverence of, 228–9; lavish lifestyle of, 36, 40, 105; letter to Col. Benwell, 73–4, 120, 157–8, 162, 178, 208, 212; life in jail, 62, 187–9; as "moral idiot," 179; nonchalance of, 61, 124, 131, 148, 167, 171; notes prepared for defence, 183–4; personal items found in jail search, 49; photograph of, 35f3.2; plan for fleecing Benwell, 181–2; pleads not guilty, 44, 164; popularity of, 217; post-verdict demeanour, 170; at preliminary hearing, 44; preparation for hanging, 227–9; property ownership, 125; psychology of, 167–8, 179–80; public sympathy for, 170; refusal to confess, 228; relationship with Benwell, 31; remanded to jail, 50; seen at Blenheim Swamp, 130; seen wearing muddy boots, 49–50, 55, 60, 87, 123, 138, 139–41; as "snake charmer," 179; as sociopath, 236; spelling of surname, 36, 65; statement made to Det. Murray, 31–2; statement to Associated Press, 30–1; suspected of murder, 4; travels in southwestern Ontario (map), 2; at trial, 118; "unmanned," 222; visited by reporters, 171; visits from wife, 174, 216, 228; in Woodstock jail, 63–6, 78–9. *See also* Birchall's autobiography; "Lord Somerset"; Somerset (Birchall)

Birchall, Mary Eleanor, 219
Birchall, Rev. Joseph, 76, 192–3, 234
Birchall, Rev. Oswald, 219
Birchall–Benwell Committee, 242
"Birchallism," 187–9
Birchall's autobiography: copyright to, 191; death of father, 193; devises swindle, 200–3; early life, 192–3; evaluation of, 210–13; events of February 17, 207–10; financial support for wife, 190–1; horse-racing, 198; jail time, 203–5; no alibi presented, 213; at Oxford University, 193–9; praise for defence lawyers, 206; prejudices expressed, 212; published in instalments, 191; return to England, 200; rights acquired by *Mail* and *New York Herald*, 190, 210; school days, 191–4; sentenced to death, 210; sojourn in Canada, 199–200; source of funds for legal expenses, 206; theatre pursuits, 198; the trial, 205–7; views of women, 195–6; wife and married life, 202, 211; work in photography, 200; written in jail, 190
Black and Tan Club, 76, 77, 195, 211
Blackstock, George Tate: assessed by news media, 166–7; courtroom

style of, 115; cross-examinations, 121–2, 125–7, 129–30, 132–5, 138–41; exhausted by trial, 172; final address to jury, 153–7, 220; later life of, 240; legal fee received, 206; presents defence case, 143–51; professional career, 115
Blackstock, Thomas Gibbs, 115
Blake, Edward, 133
Blandford Township, 135
Blenheim Swamp: as crime scene, 14f2.1, 15, 79, 144, 158; description of, 100; discovery of body, 3, 13, 125; known to Birchall, 16; location of, 19; visited by judge MacMahon, 151; visited by reporters, 151; visited by trial lawyers, 117
Blenheim Township, 54, 119, 125, 135, 237
Bluett, Detective "Charley," 116, 144–5, 151, 184, 205–6
body, discovery of: bullet wounds, 24, 127, 159; clothing, 3–4, 13–14; exhumation, 55, 129, 132; identification, 147; labels removed, 14, 20, 27, 39, 159; media accounts, 13; in Pelly's memoir, 88; witness testimony at trial, 125, 126–7. *See also* autopsy – Benwell; cigar-box/cigar case; gold pen/pencil; murder victim
Bond, Bishop William Bennett, 218
Booth, Rev. W.B., 223
Bowen, James, 239
Brandon, Manitoba, 9
Brantford, 19, 20, 25, 28, 29, 113, 134, 153
Britannic steamer: arrives in New York, 48, 86; Birchalls, Pelly, and Benwell as passengers, 31, 35, 39, 46, 48; dislike develops, 202;
Isidore Hellmuth as passenger, 34, 44, 48, 87, 115, 295; as luxury ship, 86; money spent by Benwell, 74; murder victim identified as ship passenger, 55; Pickthall mentioned, 69, 86; Youngheart and Benwell meet, 78
British Empire, 214, 223, 236
British gentry, 5
British newspapers: coverage of Benwell–Birchall case, 4, 41, 165, 169–70; and crime stories, 10; and investment scams, 57. *See also Daily News; Daily Post; Daily Telegraph; Graphic; Scotsman; Standard; The Times; Weekly Standard and Express; Weekly Times and Examiner*
brothel as site of murder, 20, 22, 128
Buck, Charles, 65–6
Buffalo, 31, 33
Buffalo Evening News, 50
Buffalo News, 169
Buffalo Times, 44, 61, 169
bullet wounds, 24, 127, 159. *See also* autopsy; body, discovery of
Bunting, C.W., 190
Burchell, John Reginald. *See* Birchall, John Reginald
Burgess, William, 147
Butcher, Nelson R., 118, 189
Bytheway, Alan J., 8

cable communications, 6
cable companies' competition, 174
Caldwell, Robert, 25–6, 145, 146, 148, 159, 161
Cambridge University, 35, 82, 191
Cameron, John, 179, 204, 216, 230
Canada – status and reputation, 4, 6, 223, 236

Canada Southern Railway, 96, 97
Canadian Breeder and Agricultural Review, 68
Canadian criminal law, 168, 236
Canadian Express Company, 32
Canadian legal history. *See* legal history, Canada
Canadian newspapers, 6–7, 76, 165. *See also Courier (Brantford); Empire; Evening Standard; Fireside Weekly; Free Press (London); Gazette (Montreal); Globe; Hamilton Spectator; Journal; Mail; National Post; News; Sentinel-Review; Spectator; Telegram; World*
Canadian Pacific Railway, 84, 115
Canadian Press Association, 7
cap worn by Birchall, 49, 50, 55; Astrakhan cap, 46, 123, 132, 133; black cap, 139, 231; black curly cap, 49, 139; dark cap, 140; dark round cap, 141; fur cap, 135; sealskin cap, 148; skin cap, 38
capital punishment, 166, 223, 224
Caron, Sir Adolphe-Phillipe, 221
Cartwright, John Robinson, 53, 116, 216
The Case of Valentine Shortis (Friedland), 9
Castle Cameron, 63, 203. *See also* Cameron, John; Woodstock Jail
Cavanagh, Professor F., 181
Caven, Rev. Dr. William, 224
cemetery, Princeton, 242
Central Methodist Church, 174, 179
Chamberlain, Dr. Theodore F., 230, 232
Chapleau, Joseph-Adolphe, 214, 221
cheese-making, 11–12, 135, 146
Cheesewright, Fred, 22

Cheltenham, Gloucestershire, 37, 45, 58, 68, 73, 85, 117, 201, 242
Cheltenham College, 40, 124, 188
Chicago Tribune, 168
Chippewa First Nation, 11
Choate, Carrie, 133–4, 155, 159, 161, 175, 207
Christie, Robert, 171, 173
Christopher, George, 119, 163
cigar-box/cigar case: attempts to identify owner of, 45, 102; description of, 21; discovery of, 17–18, 101, 126; has name "F.C. Benwell," 21, 33, 88, 89, 101, 123, 128; identified by Charles Benwell, 124–5; leads to Birchall's identification of body, 123, 208; linked to Benwell's unclaimed luggage, 33
cigar-holder, 18, 27, 101, 126. *See also* cigar-box/cigar case
circumstantial evidence, 157, 160–1, 162, 165–6, 217, 219, 233
Clarke, Dr. Daniel, 180
class on trial, 4, 234.
clemency requests, 214–19, 237–8
Clench, Johnson, 78
Clench, Mrs. Johnson, 47
clergy sermons on the case, 174
clergy views of executions, 217
clergy visits, 189. *See also* Wade, Rural Dean William H.
"the Colonel" as Benwell's murderer, 184–6
colonies, 83, 235
colonization, 11
Commercial Hotel, Woodstock, 67, 79, 110, 170
community justice system, 15, 23, 236–7

commutation, 164, 214–15, 219–21
Confederation, 214, 215, 224
confessions, false, 175
Coningham House, 81
conspiracy theory, 152
constables, 3, 15, 237. *See also* Watson, W.J.
Constitution (Atlanta), 167
Cooper, John, 175
coroners, 23. *See also* McLay, Dr. Archibald
coroner's inquest, 23–6, 53–8. *See also* McLay, Dr. Archibald
Cosby, John, 126, 135
Costin, James, 153
counterfeiting, 97
county sheriffs, 224
court reporter, 118
courtroom sketches, 54
Cox, Captain Peter H., 130
crime journalism, 10–11, 41. *See also Memoirs of a Great Detective* (Murray)
criminal cases, 53
criminal insanity, 9
Criminal Investigation Branch, 97
criminal offences, serious, 113
critical media studies, 10
Cromwell, Ida, 54, 138, 139, 155, 161
Crosby, John, 54, 134–5, 156, 160, 161
Crosby, William, 15, 54, 126
Crown attorney, 113, 115, 116. *See also* Ball, Francis Ramsay; Osler, Britton Bath
Crumb, George, 131
The Cultured Criminal (dir. Marksteiner), 8
Curtis, L. Perry, 10–11
customs officers, 60–1

Daily News, 165
Daily Post, 3
Daily Telegraph, 201
dairy industry, 11–12
Dake, Jerry, 25
Dake's Hotel, 25–6, 125, 135, 136
Dalziel Agency, 6
Davis, Natalie Zemon, 8
death sentence, 153, 164, 214, 217. *See also* capital punishment
debt (Birchall), 38, 47, 75, 76, 108
Department of Justice, Ottawa, 180, 186, 189, 214, 218, 219, 221
deputy attorney general, 53, 116, 216. *See also* Cartwright, John Robinson
deputy justice minister, 222
detective fiction, 99–100
detectives' roles and reputations, 99
Dickens, Charles, 44
direct evidence, 160–1
Dominion Day, 19, 25
Dominion government, 214, 222
Don Mills Methodist Church, 223
Donnelly murder trial, 113
Drege, Louis, 131
Drumbo, 16, 25, 25–6, 129, 140, 145–7
Dudley, S.V. ("Cholly"), 54, 70, 71f5.2, 137–8, 141, 155, 200
Duffy, James, 50, 59, 141, 154, 159, 162
Dunlop's cable, 131
Dunn, Stationmaster, 54–5, 138, 139, 140, 208
Durrant, Arthur, 89

Eastwood Station and train: Birchall seen at, 39, 49–50, 54–5, 131–2, 137, 139–41, 161, 238; Birchall's account, 207–8; men sighted at, 54; porter, 140; testimony challenged, 155
Eastwood village, 38, 134, 137

editorials: on denial of clemency, 222–3; on guilty verdict, 165, 167, 170
Edmiston, 156
effigy, 227–8
Ellis, James, 130
Elmiston, Archibald, 135
Elvidge, George, 3, 126
Elvidge, Joseph, 3, 126
Elvidge brothers, 13–15, 17–18, 19, 23–4, 100–1, 146
embalming methods, 55–6
Emery, Charles F., 92
emigration scams, 4
emigration to Canada, 67, 68
Emmanuel College, 82
Empire. *See* British Empire
Empire: contempt of court, 79; interviews with Birchall in jail, 62, 65–6; lavish lifestyle of Birchall/Somerset, 40; reports on inquest, 53; reports on preliminary hearing, 58; reports on trial, 163, 205; Toronto daily paper, 6
English Derby, 200–1
English elite, 192, 235. *See also* rich young Englishmen
Entwhistle, John, 118, 164, 171, 186, 189, 204
Evening Standard: description of Birchall, 36; early coverage of murder mystery, 14–16, 18, 20, 22; Pickthall mystery, 72–3; rival to *Sentinel-Review*, 7, 72–3; trial verdict, 165
Evening Sun, 169
evidence, direct versus circumstantial, 160–1. *See also* circumstantial evidence
executions. *See* hangings
eyeglasses, 18, 27, 124, 126, 133, 135, 159

Fallon, Ellen, 136, 156, 161
family farms, 11–12
farm, purchase of, 28, 31. *See also* farm investment fraud; stock farms
farm employment, 67–8. *See also* farm pupils business
farm investment fraud: admitted by Florence Birchall, 90; Birchall's roles in, 4, 83, 200–2, 242; detailed during trial, 120, 158, 161; perpetrated on Benwell, 4, 73; perpetrated on Pelly, 4, 37, 45, 57, 75, 83; suspicions of locals, 78
farm pupil business: Benwell as farm pupil, 87; Birchall as farm pupil, 12, 68, 120, 199, 236; Birchall's involvement, 66–9, 108, 122; disappearances associated with, 68, 106; disillusionment with, 67–8; as fraudulent, 121, 184, 236; Graeme as farm pupil, 183; operating in Canada, 83, 106; Pelly's interest in, 83; in Woodstock area, 12. *See also* farm investment fraud; Ford, Rathbone & Co.; McDonald, William
Farrer, Edward, 181
Farthing, Rev. J.C., 172
Ferguson, Ruth, 136, 156
Fifth Avenue Hotel, New York, 47, 60, 88, 89, 123, 141
Finkle, Judge H.J., 134, 172, 232
Finkle, McKay, and McMullen, 115, 206
Fireside Weekly, 79
First Concession, East Oxford, 136
Flynn, James, 49, 60–1
footstool from swamp wood, 243f14.1, 244
Forbes, James, 171, 204, 228

Ford, Rathbone & Co., 66–7, 120, 121, 183, 202
Fowler, George, 25, 147
Francis, Bessie, 132–3
fraud. *See* farm investment fraud
Fredenburg, George, 136
Free Press (Detroit), 169
Free Press (London), 6, 13, 20, 32, 34
Friedland, Martin, 9
Fry, Elizabeth, 81

gallows, 157, 166, 171, 187, 243f14.1, 244
Galt, Ontario, 21
Gartner, Rosemary, 9
Gazette (Montreal), 6, 165, 169, 217, 223
gender stereotypes, 8, 51, 237–8
gentlemanly code, 231, 235–6. *See also* masculinity
Georgetown, Guyana, 7
Gladstone, William, 200
Globe: admiration for Murray, 107; assessed Blackstock's role, 167, 240; assessment of Judge MacMahon, 113; Bessey report on Birchall, 179–80; Birchall confession to Wade, 241; "Birchall's Book," 191; Birchall's character, 168; capital punishment, 223, 233; cigar-box found, 18; clemency petitions, 219, 220; coverage of Benwell–Birchall case, 7, 36; draws on Murray's statements, 106; "partial confession," 181–2; public interest in case, 167, 183–4; reviews Murray's memoir, 108; sued by G.H. Graeme, 182–3
Gobles, 25, 137, 147
gold pen/pencil, 49, 124–5, 157, 160, 187, 202–3, 208

Goldingham, P.C., 40–1
governor general, 214, 222
Governor's Road, 26
Gowan, James Robert, 116
Gowers, Rebecca, 8
Graeme, Grosvenor Hood, 182–3
Graham – alleged murderer of Benwell, 182–3
Grand Army of the Republic, 186
Grand Hall, Woodstock, 111–12
grand jury, 116
Grand Trunk Railway, 26, 49–50, 54, 136, 141
Graphic, 54
Gray, Maria Anne, 192
Great North Western Telegraph Company, 112, 231
Great Western Telegraph, 61, 141
Gregge, John W., 129
Grenier, Mayor Jacques, 218
Grigg hotel, London, Ont., 32
GTR. *See* Grand Trunk Railway
Guillet, Edwin, 114–15
guilty verdict: editorials, 165; local reactions and impact, 170–4; news cabled to England, 163; objections to, 166
"The Gullibility of Englishmen" (*Sentinel-Review*), 56
gun, 54, 208. *See also* pistol as possible murder weapon; pistol shots; revolver

Habberton, John, 190
handwriting, 87, 120, 125, 184, 186
hanging as punishment for murder, 160
hanging of Birchall: autopsy, 232; Birchall's preparations, 227–9; convulsions and delayed death,

231, 232; date of, 164; execution, 229–34; press coverage of, 224, 230–1, 233; scaffold construction, 226; technique used, 225–6; tickets for spectators, 229
hangings in Canada, 215
hangman, 224–6, 237. *See also* Radclive, John Robert
Harrow, 81
Hay, George, 49–50, 53, 141, 154
Hayward, Alfred, 38, 54, 134, 150–1, 156, 159, 161
Hayward, George, 137
Hayward, James, 55, 138, 140, 155
Hayward, John, 54
hearing. *See* preliminary hearing
Hellmuth, Isidore F.: assisted defence lawyer, 115, 163; authors *Maclean's* article on case, 241–2; biography of, 34–5; charged local media, 79; counsel for Florence Birchall, 44, 50–1; disputes Birchall murder charge, 34; identifies Benwell, 34; later life of, 241; legal fees received, 206; and mental state of Birchall, 187; met Birchall on the *Britannic*, 46, 87, 202; as national tennis champion, 34, 241
Herbert, Sir Robert, 77, 92
Herbert, Verena Nellie, 240
Hersee, George, 130, 161
Hersee, William, 18–19
Hersee farm, 40
Hickson, Sir Joseph, 218
Hill, Andrew Gregory, 33, 42, 50, 59–60, 90–1, 94
historical legal literature, 7–11
Hodge's Case rule, 162–3
Holmes, Sherlock, 99
homosocial culture, 211–12

Hood, James, 148
horse farm allegedly owned by Birchall, 37, 83, 90
horse farm investments. *See* farm investment fraud
horse trading, 31, 36, 39, 43, 46, 83–4, 123
horse-racing, 65, 187, 198
Howie, Matthew, 21
Hull, J.H., 129

Imperial Federation, 171
Imperial Hotel, Niagara Falls, 47, 60
imperialism, 4
"Indian" war dances/songs, 16, 28, 129
Ingersoll, 12, 119, 133
inquest. *See* coroner's inquest
interference in justice system, 51, 237
investment scams. *See* farm investment fraud
Irish in jail, 63–4
Isaac, Levi, 19
Ivey, Charles H., 35, 59, 60, 61, 206

James, Henry (Harry), 138, 140
Jennings, Maureen, 241
Jesuit Estates, 218
Jewish pedlar theory, 19, 25, 26, 28, 147
Journal, 180
journalism, 171
journalists. *See individual newspapers*
judges, 113, 163, 220–1, 237. *See also* assize courts; Finkle, Judge H.J.; Gowan, James Robert; Hill, Andrew Gregory; MacMahon, Justice Hugh; Thompson, Sir John
jury: compensation for, 118; formation of, 23; at inquest, 56–7;

partiality of, 79, 216; photograph of, 173f10.1; role and responsibility of, 153–4; selection, 118–19, 169; sequestered, 123, 148, 152; verdict returned, 163–4, 169
jury system, 169
justice minister, Ottawa, 216, 219–20, 222
justice of the peace, 3, 15, 53, 126, 237. *See also* Crosby, William

Kansas, 6
Kingsville, 166
Kipp, James, 26
Knox Presbyterian, Toronto, 174
Knutsford, Lord, 74
Kramer, Rheinhold, 9

labels removed, 14, 20, 27, 39, 159
Lancaster, William, 147
Langevin, Sir Hector-Louis, 221
Lansdowne, Lord, 104
laudanum, 65
Laycock, Alfred, 25, 147
Lazier, Peter, 9
The Lazier Murder: Prince Edward County, 1884 (Sharpe), 9
Le Baron, Marina, 175
Leatham, Arthur R., 197, 218, 228, 230–2
legal history, Canada, 8–10
life sentence (versus death), 214
Lincoln College, 76, 77, 194
Lincoln County, 42, 78
Lloyd's (insurance firm), 82, 83
lockets, 189
Lockhart, Mary, 132, 134, 155, 161, 207
Logan, Alexander, 136
London, UK: Birchall's life in, 92, 102, 200–2; cable and telegraph companies of, 174; elite clubs of, 57, 201; executioner, 225; home of Benwells, 21, 202; home of David Stevenson, 74, 78; home of Florence Birchall, 37, 175, 239; location of farm-pupil agencies, 66–7, 83–5, 120, 199; news stories on Benwell murder, 2, 231; Pelly's life in, 82; shipping agent in, 26, 28. *See also* Madame Tussaud's
London and North Western Railway, 37, 200
London asylum (Ont.), 203; Benwell's alleged travel to, 31–2, 39, 45, 103, 128, 130, 208; letter allegedly sent from, 56, 129; Murray's search for evidence in, 32, 45, 103–4. *See also* *Free Press*; Hellmuth, Isidore F.; Western University
London newspapers (UK), 5–6, 41, 45, 54, 73, 76. *See also* *Daily News*; *Daily Telegraph*; *Graphic*; *Morning Post*; Reuters; *Standard*; *Weekly Standard and Express*
"Lord Somerset," 40, 65, 136, 137, 140, 141, 199. *See also* Birchall, John Reginald; Somerset (Birchall)
luggage. *See* trunks/luggage (Benwell)
Lumsden, Hugh D., 94
Lynch, Mr., 206

MacDonald, Rev. D.J., 224
Macdonald, Sir John A., 94, 113, 114, 214, 219, 221
Maclean's, 109, 241–2
MacMahon, Justice Hugh: addresses Birchall, 164; addresses jury, 151; appreciation for, 167; biography of, 113; death of father, 241;

defends grand jury system, 116; defines murder, 116–17; favours prosecution, 162; post-trial report, 220–1; questions for defence witnesses, 149–50; trial decisions, 123, 126, 138, 142, 148, 153, 163; visit to swamp, 151
MacMurchy, Dugald, 117, 143, 218, 220, 222, 233
Madame Tussaud's, 228
magistrates. *See* police magistrates
Mail: acquires Canadian rights to Birchall autobiography, 190–1; Benwell's character, 40; cigar-box, 18; on clemency petitions, 216, 218; dismissed *Globe*'s "partial confession," 182; letters to the editor on guilty verdict, 166; printed letter of "the Colonel," 185–6; reports on Birchall, 36; reports on preliminary hearing, 59; right of accused to testify, 168
Maloney, Thomas, 40
manslaughter, 117
Markey, John, 43–4
Marksteiner, Florin, 8
marriage certificate (Birchalls), 49, 74
Martin, Joseph, 146–7
Marwood, William, 225
masculine privilege, 237–8
masculinity, 8, 61, 100, 113, 188, 210–11, 231
mass readership, 5
Matlock Bath, Derbyshire, 81
Mayall & Co., 200
McCarthy, D'Alton, 114
McCarthy, Osler, Hoskin, and Creelman, 114
McDonald, George, 136, 148, 151

McDonald, William: as agent in farm-pupil business, 66–7, 108, 120, 121, 199; and Benwell, 46, 183–4; testimony of, 47–8, 120–2
McGee, Constable John, 171, 188, 204
McGuire, Richard, 125, 161
McKay, John S. (lawyer), 36, 38
McKay: John W., 25, 147; Mrs. John W., 199
McKay, Margaret, 36, 38
McKay, Samuel G. (defence attorney), 115, 116, 134, 150–1, 161, 189
McLay, Dr. Archibald, 16–17, 23–6, 53, 65, 232
McMullen, Rev. Dr., 174
McQueen, Norman, 150, 156, 160, 167
Mearns, Dr. J., 149, 232
media. *See* news industry
medical testimony at trial: Crown's case, 126–8; defence's case, 149–50
Mellersh, T.S., 45, 68, 76, 83, 122, 163, 201
Memoirs of a Great Detective (Murray): crime story genre, 100; critique of, 96, 99, 100–6, 108–9; influences assessment of case, 109
mercy of the Crown, 215
Meredith, William, 107
meteorologists, 128
Metropolitan Hotel, New York, 31, 46, 69, 86, 105, 153
Metropolitan Police Force, 100
Micham, Surrey, 80
Michigan Central train, 58
micro-history, 8–9
Midgley, Constable, 134, 161, 204
Millman, Fred, 38, 147–8, 156, 160
Minister of Justice, 217. *See also* Thompson, Sir John
Mississauga First Nation, 11

Mitchell, Tom, 9
moccasin tracks, 13, 16, 129, 145, 146
Morning Post, 41
Morton, Mabel, 175
motive for murder, 157
"moulder theory," 21, 26
Mounties, 99
Mowat, Oliver (Attorney General), 51, 97, 107, 216, 225, 233, 237, 241
Mud Lake, 130, 147, 151
muddy boots of Birchall: in Crown witnesses's testimony, 156, 158, 160; explained by Birchall, 208; mentioned by Murray, 40; seen by Cromwell, 139; seen by Crosby, 135; seen by Duffy, 60, 141; seen by Hay, 49; seen by Pelly, 87, 123; seen by Smith, 138; seen by Swayzie, 55, 140
murder, definition of, 116–17
Murder and Mysteries: A Canadian Series (Wallace), 8
Murder as a Fine Art: A Story of Fraud, Betrayal, and Murder across Two Continents (Bytheway), 8
murder case, Liverpool, 162
murder cases, procedures for, 53, 153–4
"The Murder Mystery," 4, 13, 28, 29
murder of Woodstock girl (2016), 244
murder trials, 153, 160
murder victim (Benwell): clothing of, 3–4, 16, 17, 21, 22, 27; identified as Benwell, 27–9, 31; as Indigenous man, 16, 28; as jewellery salesman, 147; as Jewish pedlar, 19, 25, 26, 28, 147; photographs of, 17, 18f2.2, 20, 21; speculation on identity of, 14, 16–22; time and date of death, 149–50, 156; viewed at undertaker's, 22

Murdering Holiness (Phillips and Gartner), 9
murders and popular press, 5
murders of rich young Englishmen. *See* rich young Englishmen
Murdoch Mysteries, 241
Murray, John Wilson: arrests Florence Birchall, 37, 51, 58; brings witnesses to identify Birchall, 65–6; at crime scene, 14; description of, 98; despatched to Niagara Falls, 48–9; despatched to Princeton, 16, 28; detective career, 97–8; dissent with Chief Young, 58; documents in his possession, 108; early life of, 96–7; expertise of, 237; group conspiracy theory, 106, 109; interactions with witnesses, 105; interviews with press, 26, 37, 39–40, 52, 106–7; later life of, 241; meets with Birchall in jail, 62; memoir of Benwell–Birchall case, 8, 98–100; methods critiqued, 108; not included as Crown witness, 108; obituary, 98; pilloried by Blackstock, 155; preparation for trial, 115; as prosecutor at preliminary hearing, 44; receives statement from Birchall, 31–2; reputation of, 97; self-promotion of, 37; shapes public opinion, 52; subpoenaed, 53; testifies at inquest, 56; testifies at preliminary hearing, 44–5, 48–9; warrant for Pelly's arrest, 90–1. *See also Memoirs of a Great Detective* (Murray)

National Post, 244
Nelles, Mrs. J.B., 38
Neutral (Indigenous) people, 11
"new journalism," 5

New Orleans, 41
New York Evening World, 41
New York Herald, 5, 10, 76, 190
New York Tribune, 167–8, 217, 219
New York World, 44, 54, 70, 70–1
New Zealand, 46, 82, 124
Newhall, Detective John, 22
News: Birchall's hanging, 230; clemency denied – Birchall's reaction, 222; clemency requests, 216; interviews Florence Birchall and sister, 177–8; right of accused to testify, 168; sermons on case, 174; trial verdict – guilty, 124, 162–4, 163, 166, 172; trial's impact on local merchants, 152
news industry: and detectives, 99; influence on public opinion, 10, 154; in nineteenth century, 5, 10; roles in criminal cases, 153–4. *See also* American newspapers; British newspapers; Canadian newspapers; editorials; sensationalism; Toronto newspapers
Niagara District Courthouse, 43
Niagara Falls: Benwell's departure from, 28; border-crossing by criminals, 42; chief of police, 33; news of arrest, 33; site of murder investigation, 30, 32; site of preliminary hearing, 57–61; source of "murder mystery" reports, 6
Niagara Falls Bank, 49, 243
Niagara Falls Town Hall, 43
Nomination Day, 16, 129
North American Hotel, 147

Office of the Attorney General, 116
Old Town Hall, Woodstock, 111

Oldham, William, 135, 156, 232
Oliver, Adam, 145
Oliver, James, 147
O'Neill House, 110
Ontario courts, 119
Ontario government, 214
Ontario High Court of Justice, 113
Ontario legislature, 7, 42
Ontario Medical Association, 149
Ontario Provincial Police Force, 97
Osler, Britton Bath: biography of, 113–14; courtroom style of, 115; cross-examinations, 144–6; description of, 114; ends Crown's case, 142; frank comments about case, 242; later life of, 240; lauded in news media, 166; opening statement at trial, 119–20; receives false evidence, 175
Ottawa Citizen, 217
Oxford Circuit, 113
Oxford County: biased jury, 216; Birchall's stay in, 120; cheese production, 11–12; colonization and settlement of, 11; commemoration of Benwell–Birchall case, 242–4; county jail, 12, 63, 203; courthouse, 12, 206; Crown attorney of, 115; demographics of, 11; departure of Pickthall from, 69–70, 72; discovery of body, 13; family farms, 11–12; high school case study, 244; public opinion in, 79, 216; religions of, 11; sheriff of, 222; trial costs, 189; witnesses sought in, 52. *See also* Ball, Francis Ramsay; Woodstock; Woodstock Jail
Oxford Hotel, 110
Oxford Men (Deslandes), 210

Oxford Times, 41
Oxford University: Birchall's time at, 64, 75–7, 83, 178, 192, 194–9, 210–12, 235; Cartwright's education at, 116; formation of elite men, 178, 191–2, 198, 210, 212
Oxford University Histrionics Club, 198

Page, Mary Ann, 234
Panama City, 7
Paris, Ontario, 31
Parker, Mary Eleanor, 192
Parti National, Quebec, 218
Patriot, 217
Patterson, George W., 153
Patterson, T.C., 22, 54, 93–4
Pattullo, Andrew, 7
Pattullo, Thomas Dufferin "Duff," 7
Pattullo family, 7
Pelly, Douglas: at Buffalo hotel, 33; careers explored, 82–5; as celebrity, 92–3; claims Birchall tried to murder him, 37, 89; as Crown witness, 8, 91; description of, 34, 84f6.1, 61, 122; early contact with Birchall, 83–5; early life of, 80–2; exposes hoax, 238; interrogated by Murray, 90–1; investment deal with Birchall, 45, 68, 85; later life of, 240; learns of Benwell's murder, 88–91; letters re Birchall's deceit, 92; memoir, 80, 94–5; questioned by police magistrate, 33, 94; returns to England, 172; sojourn in Canada, 85–8; suspicions raised, 88–9; sympathy for, 77; talks to reporters, 37; testimony at inquest, 56; testimony in preliminary hearing, 45–7, 50–1; testimony in trial, 122–3; travel to New York, 33; work during interregnum, 79, 93–4
Pelly, Louise, 81
Pelly, Raymond Percy, 75, 81, 86, 92, 189, 201
pen/pencil of Pelly. *See* gold pen/pencil
Perry, C.E. (photographer), 17, 18f2.2, 172, 173f10.1
Perry, George, 188, 204
Perry, John (Deputy Sheriff), 118, 204, 230, 231, 232
petitions for clemency, 215–21; denied, 221; from England, 215, 219; from Ontario, 215, 217; procedures for, 214–15, 220–2, 237; from Quebec, 215, 218; reasons for, 219; role of Florence Birchall, 215–16, 218, 220, 222; role of press, 215, 217; signed by thousands, 238; from Toronto, 215, 217; from Woodstock, 216–18
Phemister, George, 60, 141–2, 158, 159, 162
Philadelphia, 181
Philadelphia Inquirer, 166, 167, 169, 170
Phillips, Jim, 9
photographers, 17, 172–3
Phrenological Journal and Science of Health, 181
phrenology, 180–1
Pickthall, Miss, 127
Pickthall, Neville Hunter: biography of, 70; disappearance of, 69–73; mentioned on Britannic, 86; scheme with Birchall, 181–3, 212
Pine Pond, 100, 106, 130, 199, 207
pistol, 89, 123. *See also* pistol shots; revolver

pistol shots: and autopsy results, 24; heard by Rabb, 25, 159; and jury findings, 56; murder versus manslaughter, 117; suggested suicide, 22; witnesses' testimony, 136, 144–5, 148, 151, 156, 161, 221
Poe, Edgar Allan, 167
police court, 53, 60
Police Gazette, 7
police magistrates, 42, 53. *See also* Hill, Andrew Gregory
Poole, William H., 54, 59, 131, 154, 161, 207
popular press, 5
post-trial report, 220–1
preliminary hearing: arrangement of courtroom, 44; attended by crowds, 43, 57, 59; difference from trial, 44; Hay's testimony, 49–50; insufficient evidence re Florence Birchall, 51; interrupted by coroner's inquest, 53; McDonald's testimony, 47–8; Murray's testimony, 44–5, 48; news coverage of, 43–4, 48; part one, Princeton, 42–53; part two, Niagara Falls, 58–61; Pelly's testimony, 45–7, 50–1; procedures for, 53
press. *See* news industry
press freedoms, 154
Princeton: Birchall travels to, 31; body found near, 13; location of autopsy, 3; site of coroner's inquest, 54
Princeton Cemetery, 129
prison apparel, 173
prisons inspector, 171, 173
Privy Council order, 222
professionalization of justice, 9, 97, 236–7
psychiatry and legal defence, 9

psychological reports, 179–81, 236
public executioner, 225, 231–2, 241
public hangings, 229
Puisne Judge, 113

Quebec, 9
Queen's Hotel, Toronto, 38
Quincey, Thomas de, 8

Rabb: John R., 14f2.1, 25, 144–5, 156–7, 159; John (son), 25–6
Radclive, John Robert, 225–7, 228, 231–2, 241
Ramsgate, Kent, 81
Rants, 63, 79
Reading School, Berkshire, 193–4
reasonable doubt, 157
"Reginald Birchall: Occupation Murderer" (Murray), 100
Reid, Sally, 172
relic hunters, 228, 243–4
Remissions Branch, 221
reserve case, 163
The Return of Martin Guerre (Davis), 8
Reuters, 6, 131
revolver, 45, 89, 123, 185, 233, 244. *See also* pistol shots
"Rex." *See* Birchall, John Reginald
Rice, Dr. Andrew T., 65, 204, 228
rich young Englishmen: alleged suicides of, 41; disappearances of, 4, 68–9, 169, 236; murders of, 41; swindling of, 4, 37, 41, 76, 184, 200–2, 235. *See also* farm investment fraud
Richardson, Dr. James H., 149–50
Riel, Louis, 114, 218, 220
rights of accused persons, 168, 238
Robarts, N.F., 92
Robinson, M.J., 227–8

Roman Catholic Church, Quebec, 218–19
Roman Catholics, 212
Rossall School, 193, 192
Royal Canadian Mounted Police ("Mounties"), 99
Royal Corps of Signallers, 239
Royal Hotel, 123, 129, 152
Rutherford, Robert, 53

Saffron Walden, 43, 75, 82–3, 85, 201, 240
Saint Paul, 41
Salvation Army, 204
San Francisco, 41; *San Francisco Chronicle*, 72
Sandhurst, 194
scaffold, 226, 230, 232
Scarff, Oscar, 22
Scotland Yard, 68, 92, 105
Scotsman, 165, 169
Seattle, 9
Second Concession, 26, 135, 136, 137, 145
Secretary of State, Department of, 214, 221
sensationalism, 5, 6, 10, 39, 41
Sentinel-Review: anti-Quebec sentiment, 218; article in Feb. 28 issue, 132–3, 155; badgering of witnesses, 168; Benwell's behaviour during trial, 131; Benwell's character, 40; Birchall in jail, 62–3; "Birchallism," 187; Birchall's hanging, 230; clemency petitions, 216; corroboration of Choate testimony, 175; cost of trial, 152; coverage of inquest, 25, 43–4, 52, 54, 56; coverage of murder mystery, 7, 14, 30, 52; coverage of trial, 112, 132, 133, 139; dismissed *Globe*'s "partial confession," 182; hangman Radclive, 225; identity of murder victim, 16, 19, 21, 27–8; letter from "the Colonel," 185; letter to the editor opposing verdict, 166; news of clemency denied, 222; ownership of, 7; Pelly's testimony, 48; Pickthall mystery, 70–2; reports on Birchall, 36, 179, 184; sells out print run, 39, 52; subscription to, 137; witnesses obtained by, 54
Shannon, H.M., 38–9
Sharpe, Robert, 9
Sherbourne Street Methodist Church, 223
shots fired/heard. *See* pistol shots
Shultz, Rachel, 144–5
signatures copied, 87, 120, 123, 125, 202
small-town journalism, 7, 28
Smith, Alice, 54, 137–9, 140, 159, 161
Smith, Goldwin, 233
Smith, Sheriff of Welland, 58
Smith, Sir John A., 218
sociopath, 236
Somerset (Birchall): as identified by inquest jury, 56; as identified in trial testimony, 130, 137, 140, 141, 155; as known by Pickthall, 70; as known in Eastwood, 55; as known in Woodstock, 38, 40, 47, 50, 75, 77; no property in this name, 125; used as business alias, 36, 39, 90, 108, 121, 199. *See also* Birchall, John Reginald; "Lord Somerset"
Somerset, Mr. and Mrs. (Lord and Lady), 36. *See also* Birchall, Florence; Birchall, John Reginald; "Lord Somerset"

southwestern Ontario, 2, 3, 7, 11, 28, 35, 215
spectacles. *See* eyeglasses
Spectator: on Birchall's hanging, 225, 227, 230; defence performance at trial, 127–8, 133, 166–7; on hangman Radclive, 227; judge's performance, 167; jury decision, 169; on Osler's testimony, 159, 166; source of news stories, 6; use of typewriter, 120
Speer, Victor, 98
Spooner, Rev. George, 219
St. Catharines, 43
St. John's, Stratford, Essex, 81
stables with electricity, 40, 43, 57
Stafford, Rev. Dr., 223
Stafford House, Buffalo, 31, 46, 49, 60, 87, 105, 243
Standard, 45, 57, 68–9, 83, 168, 170
Stanley, Frederich Arthur (Lord Stanley), 92, 214, 221
Staples, Dr. Charles R., 24, 126, 127, 208
Starnes, Hon. Henry, 218
Stevens, George, 186
Stevenson, David, 37, 74–5, 78, 84, 93, 152, 200, 206
stock farms, purchase of, 28, 44, 45
stomach empty (Benwell's body), 123, 156, 158, 207
Strange, Carolyn, 215
Street, W., 216
Stroud, John, 145
Stroud, Samuel, 25, 146
Stroud's Hotel, Princeton, 146
suicide, 22, 41
suicide watch (Birchall), 171
Sunnyside Boating Club, 225, 241
Sutherland, MP, 134

"Swamp of Death," 130. *See also* Blenheim Swamp
The Swamp of Death: A Tale of Victorian Lies and Murder (Gowers), 8
The Swamp of Death or, The Benwell Murder (Rose Publishing), 7
Swartz, James H.: body delivered to, 14; claimed body was Indigenous man, 16, 129; embalmed body for viewing, 17, 18f2.2, 22, 55–6; prepared body for autopsy, 24; testimony of, 128–9, 155
Swartz, Mary, 138
Swayzie, Mary, 54, 139–40, 155
swindling of wealthy Englishmen, 4, 37, 41, 76, 184, 200–2, 235. *See also* farm investment fraud
Switzerland, 82, 124

Taylor, Dr. Oliver, 16, 24, 126–8, 208, 209
Tecumseh hotel, London, Ont., 32
Telegram, 41, 65, 171, 172, 184, 187, 231
telegrams: as evidence, 61, 125, 141–2, 158–60, 162; used by news media, 6
telegraph, 6, 174
telegraphic equipment, 112
telephone lines, 112
Tennis Canada Hall of Fame, 241
Thompson, Joe, 227
Thompson, Phillips, 99
Thompson, Sir John, 214, 218–21, 241
Thomson House, Woodstock, 185
The Times, 3, 68, 74, 165, 166, 169–70
Tolstoy, Leo, 191
Topping, E., 167
Toronto Asylum, 180
Toronto News, 54, 57
Toronto newspapers, 5, 6–7. *See also Empire; Globe; Mail; National Post; Telegram; World*

Toronto Police Force, 99
Toronto Presbytery, 224
Toronto School of Medicine, 149
Toronto Telegram, 41
train tickets, 40, 131, 154, 158, 161
train travel: of Carrie Choate, 133–4, 175; Hellmuth and Osler meet, 242; to London, Ontario, 103; London to Liverpool, 45–6, 123, 233; New York to Buffalo, 31, 87; Niagara Falls to New York, 47, 89; to Ottawa, 220; to Paris, Ontario, 31, 47; of Pelly, 92–3, 94; of Pickthall, 71–2; to Princeton, 53, 89; to Toronto, 216; to/from Welland Jail, 50, 57–9; to Woodstock, 62–3; Woodstock to Buffalo, 207. *See also* Eastwood Station and train
trainmen's testimony, 49–50, 54, 60
treaties, 11
trial of Birchall: assessed by news media, 166, 168; Birchall in vicinity of swamp, 131–6; Birchall's knowledge of swamp, 130–1; Birchall's return alone, 136–7; Birchall's return to Niagara Falls, 137–42; Blackstock's closing address, 153–7, 220; cost of, 152, 189; crowds in attendance, 143, 163; Crown's closing address, 157–60; day one, 117–24; fairness of, 167, 171; identification of body, 128–30; judge's closing words to jury, 160–3; jury selection, 118–19; jury sequestered, 123; legal teams, 113–16; medical evidence, 126–8; presentation of Crown's case, 124–6; presentation of defence's case, 142–51, 153; press gathered to cover, 110, 117, 131; role of press in influencing public opinion, 217; setting and preparations, 110–13; transcript of, 189; verdict returned, 163–4; women's presence at, 124, 131, 143
trial transcript, 189
trunks/luggage (Benwell): bond receipt for, 31, 49, 160; and customs, 33, 47, 48, 123; examined by Murray, 40; instructions to send to New York, 47, 88, 103, 123, 125, 160, 208; keys for, 49, 123, 129, 160; left in Niagara Falls, 31, 46, 102
Tupper, Sir Charles, 221
Turnbull family, 22
Twain, Mark, 60
typewriter, use of, 120

undertaker, Princeton, 126, 127, 128. *See also* Swartz, James H.
United Kingdom. *See* British newspapers; London, England
United Press, 6
United States of America. *See* American newspapers

Valleyfield, Quebec, 9
Victorian England – social mores, 10–11
Victorian gender norms, 172. *See also* masculinity; women's rights and roles
Vineberg & Co., 78
Virtue, Matthew, 54, 132, 132–3, 155, 207
Volunteer Force, 81, 82

Wade, Rural Dean William H., 189, 205, 210, 228–31, 231, 241
Walk Toward the Gallows (Kramer and Mitchell), 9

Walker, Rev. (East Hastings), 219
Wallace, Stewart, 8, 109
Warren, J.B., 217
Waterford, 25, 147
Waters, John Frances, 180, 204
Watson, Constable W.J.: contacts attorney general, 28, 100; demands payment from defence, 206; investigates crime, 23, 100–1; mentioned in others' testimony, 129, 135, 162, 209; occupation as house painter, 15; testimony of, 56, 126, 128
weapon, 13. *See also* gun; pistol as murder weapon; pistol shots; revolver
weather, 159–60
Weekly Standard and Express, 75–6
Weekly Times and Examiner, 170
Weldon Library, Western University, 80
Welford, Dr. A.B., 127–8, 149
Welland County, 42
Welland Jail, 50, 58, 62, 65
Wentworth County, 113–14
West Yorkshire Regiment, 239
Western Union, 174
Western University, 80
West-Jones, Marion, 78–9, 93, 152, 176f10.2, 189, 220, 232, 239
Westlake, A.G., 17, 172–3
Wickson, D.G., 54
Willis, H.R. (Chief of Police, Woodstock), 62, 63, 229
witnesses: in coroner's inquest, 25–6, 54–7; Crown witnesses in trial, 120–6; to identify Birchall, 65–6; payments to, 206; in preliminary trial, 44–50, 60–1; treatment by defence, 168

women's rights and roles, 51, 124, 237–8
"Wonderland," 79, 227
Woodford Wells, Essex, 81
Woodstock: bailiff, 54; Birchalls' stay in, 38; and "farm pupils," 12; horse culture, 12; incorporation of, 111; murder of girl, 2016, 244; newspapers of, 7; settled by British officers, 12; site of trial, 7, 110; source of "murder mystery" reports, 6; tourism on Birchall case, 244. *See also Evening Standard*; *Sentinel-Review*
Woodstock Jail: Birchall's stay in, 63–6, 203–5; design of, 63; photograph of, 64f5.1; tourism, 244. *See also* Cameron, John
Woodstock Museum, 111, 242–4
Woodstock Town Hall, 110–12, 242
World: aftermath of verdict, 170; announces murder "solved," 30; arrest of Florence Birchall, 37; assessment of jurors, 119; autopsy results, 17; Birchall's flamboyance, 38; body found, 13; coverage of Benwell–Birchall case, 6–7, 20–1; hangman Radclive, 225, 228; identity of Birchall and Benwell, 73; identity of murderers, 26; influences public opinion, 52; interview with Det. Murray, 26, 52; list of dead man's effects, 27; questions for readers, 39; reports on inquest, 54–5, 56, 57; reports on preliminary hearing, 58–9; reports on trial, 139, 143, 144, 148, 167; special treatment accorded Birchall, 174; stable with electricity, 40

wrongful conviction, 9
www.newspapers.com, 6

Young, Andrew, 146
Young, Chief Thomas H.: arrests Reginald Birchall, 33, 37, 43f4.1, 49, 104, 118; assists in preparation for trial, 115; attends Birchall trial, 118; as chief of police, Niagara Falls, 42–3, 107; conducted prosecution, 44; investigates murder, 33; at loggerheads with Murray, 57; searches Benwell boxes, 60–1; searches Birchalls' goods, 49; surveillance of Birchalls, 209; testimony of, 48–9; visit to swamp, 117
Youngheart, Joseph, 78

Zorra Township, 204
Zyback, Mr., 137, 138

PUBLICATIONS OF THE OSGOODE SOCIETY FOR CANADIAN LEGAL HISTORY

2024 Adam Dodek, *Heenan Blaikie: The Making and Unmaking of a Great Canadian Law Firm*
Colin Campbell and Robert Raizenne, *A History of Canadian Income Tax Volume II, 1948–71*
Wayne Sumner, *Prairie Justice: The Hanging of Mike Hack*
Ian Radforth, *Deadly Swindle: An 1890 Murder in Backwoods Ontario That Gripped the World*

2023 Lori Chambers and Joan Sangster, eds., *Essays in the History of Canadian Law Volume XII: New Perspectives on Gender and the Law*
Ian Kyer, *The Ontario Bond Scandal of 1924 Re-examined*
Jonathan Swainger, *The Notorious Georges: Crime and Community in British Columbia's Northern Interior, 1909–25*

2022 Jim Phillips, Philip Girard, and R. Blake Brown, *A History of Law in Canada Volume II: Law for the New Dominion, 1867–1914*
J. Barry Wright, Susan Binnie, and Eric Tucker, eds., *Canadian State Trials Volume V: World War, Cold War and Challenges to Sovereignty, 1939–1990*
Constance Backhouse, *Reckoning with Racism: Police, Judges and the RDS Case*

2021 Daniel Rûck, *The Laws and the Land: The Settler Colonial Invasion of Kahnawà:ke in Nineteenth-Century Canada*
Lyndsay Campbell, *Truth and Privilege: Libel Law in Massachusetts and Nova Scotia, 1820–1840*
Martine Valois, Ian Greene, Craig Forcese, and Peter McCormick, eds. *The Federal Court of Appeal and the Federal Court: Fifty Years of History*
Colin Campbell and Robert Raizenne, *A History of Canadian Income Tax Volume I: The Income War Tax Act 1917–1948*

2020 Heidi Bohaker, *Doodem and Council Fire: Anishinaabe Governance through Alliance*
Carolyn Strange, *The Death Penalty and Sex Murder in Canadian History*

2019 Harry Arthurs, *Connecting the Dots: The Life of an Academic Lawyer*
Eric Reiter, *Wounded Feelings: Litigating Emotions in Quebec, 1870–1950*

2018 Philip Girard, Jim Phillips, and Blake Brown, *A History of Law in Canada Volume 1: Beginnings to 1866*
Suzanne Chiodo, *The Class Actions Controversy: The Origins and Development of the Ontario Class Proceedings Act*

2017 Constance Backhouse, *Claire L'Heureux-Dube: A Life*

Dennis G. Molinaro, *An Exceptional Law: Section 98 and the Emergency State, 1919–1936*

2016 Lori Chambers, *A Legal History of Adoption in Ontario, 1921–2015*
Bradley Miller, *Boarderline Crime: Fugitive Criminals and the Challenge of the Boarder, 1819–1914*
James Muir, *Law, Debt, and Merchant Power: The Civil Courts of Eighteenth-Century Halifax*

2015 Barry Wright, Eric Tucker, and Susan Binnie, eds., *Canadian State Trails Volume IV: Security, Dissent and the Limits of Toleration in War and Peace, 1914–1939*
David Fraser, *"Honorary Protestants": The Jewish School Question in Montreal, 1867–1997*
C. Ian Kyer, *A Thirty Years' War: The Failed Public /Private Partnership that Spurred the Creation of The Toronto Transit Commission, 1891–1921*

2014 Christopher Moore, *The Court of Appeal for Ontario: Defining the Right of Appeal, 1792–2013*
Dominique Clément, *Equality Deferred: Sex Discrimination and British Columbia's Human Rights State, 1953–84*
Paul Craven, *Petty Justice: Low Law and the Sessions System in Charlotte County, New Brunswick, 1785–1867*
Thomas Telfer, *Ruin and Redemption: The Struggle for a Canadian Bankruptcy Law, 1867–1919*

2013 Roy McMurtry, *Memoirs and Reflections*
Charlotte Gray, *The Massey Murder: A Maid, Her Master and the Trial That Shocked a Nation*
C. Ian Kyer, *Lawyers, Families, and Businesses: The Shaping of a Bay Street Law Firm, Faskens 1863–1963*
G. Blaine Baker and Donald Fyson, eds., *Essays in the History of Canadian Law Volume 11: Quebec and the Canadas*

2012 R. Blake Brown, *Arming and Disarming: A History of Gun Control in Canada*
Eric Tucker, James Muir, and Bruce Ziff, eds., *Property on Trial: Canadian Cases in Context*
Shelley A.M. Gavigan, *Hunger, Horses, and Government Men: Criminal Law on the Aboriginal Plains, 1870–1905*
Barrington Walker, ed., *The African Canadian Legal Odyssey: Historical Essays*

2011 Robert J. Sharpe, *The Lazier Murder: Prince Edward County, 1884*
Philip Girard, *Lawyers and Legal Culture in British North America: Beamish Murdoch of Halifax*

John McLaren, *Dewigged, Bothered, and Bewildered: British Colonial Judges on Trial*

Lesley Erickson, *Westward Bound: Sex, Violence, the Law, and the Making of a Settler Society*

2010 Judy Fudge and Eric Tucker, eds., *Work on Trial: Canadian Labour Law Struggles*

Christopher Moore, *The British Columbia Court of Appeal: The First Hundred Years*

Frederick Vaughan, *Viscount Haldane: The Wicked Step-father of the Canadian Constitution*

Barrington Walker, *Race on Trial: Black Defendants in Ontario's Criminal Courts, 1850–1950*

2009 William Kaplan, *Canadian Maverick: The Life and Times of Ivan C. Rand*

R. Blake Brown, *A Trying Question: The Jury in Nineteenth-Century Canada*

Barry Wright and Susan Binnie, eds., *Canadian State Trials Volume 3: Political Trials and Security Measures, 1840–1914*

Robert J. Sharpe, *The Last Day, the Last Hour: The Currie Libel Trial*

2008 Constance Backhouse, *Carnal Crimes: Sexual Assault Law in Canada, 1900–1975*

Jim Phillips, R. Roy McMurtry, and John Saywell, eds., *Essays in the History of Canadian Law. Volume 10: A Tribute to Peter N. Oliver*

Gregory Taylor, *The Law of the Land: Canada's Receptions of the Torrens System*

Hamar Foster, Benjamin Berger, and A.R. Buck, eds., *The Grand Experiment: Law and Legal Culture in British Settler Societies*

2007 Robert Sharpe and Patricia McMahon, *The Persons Case: The Origins and Legacy of the Fight for Legal Personhood*

Lori Chambers, *Misconceptions: Unmarried Motherhood and the Ontario Children of Unmarried Parents Act, 1921–1969*

Jonathan Swainger, ed., *The Alberta Supreme Court at 100: History and Authority*

Martin Friedland, *My Life in Crime and Other Academic Adventures*

2006 Donald Fyson, *Magistrates, Police and People: Everyday Criminal Justice in Quebec and Lower Canada, 1764–1837*

Dale Brawn, *The Court of Queen's Bench of Manitoba 1870–1950: A Biographical History*

R.C.B. Risk, *A History of Canadian Legal Thought: Collected Essays*, edited and introduced by G. Blaine Baker and Jim Phillips

2005 Philip Girard, *Bora Laskin: Bringing Law to Life*

Christopher English, ed., *Essays in the History of Canadian Law Volume 9: Two Islands, Newfoundland and Prince Edward Island*
Fred Kaufman, *Searching for Justice: An Autobiography*

2004 John D. Honsberger, *Osgoode Hall: An Illustrated History*
Frederick Vaughan, *Aggressive in Pursuit: The Life of Justice Emmett Hall*
Constance Backhouse and Nancy Backhouse, *The Heiress versus the Establishment: Mrs. Campbell's Campaign for Legal Justice*
Philip Girard, Jim Phillips, and Barry Cahill, eds., *The Supreme Court of Nova Scotia, 1754–2004: From Imperial Bastion to Provincial Oracle*

2003 Robert Sharpe and Kent Roach, *Brian Dickson: A Judge's Journey*
George Finlayson, *John J. Robinette: Peerless Mentor*
Peter Oliver, *The Conventional Man: The Diaries of Ontario Chief Justice Robert A. Harrison, 1856–1878*
Jerry Bannister, *The Rule of the Admirals: Law, Custom and Naval Government in Newfoundland, 1699–1832*

2002 John T. Saywell, *The Law Makers: Judicial Power and the Shaping of Canadian Federalism*
David Murray, *Colonial Justice: Justice, Morality and Crime in the Niagara District, 1791–1849*
F. Murray Greenwood and Barry Wright, eds., *Canadian State Trials Volume 2: Rebellion and Invasion in the Canadas, 1837–1838*
Patrick Brode, *Courted and Abandoned: Seduction in Canadian Law*

2001 Ellen Anderson, *Judging Bertha Wilson: Law as Large as Life*
Judy Fudge and Eric Tucker, *Labour before the Law: Collective Action in Canada, 1900–1948*
Laurel Sefton MacDowell, *Renegade Lawyer: The Life of J.L. Cohen*

2000 Barry Cahill, *"The Thousandth Man": A Biography of James McGregor Stewart*
A.B. McKillop, *The Spinster and the Prophet: Florence Deeks, H.G. Wells, and the Mystery of the Purloined Past*
Beverley Boissery and F. Murray Greenwood, *Uncertain Justice: Canadian Women and Capital Punishment*
Bruce Ziff, *Unforeseen Legacies: Reuben Wells Leonard and the Leonard Foundation Trust*

1999 Constance Backhouse, *Colour-Coded: A Legal History of Racism in Canada, 1900–1950*
G. Blaine Baker and Jim Phillips, eds., *Essays in the History of Canadian Law Volume 8: In Honour of R.C.B. Risk*
Richard W. Pound, *Chief Justice W.R. Jackett: By the Law of the Land*
David Vanek, *Fulfilment: Memoirs of a Criminal Court Judge*

1998 Sidney Harring, *White Man's Law: Native People in Nineteenth-Century Canadian Jurisprudence*
Peter Oliver, *"Terror to Evil-Doers": Prisons and Punishments in Nineteenth-Century Ontario*
1997 James W. St. G. Walker, *"Race," Rights and the Law in the Supreme Court of Canada: Historical Case Studies*
Lori Chambers, *Married Women and Property Law in Victorian Ontario*
Patrick Brode, *Casual Slaughters and Accidental Judgments: Canadian War Crimes and Prosecutions, 1944–1948*
Ian Bushnell, *The Federal Court of Canada: A History, 1875–1992*
1996 Carol Wilton, ed., *Essays in the History of Canadian Law Volume 7: Inside the Law – Canadian Law Firms in Historical Perspective*
William Kaplan, *Bad Judgment: The Case of Mr. Justice Leo A. Landreville*
Murray Greenwood and Barry Wright, eds., *Canadian State Trials Volume 1: Law, Politics and Security Measures, 1608–1837*
1995 David Williams, *Just Lawyers: Seven Portraits*
Hamar Foster and John McLaren, eds., *Essays in the History of Canadian Law Volume 6: British Columbia and the Yukon*
W.H. Morrow, ed., *Northern Justice: The Memoirs of Mr. Justice William G. Morrow*
Beverley Boissery, *A Deep Sense of Wrong: The Treason, Trials and Transportation to New South Wales of Lower Canadian Rebels after the 1838 Rebellion*
1994 Patrick Boyer, *A Passion for Justice: The Legacy of James Chalmers McRuer*
Charles Pullen, *The Life and Times of Arthur Maloney: The Last of the Tribunes*
Jim Phillips, Tina Loo, and Susan Lewthwaite, eds., *Essays in the History of Canadian Law Volume 5: Crime and Criminal Justice*
Brian Young, *The Politics of Codification: The Lower Canadian Civil Code of 1866*
1993 Greg Marquis, *Policing Canada's Century: A History of the Canadian Association of Chiefs of Police*
Murray Greenwood, *Legacies of Fear: Law and Politics in Quebec in the Era of the French Revolution*
1992 Brendan O'Brien, *Speedy Justice: The Tragic Last Voyage of His Majesty's Vessel* Speedy
Robert Fraser, ed., *Provincial Justice: Upper Canadian Legal Portraits from the Dictionary of Canadian Biography*
1991 Constance Backhouse, *Petticoats and Prejudice: Women and Law in Nineteenth-Century Canada*

1990   Philip Girard and Jim Phillips, eds., *Essays in the History of Canadian Law Volume 3: Nova Scotia*

Carol Wilton, ed., *Essays in the History of Canadian Law Volume 4: Beyond the Law – Lawyers and Business in Canada 1830–1930*

1989   Desmond Brown, *The Genesis of the Canadian Criminal Code of 1892*

Patrick Brode, *The Odyssey of John Anderson*

1988   Robert Sharpe, *The Last Day, the Last Hour: The Currie Libel Trial*

John D. Arnup, *Middleton: The Beloved Judge*

1987   C. Ian Kyer and Jerome Bickenbach, *The Fiercest Debate: Cecil A. Wright, the Benchers and Legal Education in Ontario, 1923–1957*

1986   Paul Romney, *Mr. Attorney: The Attorney General for Ontario in Court, Cabinet and Legislature, 1791–1899*

Martin Friedland, *The Case of Valentine Shortis: A True Story of Crime and Politics in Canada*

1985   James Snell and Frederick Vaughan, *The Supreme Court of Canada: History of the Institution*

1984   Patrick Brode, *Sir John Beverley Robinson: Bone and Sinew of the Compact*

David Williams, *Duff: A Life in the Law*

1983   David H. Flaherty, ed., *Essays in the History of Canadian Law Volume 2*

1982   Marion MacRae and Anthony Adamson, *Cornerstones of Order: Courthouses and Town Halls of Ontario, 1784–1914*

1981   David H. Flaherty, ed., *Essays in the History of Canadian Law Volume 1*